SOURCEBOOK
FOR
RESEARCH
IN
MUSIC

SOURCEBOOK FOR RESEARCH IN MUSIC

Second Edition

PHILLIP D. CRABTREE AND
DONALD H. FOSTER

REVISED AND EXPANDED BY
ALLEN SCOTT

INDIANA UNIVERSITY PRESS
BLOOMINGTON & INDIANAPOLIS

This book is a publication of

Indiana University Press
601 North Morton Street
Bloomington, IN 47404–3797 USA

http://iupress.indiana.edu

Telephone orders 800-842-6796
Fax orders 812-855-7931
Orders by e-mail iuporder@indiana.edu

First edition published in 1993
© 2005 by Indiana University Press
All rights reserved

The paper used in this publication meets the minimum requirements of American National
Standard for Information Sciences—Permanence of Paper for Printed Library Materials,
ANSI Z39.48–1984.

Manufactured in the United States of America

The Library of Congress has cataloged the original hardcover edition as follows:

Crabtree, Phillip.
    Sourcebook for research in music / Phillip D. Crabtree and Donald H. Foster.
      p.   cm.
    Includes indexes.
    ISBN 0–253–31476–3 (cloth : alk. paper)
      1. Music—Bibliography.   2. Music—History and criticism—Bibliography
    3. Bibliography—Bibliography—Music.   I. Foster, Donald H.   II. Title.   III. Title:
    Source book for research in music.
    ML113.C68   1993
    016.7—dc20   92-32038

    2nd ed.: ISBN 978-0-253-34611-7 (cloth)   ISBN 978-0-235-21780-6 (pbk.)

        2   3   4   5   6   12   11   10   09   08   07

C ONTENTS

Preface to the Second Edition

During the past twelve years the *Sourcebook for Research in Music* has become one of the standard resources in musical scholarship. The balance between depth of content and brevity of format makes it ideal for use as a textbook for graduate music students, as a reference work for music faculty and professional musicians, and as an aid to collection evaluation and development for music librarians.

Because it has been a dozen years since the *Sourcebook for Research in Music* was first published, the time has come for a second edition. Since 1993 many of the listed sources have been updated and many new sources have appeared. Musical scholars have been quite active in some specialized areas of music research (such as music and technology, performance practice issues, and the study of women in music, for example), and I have striven to reflect this increase in scholarship. In addition, the usefulness, accessibility, and popularity of the Internet has changed many facets of the research process. The revised and expanded second edition incorporates these additions and changes using the same editorial method as the original edition. Although I have worked closely with the original authors in preparing the second edition, I bear all responsibility for any errors that may have crept in, and ask that any updates and corrections be addressed to me.

I am deeply indebted to Phillip Crabtree and Donald Foster for their encouragement, advice, and, above all, for the willingness to place the fruit of their long labor into new hands. It has been a joy and pleasure to work with such wise colleagues. In addition, I wish to thank the reference and cataloging staff of Oklahoma State University's Edmon Low Library, especially cataloging librarian Linda Taylor, for their kind assistance. Special thanks also go to Dan Clark, Director of The Florida State University's Warren D. Allen Music Library.

Allen Scott

Oklahoma State University

August 2004

Preface to the First Edition

This book is intended as an introductory reference source of varied information, largely bibliographical, pertaining to research in the field of music. It has come largely out of the authors' years of experience in teaching Introduction to Graduate Study and Senior Research, two courses in music bibliography, research, and writing at the College-Conservatory of Music, University of Cincinnati, and it may function as a text in such courses, as well as in any music research class or seminar, graduate or upper-class undergraduate. If so used, it is not necessarily meant to be followed page by page from beginning to end, but adapted in accordance with the needs and emphases of different instructors and schools or individuals using the book. Its use is by no means limited to the classroom; it may also serve as a guide to current important sources in music for music researchers, faculty members, librarians, performing and teaching musicians, and musical amateurs.

The *Sourcebook for Research in Music* consists of seven chapters of bibliographies, each of a different type of source, preceded by a chapter of introductory materials pertaining to research in music. The bibliographies are usually divided into subcategories in order to avoid the confusion of long, undifferentiated lists of variously related items. The organization of the book is evident in the detailed table of contents, with all of the subheadings included, which should facilitate fairly rapid access to particular categories or types of sources. Furthermore, there are collective annotations throughout the book that introduce and identify specific items within the bibliographies they precede, often singling out sources of particular importance or distinguishing between different ones; where appropriate, cross references are made to items appearing elsewhere in the book. Finally, there are two indexes: the first of authors, editors, compilers, and translators; the second of titles of books, articles, and series.

The past decade or so has witnessed an extraordinary expansion of the materials of music, and the field is growing ever more rapidly. It has become a Herculean task to try to keep up with the many effort-saving sources that are constantly becoming available. Thus, in the interest of practicality and usefulness, emphasis has been placed on the more recent and up-to-date ones rather than on those of more purely historical or musicological interest, and on English-language sources rather than on those in foreign languages. Certain major early sources have occasionally been included, usually under the heading "Of Historical Interest," and some of the bibliographies include more recent sources in other languages as well, chiefly German and French, when considered to be of particular importance. (Brief lists of bibliographical terms in these languages have been provided in chapter 1 to assist further in confronting such sources.) Some of the bibliographies—in particular the "Basic Bibliographical Tools for Research in Music" in chapter 2—are meant to provide the means of direct access to materials of research; others emphasize the basic or current representative sources of significance. In other words, in the bibliographies and other materials that follow, the guiding principle, to one extent or another, is selectivity rather than comprehensiveness, as detailed in the chapter introductions and collective annotations throughout.

We have not tried to cover every conceivable area in which research might be conducted in music. For exhaustive lists of sources in areas such as, for example, the literature of specific instruments and performing ensembles, the music of individual countries throughout the world, popular music, and folk music, the reader should consult Vincent H. Duckles and Michael A. Keller, *Music Reference and Research Materials: An Annotated Bibliography*, 4th ed., rev.; and Guy A. Marco, ed., *Information on Music: A Handbook of Reference Sources in European Languages* (both listed on p. 49 below).

Three sources, *The New Grove Dictionary of Music and Musicians*, *The New Harvard Dictionary of Music*, and, to a lesser extent, *Die Musik in Geschichte und Gegenwart*, are cited fairly often throughout these pages, so they are given in abbreviated form whenever they occur (full citations appear in chapter 4 below on pp. 146, 152, and 146 respectively).

The stylistic and bibliographical format followed throughout is the one specified in Kate L. Turabian's *A Manual for Writers of Term Papers, Theses, and Dissertations*, 5th ed. (listed on p. 286 below). We have made a few adaptations, the most important of which are: (1) In the case of sources in second or later editions, or of translations of sources published earlier, the date of the original edition is also given (e.g., "First published in 1963"). (2) In the interest of simplicity, information about reprint and microform editions is usually omitted, the main exceptions being those instances in which something new has been added in the reprint, such as a list of corrections or a new preface. (3) Normally, when more than one city and/or publishing firm is listed in a source, only one of each is cited here, the city usually being the one where the principal headquarters is located. (4) Ordinarily, complicated or frequently changing publication information in serial publications, e.g., in the case of sets and monuments of music, has been abbreviated. For complete publication data related to music editions, see Hill and Stephens's recent *Collected Editions, Historical Series and Sets, and Monuments of Music: A Bibliography* (listed on p. 60 below).

We wish to extend our thanks to the following persons whose expertise and assistance have helped in various ways in the preparation of this book: Charles Benner, J. Bunker Clark, Carl Dahlgren, Karen Faaborg, Warren George, Lewis B. Hilton, Roland Jackson, David Lasocki, Michael Luebbe, bruce d. mcclung, Severine Neff, Bruno Nettl, Edward Nowacki, Karin Pendle, Lewis Peterman, Jennifer Stasack, Jennifer Thomas, J. Randall Wheaton, Lizabeth Wing, and Robert Zierolf; and to Robert Johnson and his staff at the Gorno Memorial Music Library of the University of Cincinnati: Paul Cauthen, Sharon Downing, Ollie Meyer, Mark Palkovic, and Rebecca Willingham. Finally, we are grateful to E. Eugene Helm, Jon Piersol, and Ruth Watanabe for their initial encouragement in this project.

University of Cincinnati

June 1992

SOURCEBOOK
FOR
RESEARCH
IN
MUSIC

CHAPTER ONE

Introductory Materials

As a preliminary to the bibliographies that constitute the main body of this volume, this chapter presents some general information pertaining to research in music. First, there is a list of standard English terms that relate to the scholarly study of music or to general bibliography and library research, with definitions. Next follow lists of such terms in the two other most important languages of research in music, German and French, together with English equivalents. The final list is a general outline of the music classification numbers in the two standard library cataloging systems in North America, the Library of Congress Classification system and the Dewey Decimal Classification system.

COMMON BIBLIOGRAPHICAL TERMS

The terms that follow have been brought together because of their application to scholarship in general and the scholarly study of music in particular. Some (e.g., *abstract, anthology, catalog, discography*) will be quite familiar and are generally known, whereas others might be confusing (*congress report, journal, magazine, periodical*). Many, even most, are likely to be less familiar because they are new or relate to the study of books (*codex, foliation, incunabula, siglum, watermark*), manuscripts (*autograph, choirbook, holograph*), printing (*colophon, facsimile, frontispiece*), research libraries (*archive, carrel, microforms, serial, stacks*), or scholarship (*collate, historical set, iconography, Urtext*). Some are technical or specialized enough so that they are not to be found in most dictionaries. For further information and other terms, see Heartsill Young, ed., *A.L.A. Glossary of Library and Information Science* (Chicago: American Library Association, 1983); and Jean Peters, *The Bookman's Glossary*, 6th ed., rev. and enl. (New York: R. R. Bowker, 1983).

abstract—a summary of a book, article, etc.; also called **précis** (e.g., *Dissertation Abstracts, RILM Abstracts*).

anthology—a representative collection of selected musical or literary works or excerpts.

archive—a place in which public or institutional records are systematically preserved, or a repository of any documents or other materials, especially those of historical value.

arrangement—a reworking of a musical composition so that the performing forces, the musical content, or the form are substantially different from the original (compare **edition,** definition c, and **transcription**).

autograph—a document (music manuscript, letter, etc.) written or signed in a person's own hand; thus, a primary source (see **sources, primary and secondary;** compare **holograph, manuscript**).

carrel—an alcove or desk in a library: often in the **stacks**— comprising a table and shelves for private study, to which books in a library's collection may be charged for research use.

catalog, catalogue—(a) a list of the contents of a library, book collection, or group of libraries (see **union catalog**); (b) a list or index of compositions, usually by a single composer rather than of a collection or a repertory of music (see **thematic catalog**).

CD-ROM ("compact disk read-only memory")—any information, such as a database, stored on compact disks and readable on the screen of a computer designed for this purpose, or one equipped with a CD-ROM drive (see **online catalog, database**).

choirbook—a music manuscript in a large enough **format** and with the separate voice parts of the compositions contained in it written large enough on the same or on facing pages so that an entire choir could sing from it (in use especially in the fifteenth and early sixteenth centuries). (See also **partbook, manuscript.**)

codex (pl.: codices)—an ancient book or unbound sheets in **manuscript** (e.g., Squarcialupi Codex, Trent Codices; see *The New Harvard Dictionary of Music,* "Sources [pre-1500]").

collate—to compare minutely in order to determine whether two or more books or manuscripts are identical copies or variants.

collected works, complete edition—the publication of the entire compositional output of a single composer in a scholarly edition (compare **edition,** definition c, **historical set, monument**).

colophon—(a) an inscription usually placed at the end of a book or manuscript and containing facts relative to its production; (b) an identifying mark, emblem, or device sometimes used by a printer or publisher on the title page, cover, spine, or jacket, i.e., a logotype (commonly called "logo") (compare **imprint**).

congress report—a publication containing the texts of the papers read at a congress or conference, either a one-time event on a particular topic, such as an individual composer, or the regular meeting of a society; in the first instance, the report would normally be an independent publication, and, in the second, it could be one of a series of such volumes (see **proceedings**) or published in the association's **journal.**

copyright (©)—the "right to copy"; the exclusive, legally secured right to reproduce, publish, record, and sell the matter and form of a literary, musical, or artistic work for a period in the United States of fifty years beyond the death of the writer, with no right of renewal (Copyright Act of 1976); different rules apply for works copyrighted before January 1, 1978, when the new law went into effect.

discography—a listing of phonograph records, compact disks, videotapes, and/or tape recordings.

edition—(a) all the impressions of a literary work printed at any time or times from one setting-up of type (excluding a **facsimile** reproduction, which constitutes a different edition); (b) one of the successive forms—e.g., second, revised, enlarged, corrected, etc.—in which a work is published, either by the author or a subsequent editor (see also **reprint edition, revised edition**); (c) the presentation of an older musical composition in a version that makes it accessible to modern performers (compare **arrangement, transcription**).

engraving—the process of incising a design, musical composition, etc., on a metal plate, or the resulting print made from it when the incised lines are inked.

facsimile—an exact reproduction (but not necessarily the original color or size) of a **manuscript** or printed source (compare **reprint edition**).

fair copy—a neat copy of a corrected document.

fascicle—one of the temporary divisions of a work which is issued in small installments intended to be bound together permanently at a later time.

Festschrift—a publication on the occasion of a celebration, or in honor of someone (e.g., on the occasion of a renowned scholar's sixtieth birthday), usually consisting of articles by practicing scholars in the field of the one honored, e.g., colleagues, former students, or other professionals.

foliation—the consecutive numbering of the leaves (i.e., the sheets of paper with a page on each side) of a book or manuscript, as opposed to the numbering of the pages (see also **recto, verso**).

folio (f., fo., fol.)—(a) a leaf of a **manuscript** or book (see **recto, verso**); (b) formed of sheets each folded once into two leaves or four pages ("in folio"); (c) a page size more than 15 inches/38 centimeters high; (d) a volume of this size.

format—the general makeup of a book as to size and other features (see also **folio, oblong, octavo, quarto**).

frontispiece—an illustration preceding and facing the title page of a book.

historical set—a set of volumes of music of historical significance (compare **anthology, monument;** see chapter 7 of this book).

holograph—a document (music manuscript, letter, etc.) *wholly* in the handwriting of its author (from the Greek word *holos*, "whole" or "complete"; thus, a primary source (see **sources, primary and secondary;** compare **autograph, manuscript**).

iconography—the study of the representation of objects by means of images or statues, reliefs, mosaics, paintings, etc.

imprint—the publisher's name, often with address and date of publication, placed at the foot of the title page or elsewhere in a book (compare **colophon**).

incipit—the first few notes or words of text used to identify a musical composition.

incunabula (pl.)—Latin, "cradle"; books printed from movable type before 1500 (i.e., the cradle of printing).

ISBN, ISSN (International Standard Book Number; International Standard Serial Number)—code numbers in an international identification system first developed in the United Kingdom in 1967 and adopted in the United States in 1968; the identifying code is placed at the front of books and **serials** respectively (e.g., ISBN 0–697–03342–2, ISSN 1044–1608).

journal—(a) a generic term to refer to, or sometimes used in the title of, a scholarly periodical (e.g., *Journal of the American Musicological Society*); (b) a diary or daily record of occurrences, transactions, or reflections. (Compare **magazine, periodical, proceedings, review, yearbook;** see chapter 6 of this book.)

lacuna (pl.: **lacunae**)—a hiatus, gap, or missing portion in a source or body of works.

lexicon—a book containing an alphabetical or other systematic arrangement of words and their definitions; a dictionary.

magazine—a **periodical** containing articles, pictures, reviews, advertisements, etc., often of popular interest and sometimes focusing on a specific subject area.

manuscript (MS, ms)—(a) a book, document, musical composition, letter, etc., written by hand; (b) an author's written or typed copy of a work before it is printed; thus, a primary source (see **sources, primary and secondary;** compare **autograph, holograph**).

microforms—a general term for microfilm and other miniature processes of reproduction such as the following:
> **microcard**—a card on which numerous pages of a book are reproduced in greatly reduced size.
> **microfiche**—a cardlike transparency on which appear multiple frames of microfilm.
> **microfilm**—a photographic reproduction in which the image is reduced to fit a frame of 35 millimeter or 16 millimeter film.

monograph—a scholarly study (book or article) treating a single subject or a limited aspect of a subject (see also **treatise**).

monument, musical—a scholarly edition of music from one region or country (*Denkmal* [pl.: *Denkmäler*] is the German equivalent) (see **edition,** definition c; refer to chapter 7 of this book).

necrology—(a) a notice of the death of a person; obituary; (b) a list or record of people who have died within a certain period of time; in either sense there may or may not be biographical information included.

oblong (ob., obl.)—a book size wider than it is high (e.g., 4' obl., 8' obl.).

octavo (8', 8vo) the size of a piece of paper cut eight from a sheet, or a page size about 9 3/4 inches/25 centimeters high.

online catalog, database—a catalog of information (such as a library's holdings with information about each item) loaded into a computer, which may be called up by author, title, subject, keyword(s), type or set of composition(s), etc., on a computer terminal (see **catalog, catalogue,** definition a).

opus (pl. opera, opuses)—a creative work, usually a composition, to which a number is assigned by a composer or publisher to indicate its order in a composer's written and/or published output.

partbook—one of a set of printed or manuscript books, each containing the music for only one voice or instrument part in an ensemble (in use throughout the sixteenth century and into the seventeenth).

periodical—a **journal** or **magazine** ordinarily with a fixed interval between issues (compare **serial**).

précis—a summary of a book, article, etc.; also called **abstract.**

proceedings—a published report of a conference or meeting of a society or congress, frequently accompanied by abstracts or texts of the papers presented there (see also **congress report**).

pseudonym—pen name; nom de plume.

quarto (4', 4to)—the size of a piece of paper cut four from a sheet, or a page size about 12 inches/30 centimeters high.

rastrology—the study of musical staves drawn by hand using a rastrum (Latin, "rake"), a pen with five or more points used to draw one or more staves at a time; the comparison of differences and irregularities between the lines and staves thus drawn may lead to conclusions such as probable date, identity of the scribe, etc., of a manuscript.

recto (r)—the side of a **folio** that is to be read first, i.e., the right-hand page (e.g., "fol. 2r"; see also **verso**).

reprint edition—a later unaltered printing of a work that ordinarily is no longer in print, often issued by another publisher who specializes in these editions, such as Da Capo or Dover (compare **facsimile, revised edition**).

reprography—the process of copying documents by xerography, photography, etc.

review—(a) a writing which gives a critical assessment of something, such as a written work or musical performance; (b) a term often used in titles of scholarly periodicals (e.g., *Performance Practice Review, La revue musicale*).

revised edition—an edition of a work incorporating major revisions by the author or an editor and often supplementary matter designed to bring it up to date (compare **reprint edition**).

serial—any publication usually appearing at regular intervals, including **periodicals,** annuals (**yearbooks**), newspapers, **proceedings,** etc.

shelflist—a bibliographical record of a library collection in call-number order.

siglum (pl.: sigla)—a letter or letters with or without numbers used to identify a manuscript or printed source, library, or archive (see *The New Harvard Dictionary of Music,* "Sources [Pre-1500]").

sources, primary and secondary—a primary source is a composition, letter, or document by a composer, author, or some other person, or any document dating from the historical period in question that gives the words of the witnesses or recorders of an event; a secondary source is second- or third-hand information and may be based on a primary source.

stacks—a library term for the main area in a library where books are shelved. Stacks are either "open," if the general public is admitted to them, or "closed," if it is not.

stemmatics—from stemma (Latin, "garland, wreath"); the genealogical study of musical or literary manuscripts.

thematic catalog—a list or index of compositions, usually by a single composer rather than of a collection or repertory of music, in which each composition or movement is identified by an **incipit** (compare **catalog, catalogue,** definition b).

transcription—(a) the transliteration of an early work into modern musical notation; (b) the process or result of adapting a musical composition (usually instrumental) to a medium other than its original one, which may vary from little more than a transference from one medium to another to a modification of the original necessitated by the change of medium (compare **arrangement, edition**).

treatise—a learned, formal writing on a subject, usually in book form (see also **monograph**).

union catalog—a library catalog listing the holdings of a group of cooperating libraries (see **catalog, catalogue,** definition a).

Urtext—original text, often a prototype from which later variants (texts, compositions, etc.) are derived.

verso (v)—the side of a **folio** that is to be read second, i.e., the reverse side or left-hand page (e.g., "fol. 2v"; see also **recto**).

watermark—a manufacturer's identifying mark or design embedded in a sheet of paper, resulting from different thicknesses in the paper and visible when held up to light.

yearbook—a publication issued annually, such as the *Bach-Jahrbuch* or *"Recherches" sur la musique française classique,* that contains scholarly contributions and information, often limited to a specific area.

GERMAN BIBLIOGRAPHICAL TERMS

The English equivalents given for the following German terms are those that concern bibliography and scholarship (e.g., *Folge* can also mean "sequel," "result," "inference," etc., as well as "series"); in particular, note terms that are not obvious cognates or are even misleading ones, sometimes called "false friends" (e.g., *Band,*

Brief, Kapitel, Register). Abbreviations commonly used in scholarly German are given here, and other standard ones may be found listed in any good German-English dictionary. The abbreviations of musical terms have been taken largely from Richard Schaal's *Abkürzungen in der Musik-Terminologie* (see p. 152 below), which is devoted entirely to abbreviations in music; and from *Die Musik in Geschichte und Gegenwart* [*MGG*] (see chapter 4 under "General Dictionaries and Encyclopedias"), whose abbreviations are listed at the beginning of each volume.

Abbildung (Abb.)—illustration, figure
Abdruck (Abdr.)—impression, print, reproduction
Abhandlung (Abh.)—treatise
Abkürzung (Abk.)—abbreviation
Abschrift (Abschr.)—reprint, copy
Anhang (Anh.)—appendix, supplement (see also **Beilage, Beiheft**)
Anmerkung (Anm.)—footnote (see also **Fussnote**)
Anthologie (Anth.)—anthology
Archiv (Arch.)—record office, archive
Aufführungspraxis—performance practice
Auflage (Aufl.)—edition (see also **Ausgabe, Gesammelte Werke, Gesamtausgabe, Sammelwerk, Sämtliche Werke**)
Ausgabe (Ausg.)—edition (see also **Auflage, Gesammelte Werke, Gesamtausgabe, Sammelwerk, Sämtliche Werke**)
Ausgewählte Werke (AW)—selected works
Band (Bd.)—volume
Bearbeiter; Bearbeitung (Bearb.)—compiler, author, reviser; compilation, edition, arrangement
Beiheft (Beih.)—supplement (see also **Anhang, Beilage**)
Beilage (Beil.)—supplement, appendix (see also **Anhang, Beiheft**)
Beispiel (Beisp.)—example ("zum Beispiel" [z.B.]: for example, e.g.)
Beitrag (Beitr.)—contribution (i.e., to a journal)
Bemerkungen (Bem.)—remarks, annotations, commentary
Bericht (Ber.)—report, commentary (see also **Kritischer Bericht, Revisionsbericht**)
Besprechung—review, criticism, conference
beziehungsweise (bzw.)—respectively; or, or else; more specifically
Bibliothek (Bibl.)—library
Bildnis (Bildn.)—portrait, likeness
Bildtafel—plate in a book
Blatt (Bl.)—leaf, folio; newspaper
Brief—letter, epistle

Buchhändler; Buchhandlung (Buchh.)—bookseller; bookshop
das heisst (d.h.)—that is, i.e. (also "das ist")
Denkmäler (Dkm.) (pl.)—monuments
Doktorarbeit; Dissertation (Diss.)—doctoral dissertation
Druck (Dr.)—print, printing, impression
ebenda(selbst) (ebd.)—in the same place, ibidem
Einleitung (Einl.)—introduction
erscheinen (ersch.)—to appear, come out, be published
Festschrift (Fs.)—publication on the occasion of a celebration
    or in honor of someone
Folge (F.); Neue Folge (N.F.)—series, continuation, issue; new
    series or issue ("und folgende" [u.ff.]: and following)
Fussnote—footnote (see also **Anmerkung**)
geboren (geb.)—born
gedruckt (gedr.)—printed
Gegenwart (Gegenw.)—present time
Gesammelte Werke (GW)—complete works (see also **Auflage,**
    Ausgabe, Gesamtausgabe, Sammelwerk, Sämtliche
    Werke)
Gesamtausgabe (GA)—complete works (see also **Auflage,**
    Ausgabe, Gesammelte Werke, Sammelwerk, Sämtliche
    Werke)
Geschichte (Gesch.)—history
Gesellschaft (Ges.)—society, association, club (see also **Verein,**
    Musikverein)
gestorben (gest.)—died
getauft (get.)—baptized
Handbuch (Hdb.)—handbook, manual
Handexemplar—composer's or author's copy
Handschrift (Hs.)—manuscript (see also **Manuskript**)
Heft (H.)—number, part
Herausgeber (Hrsg.); herausgegeben (hg.)—editor (see also
    Redakteur); edited, published (see also **publiziert**)
Inhalt (Inh.)—table of contents
insbesondere (insb.)—especially, particularly
Jahr (J.)—year
Jahrbuch (Jb.)—yearbook
Jahreszahl (JZl.)—date, year
Jahrgang (Jg.)—the bound issues of a periodical for one year
Jahrhundert (Jh.)—century
Kapitel (Kap.)—chapter
Katalog (Kat.)—catalog
Komponist (Komp.)—composer
Kritischer Bericht (Krit. Ber.)—critical report or commentary
    (see also **Revisionsbericht**)
Kunst—art ("Tonkunst": music [tonal art])

Lexikon (L)—dictionary (abb. used in combination with an
  author, e.g., RiemannL) (see also **Wörterbuch**)
Lieferung (Lfg.)—part of a work, fascicle
Literatur (Lit.)—literature, letters, bibliography
Manuskript (Ms.)—manuscript (see also **Handschrift**)
Mitarbeiter (Mitarb.)—collaborator
Mitteilung (Mitt.)—announcement, communication (see also
  Nachricht)
Mitwirkung (Mitw.)—cooperation
Monatsheft—monthly periodical
Musik Lexikon (M Lex.)—music lexicon, dictionary (see also
  Wörterbuch)
Musikforschung (Mf.)—music research (see also **Musikwis-
  senschaft**)
Musikgeschichte (Mg.)—music history
Musikverein (MV)—musical society (see also **Gesellschaft**)
Musikwissenschaft (Mw.)—musicology (see also **Musik-
  forschung**)
Nachricht (Nachr.)—communication, report, notice (see also
  Mitteilung)
Nachwort (Nachw.)—concluding remarks, epilogue
Neudruck (Neudr.)—reprint
Neuausgabe, Neue Ausgabe (NA)—new edition
ohne (o.)—without ("ohne Jahr" [o.J.]: no year [of publication];
  "ohne Ort" [o.O.]: no place [of publication], no opus
  [number])
Partitur (P., Part.)—musical score
publiziert (publ.)—published (see also **herausgegeben**)
Quelle—source
Redakteur; Redaktion (Red.)—editor (see also **Herausgeber**);
  editorial matter, editorial staff
Register—index
Reihe (R.)—series, set, tone row ("Neue Reihe" [N.R.]: new
  series)
revidiert (rev.)—revised
Revisionsbericht—critical commentary (see also **Kritischer
  Bericht**)
Sammelband (Sbd., Smlbd.)—volume containing a collection
  of essays
Sammelwerk (Sw., Swk.)—collected works (see also **Auflage,
  Ausgabe, Gesammelte Werke, Gesamtausgabe,
  Sämtliche Werke**)
Sammlung (Samlg., Samml., Slg., Slng.)—collection, compila-
  tion, set
Sämtliche Werke—complete works (see also **Auflage, Ausgabe,
  Gesammelte Werke, Gesamtausgabe, Sammelwerk**)

Schrift—writing, book, periodical, etc.
Schriftleiter; Schriftleitung (Schriftl.)—editor (see also **Herausgeber, Redakteur**); editorship, editorial staff (see also **Redaktion**)
Seite (S.)—page
siehe oben (s.o.)—see above, supra
siehe unten (s.u.)—see below, infra
Skizzen (SK)—sketches, outlines
Stimmbuch (Stb.)—part book
Tabelle (Tab.)—table, chart, graph (see also **Tafel**)
Tafel (Taf.)—table (see also **Tabelle**)
Teil (Tl.)—part, division ("zum Teil" [z.T.]: in part)
Titelblatt—title page
Überlieferung—tradition, inheritance, surviving original sources, etc.
Übertragung (Übtr.)—translation, transcription
und andere (u.a.)—and others, et al.
und so weiter (usw.)—and so forth, etc.
unter anderem (u.a.)—among others
Urtext—original text
Verein (Ver.)—association, society (see also **Gesellschaft**)
Verfasser (Verf.)—composer, writer
vergleich (vgl., vergl.)—compare
Verlag (Vlg.)—publishing house
Verzeichnis (Verz.)—catalog
Vierteljahrsschrift (Vjs.)—quarterly periodical
in Vorbereitung (in Vorb.)—in preparation
Vorrede (Vorr.)—preface (see also **Vorwort**)
Vortrag (Vortr.)—lecture, discourse, report
Vorwort (Vorw.)—foreword (see also **Vorrede**)
Wochenblatt—weekly periodical
Wörterbuch (Wb.)—dictionary (see also **Lexikon**)
Zahl (Zl.)—number, numeral, figure
Zeitschrift (Zs., Ztschr.)—periodical
Zeitung (Ztg.)—newspaper
zugleich (zugl.)—at the same time, together, conjointly, with (see also **zusammen**)
zur Zeit (z.Z., z.Zt.)—now, at present
zusammen (zus.)—together, jointly (see also **zugleich**)

FRENCH BIBLIOGRAPHICAL TERMS

As in the preceding list of German terms, the English equivalents for the following French terms concern bibliography and scholarship only (e.g., besides "sheet of paper" or "folio," *feuille* can mean "leaf," "veneer," etc.), and similarly include "false friends" (e.g., *avertissement, dessin, libraire*).

abréger—to abbreviate
analyse—book review (see also **compte rendu**); analysis
annexe—appendix (to a book)
annuaire—yearbook
aperçu—literary sketch, outline, summary (see also **esquisse**)
augmenté(e)—enlarged ("édition augmentée")
auteur—author ("du même auteur": by the same author) (see
        also **écrivain**)
avant-propos—preface, foreword; introduction (see also **aver-
        tissement, avis**)
avertissement—preface, foreword (see also **avant-propos, avis**)
avis—notice ("avis au lecteur": preface, foreword) (see also
        avant-propos, avertissement)
beaux-arts—fine arts
bibliothèque—library
cahier—short book or magazine; copybook
catalogue raisonné—descriptive catalog
chapitre—chapter
chez—at the (publishing) house of
collection—set or series of books (see also **fonds, recueil, série**)
compositeur—composer
compte rendu—book review or résumé (see also **analyse**)
corrigé(e)—corrected ("édition corrigée")
côte—call number
dépôt légal—registration of copyright
dessin—drawing, sketch
dictionnaire—dictionary (see also **lexique**)
dirigé(e)—directed ("collection dirigée par Jean Marin": series
        of books under the general editorship of . . .)
écrit—writing, written work
écrivain—writer (see also **auteur**)
éditer—to publish, issue (usually not "to edit") (see also **publier**)
éditeur—publisher (usually), editor (rarely)
esquisse—literary or pictorial sketch, outline (see also **aperçu**)
étude—study (noun)
feuille, feuillet—sheet of paper, folio
fonds—collection in a library ("les fonds Dupont": the Dupont
        collection) (see also **collection, recueil**)
gravure—engraving
hebdomadaire—weekly (see also **mensuel, trimestriel**)
impression—printing ("2e impression": 2nd printing) (see also
        tirage)

imprimer—to print
inédit—unpublished
journal—newspaper
lexique—lexicon, dictionary (see also **dictionnaire**)
libraire—bookseller (not "library")
librairie—bookshop (not "library")
livre—book
livret—libretto
mélange—miscellany (see also **recueil**)
mensuel(le)—monthly (see also **hebdomadaire, trimestriel**)
musicographe; musicographie—writer on music; works about music
oeuvre—work, output
oeuvres complètes (o.c.)—complete works
ouvrage—work of literature, art, etc.
page de titre—title page
partie—part of a book, etc.
partition—musical score
paru—published ("déjà paru": already published)
périodique—periodical (see also **revue**)
planche—plate in a book ("planches hors texte": plates not numbered with the pages of text)
précis—abstract
publier—edit, publish (see also **éditer**)
recueil—collection, selection, miscellany ("recueil choisi": anthology) (see also **collection, fonds, mélange**)
rédacteur; rédaction—editor ("rédacteur en chef": chief editor); editorial staff
rédiger—to edit (a newspaper), to draft or write (an article, etc.)
réimpression—reprinting
reliure—bookbinding
revu(e)—revised ("édition revue")
revue—magazine, periodical (see also **périodique**)
série—series (see also **collection**)
siècle—century
sommaire—short, brief ("bibliographie sommaire"); table of contents (see also **table des matières**)
table des matières—table of contents (see also **sommaire**)
tableau—table in a book (e.g., "tableau chronologique")
thèse—thesis, doctoral dissertation
tirage—printing (see also **impression**)
titre—title
tome (t.)—volume; division of a book
traduction—translation
traité—treatise

travail—work, piece of work
trimestriel(le)—quarterly (every three months) (see also **hebdo-madaire, mensuel**)
voir (v.)—see (e.g., "v. Annexe 2": see appendix 2)

LIBRARY OF CONGRESS MUSIC CLASSIFICATION

The holdings of most North American research and university libraries are arranged according to the Library of Congress classification system, although other systems, chiefly the Dewey Decimal, are sometimes used. Because of the wide application of the Library of Congress (LC) system, the portions that pertain to music and music literature are listed below in some detail. In a library that uses the system, these letter(s) and number(s) are followed by a decimal point and further letter(s) and number(s) (the so-called cutter or author number; e.g., ML 1255 .B23 1983, ML 410 .B4H92, etc.), which may or may not be the same as those in the Library of Congress's own complete call numbers. The initial letter-number combinations, however, are the same from one library to another (e.g., oratorios are always cataloged between M 2000 and M 2007, biographies of individual composers under ML 410, analytic guides between MT 90 and MT 145). This greatly facilitates searching or browsing in any LC-based library's stacks or shelflist. The following list is adapted from *M, Music and Books on Music: Library of Congress Classification, 1998 edition* (Washington, D.C.: Library of Congress, Cataloging Distribution Service, 1999). For the complete alphabetical listing of subject headings, in music as well as in all other areas, consult *Library of Congress Subject Headings,* 25th ed., 5 vols. (Washington, D.C.: Cataloging Distribution Service, Library of Congress, 2002).

Music

1.A1–.A15	Music printed or copied in manuscript in the United States or the colonies before 1860
1.A5–2.3	Collections
2–2.3	Collections of musical sources
3–3.3	Collected works of individual composers
3.3	First editions

Instrumental Music

5	Collections
6–175.5	Solo instruments
176	Instrumental music for motion pictures

176.5	Instrumental music for radio and television
177–990	Music for two or more solo instruments
180–298.5	Duets
300–386	Trios
400–486	Quartets
500–586	Quintets
600–686	Sextets
700–786	Septets
800–886	Octets
900–986	Nonets and larger combinations of purely chamber music
990	Chamber music for instruments of the 18th century and earlier
1000–1075	Orchestra
1100–1160	String orchestra
1200–1269	Band
1270	Fife (bugle) and drum music, field music, etc.
1350–1353	Reduced orchestra
1356–1356.2	Dance orchestra and instrumental ensembles
1360	Mandolin and similar orchestras of plucked instruments
1362	Accordion band
1365	Minstrel music
1366	Jazz ensembles
1375–1420	Instrumental music for children
1450	Dance music
1470	Chance compositions
1473	Electronic music
1480	Music with color or light apparatus
1490	Music, printed or copied in manuscript, before 1700

Vocal Music

1497–1998	Secular vocal music
1500–1527.8	Dramatic music
1528–1529.5	Duets, trios, etc., for solo voices
1530–1546.5	Choruses with orchestra or other ensemble
1547–1600	Choruses, part-songs, etc., with accompaniment of keyboard or other solo instrument, or unaccompanied
1608	Choruses, etc., in tonic sol-fa notation
1609	Unison choruses

1610	Cantatas, choral symphonies, etc., for unaccompanied chorus (secular and sacred) with or without solo voices
1611–1624.8	Songs
1625–1626	Recitations with music
1627–1853	National music
1900–1978	Songs (part and solo) of special character
1985	Musical games
1990–1998	Secular music for children
1999–2199	Sacred vocal music
1999	Collections
2000–2007	Oratorios
2010–2017.6	Services
2018–2019.5	Duets, trios, etc., for solo voices
2020–2036	Choruses, cantatas, etc.
2060–2101.5	Choruses, part-songs, etc., with accompaniment of keyboard or other solo instrument, or unaccompanied
2102–2114.8	Songs
2115–2146	Hymnals, hymn collections
2147–2188	Liturgy and ritual
2147–2155.6	Roman Catholic Church
2156–2160.87	Orthodox churches
2161–2183	Protestant churches
2184	Other Christian churches
2186–2187	Jewish
2188	Other non-Christian religions
2190–2196	Sacred vocal music for children
2198–2199	Gospel, revival, temperance, etc., songs
5000	Unidentified compositions

ML   Literature on Music

1–5	Periodicals
12–21	Directories, almanacs
25–28	Societies, organizations
29–33	Special collections and institutions
35–38	Festivals, Congresses
40–44	Programs
47–54.8	Librettos and scenarios
55–60	Collected essays, etc., by several authors, including Festschriften
62–90	Special aspects
90	Writings of musicians (collections)

1091.8–1093	Electronic instruments
1100–1165	Chamber music
1200–1270	Orchestra music
1300–1354	Band music
1370–1380	Electronic music, computer music
1400–3275	Vocal music
1499–1554	Choral music
1600–2881	Secular vocal music
2900–3275	Sacred vocal music
3300–3354	Program music
3400–3465	Dance music
3544–3775	National music
3790	Music industry
3797	General works on music history and musicology
3800–3923	Philosophy and physics of music
3830	Psychology
3845–3877	Aesthetics
3880–3915	Criticism
3928–3930	Literature for children

MT   Musical Instruction and Study

1–5	History and criticism
5.5–7	Music theory
20–32	Special methods
40–67	Composition, elements, and techniques of music
58–67	Forms
68	Improvisation, accompaniment, transposition
70–74	Instrumentation and orchestration
73	Band
90–146	Analysis and appreciation of musical works
95–100	Opera, ballet, opéra-ballet, etc.
110–115	Oratorios, cantatas, etc.
125–130	Orchestral music
140–145	Chamber and solo instrumental music
146	Popular music
150	Audio-visual aids
170–810	Instrumental techniques
180–198	Organ
192	Electronic keyboard instruments
200–208	Reed organ
220–255	Piano

259–338	String instruments
260–279.7	Violin
280–298	Viola
300–318	Violoncello
320–334	Double bass
339–533	Wind instruments
340–359	Flute
360–379	Oboe
380–392	Clarinet (A, B-flat, C, E-flat, etc.)
400–415	Bassoon
418	Brass instruments
420–432	Horn
440–456	Trumpet
460–472	Trombone
480–488	Tuba
500–510	Saxophone
539–654	Plucked instruments
540–557	Harp
560–570	Banjo
580–599	Guitar
600–612	Mandolin
620–634	Zither
640–654	Lute, balalaika, etc.
655–725	Percussion and other instruments
728	Chamber music
730	Orchestra
733–733.6	Band
740–810	Instrumental techniques for children
820–915	Singing and vocal technique
825–850	Systems and methods
855–883	Special techniques
885–893	Studies and exercises
898–915	Techniques for children
918–948	School music
955–956	Musical theater

SOME NONMUSICAL GENERAL CLASSIFICATIONS RELATING TO RESEARCH IN MUSIC

A	General Works	L	Education
B	Philosophy, Psychology, Religion	N	Fine Arts
D	History	P	Languages, Literature
GV	Dance	Q, T	Science, Technology
K	Law	Z	Bibliography

Dewey Decimal Classification: Music

Although a majority of North American research and university libraries use the Library of Congress Classification system, approximately 25 percent of academic libraries and most public and civic libraries in the United States use the Dewey Decimal Classification system (DDC). In addition, libraries in more than 135 countries use the DDC to organize their collections. The DDC is maintained by the Decimal Classification Division of the Library of Congress, and all copyright rights are owned by the Online Computer Library Center (OCLC). A full introduction to the DDC is available at the OCLC website (http://www.oclc.org/dewey).

According to OCLC, in the DDC basic classes are organized by disciplines or fields of study. At the broadest level, the DDC is divided into ten main classes, which together cover the entire world of knowledge. Each main class is further divided into ten divisions, and each division into ten sections. Music is assigned the classification range 780–789 (class 700, division 80, sections 1–9).

Because the DDC was created in the nineteenth century, librarians have had to make adjustments periodically in the system to accommodate new knowledge and new disciplines. Therefore, throughout the twentieth century different versions of the DDC contain reassigned or revised meanings of parts of the system. A complete revision of a division is known as a phoenix schedule.

The version of the DDC currently in use is the twenty-first edition (called the DDC21). The last complete revision (phoenix schedule) of the music division 780 occurred in 1989 with edition 20 (DDC20). These revisions present problems with DDC collections. Most libraries do not routinely reclassify their existing collections when a phoenix schedule is published; therefore, such collections contain items cataloged under two or more systems. This situation can severely restrict the facility of browsing in a DDC collection. Both DDC19 and DDC21 are listed here to aid the researcher working in a collection that is not consistently cataloged.

The following table compares the differences of the main sections between DDC19 (the last edition before the most recent phoenix schedule) and DDC21 (the current edition).

DDC21		DDC19
780	Relation of music to other subjects	Music
781	General principles and musical forms	General principles and considerations

782	Vocal music	Dramatic music and musical drama
783	Music for single voices, the voice	Specific kinds of music and performing groups
784	Instruments and instrumental ensembles and their music	Voice and vocal music
785	Ensembles with only one instrument per part	Instrumental ensembles and their music
786	Keyboard, mechanical, electrophonic, percussion instruments	Keyboard instruments and their music
787	Stringed instruments, bowed string instruments	String instruments and their music
788	Wind instruments	Wind instruments and their music
789	Composers and traditions of music (optional number)	Percussion, mechanical, electrical instruments

The following list of the DDC21 music classification is adapted from *Dewey Decimal Classification and Relative Index, Edition 21* (Albany, N.Y.: Forest Press, 1996).

Dewey Decimal Classification 21: Music

780	**Relation of Music to Other Subjects**
780.1	Philosophy and theory
780.2	Miscellany
780.7	Education, research, performances, related topics
780.8	History and description of music with respect to kinds of persons
780.9	Historical, geographic, persons treatment
780.901–.905	Periods of stylistic development of music
780.901	Ancient times through 499
780.902	500–1449 (including Gothic style, ars antiqua, ars nova, medieval music)
780.903	1450+
780.903 1	Ca. 1450–ca. 1600 (including Renaissance music)
780.903 2	Ca. 1600–ca. 1750 (including Baroque music, nuove musiche)

780.903 3	Ca. 1750–ca. 1825 (including preclassicism, classicism, rococo style)
780.903 4	Ca. 1825–ca. 1900 (including nationalism, romanticism)
780.904	1900–1999 (including avant-garde music, impressionism, neoclassicism)
780.905	2000–2099
780.92	Persons associated with music (biographies and studies of composers, performers, and critics; thematic catalogs of individual composers)
780.94	Europe, Western Europe
781	**General Principles and Musical Forms**
781.1	Basic principles of music
781.11	Psychological principles
781.12	Religious principles
781.17	Artistic principles
781.2	Elements of music
781.22	Time (including pulse, rhythm, meter)
781.23	Musical sound (including pitch, volume, timbre)
781.24	Melody (including scales, ornaments, themes)
781.25	Harmony (including chords, harmonic rhythm, tonality)
781.26	Tonal systems (including modes, atonality, dodecaphony)
781.28	Texture
781.3	Composition
781.32	Indeterminacy and aleatory composition
781.33	Serialism
781.34	Computer composition
781.36	Extemporization (improvisation)
781.37	Arrangement (including transcription and orchestration)
781.38	Arrangements
781.4	Techniques of music
781.42	Techniques for acquiring musical skills and learning a repertoire
781.43	Performance techniques
781.44	Rehearsal and practice
781.45	Conducting
781.46	Interpretation
781.47	Accompaniment (including continuo)
781.48	Breathing and resonance

781.49	Recording of music
781.5	Kinds of music
781.52	Music for specific times (days, times of day, seasons)
781.53	Music in specific settings (including court, theater, concert hall)
781.54	Music for specific media (including film, radio, television)
781.55	Music accompanying public entertainments (dramatic music, dance, ballet)
781.56	Program music
781.57	Music accompanying activities
781.58	Music accompanying stages of the life cycle
781.59	Music reflecting other themes and subjects (including work, recreation, and military music)
781.6	Traditions of music (works emphasizing a specific tradition)
781.62	Folk music
781.621–.629	Folk music of specific racial, ethnic, national groups
781.63	Popular music
781.64	Western popular music (including country, blues, ragtime, rap, etc.)
781.65	Jazz
781.66	Rock (rock 'n' roll)
781.68	Western art (classical) music (comprehensive works on art music)
781.69	Non-Western music
781.7	Sacred music
781.71	Christian sacred music
781.711–.718	Christian sacred music of specific denominations
781.72	Music of the Christian church year
781.73	Sacred music of classical (Greek and Roman) and Germanic religions
781.74–.79	Sacred music of other religions
781.8	Musical forms
781.82	Specific musical forms (including binary, ternary, strophic, rondos, variations, etc.)
782	**Vocal Music**
782.1	Dramatic vocal forms, operas
782.12	Operettas

782.13	Singspiels
782.14	Musical plays
782.2	Nondramatic vocal forms
782.22	Sacred vocal forms
782.23	Oratorios
782.24	Large-scale vocal works, cantatas
782.25	Sacred songs
782.26	Motets
782.27	Hymns
782.28	Carols
782.29	Liturgical forms
782.292	Chant
782.294–.298	Specific texts
782.3	Services (liturgy and ritual)
782.32	Christian services
782.322	Services of specific denominations
782.323	Mass
782.324	Divine office
782.33	Services of classical (Greek and Roman) and Germanic religions
782.34–.39	Services of other specific religions
782.4	Secular forms
782.42	Songs
782.43	Forms derived from poetry, madrigals
782.47	Song cycles
782.48	Secular cantatas
782.5	Mixed voices (choral music, choral music with solo parts, unison voices)
782.6	Women's voices
782.7	Children's voices
782.8	Men's voices
782.9	Other types of voices
782.96	Speaking voices (choral speech)
782.97	Sprechgesang
783	**Music for Single Voices, the Voice**
783.1	Single voices in combination (part songs)
783.12–.19	Ensembles by size (duets, trios, quartets, etc.)
783.2	Solo voice
783.3	High voice
783.4	Middle voice
783.5	Low voice
783.6–.8	Woman's, child's, man's voice
783.9	Other types of voice
783.96	Speaking voice
783.97	Sprechgesang

784	**Instruments and Instrumental Ensembles and Their Music**
784.1	General principles, musical forms, instruments
784.18	Musical forms
784.182	General musical forms
784.183	Sonata form and sonatas
784.184	Symphonies
784.185	Suites and related forms
784.186	Concerto form
784.187	Contrapuntal forms
784.188	Dance forms
784.189	Other instrumental forms
784.2	Full (symphony) orchestra (comprehensive works on orchestral combinations, music intended equally for orchestral or chamber performance)
784.3	Chamber orchestra
784.4	Light orchestra (salon, school, and dance orchestras)
784.6	Keyboard, mechanical, electronic, percussion bands
784.7	String orchestra
784.8	Wind band (marching, military, and woodwind bands)
784.9	Brass band
785	**Ensembles with Only One Instrument per Part**
785.1	Ensembles by size (duets, trios, quartets, etc.)
785.2	Ensembles with keyboard
785.3	Ensembles without electrophones and with percussion and keyboard
785.4	Ensembles without keyboard
785.5	Ensembles without keyboard and with percussion
785.6	Keyboard, mechanical, aeolian, electrophone, percussion ensembles
785.7	String ensembles, bowed string ensembles
785.8	Woodwind ensembles
785.9	Brass ensembles
786	**Keyboard, Mechanical, Electrophonic, Percussion Instruments**
786.2	Pianos
786.3	Clavichords
786.4	Harpsichords (spinets, virginals)

786.5	Keyboard wind instruments, organs
786.6	Mechanical and aeolian instruments (including carillons, music boxes, player pianos)
786.7	Electrophones, electronic instruments (including synthesizers and *musique concrète*)
786.8	Percussion instruments (idiophones)
786.9	Drums and devices used for percussive effects (membranophones)
787	**Stringed Instruments (Chordophones), Bowed Stringed Instruments**
787.2	Violins
787.3	Violas
787.4	Violoncellos
787.5	Double basses
787.6	Other bowed stringed instruments (viols, violas d'amore, hurdy-gurdies)
787.7	Plectral instruments (zithers, lyres)
787.8	Plectral lute family (lutes, mandolins, guitars, etc.)
787.9	Harps and musical bows
788	**Wind Instruments (Aerophones)**
788.2	Woodwind instruments and free aerophones
788.3	Flute family
788.4	Reed instruments (bagpipes)
788.5	Double-reed instruments (oboes, bassoons, etc.)
788.6	Single-reed instruments (clarinets)
788.7	Saxophones
788.8	Free reeds (harmonicas, accordions, etc.)
788.9	Brass instruments (lip-reed instruments)
789	**Composers and Traditions of Music (Optional Number)**

The following list of the DDC19 music classification is adapted from *Dewey Decimal Classification and Relative Index, Edition 19* (Albany, N.Y.: Forest Press, 1979).

Dewey Decimal Classification 19: Music

780	**Music**
780.1	Philosophy and aesthetics
780.15	Appreciation
780.2	Miscellany

780.4	Special topics of general applicability
780.42	Popular music
780.43	Art ("classical") music
780.7	Study, teaching, performances
780.729 01–.729 05	Historical periods
780.8	Scores and parts, and treatment among groups of persons
780.81–.82	Collected scores and parts of conventional size
780.9	Historical and geographical treatment
780.901–.905	Periods of development of music, of European music
780.901	Ancient times to 450 A.D.
780.902	450–1450 (including Gothic style, ars antiqua, ars nova)
780.903	Modern period, 1450+
780.903 1	1450–1600 (including Renaissance style)
780.903 2	1600–1750 (including Baroque style, nuove musiche)
780.903 3	1750–1825 (including classicism, rococo style)
780.903 4	1825–1900 (including nationalism, romanticism)
780.904	Twentieth century, 1900–1999 (including new music, impressionism, neoclassicism)
780.905	Twenty-first century, 2000–2099
780.91	Treatment by areas, regions, places in general
780.92	Persons associated with music (composers, performers, critics)
780.93	Treatment by specific continents, countries, localities
781	**General Principles and Considerations**
781.1	Scientific principles (mathematical, physical, physiological)
781.2	Other basic considerations
781.22	Musical sound (pitch, scales, intervals, tonalities, chords)
781.3	Harmony (including harmonic analysis, twelve-tone system)
781.32	Thorough bass (basso continuo)
781.4	Melody and counterpoint
781.41	Melody
781.42	Counterpoint (including canon, fugue)
781.5	Musical forms

781.52	Sonata
781.55	Dance music
781.56	Program music
781.57	Jazz and related forms
781.6	Composition and performance
781.61	Composition
781.62	Rhythm and meter
781.63	Performance (execution, interpretation, expression)
781.64	Arrangement (transcription)
781.65	Improvisation (extemporization)
781.66	Accompaniment
781.67	Embellishment
781.7	Music of ethnic groups and various specific countries and localities
781.71	Of nonliterate peoples
781.72–.79	Of literate peoples
781.9	Other topics
781.91	Musical instruments (including design, description, hand construction, care, tuning, repairing, verification)
781.96	Words to be sung or recited with music
782	**Dramatic Music and Production of Musical Drama**
782.01	Philosophy, theory, aesthetics
782.02	Miscellany
782.07	Study, teaching, production, productions
782.08	Collections and treatment among groups of persons
782.1	Opera (grand, light, comic, satiric, chamber)
782.8	Theater music
782.9	Music for ballets, masques, pageants, pantomimes
783	**Specific Kinds of Music and Performing Groups**
783.1	Instrumental music (treatises on instrumental music and instrumental accompaniment to vocal music)
783.2	Liturgical and ritualistic music
783.21–.29	Liturgical music of a Christian church
783.3	Oratorios (including Passions)
783.4	Nonliturgical choral works (anthems, motets, choruses, cantatas)
783.5	Nonliturgical chants (Gregorian, Ambrosian, Anglican, Jewish chants)

783.6	Songs (including carols and Negro spirituals)
783.7	Evangelistic music (treatises on mission, revival, Sunday school, gospel music)
783.8	Choirs and vocal groups (in churches and other local units of worship; including training, conducting)
783.9	Hymns (songs for congregational singing)
783.952	Collections by more than one composer (hymnals)
784	**Voice and Vocal Music** (with or without instrumental accompaniment)
784.1	Choruses and part songs (choral pieces not originally composed for orchestral accompaniment)
784.2	Complete choral works (originally composed for chorus with or without solo voices)
784.3	Songs for from one to nine parts (vocal chamber music, art songs, dance songs, ballads, ballades, canzonets)
784.4	Folk songs
784.5	Popular songs (including country, blues, rock, soul)
784.6	Songs for specific groups and on specific subjects (including home and community, students and children, college and university, high school, etc.)
784.7	Other kinds of songs (including national airs, songs, hymns; songs of ethnic and cultural groups in the United States and Canada)
784.8	Collections of vocal music (solos, duets, trios, quartets, etc.)
784.9	The voice (training and performance for both solo and vocal ensemble)
785	**Instrumental Ensembles and Their Music**
785.1	Symphonies and band music
785.2	Music for orchestra with incidental vocal parts
785.3	Miscellaneous music for orchestra (including salon, string orchestras)
785.4	Music for small ensembles (including dance music and jazz)
785.5	Independent overtures for orchestra
785.6	Concertos (one or more solo instruments

	with orchestra or band, including concerti grossi)
785.7	Chamber music (compositions for two or more different solo instruments)
785.71–.79	Scores and parts for duets, trios, quartets, etc.
785.8	Suites for orchestra
786	**Keyboard Instruments and Their Music**
786.1	Keyboard string instruments and their music
786.2	Keyboard string instruments (including pianoforte, harpsichord, spinet, virginal, etc.)
786.3	Training in and performance on keyboard string instruments (including studies and exercises, graded instruction)
786.4	Music for keyboard string instruments
786.41–.49	Scores for specific forms (sonatas, rondos, fantasias, dances, suites, etc.)
786.5	Organ and its music
786.6	Organ
786.7	Training in and performance on organ (including studies and exercises, graded instruction)
786.8	Music for organ
786.81–.89	Scores for specific forms (sonatas, preludes and fugues, offertories, voluntaries, etc.)
786.9	Other keyboard instruments and their music
786.92	Electronic organ
786.94	Reed organ
786.97	Accordion and concertina
787	**String Instruments and Their Music**
787.1	Violin
787.2	Viola
787.3	Violoncello
787.4	Other bowed string instruments (double bass, viols, etc.)
787.5	Harp
787.6	Guitar, mandolin, lute
787.7	Banjo
787.8	Zither
787.9	Other plectral instruments (hurdy-gurdy, dulcimer, etc.)
788	**Wind Instruments and Their Music**
788.1	Trumpet, cornet, bugle

788.2	Trombone
788.4	Horns and other brass wind instruments (euphonium, tuba, etc.)
788.5	Flute group
788.6	Single reed instruments
788.7	Oboe and English horn
788.8	Bassoon
788.9	Other reed instruments (harmonica, bagpipe, etc.)
789	**Percussion, Mechanical, Electrical Instruments**
789.1	Membranophones (tympani, drum, tambourine, tom-tom)
789.2	Cymbals
789.3	Triangle
789.4	Anvil, castanets, gong, maracas, rattle
789.5	Bells, carillon, chimes
789.6	Other percussion instruments of definite pitch (including marimba, xylophone, vibraphone, celesta, etc.)
789.7	Mechanical instruments and devices
789.8	Music box
789.9	Electronic musical instruments and music recording
789.91	Music recording
789.98	*Musique concrète*
789.99	Electronic music

Researchers who work in both Library of Congress and Dewey Decimal collections or those who find themselves faced with learning a different system can consult Mona L. Scott's *Conversion Tables*, 2nd ed. (Englewood, Colo.: Libraries Unlimited, 1999). This three-volume work converts LC classifications to DDC21 classifications (volume 1), DDC21 classifications to LC classifications (volume 2), and provides the DDC21 and LC classifications of the Library of Congress subject headings (volume 3).

CHAPTER TWO

Basic Bibliographical Tools for Research in Music

This chapter consists of lists of the most important current basic sources, to be used as the point of departure for researching virtually any topic in the field of music. The sources listed in the various categories should be consulted, as appropriate, along with related books on the subject in question—period or regional music histories, biographies, histories of genres or forms, general and specialized music dictionaries and encyclopedias, chief texts on the subject, etc.—for the preliminary compilation of a working bibliography. Sources may be found under subject headings in a particular library's card catalog or online catalog, and also by browsing in appropriate areas of its stacks, but these are just two of many initial steps that need to be taken, casual and unsystematic ones at that, and they rarely if ever uncover materials such as periodical articles, chapters in jointly authored publications or Festschriften, prefaces in volumes of collected sets and monuments, etc. One methodical way to begin to find materials of this sort is to consult the relevant bibliographical tools listed here.

The following list consists of four categories, each further divided: "Music Literature Sources," in which indexes to twelve basic categories of music literature are listed; "Directories and Catalogs of Institutions," subdivided into "Libraries," "Library and Union Catalogs," "Private Music Collections," "Musical Instrument Collections," "Schools of Music," and "International Music Guides"; "Music Sources," comprising five categories of reference sources pertaining to music itself; and "Selected General Bibliographies." The first category, "Music Literature Sources," provides access to the most generally useful categories of music literature; the third, "Music Sources," gives access to music, and it is also a further avenue into prefaces in scholarly editions and recording program notes, both of which may contain valuable information.

A few of the items (e.g., *WorldCat*, *RLIN*, *INGENTA*) exist exclusively in the form of remote databases readable only on a computer terminal. These and another popular format, CD-ROM ("compact disk read-only memory"), are technologies which promise to revolutionize scholarly research. Whereas remote databases can be added to on a continuing basis, CDs can hold up to 260,000 pages of text and are automatically searchable in a variety of ways that can also greatly increase the speed of the search. The holdings of such foreign libraries as the British Library and the French Bibliothèque Nationale, as well as various other bibliographic sources, are also now available on the Internet and CD-ROM (in addition to hard copy). For further information, consult *CD-ROMs in Print: An International Guide* (17th ed., Detroit: Thomson/Gale, 2003 [print version] and Westport, Conn.: Meckler [CD-ROM version]).

It must be remembered that no part of this bibliography is all-inclusive—there exist many additional sources that are specialized, regional, rare, obsolete, or superseded, etc.—but a thorough consultation of the following sources, as appropriate, will take the researcher far into the existing literature in a vast range of musical topics.

MUSIC LITERATURE SOURCES

Current Writings about Music

The sources listed below each index several types of works. Each has different features and limitations, however—period of time covered, subjects included or emphasized, number and types of publications included, etc.—so wherever possible, all or more than one of them should be consulted for accuracy and completeness of coverage. Three are ongoing: The oldest is the *Bibliographie des Musikschrifttums,* a yearly listing of books, dissertations, and articles, including many in nonmusic periodicals, in all European languages. *RILM* is the most comprehensive and informative, the only one of the three that provides abstracts. It lists current scholarly writings about music in all languages: books, dissertations, articles, and prefaces to editions. The *Bibliographic Guide to Music* lists publications cataloged each year by the Research Libraries of the New York Public Library and the Library of Congress, including books, periodicals, music, and sound recordings. The remaining source, the *Bibliographia Musicologica,* indexes only items published in the period 1968–76, but it is international in coverage and includes books, dissertations, musical editions, and facsimile editions.

Bibliographia Musicologica: A Bibliography of Musical Litera-
ture. 9 vols. Utrecht: Joachimsthal, 1970–80.
Bibliographic Guide to Music. Boston: G. K. Hall, 1975–.
Bibliographie des Musikschrifttums. Institut für Musikforschung
Preussischer Kulturbesitz, Berlin. Leipzig: F. Hofmeister,
1936–38, 1950–.
RILM Abstracts of Music Literature: Répertoire international de
littérature musicale/International Repertory of Music
Literature/Internationales Repertorium der Musikliter-
atur. New York: RILM International Center, 1967–. Internet
address: http://www.rilm.org (The listings for the years
1970–90 are also available on the CD-ROM version of
RILM, MUSE, a database that also includes listings from
the Library of Congress *National Union Catalog* from 1960
to the present.)

Periodicals

Robinson's bibliography is an annotated list of 1,867 periodicals
in all fields of music and dance. Basart's is an annotated list of music research journals in English whose chief purpose is to serve as
a guide to authors wishing to submit articles, but the information
provided is of use to general researchers as well. Fidler and James,
which comprises commissioned essays on over 150 of the most important music periodicals, historic as well as modern, constitutes
a valuable source of information on topic areas, editorial policies
and biases, etc.

The remaining items are lists of music periodicals that span the
nearly three hundred years of the genre's history. The *MGG* and *New
Grove* lists are both very comprehensive, the latter more so and also
more recent. They each list periodicals by country; in *The New Grove*
they are arranged chronologically (with an index), making it much
easier to identify those published in a given period; in *MGG* the
arrangement is alphabetical. *The New Harvard Dictionary* treats the
subject in brief. Further lists of music periodicals are cited in chapter 6 of Meggett's *Music Periodical Literature* (see p. 36 below). See
also the selective list of research periodicals in chapter 6 below.

Basart, Ann P. *Writing about Music: A Guide to Publishing*
Opportunities for Authors and Reviewers. Fallen Leaf
Reference Books in Music, no. 11. Berkeley, Calif.: Fallen
Leaf Press, 1989.
Fellinger, Imogen. "Periodicals." In *The New Grove Dictionary*
of Music and Musicians. 2nd ed. Vol. 19, pp. 404–36. Lists
of periodicals arranged by continent and subdivided by
country in vol. 28, pp. 339–573.

———. "Zeitschriften." In *Die Musik in Geschichte und Gegen-wart.* 2nd rev. and exp. ed. Vol. 9 (1998), cols. 2252–75.
Fidler, Linda M., and Richard S. James, eds. *International Music Journals.* New York: Greenwood Press, 1990.
Robinson, Doris. *Music and Dance Periodicals: An International Directory & Guidebook.* Voorheesville, N.Y.: Peri Press, 1989.
Samuel, Harold E. "Periodicals." In *The New Harvard Dictionary of Music.* Pp. 625–28.

Periodical Articles

All of these items are indexes or bibliographies of periodical articles except Meggett's *Music Periodical Literature,* the bulk of which (chapters 3, 4, and 5) is an annotated bibliography of many such indexes, largely specialized ones. Of the other sources, *The Music Index,* begun in 1949 and international in scope, is the most standard and comprehensive index to music periodical literature; *Music Article Guide,* begun in 1966, is limited to American periodicals, only a few of which duplicate those in *The Music Index,* and includes a brief annotation for each item. *A Bibliography . . . Oct. 1938–Sept. 1940* pushes the indexing back to a brief pre–World War II period.

RIPM and Warner's *Periodical Literature on American Music* are important recent specialized indexes, the first being the beginning of a series that will "provide access to a selected corpus of 18th-, 19th-, and early 20th-century periodical literature dealing with music," and the second a comprehensive bibliography of articles on American music. The *Arts and Humanities Citation Index,* as its title suggests, indexes a large number of periodicals in essentially all arts and humanities fields, so while it is not the most comprehensive in music, it is of particular value in many cross-disciplinary subjects.

Of the H. W. Wilson indexes listed, one is the well-known general *Readers' Guide to Periodical Literature,* whereas each of the others addresses a specific area of study. The ten final sources, listed under "Bibliographic Databases," are only readable on a computer terminal.

It should be recalled that the *Bibliographie des Musikschrifttums* and *RILM,* listed above under "Current Writings about Music," include periodical articles as well.

Art Index: A Cumulative Author and Subject Index to a Selected List of Fine Arts Periodicals and Museum Bulletins. New York: H. W. Wilson, 1929–. (Also available on CD-ROM and online through OCLC FirstSearch [subscription required].)

Arts and Humanities Citation Index (A&HCI). Philadelphia:
Institute for Scientific Information, 1976–. (Also available
on CD-ROM and online at http://www.isinet.com/prod-
ucts/citation/ahci [subscription required].)

*A Bibliography of Periodical Literature in Musicology . . . Oct.
1938–Sept. 1940.* Washington, D.C.: American Council of
Learned Societies, 1940–43. Reprint: New York: Da Capo
Press, 1973.

*Biography Index: A Cumulative Index to Biographical Material
in Books and Magazines.* New York: H. W. Wilson, 1946–.
(Also available on CD-ROM and online at
http://www.hwwilson.com/databases/bioind.htm
[subscription required].)

Education Index. New York: H. W. Wilson, 1929–. (Also available
on CD-ROM and online at
http://www.hwwilson.com/databases/educat.htm
[subscription required].)

Humanities Index. New York: H. W. Wilson, 1974–. (Also available on CD-ROM and online at
http://www.hwwilson.com/databases/humani.htm
[subscription required].)

Meggett, Joan M. *Music Periodical Literature: An Annotated
Bibliography of Indexes and Bibliographies.* Metuchen,
N.J.: Scarecrow Press, 1978.

*Music Article Guide: A Comprehensive Quarterly Reference
Guide to Significant Signed Feature Articles in American
Music Periodicals.* Philadelphia: Music Article Guide,
1966–76; Philadelphia: Information Services, 1977–.

*The Music Index: A Subject-Author Guide to Music Periodical
Literature.* Detroit: Information Services, 1949–63; Detroit:
Information Coordinators, 1963–87; Warren, Mich.:
Harmonie Park Press (Information Coordinators), 1987–.
(Also available on CD-ROM and online at
http://www.harmonieparkpress.com/musicindex.htm
[subscription required].)

Readers' Guide to Periodical Literature. New York: H. W.
Wilson, 1900–. (Also available on CD-ROM and online at
http://hwwilson.com/databases/readersg.htm [subscrip-
tion required].)

*Répertoire international de la presse musicale: Retrospective
Index to Music Periodicals 1800–1950 (RIPM).* H. Robert
Cohen, gen. ed. University of Maryland at College Park
and Baltimore, Md.: National Information Services Corporation, 1988–. (Internet address:
http://www.nisc.com/ripm [subscription required].)

Social Sciences Index. New York: H. W. Wilson, 1974–. (Also available on CD-ROM and online at http://www.hwwilson.com/databases/socsci.htm [subscription required].)

Warner, Thomas E. *Periodical Literature on American Music, 1620–1920: A Classified Bibliography with Annotations.* Bibliographies in American Music, no. 12. Warren, Mich.: Harmonie Park Press, for the College Music Society, 1988.

Bibliographic Databases

ABI/Inform. Ann Arbor, Mich.: University Microfilms International, 1989–. A database of business-related periodicals; includes articles on music that are not contained in *Music Index*. (Also available on CD-ROM and online through ProQuest [subscription required].)

CAIRSS for MUSIC. Charles T. Eagle, Jr., ed. San Antonio: Institute for Music Research (Donald A. Hodges, dir.), University of Texas at San Antonio, 1993–. Internet address: http://imr.utsa.edu/cairss.html. This "Computer-Assisted Information Retrieval Service System" is a bibliographic database of music research literature that emphasizes music education, music therapy, music psychology, and medicine. Currently there are eighteen "primary" journals in these areas that are completely indexed, with selected articles from more than thirteen hundred "secondary" journals that are also in the database.

Education Full Text. New York: H. W. Wilson. Internet address: http://www.hwwilson.com/Databases/educat.htm. Full text articles, abstracts, and page images from English-language periodicals, monographs, and yearbooks.

Humanities Full Text. New York: H. W. Wilson. Internet address: http://www.hwwilson.com/Databases/humani.htm. Full text articles, abstracts, and bibliographic indexing from scholarly journals. Subjects include music, the performing arts, dance, film, and gender studies.

Ingenta (formerly *UNCOVER/UNCOVER2*). An online database and document delivery service (that is, entire articles can be delivered via FAX to private office or home, or Interlibrary Loan office) that includes over twenty-seven thousand periodicals, general as well as musical. Articles from fifty-four hundred publications also are available in full-text electronic form.

International Index to Music Periodicals. Ann Arbor, Mich.: ProQuest. Online (by subscription) and CD-ROM index to articles in over four hundred international music journals. Most records date from 1996 to the present; some records date back to 1874.

International Index to Music Periodicals Full Text. Ann
Arbor, Mich.: ProQuest. Online (by subscription) index
to all of the articles cited in the *International Index to
Music Periodicals* plus selected articles from an additional sixty-one music journals. Most records date
from 1996 to the present; some records date back to
1874.

Periodicals Abstracts. 1971–. A database containing abstracts
of articles in more than two thousand general periodicals,
including some in music. Available on CD-ROM and
online by subscription.

ProQuest General Periodicals (formerly *General Periodicals
Ondisc*). Ann Arbor, Mich.: ProQuest. Exists only on CD-
ROM; the earliest year indexed is 1986. The source may
also be accessed under other titles, e.g., *ProQuest* and
Periodicals Abstracts. Over eighteen hundred general
periodicals are indexed; an abstract is usually included
with the article citation.

Social Sciences Full Text. New York: H. W. Wilson. Internet address: http://www.hwwilson.com/Databases/humani
.htm. Full text articles, abstracts, and page images from
English-language periodicals, monographs, and yearbooks.

Music Dictionaries and Encyclopedias

Of these three lists of music dictionaries and encyclopedias,
Coover's *Music Lexicography,* in a single alphabetical list, is the most
thorough available; his article in *The New Grove Dictionary,* also
comprehensive and more recent, is divided by period into several
lists; and Samuel's article in *The New Harvard Dictionary* is a concise treatment of the subject featuring several lists of works. For selective lists of music dictionaries and encyclopedias, see chapter 4
below.

Coover, James B., and John C. Franklin. "Dictionaries and
Encyclopedias of Music." In *The New Grove Dictionary of
Music and Musicians.* 2nd ed. Vol. 7, pp. 306–20. Lists of
dictionaries and encyclopedias of music in chronological
order in vol. 28, pp. 109–66.
———. *Music Lexicography, Including a Study of Lacunae in
Music Lexicography and a Bibliography of Music Dictio-
naries.* 3rd ed., rev. and enl. Carlisle, Pa.: Carlisle Books,
1971. First published in 1952.
Samuel, Harold E. "Dictionaries and Encyclopedias." In *The New
Harvard Dictionary of Music.* Pp. 226–30.

Festschriften

These three sources are virtually the only available specialized indexes to musical Festschriften of any importance, Gerboth's more thorough and more recent, Krohn's shorter and earlier, both published in the 1960s. *MUSE,* the CD-ROM version of *RILM,* and the online version of *RILM* index individual articles in Festschriften, currently cover the years 1970–90; the hard copy version of *RILM* does not.

Gerboth, Walter. *An Index to Musical Festschriften and Similar Publications.* New York: W. W. Norton, 1969.
Krohn, Ernst C. "Musical Festschriften and Related Publications." In *Notes* 21 (Winter–Spring 1963–64): 94–108.
MUSE (RILM Abstracts of Music Literature: Répertoire international de littérature musicale/International Repertory of Music Literature/Internationales Repertorium der Musikliteratur). New York: RILM International Center, 1984–.

Monographs in Series

The two important indexes to series of monographs on music are Blum's, covering 1945 to the early 1960s, and Charles's, which complements it by including both earlier series and others that go up to about 1970. One of the chief values of these sources, dated as they are, is that they list the volumes in various series that emphasize certain historical periods or subjects, thus leading the researcher to works related to a given area of investigation.

Blum, Fred. *Music Monographs in Series: A Bibliography of Numbered Monograph Series in the Field of Music Current since 1945.* New York: Scarecrow Press, 1964.
Charles, Sydney Robinson. *A Handbook of Music and Music Literature in Sets and Series.* New York: Free Press, 1972. Section C: "Music Literature Monograph and Facsimile Series," pp. 326–405.

Congress Reports

The Simeone *New Grove Dictionary* article is the most complete listing of published congress reports to date; the Tyrrell and Wise volume is still useful for pre-1975 information, however. Briquet is a list of titles of papers on musical subjects read in congresses between 1835 and 1939.

Briquet, Marie. *La musique dans les congrès internationaux*

(1835–1939). Publications de la Société Française de
Musicologie, ser. 2, vol. 10. Paris: Heugel, 1961.

Simeone, Nigel. "Congress reports." In *The New Grove Dictionary of Music and Musicians.* 2nd ed. Vol. 6, pp. 300–302.
List of published congress reports in chronological order
from 1860 to 1998 in vol. 28, pp. 43–105.

Tyrrell, John, and Rosemary Wise. *A Guide to International
Congress Reports in Musicology, 1900–1975.* New York:
Garland Publishing, 1979.

Dissertations

Since its inception in 1951, there have been two series of *Doctoral Dissertations in Musicology* listing dissertations completed and
in progress, covering only American ones up to 1971 and international ones since 1972 (the annotation in Duckles, *Music Reference
and Research Materials*—see p. 49 below—covers its publication history in detail and also refers to other lists of non-American dissertations). The *International Directory* lists dissertations in progress
not only directly related to music education but on a wide range
of other musical topics as well, including biography, church music, humanities and the arts, ethnomusicology, jazz, etc. The *Music
Theory Online Dissertation Index* is a listing of in-progress and completed dissertations that have appeared in *Music Theory Online.*
Each entry is linked to an abstract and a table of contents.

Dissertation Abstracts International, begun in 1938 as *Microfilm
Abstracts* of American dissertations and broadened to its present
international status in 1969, is the well-known guide to dissertations in all fields, to which there are both author and keyword-
in-title indexes. (Each monthly issue is also indexed in *The Music
Index;* see p. 36 above.) ProQuest Information and Learning now
maintains online searchable databases of dissertation citations and
abstracts.

Adkins, Cecil, and Alis Dickinson, eds. *Doctoral Dissertations
in Musicology.* 7th North American ed./2nd International
ed. (1st ser., cumulative ed.) Philadelphia: American
Musicological Society/International Musicological Society,
1984. First published in 1951.

———. *Doctoral Dissertations in Musicology.* 2nd ser., 1st
cumulative ed. Philadelphia: American Musicological
Society/International Musicological Society, 1990. Suppls.,
1991–. (Also available online at http://www.music.indiana
.edu/ddm)

Dissertation Abstracts International. Ann Arbor, Mich.: University Microfilms, 1938–. The most current of the printed

sources for the Dissertation Abstracts database; published monthly and cumulated annually. Available in print, microfiche, and on CD-ROM.

Dissertation Abstracts Online and *ProQuest Digital Dissertations*. Ann Arbor, Mich.: ProQuest Information and Learning. Subject, title, and author indexes to every American dissertation accepted at accredited institutions since 1861. Abstracts are included for doctoral records from July 1980 to the present. Abstracts are included for masters theses from spring 1988 to the present. Citations and abstracts from dissertations worldwide are included from 1988 to the present.

International Directory of Approved Music Education Doctoral Dissertations in Progress. Ed. Richard J. Colwell. Council for Research in Music Education, University of Illinois, in behalf of The Graduate Program in Music Education. Urbana: University of Illinois, 1989–.

Music Theory Online Dissertation Index. Internet address: http://boethius.music.ucsb.edu/mto/docs/diss-index.html. This index lists announcements of completed and in-progress dissertations that have appeared in *Music Theory Online*, the refereed online journal of the Society for Music Theory. Each entry is linked to an abstract and table of contents.

Guides to Historical Periods

The Baron *Guide* is an annotated bibliography of 1,422 secondary sources covering all aspects of Baroque music, from studies of the various genres to such subjects as musical patronage, pedagogy, printing, and iconography. Hughes's book is a selective but comprehensive annotated index to sources from and about the entire medieval period, including the transition to the Renaissance.

Baron, John H. *Baroque Music: A Research and Information Guide*. Music Research and Information Guides, vol. 16. Garland Reference Library of the Humanities, vol. 871. New York: Garland Publishing, 1993.

Hughes, Andrew. *Medieval Music: The Sixth Liberal Art*. Rev. ed. Toronto Medieval Bibliographies, no. 4. Toronto: University of Toronto Press, 1980. First published in 1974.

Guides to National Music

Morey's *Guide* is an annotated bibliography of a broad spectrum of specialized studies covering all aspects of Canadian music, including both "classical" and popular music. Smialek's work, which concentrates primarily on "classical" music, contains references to the most useful Polish writings and sources in Western publications. Turbet's *Guide* is more limited in scope, covering the time period from the Eton choirbook to the end of the sixteenth century.

Morey, Carl. *Music in Canada: A Research and Information Guide.* Music Research and Information Guides, vol. 20. Garland Reference Library of the Humanities, vol. 1223. New York: Garland Publishing, 1997.
Smialek, William. *Polish Music: A Research and Information Guide.* Music Research and Information Guides, vol. 11. Garland Reference Library of the Humanities, vol. 1093. New York: Garland Publishing, 1989.
Turbet, Richard. *Tudor Music: A Research and Information Guide, with an Appendix Updating William Byrd: A Guide to Research.* Music Research and Information Guides, vol. 18. Garland Reference Library of the Humanities, vol. 1122. New York: Garland Publishing, 1994.

Biographies of Musicians

Of these sources, Green's *Index* differs from the others in that it is an annotated index of bibliographies on composers, and it is thus the work to consult when looking for other, earlier bibliographies than those given here. The remaining works, each addressing a different category of musician, all concern biographical materials themselves. Of these, only the Adams and Farkas books are significantly annotated. For guides to biographies in special areas, see chapter 3 below under "Bibliographies and Research Guides in Other Selected Areas." For further information about biographies, see the appropriate sections in Marco's *Information on Music* (p. 49 below).

See also chapter 5 under "Biographies of Composers in English" and "Series of Composers' Biographies in English," and appropriate articles in such sources as *The New Grove Dictionary.* Selected periodicals devoted to individual composers are listed in chapter 6 under "Limited to a Single Composer," pp. 238–39 below.

Two other valuable sources of information for those composers included in them are the Bio-Bibliographies in Music series and the Routledge Music Bibliographies series, listed alphabetically by composer in full below.

Adams, John L., comp. *Musicians' Autobiographies: An Annotated Bibliography of Writings Available in English, 1800 to 1980.* Jefferson, N.C.: McFarland, 1982.

Bull, Storm. *Index to Biographies of Contemporary Composers.* 3 vols. New York: Scarecrow Press, 1964–87.

Cowden, Robert H., comp. *Classical Singers of the Opera and Recital Stages: A Bibliography of Biographical Materials.* Music Reference Collection, no. 42. Westport, Conn.: Greenwood Press, 1994.

———, comp. *Concert and Opera Conductors: A Bibliography of Biographical Materials.* Music Reference Collection, no. 14. Westport, Conn.: Greenwood Press, 1987.

———, comp. *Concert and Opera Singers: A Bibliography of Biographical Materials.* Music Reference Collection, no. 5. Westport, Conn.: Greenwood Press, 1985.

———, comp. *Instrumental Virtuosi: A Bibliography of Biographical Materials.* Music Reference Collection, no. 18. Westport, Conn.: Greenwood Press, 1989.

Farkas, Andrew. *Opera and Concert Singers: An Annotated International Bibliography of Books and Pamphlets.* Garland Reference Library of the Humanities, vol. 466. New York: Garland Publishing, 1985.

Glennon, Maura. *Pianists: A Research and Information Guide.* New York: Routledge, 2003.

Green, Richard D. *Index to Composer Bibliographies.* Detroit Studies in Music Bibliography, no. 53. Detroit: Information Coordinators, 1985.

Greene, Frank, comp. *Composers on Record: An Index to Biographical Information on 14,000 Composers Whose Music Has Been Recorded.* Metuchen, N.J.: Scarecrow Press, 1985.

BIO-BIBLIOGRAPHIES IN MUSIC
(WESTPORT, CONN.: GREENWOOD PRESS, 1984–)

Joachim Andersen: A Bio-Bibliography. By Kyle J. Dzapo. 1999.
Violet Archer: A Bio-Bibliography. By Linda Hartig. 1991.
Malcolm Arnold: A Bio-Bibliography. By Stewart R. Craggs. 1998.
Esther Williamson Ballou: A Bio-Bibliography. By James R. Heintze. 1987.
Samuel Barber: A Bio-Bibliography. By Don A. Hennessee. 1985.
Leslie Bassett: A Bio-Bibliography. By Ellen S. Johnson. 1994.
Irwin Bazelon: A Bio-Bibliography. By David Harold Cox. 2000.
Richard Rodney Bennett: A Bio-Bibliography. By Stewart R. Craggs. 1990.
Robert Russell Bennett: A Bio-Bibliography. By George J. Ferencz. 1990.
Arthur Bliss: A Bio-Bibliography. By Stewart R. Craggs. 2001.
Frank Bridge: A Bio-Bibliography. By Karen R. Little. 1991.

Radie Britain: A Bio-Bibliography. By Walter B. Bailey and
　　Nancy Gisbrecht Bailey. 1990.
Benjamin Britten: A Bio-Bibliography. By Stewart R. Craggs.
　　2001.
Ferruccio Busoni: A Bio-Bibliography. By Marc-André Roberge.
　　1991.
John Alden Carpenter: A Bio-Bibliography. By Joan O'Connor.
　　1994.
Elliott Carter: A Bio-Bibliography. By William T. Doering. 1993.
George Whitefield Chadwick: A Bio-Bibliography. By Bill F.
　　Faucett. 1998.
Cécile Chaminade: A Bio-Bibliography. By Marcia J. Citron.
　　1988.
Aaron Copland: A Bio-Bibliography. By JoAnn Skowronski.
　　1985.
Elvis Costello: A Bio-Bibliography. By James E. Perone. 1998.
Paul Creston: A Bio-Bibliography. By Monica J. Slomski. 1994.
George Crumb: A Bio-Bibliography. By David Cohen. 2002.
Peter Maxwell Davies: A Bio-Bibliography. By Carolyn J. Smith.
　　1995.
Emma Lou Diemer: A Bio-Bibliography. By Ellen Grolman
　　Schlegel. 2001.
Ernst von Dohnányi: A Bio-Bibliography. By James A. Grymes.
　　2001.
Manuel de Falla: A Bio-Bibliography. By Nancy Lee Harper.
　　1998.
Vivian Fine: A Bio-Bibliography. By Judith Cody. 2001.
Ross Lee Finney: A Bio-Bibliography. By Susan Hayes Hitchens.
　　1996.
Gerald Finzi: A Bio-Bibliography. By John C. Dressler. 1997.
Lukas Foss: A Bio-Bibliography. By Karen L. Perone. 1991.
George Gershwin: A Bio-Bibliography. By Norbert Carnovale.
　　2000.
Peggy Glanville-Hicks: A Bio-Bibliography. By Deborah Hayes.
　　1990.
Louis Moreau Gottschalk: A Bio-Bibliography. By James E.
　　Perone. 2002.
Enrique Granados: A Bio-Bibliography. By Carol A. Hess. 1991.
Howard Hanson: A Bio-Bibliography. By James E. Perone. 1993.
Roy Harris: A Bio-Bibliography. By Dan Stehman. 1991.
Edward Burlingame Hill: A Bio-Bibliography. By Linda L. Tyler.
　　1989.
Alun Hoddinott: A Bio-Bibliography. By Stewart R. Craggs.
　　1993.
Karel Husa: A Bio-Bibliography. By Susan Hayes Hitchens. 1991.
Charles Ives: A Bio-Bibliography. By Geoffrey Block. 1988.

Ulysses Kay: A Bio-Bibliography. By Constance Tibbs Hobson and Deborra A. Richardson. 1994.

Carole King: A Bio-Bibliography. By James E. Perone. 1999.

Ernst Krenek: A Bio-Bibliography. By Garrett H. Bowles. 1989.

Jean Langlais: A Bio-Bibliography. By Kathleen Thomerson. 1988.

György Ligeti: A Bio-Bibliography. By Robert W. Richart. 1990.

Otto Luening: A Bio-Bibliography. By Ralph Hartsock. 1991.

Witold Lutoslawski: A Bio-Bibliography. By Stanislaw Bedkowski and Stanislaw Hrabia. 2000.

Frank Martin: A Bio-Bibliography. By Charles W. King. 1990.

Pietro Mascagni: A Bio-Bibliography. By Roger Flury. 2000.

Lowell Mason: A Bio-Bibliography. By Carol A. Pemberton. 1988.

William Mathias: A Bio-Bibliography. By Stewart R. Craggs. 1995.

John McCabe: A Bio-Bibliography. By Stewart R. Craggs. 1991.

William Thomas McKinley: A Bio-Bibliography. By Jeffrey S. Sposato. 1995.

Gian Carlo Menotti: A Bio-Bibliography. By Donald L. Hixon. 2000.

André Messager: A Bio-Bibliography. By John Wagstaff. 1991.

Anthony Milner: A Bio-Bibliography. By James Siddons. 1989.

Thea Musgrave: A Bio-Bibliography. By Donald L. Hixon. 1984.

Phil Ochs: A Bio-Bibliography. By David Cohen. 1999.

Vincent Persichetti: A Bio-Bibliography. By Donald L. Patterson and Janet L. Patterson. 1988.

Daniel Pinkham: A Bio-Bibliography. By Kee Deboer and John B. Ahouse. 1988.

Francis Poulenc: A Bio-Bibliography. By George R. Keck. 1990.

Sergei Rachmaninoff: A Bio-Bibliography. By Robert E. Cunningham, Jr. 2000.

Gardner Read: A Bio-Bibliography. By Mary Ann Dodd and Jayson Rod Engquist. 1996.

Alfred Reed: A Bio-Bibliography. By Douglas M. Jordan. 1999.

Max Reger: A Bio-Bibliography. By William E. Grim. 1988.

Steve Reich: A Bio-Bibliography. By D. J. Hoek. 2001.

Ned Rorem: A Bio-Bibliography. By Arlys L. McDonald. 1989.

Hans Rosbaud: A Bio-Bibliography. By Joan Evans. 1992.

Albert Roussel: A Bio-Bibliography. By Robert Follet. 1988.

Carl Ruggles: A Bio-Bibliography. By Jonathan D. Green. 1995.

Allen Sapp: A Bio-Bibliography. By Alan Green. 1996.

Henri Sauguet: A Bio-Bibliography. By David L. Austin. 1991.

Peter Schickele: A Bio-Bibliography. By Tammy Ravas. 2004.

Gunther Schuller: A Bio-Bibliography. By Norbert Carnovale. 1987.

William Schuman: A Bio-Bibliography. By K. Gary Adams. 1998.
Cyril Scott: A Bio-Bibliography. By Laurie J. Sampsel. 2000.
Peter Sculthorpe: A Bio-Bibliography. By Deborah Hayes. 1993.
Paul Simon: A Bio-Bibliography. By James E. Perone. 2000.
Larry Sitsky: A Bio-Bibliography. By Robyn Holmes, Patricia
     Shaw, and Peter Campbell. 1997.
William Grant Still: A Bio-Bibliography. By Judith Anne Still,
     Michael J. Dabrishus, and Carolyn L. Quin. 1996.
Germaine Tailleferre: A Bio-Bibliography. By Robert Shapiro.
     1993.
Toru Takemitsu: A Bio-Bibliography. By James Siddons. 2001.
Alexander Tcherepnin: A Bio-Bibliography. By Enrique Alberto
     Arias. 1989.
Randall Thompson: A Bio-Bibliography. By Caroline Cepin
     Benser and David Francis Urrows. 1991.
Virgil Thomson: A Bio-Bibliography. By Michael Meckna. 1986.
Vladimir Ussachevsky: A Bio-Bibliography. By Ralph Hartsock
     and Carl Rahkonen. 2000.
Heitor Villa-Lobos: A Bio-Bibliography. By David P. Appleby.
     1988.
William Walton: A Bio-Bibliography. By Carolyn J. Smith. 1988.
Robert Ward: A Bio-Bibliography. By Kenneth Kreitner. 1988.
Elinor Remick Warren: A Bio-Bibliography. By Virginia Bortin.
     1993.
Alec Wilder: A Bio-Bibliography. By David Demsey and Ronald
     Prather. 1993.
Charles Wuorinen: A Bio-Bibliography. By Richard D. Burbank.
     1993.

ROUTLEDGE MUSIC BIBLIOGRAPHIES (FORMERLY THE GARLAND
COMPOSER RESEARCH MANUALS, 1983–2000), BRAD L. EDEN,
SERIES ED. (NEW YORK: ROUTLEDGE, 1993–)

Adolphe Adam and Léo Delibes: A Guide to Research. By
     William E. Studwell. 1987.
Isaac Albéniz: A Guide to Research. By Walter A. Clark. 1998.
C. P. E. Bach: A Guide to Research. By Doris Powers. 2002.
Samuel Barber: A Guide to Research. By Wayne Wentzel. 2001.
Béla Bartók: A Guide to Research. 2nd ed. By Elliott Antokoletz.
     1997. First published in 1988.
Vincenzo Bellini: A Guide to Research. By Stephen A. Willier.
     2002.
Alban Berg: A Guide to Research. By Bryan R. Simms. 1996.
Hector Berlioz: A Guide to Research. By Jeffrey Alan Langford
     and Jane Denker Graves. 1989.
Leonard Bernstein: A Guide to Research. By Paul Laird. 2001.

Ernest Bloch: A Guide to Research. By David Z. Kushner. 1988.

Johannes Brahms: A Guide to Research. By Heather Platt. 2003.

Benjamin Britten: A Guide to Research. By Peter J. Hodgson. 1996.

Elliott Carter: A Guide to Research. By John F. Link. 2000.

Carlos Chávez: A Guide to Research. By Robert L. Parker. 1998.

Frédéric Chopin: A Guide to Research. By William Smialek. 1999.

Aaron Copland: A Guide to Research. By Marta Robertson and Robin Armstrong. 2001.

Claude Debussy: A Guide to Research. By James R. Briscoe. 1990.

Gaetano Donizetti: A Guide to Research. By James P. Cassaro. 2000.

Edward Elgar: A Guide to Research. By Christopher Kent. 1993.

Gabriel Fauré: A Guide to Research. By Edward R. Phillips. 1999.

Stephen Collins Foster: A Guide to Research. By Calvin Elliker. 1988.

Girolamo Frescobaldi: A Guide to Research. By Frederick Hammond. 1988.

Christoph Willibald Gluck: A Guide to Research. 2nd ed. By Patricia Howard. 2003. First published in 1987.

G. F. Handel: A Guide to Research. By Mary Ann Parker-Hale. 1988.

Franz Joseph Haydn: A Guide to Research. By Floyd K. Grave and Margaret G. Grave. 1990.

Henricus Isaac: A Guide to Research. By Martin Picker. 1991.

Charles Ives: A Guide to Research. By Gayle Sherwood. 2002.

Scott Joplin: A Guide to Research. By Nancy R. Ping Robbins and Guy A. Marco. 1998.

Josquin des Prez: A Guide to Research. By Sydney Robinson Charles. 1983.

Zoltán Kodály: A Guide to Research. By Michael Houlahan and Philip Tacka. 1998.

Orlando di Lasso: A Guide to Research. By James Erb. 1990.

Franz Liszt: A Guide to Research. By Michael Saffle. 2003. First published in 1991.

Guillaume de Machaut: A Guide to Research. By Lawrence Earp. 1995.

Gustav and Alma Mahler: A Guide to Research. By Susan Melanie Filler. 1989.

Felix Mendelssohn Bartholdy: A Guide to Research with an Introduction to Research Concerning Fanny Hensel. By John Michael Cooper. 2001.

Claudio Monteverdi: A Guide to Research. By K. Gary Adams and Dyke Kiel. 1989.

Wolfgang Amadeus Mozart: A Guide to Research. By Baird Hastings. 1989.

Carl Nielsen: A Guide to Research. By Mina F. Miller. 1987.
Johannes Ockeghem and Jacob Obrecht: A Guide to Research.
    By Martin Picker. 1988.
Giovanni Battista Pergolesi: A Guide to Research. By Marvin E.
    Paymer and Hermine Weigel Williams. 1989.
Giovanni Pierluigi da Palestrina: A Guide to Research. By Clara
    Marvin. 2002.
Giacomo Puccini: A Guide to Research. By Linda B. Fairtile. 1998.
Henry Purcell: A Guide to Research. By Franklin B. Zimmerman.
    1989.
Sergei Vasil'evich Rachmaninoff: A Guide to Research.
    By Robert Palmieri. 1985.
Jean-Philippe Rameau: A Guide to Research. By Donald H.
    Foster. 1989.
Nikolai Andreevich Rimsky-Korsakov: A Guide to Research.
    By Gerald R. Seaman. 1988.
Gioachino Rossini: A Guide to Research. By Denise P. Gallo.
    2002.
Camille Saint-Saëns: A Guide to Research. By Timothy Flynn.
    2003.
Alessandro and Domenico Scarlatti: A Guide to Research.
    By Carole F. Vidali. 1993.
Heinrich Schenker: A Guide to Research. By Benjamin Ayotte.
    2003.
Jean Sibelius: A Guide to Research. By Glenda Dawn Goss. 1997.
Ralph Vaughan Williams: A Guide to Research. By Neil Butter-
    worth. 1990.
Giuseppe Verdi: A Guide to Research. By Gregory W. Harwood.
    1998.
Tomás Luis de Victoria: A Guide to Research. By Eugene Casjen
    Cramer. 1998.
Antonio Vivaldi: A Guide to Research. By Michael Talbot. 1988.
Richard Wagner: A Guide to Research. By Michael Saffle. 2002.
Carl Maria von Weber: A Guide to Research. By Donald G.
    Henderson and Alice H. Henderson. 1990.
Hugo Wolf: A Guide to Research. By David Ossenkop. 1988.

Other Bibliographies of Music Literature Sources

The sources listed here are of several kinds. Brockman, Duckles, and Marco are all annotated bibliographies of reference materials in the field of music; Duckles aims at near-comprehensiveness,
whereas Brockman is more selective. The *Basic Music Library* offers
suggestions for the stocking of a music library; Baily and *Performing Arts Books* are specialized bibliographies. Foreman's work is a
collection of essays and bibliographies on various research areas,

ranging from traditional topics ("Standard Reference Sources and Collected Editions" and "Composer Catalogues, Thematic Catalogues, and Bibliographies") to more recent or relatively neglected ones ("The Second-Hand Trade: Dealers and Auctions" and "Film and Its Music").

Baily, Dee. *A Checklist of Music Bibliographies and Indexes in Progress and Unpublished.* 4th ed. MLA Index and Bibliography Series, vol. 3. Philadelphia: Music Library Association, 1982. First published in 1974.

A Basic Music Library: Essential Scores and Books. 3rd ed. Compiled by the Music Library Association, Resource Sharing and Collection Development Committee, under the direction of Daniel Zager and Elizabeth Davis. Chicago: American Library Association, 1997. First published in 1978.

Brockman, William S. *Music: A Guide to the Reference Literature.* Reference Sources in the Humanities Series. Littleton, Colo.: Libraries Unlimited, 1987.

Duckles, Vincent H., and Ida Reed. *Music Reference and Research Materials: An Annotated Bibliography.* 5th ed. New York: Schirmer Books, 1997. First published in 1964.

Foreman, Lewis, ed. *Information Sources in Music.* Munich: K. G. Saur Verlag, 2003.

Marco, Guy A., ed. *Information on Music: A Handbook of Reference Sources in European Languages.* 3 of 8 vols. published; series then abandoned. Littleton, Colo.: Libraries Unlimited, 1975–84.

> 1. *Basic and Universal Sources.* By Guy A. Marco. 1975.
> 2. *The Americas.* By Guy A. Marco and Ann M. Garfield. 1977.
> 3. *Europe.* By Guy A. Marco with the assistance of Sharon Paugh Ferris and Ann G. Olszewski. 1984.

Performing Arts Books, 1876–1981, Including an International Index of Current Serial Publications. New York: R. R. Bowker, 1981.

DIRECTORIES AND CATALOGS
OF INSTITUTIONS

Libraries

The *Directory of Music Research Libraries,* begun by Rita Benton, series C of *RISM,* is the standard international guide in the area, and it is now essentially complete. Penney gives similar information for British libraries. Whereas the chief focus in Bradley is chronicling the growth of music collections in American libraries, it does list special collections where they exist. Post provides a brief history of recording technology and the development of recorded collections, discusses the various kinds of sound archives, and lists sound and audiovisual archives with significant music holdings worldwide.

Benton, Rita. "Libraries." In *The New Grove Dictionary of Music and Musicians.* 2nd ed. Vol. 14, pp. 638–45. Lists and histories of libraries arranged by geographical region and subdivided by country in vol. 28, pp. 199–336.

Bradley, Carol June, comp. *Music Collections in American Libraries: A Chronology.* Detroit Studies in Music Bibliography, no. 46. Detroit: Information Coordinators, 1981.

Directory of Music Research Libraries. **Répertoire international des sources musicales [RISM],** ser. C. [2nd ed., rev. and enl.] Kassel: Bärenreiter, 1983–2001.

1. C/I: *Canada and the United States.* 2nd rev. ed. Ed. Marian Kahn, Helmut Kallmann, and Charles Lindahl. Kassel: Bärenreiter, 1983. First published in 1967.

2. C/II: *Sixteen European Countries.* 2nd rev. ed. Ed. Elizabeth Davis. Kassel: Bärenreiter, 2001. Austria, Belgium, Switzerland, Germany, Denmark, Spain. First published in 1970–72.

3. C/III/1–2: *Sixteen European Countries.* 2nd rev. ed. Ed. Elizabeth Davis. Kassel: Bärenreiter, 2001. Part 1: France, Finland, United Kingdom, Ireland, Luxembourg, Norway, Netherlands, Portugal, Sweden. Part 2: Italy. First published in 1970–72.

4. C/IV: *Australia, Israel, Japan, New Zealand.* Ed. Cecil Hill, Katya Manor, James Siddons, and Dorothy Freed. Kassel: Bärenreiter, 1979.

5. C/V: *Czechoslovakia, Hungary, Poland, Yugoslavia.* Ed. James B. Moldovan and Lillian Pruett. Kassel: Bärenreiter, 1985.

Penney, Barbara, comp. and ed. *Music in British Libraries: A Directory of Resources.* 4th ed. London: Library Association Publishing, 1992. First published in 1971.

Post, Jennifer. "Sound archives." In *The New Grove Dictionary of Music and Musicians.* 2nd ed. Vol. 23, pp. 776–78. Lists of sound and audiovisual archives with significant music holdings in vol. 28, pp. 577–87.

Library and Union Catalogs

The items in the American section pertain to the printed card and online catalogs of the largest and most important U.S. libraries. The next section includes printed and online catalogs of the major research libraries in Europe. The international items, all online union catalogs, represent an immense repository of information from cooperating libraries located primarily in America and Europe. A worldwide directory of library home pages and online catalogs is available at LibDex: The Library Index (Internet address: http://www.libdex.com).

AMERICAN

Boston Public Library. *Dictionary Catalog of the Music Collection of the Boston Public Library.* 20 vols. Boston: G. K. Hall, 1972. First Suppl., 4 vols., 1977.

Boston Public Library Online Catalogs: http://www.bpl.org/catalogs/index.htm

Library of Congress. *National Union Catalog: Music and Phonorecords: A Cumulative Author List Representing Library of Congress Printed Cards and Titles Reported by Other American Libraries.* Ann Arbor, Mich.: J. W. Edwards, [1956]–.

————. *National Union Catalog: Music and Phonorecords 1953–72.* Washington, D.C.: Library of Congress, 1966–73. Also available on CD-ROM.

————. *National Union Catalog: Music, Books on Music, and Sound Recordings 1973–1977.* Totowa, N.J.: Rowman and Littlefield, 1978. Continuation of previous item. Also available on CD-ROM.

————. *National Union Catalog: Music, Books on Music, and Sound Recordings.* Published quinquennially. Totowa, N.J.: Rowman and Littlefield, 1977–. Continuation of previous item.

————. *The National Union Catalog: Pre-1956 Imprints.* 754 vols. London: Mansell, 1968–81.

Library of Congress Online Catalog: http://catalog.loc.gov

MUSE (CD-ROM version of *RILM Abstracts of Music Literature: Répertoire international de littérature musicale/ International Repertory of Music Literature/Internationales Repertorium der Musikliteratur*). Music literature sources from the Library of Congress catalog 1970 to the present also included in the database. (See p. 39 above.)

Music Library Association Catalog of Cards and Printed Music 1953–1972: A Supplement to the Library of Congress

Catalogs. Ed. Elizabeth H. Olmstead. 2 vols. Totowa, N.J.: Rowman and Littlefield, 1974.

The New York Public Library. Reference Department. *Dictionary Catalog of the Music Collection, New York Public Library.* 2nd ed. 45 vols. Boston: G. K. Hall, 1982. First published in 1964. (See *Bibliographic Guide to Music*, p. 34 above.)

The New York Public Library Research Libraries Online Catalog (CATNYP): http://catnyp.nypl.org

EUROPEAN

Austrian National Library (Österreichische Nationalbibliothek) home page with link to online catalog: http://www.onb.ac.at (Available in English.)

Bavarian State Library. *Bayerische Staatsbibliothek, Katalog der Musikdrucke: BSB-Musik.* 17 vols. Munich: K. G. Saur, 1988–90.

Bavarian State Library home page with link to online catalog: http://www.bsb-muenchen.de/index.htm (Available in English.)

British Library. *The British Library General Catalogue of Printed Books to 1975.* 360 vols. London: Bingley; K. G. Saur, 1979–87. (Also available on CD-ROM.)

———. *The British Library General Catalogue of Printed Books 1976 to 1982.* London: K. G. Sauer, 1983.

———. *The British Library General Catalogue of Printed Books 1982 to 1985.* London: K. G. Sauer, 1986.

———. *The British Library General Catalogue of Printed Books 1986 to 1987.* London: K. G. Sauer, 1988.

———. *The British Library General Catalogue of Printed Books 1988 to 1989.* London: K. G. Sauer, 1990.

———. *The British Library General Catalogue of Printed Books 1990 to 1992.* London: K. G. Sauer, 1993.

———. *The British Library General Catalogue of Printed Books 1993 to 1994.* London: K. G. Sauer, 1995.

———. *The British Library General Catalogue of Printed Books 1995 to 1996.* London: K. G. Sauer, 1997.

———. *The British Library General Catalogue of Printed Books 1997 to 1998.* London: K. G. Sauer, 1999.

———. *The British Library General Catalogue of Printed Books 1999 to 2000.* London: K. G. Sauer, 2001.

———. *The British Library General Catalogue of Printed Books 2001 to 2002.* London: K. G. Sauer, 2003.

———. *The British Library General Catalogue of Printed Books to 1995.* Alexandria, Va.: Chadwyck-Healey, 1997. (Four CD-ROM disks.)

———. *The Catalogue of Printed Music in the British Library to 1980.* 62 vols. London: K. G. Saur, 1981–87.

———. *CPM Plus (Catalogue of Printed Music in the British Library),* 2nd ed. London: Bowker-Saur, 1993. (CD-ROM of cataloging records of printed music published between 1503 and 1992.)

British Library home page with link to online catalog: http://blpc.bl.uk

National Library of Germany (Die Deutsche Bibliothek) home page with link to online catalog: http://www.ddb.de (Available in English.)

National Library of Spain (Biblioteca Nacional de Espana) home page with link to online catalog: http://www.bne.es (Available in English.)

Paris. Bibliothèque Nationale. *Catalogue général des livres imprimés: Auteurs.* 231 vols. Paris: Imprimerie Nationale, 1897–1981. (Also available on CD-ROM.)

———. *Catalogue général des livres imprimés: Auteurs—collectivités-auteurs—anonymes, 1960–1969.* 27 vols. Paris: Imprimerie Nationale, 1972–78.

Paris. Bibliothèque Nationale home page with link to online catalog: http://www.bnf.fr (Available in English.)

Vatican Library (Biblioteca Apostolica Vaticana) home page with link to online catalog: http://www.vatican.va/library_archives/index.htm (Available in English.)

INTERNATIONAL

RLIN (Research Libraries Information Network). RLIN is an interface and system for viewing and working with RLG (Research Libraries Group [http://www.rlg.org]) bibliographic records. These bibliographic records are distributed by RLG Library Resources through a set of online catalogs, including the RLG Union Catalog, the CURL (Consortium of University Research Libraries in Britain) Union Catalogue, the union catalog of the National Library of Germany (the Deutsche Bibliothek), the National Library of Australia Catalogue, the English Short Title Catalogue, the Hand Press Book database, and SCIPIO (a union catalog of art and rare book sales catalogs).

WorldCat. WorldCat, the online union catalog of OCLC (Online

Computerized Library Center [http://www.oclc.org]), is the first online union library database in the United States, and the world's largest, with data storage (books, musical scores, recordings, visual materials, computer files, Internet resources, etc.) from over nine thousand libraries in over eighty countries and territories worldwide. Library of Congress acquisitions are being added continuously to the database.

Private Music Collections

Albrecht, Otto E., and Stephen Roe. "Collections, Private." In *The New Grove Dictionary of Music and Musicians.* 2nd ed. Vol. 6, pp. 115–16. Lists of current and historical private collections arranged by country in vol. 28, pp. 5–39.

Coover, James. *Private Music Collections: Catalogs and Cognate Literature.* Detroit Studies in Music Bibliography, vol. 81. Warren, Mich.: Harmonie Park Press, 2000.

Musical Instrument Collections

The following sources are the standard ones in the area. The MLA *Survey* and the *International Directory,* both dating from the 1970s, complement each other; the former covers North American collections and catalogs, the latter the rest of the world, with an American addendum that supplements the former. Coover's book is more recent, is worldwide in coverage, includes catalogs of expositions as well as collections, and is much more thorough on private collections than either of the previous sources. The Libin article in *The New Grove Dictionary* is a particularly accessible listing of instrument collections around the world. Bevan's book is similar in scope and content to the MLA *Survey.* Kottick and Lucktenberg's work contains descriptions of the most significant keyboard instruments found in selected European museums. None of the directories, however, is all-inclusive, and to be thorough one should consult them all.

Bevan, Clifford, ed. *Musical Instrument Collections in the British Isles.* Winchester, England: Piccolo, 1990.

Coover, James B. *Musical Instrument Collections: Catalogues and Cognate Literature.* Detroit Studies in Music Bibliography, vol. 47. Detroit: Information Coordinators, 1981.

International Council of Museums. *International Directory of Musical Instrument Collections.* Ed. Jean Jenkins. Buren, The Netherlands: Frits Knuf for the International Council of Museums, 1977.

Kottick, Edward L., and George Lucktenberg. *Early Keyboard Instruments in European Museums.* Bloomington: Indiana University Press, 1997.
Libin, Laurence, et al. "Instruments, Collections of." In *The New Grove Dictionary of Music and Musicians.* 2nd ed. Vol. 12, pp. 428–68.
Music Library Association. *A Survey of Musical Instrument Collections in the United States and Canada.* Chapel Hill, N.C.: Music Library Association, 1974.

Schools of Music

Uscher's *Schirmer Guide* is an international guide to music schools, whereas the European Union guide is limited to E.U. member countries. The other sources apply to North America, the CMS *Directory* listing music faculty members, and the NASM *Directory* listing academic degrees granted.

The College Music Society. *Directory of Music Faculties in Colleges and Universities, U.S. and Canada.* Published annually. Binghamton, N.Y.: College Music Society, 1972–.
European Union of Music Schools. *Music Schools in Europe: Handbook of the European Union of Music Schools.* Mainz: Schott Music International, 1995.
National Association of Schools of Music. *Directory.* Published annually. N.p.: 19[6–].
Uscher, Nancy. *The Schirmer Guide to Schools of Music and Conservatories throughout the World.* New York: Schirmer Books, 1988.

International Music Guides

These useful guides are annotated lists of concert halls, festivals, famous musicians' residences, instrument collections, archives and libraries, conservatories, etc., in various European countries. For further information concerning music festivals and the like, see chapter 8 under "Performing Arts, Competitions, and Festivals," pp. 292–93 below.

Adelmann, Marianne, ed. *Musical Europe: An Illustrated Guide to Musical Life in 18 European Countries.* New York: Two Continents Publishing Group, 1974.
British and International Music Yearbook. London: Rhinegold Publishing, 1999–.
British Music Yearbook. London: Classical Music, 1975–98; New York: Schirmer Books, 1984–98.

Brody, Elaine, and Claire Brook. *The Music Guide to Austria and Germany.* New York: Dodd, Mead, 1975; reprint, London: Macmillan, 1979.

————. *The Music Guide to Belgium, Luxembourg, Holland and Switzerland.* New York: Dodd, Mead, 1977.

————. *The Music Guide to Great Britain: England, Scotland, Wales, Ireland.* New York: Dodd, Mead, 1975; reprint, London: Hale, 1976.

————. *The Music Guide to Italy.* New York: Dodd, Mead, 1978; reprint, London: Macmillan, 1979.

Goertz, Harald. *Musikhandbuch für Österreich: Struktur und Organisation in 2500 Stichworten, Namen, Adressen, Information.* Vienna: Doblinger, 1993.

Gottesman, Roberta, ed. *The Music Lover's Guide to Europe: A Compendium of Festivals, Concerts, and Opera.* New York: John Wiley & Sons, 1992.

Musik-Almanach. Kassel: Bärenreiter, 1986–.

Norris, Gerald. *A Musical Gazetteer of Great Britain and Ireland.* Newton Abbot, England: David and Charles, 1981.

Plantamura, Carol. *The Opera Lover's Guide to Europe.* London: Robson, 1997.

Schweizer Musik-Handbuch: Informationen über Struktur und Organisation des Schweizer Musiklebens/Guide musicale suisse: Informations sur la structure et l'organisation de la vie musicale suisse/Guida musicale svizzera: Informazioni sulla struttura e l'organizzazione della vita musicale svizzera. Zurich: Atlantis Musikbuch-Verlag, 1991.

Schweizer Musik-Handbuch/Guide musical suisse. Published biennially. Zurich: Atlantis Musikbuch-Verlag, 1979–.

Simeone, Nigel. *Paris—A Musical Gazetteer.* New Haven, Conn.: Yale University Press, 2000.

MUSIC SOURCES

Primary Sources of Early Music: Manuscripts and Prints

In the "General" list of bibliographies of primary sources, *RISM* stands out from all the others in its all-inclusiveness. When finished, its series A and B will constitute an international index of all known sources of manuscript and printed music and writings about music up to 1800 (for further information, see *The New Harvard Dictionary* article "RISM," as well as Duckles, *Music Reference and Research Materials*—p. 49 above—where the individually annotated volumes in the series are listed under the full title: *Répertoire international des sources musicales*). Wettstein's *Thematische Sammelverzeichnisse,* an annotated list of catalogs of selected music collections in libraries and archives arranged alphabetically by city, is the only such source in print.

The *New Grove* article "Sources, MS" is also large in scope, listing in numerous separate bibliographies the manuscript sources of Western vocal music through the Renaissance. The *Census-Catalogue* is a more thorough treatment of polyphonic music in the period 1400–1550. The three other *New Grove* articles list both manuscript and printed sources of early instrumental music. The Brown and Vogel works are fundamentally important as representative bibliographies of early printed music. Samuel's article in *The New Harvard Dictionary* is a useful brief list of the chief manuscript sources of polyphonic music before 1500. The two Eitner sources, although largely superseded by *RISM,* are still of some value.

The "American" category consists of six principal bibliographies of sacred and secular music in prints and manuscripts collectively covering music up into the first quarter of the nineteenth century.

GENERAL

Boorman, Stanley, et al. "Sources, MS." In *The New Grove Dictionary of Music and Musicians.* 2nd ed. Vol. 23, pp. 791–930.

Brown, Howard Mayer. *Instrumental Music Printed before 1600: A Bibliography.* Cambridge, Mass.: Harvard University Press, 1965; reprint, San Jose, Calif.: toExcel, 1999.

Bryden, John R., and David G. Hughes. *An Index of Gregorian Chant.* 2 vols. Cambridge, Mass.: Harvard University Press, 1969.

Caldwell, John. "Sources of Keyboard Music to 1660." In *The New Grove Dictionary of Music and Musicians.* 2nd ed. Vol. 24, pp. 19–39.

Census-Catalogue of Manuscript Sources of Polyphonic Music, 1400–1550. Compiled by the University of Illinois Musicological Archives for Renaissance Manuscript Studies. 5 vols. Middleton, Wisc.: A-R Editions, for the American Institute of Musicology, 1979–88.

Edwards, Warwick. "Sources of Instrumental Ensemble Music to 1630." In *The New Grove Dictionary of Music and Musicians.* 2nd ed. Vol. 24, pp. 1–19.

Eitner, Robert. *Bibliographie der Musik-Sammelwerke des XVI. und XVII. Jahrhunderts.* In collaboration with Franz X. Haberl, A. Lagerberg, and C. F. Pohl. Berlin: L. Liepmannssohn, 1877. Suppls. in *Monatshefte für Musikge-*

schichte 14 (1882): 152–55, 161–64. Reprint, Hildesheim: Olms, 1977.

————. *Biographisch-bibliographisches Quellen-Lexikon der Musiker und Musikgelehrten christlicher Zeitrechnung bis Mitte des neunzehnten Jahrhunderts.* 2nd ed., improved and enl. 11 vols. Graz: Akademische Druck-und Verlagsanstalt, 1959. First published in 1898–1904.

Jackson, Barbara Garvey. *"Say Can You Deny Me": A Guide to Surviving Music by Women from the 16th through the 18th Centuries.* Fayetteville: University of Arkansas Press, 1994.

Klimisch, Mary Jane. *A Cumulative Index of Gregorian Chant Sources.* Yankton, S.D.: Sacred Music Resource Center, 1975.

Ness, Arthur J. "Sources of Lute Music." In *The New Grove Dictionary of Music and Musicians.* 2nd ed. Vol. 24, pp. 39–63.

Répertoire international des sources musicales/Internationales Quellen-lexikon der Musik/International Inventory of Musical Sources (RISM). Ser. A, individual composers, Kassel: Bärenreiter, 1971; ser. B, multiple-composer collections, music manuscripts, and writings about music, Munich: G. Henle, 1960–. One of the series, Ser. A/II, music manuscripts 1600–1800, was issued in its 1st and 2nd eds., 1983 and 1986, on microfiches, but beginning with the 3rd cumulated ed., 1995, the format has been changed to CD-ROM. Currently Ser. A/II is available in two formats: the 10th cumulative ed. on CD-ROM (Munich: K. G. Saur, 2002) and as an online database from N.I.S.C. (National Information Services Corporation) BiblioLine (Internet address: http://www.nisc.com). Both the CD-ROM and online database versions include four linked databases: The Ser. A/II Database contains the bibliographic records of music manuscripts written after 1600, the Composer Database contains more than twenty-four thousand composer names taken from Ser. A/I and A/II, the Libraries Sigla Database identifies more than six thousand libraries worldwide that hold music materials relevant to RISM, and the Bibliographic Citations Database contains references to all thematic catalogs and other secondary sources cited in the Ser. A/II database.

Samuel, Harold E. "Sources (Pre-1500)." In *The New Harvard Dictionary of Music.* Pp. 773–78.

Vogel, Emil, Alfred Einstein, François Lesure, and Claudio Sartori. *Bibliografia della musica italiana vocale profane pubblicata dal 1500 al 1700.* New ed. 2 vols. + suppl.

Staderini, Switzerland: Minkoff, 1977–82. First published in 1892.

Wettstein, Hermann. *Thematische Sammelverzeichnisse der Musik: Ein bibliographischer Führer durch Musikbibliotheken und -archive.* [Laaber, Germany]: Laaber-Verlag, 1982.

AMERICAN

Britton, Allen Perdue, and Irving Lowens, completed by Richard Crawford. *American Sacred Music Imprints, 1698–1810: A Bibliography.* Worcester, Mass.: American Antiquarian Society, 1990.

Dox, Thurston, comp. *American Oratorios and Cantatas: A Catalog of Works Written in the United States from Colonial Times to 1985.* Lanham, Md.: Scarecrow Press, 1986.

Fuld, James J., and Mary Wallace Davidson. *18th-Century American Secular Music Manuscripts: An Inventory.* MLA Index and Bibliography Series, no. 20. Philadelphia: Music Library Association, 1980.

Heard, Priscilla S. *American Music, 1698–1800: An Annotated Bibliography.* Waco, Tex.: Baylor University Press, 1975.

Heintze, James R. "Music in Performance and Other Editions," "Music in Facsimile Reprints." In *American Music before 1865 in Print and on Records: A Biblio-Discography.* Rev. ed. I.S.A.M. Monographs, no. 30. Brooklyn: Institute for Studies in American Music, Conservatory of Music, Brooklyn College of the City University of New York, 1990. Pp. 1–67, 68–87. First published in 1976.

Sonneck, Oscar George Theodore. *A Bibliography of Early Secular American Music (18th Century).* Rev. and enl. ed. Revised by William Treat Upton. Washington, D.C.: Library of Congress, Music Division, 1945; reprint with new preface by Irving Lowens, New York: DaCapo Press, 1964; reprint of 1945 ed., Temecula, Calif.: Reprint Services, 2003. First published in 1902.

Wolfe, Richard J. *Secular Music in America, 1801–1825: A Bibliography.* 3 vols. New York: New York Public Library, 1964.

Editions of Music

Each of these indexes is different in its organization, comprehensiveness, amount of information, and recentness; none of them covers absolutely everything, and there is some degree of overlap among them. The recent index by Hill and Stephens, covering over five thousand items, supersedes all other such sources, including

Heyer, which was long the standard one. The 1991 *Monuments of Music* catalog of the European bookseller Otto Harrassowitz is also recent, although limited to series published in Europe. Samuel's *New Harvard Dictionary* article and the two items by Charles are included for the sake of completeness; in Charles's book, section A lists sets and monuments, and section B, complete works as well as thematic catalogs. Her *New Grove* article is a bibliography only and is differently organized: complete works, other collected editions, editions of theoretical works, and anthologies.

Of the two sources that concern composers' complete works only, Coover's list is of limited value because of its age; Harrassowitz's 1992 *Composers' Collected Editions* catalog is a practical update presenting works from European publishers.

The remaining sources are indexes of anthologies of music. Hilton's is older, shorter, and limited to early music; it covers fewer anthologies, but some of them are as old as the late nineteenth century. Murray's is more recent and covers many more anthologies, emphasizing current ones. Perone's is a reference source book for music theory teachers; historical anthologies and anthologies specifically intended for score reading are not included.

Charles, Sydney Robinson. *A Handbook of Music and Music Literature in Sets and Series.* New York: Free Press, 1972. Section A: "Sets and Series Containing Music of Several Composers and Sets and Series Containing Both Music and Music Literature," pp. 1–144; section B: "Sets and Series Devoted to One Composer," pp. 145–325.

Charles, Sydney Robinson, et al. "Editions, Historical." In *The New Grove Dictionary of Music and Musicians.* 2nd ed. Vol. 7, pp. 895–98. A comprehensive list of historical editions in vol. 28, pp. 169–96.

Composers' Collected Editions from Europe. 7th rev. ed. Special Music Catalog no. 15. Wiesbaden: Otto Harrassowitz, 1992. First published in 1981.

Coover, James B. *Gesamtausgaben: A Checklist.* N.p.: Distant Press, 1970.

Heyer, Anna Harriet, comp. *Historical Sets, Collected Editions, and Monuments of Music: A Guide to Their Contents.* 3rd ed. 2 vols. Chicago: American Library Association, 1980. First published in 1957.

Hill, George R., and Norris L. Stephens. *Collected Editions, Historical Series and Sets, and Monuments of Music: A Bibliography.* Fallen Leaf Reference Books in Music, no. 14. Berkeley, Calif.: Fallen Leaf Press, 1997. (Forthcoming indexes to be published on CD-ROM.)

Hilton, Ruth B. *An Index to Early Music in Selected Anthologies.*

Music Indexes and Bibliographies, no. 13. Clifton, N.J.:
   European American Music, 1978.
Monuments of Music from Europe. 2nd rev. ed. Special Music
   Catalog no. 13. Wiesbaden: Otto Harrassowitz, 1991. First
   published in 1988.
Murray, Sterling E. *Anthologies of Music: An Annotated Index.*
   2nd ed. Detroit Studies in Music Bibliography, no. 68.
   Warren, Mich.: Harmonie Park Press, 1992. First published
   in 1987.
Perone, James E. *Musical Anthologies for Analytical Study: A
   Bibliography.* Westport, Conn.: Greenwood Press, 1995.
Samuel, Harold E. "Editions, Historical." In *The New Harvard
   Dictionary of Music.* Pp. 264–76.

Thematic Catalogs

There are two standard lists of thematic catalogs of individual
composers' works, Brook's *Thematic Catalogues* and Wettstein's
Bibliographie, both originating in the 1970s and both annotated. The
1997 edition of Brook's catalog, co-authored by Richard J. Viano, is
now by far the more complete source of such information. (Recall
that thematic catalogs are also included in section B of Charles's *A
Handbook of Music and Music Literature in Sets and Series;* see p. 60
above.)

Brook, Barry S., and Richard J. Viano. *Thematic Catalogues in
   Music: An Annotated Bibliography.* 2nd ed. RILM Retro-
   spectives, no. 4. Stuyvesant, N.Y.: Pendragon Press, 1997.
   First published in 1972.
Wettstein, Hermann. *Bibliographie musikalischer thematischer
   Werkverzeichnisse.* [Laaber, Germany]: Laaber-Verlag,
   1978.

Catalogs of Librettos

Following are three essential listings of opera librettos: the classic catalog by Sonneck and its new Italian counterpart, and the
recent, ongoing, comprehensive *RISM-U.S. Libretto Database.* See
also chapter 5 under "Dramatic Music—Libretto Studies," p. 187
below.

RISM-U.S. Libretto Database. Available through the library catalog VIRGO of the University of Virginia (Internet address:
   http://virgo.lib.virginia.edu). Searching for a combination
   of the two key words "operas" and "librettos" produces
   more than eleven thousand results.

Sartori, Claudio. *I libretti italiani a stampa dalle origini al 1800: Catalogo analitico con 16 indici.* 5 vols. + 2 index vols. Cuneo, Italy: Bertola & Locatelli, 1990–94. (Also exists as a database at the University of Michigan.)

Sonneck, Oscar. *Catalogue of Opera Librettos Printed before 1800.* Washington, D.C.: Government Printing Office, 1914; reprint, New York: Johnson Reprints, 1970.

Discographies

These items were selected from many such sources and represent a wide spectrum of musical traditions, from "classical" to world music to popular music. The first category is "Bibliographies of Discographies," works that are—or contain, in the case of *Brian Rust's Guide*—lists of discographies.

The second category, "Guides to Currently Available Recordings," consists of the most important periodically updated lists of available recordings.

The third category, "Specialized Discographies," lists some important sources with special emphases—classical, opera, choral, early music, women composers, etc.—some of them annotated, some not. Holmes's two discographies of performances organized by conductors' names, virtually the only such specialized works on the subject, are particularly detailed; the same may be said for the more recent lists of ethnic and Gregorian chant recordings, by Spottswood and Weber respectively.

Within the third category, "Ethnomusicology and World Music" reflects the increased interest in non-Western music over the past several decades. "Jazz, Blues, and Popular Music," concentrates primarily on jazz, but also includes Erlewine's *All Music Guide,* which lists recordings of all types of popular music.

Bibliographies of Discographies

Bibliography of Discographies. New York: R. R. Bowker, 1977–83.

> 1. *Classical Music, 1925–1975.* By Michael H. Gray and Gerald D. Gibson. 1977. Suppl.: *Classical Musical Discographies, 1976–1988: A Bibliography.* Compiled by Michael H. Gray. New York: Greenwood Press, 1989.
> 2. *Jazz.* By Daniel Allen. 1981.
> 3. *Popular Music.* By Michael H. Gray. 1983.

Cooper, David Edwin. *International Bibliography of Discographies: Classical Music and Jazz and Blues, 1962–1972: A*

Reference Book for Record Collectors, Dealers, and Libraries. Littleton, Colo.: Libraries Unlimited, 1975.

Rust, Brian A. L. *Brian Rust's Guide to Discography.* Discographies, no. 4. Westport, Conn.: Greenwood Press, 1980.

Guides to Currently Available Recordings

Bielefelder Katalog Klassik. Published semiannually. Stuttgart: Vereinigte Motor-Verlage, 1953–. Also available on CD-ROM.

R.E.D. Classical Catalogue (formerly *Gramophone Classical Catalogue*). Published semiannually. London: Retail Entertainment Data, 1953–.

MUZE. CD-ROM and Internet databases of sound recordings that are commercially available. Provides access to more than 665,000 musical works, album facts, and recording information. Available for commercial use only.

Specialized Discographies

Classical, Opera, and Choral

Blyth, Alan, ed. *Choral Music on Record.* Cambridge: Cambridge University Press, 1991.

———. *Opera on CD: The Essential Guide to the Best CD Recordings of 100 Operas.* Rev. and updated 3rd ed. London: Kyle Cathie, 1994. First published in 1992.

Cohn, Arthur. *Recorded Classical Music: A Critical Guide to Compositions and Performances.* New York: Schirmer Books, 1981.

Evans, Gary. *Music Inspired by Art: A Guide to Recordings.* M.L.A. Index and Bibliography Series, no. 30. Lanham, Md.: Scarecrow Press, 2002.

Gramophone Opera Catalogue. London: Retail Entertainment Data Publishing, 1995–.

Gramophone Opera Good CD Guide. Harrow, England: Gramophone Publications, 1998–.

Gruber, Paul, ed. *The Metropolitan Opera Guide to Recorded Opera.* New York: W. W. Norton, 1993.

McCants, Clyde T. *Opera for Libraries: A Guide to Core Works, Audio and Video Recordings, Books and Serials.* Jefferson, N.C.: McFarland, 2003.

Mordden, Ethan. *A Guide to Opera Recordings.* New York: Oxford University Press, 1987.

Opera on CD. Published annually. Port Melbourne, Victoria, Australia: William Heinemann, 1994–.

Parsons, Charles H. *The Mellen Opera Reference Index.* Vols.

10–12: *An Opera Discography.* Lewiston, N.Y.: Edwin
   Mellen Press, 1990.
Rosenberg, Kenyon C. *A Basic Classical and Operatic Record-
   ings Collection for Libraries.* Metuchen, N.J.: Scarecrow
   Press, 1987.
———. *A Basic Classical and Operatic Recordings Collection
   on Compact Discs for Libraries: A Buying Guide.*
   Metuchen, N.J.: Scarecrow Press, 1990.
*The Rough Guide to Classical Music: An A-Z of Composers,
   Key Works and Top Recordings.* London: Rough Guides,
   Ltd., 2001.
The Rough Guide to Classical Music: 100 Essential CDs. Lon-
   don: Rough Guides, Ltd., 1999.
The Rough Guide to Opera. 3rd ed., exp. and completely rev.
   London: Rough Guides, Ltd., 2002. First published as
   Opera: The Rough Guide in 1997.
The Rough Guide to Opera: 100 Essential CDs. London: Rough
   Guides, Ltd., 1999.

Gregorian Chant and Early Music

Barker, John W. *The Use of Music and Recordings for Teaching
   About the Middle Ages: A Practical Guide with Comprehensive Discography and Selective Bibliography.* Kalamazoo, Mich.: Medieval Institute Publications, 1988.
Croucher, Trevor, comp. *Early Music Discography: From Plainsong to the Sons of Bach.* 2 vols. Phoenix: Oryx Press,
   1981.
Weber, Jerome F., comp. *A Gregorian Chant Discography.* 2 vols.
   Discography Series, no. 20. New York: J. F. Weber, 1990.

American Music

Davis, Elizabeth A. *Index to the New World Recorded Anthology
   of American Music: A User's Guide to the Initial One
   Hundred Records.* New York: W. W. Norton, 1981.
DeVenney, David P. *From Billings to Ives: American Choral
   Music Recordings II.* Research Memorandum Series, no. 2.
   Washington, D.C.: American Choral Foundation, 2001.
Heintze, James R. "Discography." In *American Music before 1865
   in Print and on Records: A Biblio-Discography.* Rev. ed.
   I.S.A.M. Monographs, no. 30. Brooklyn: Institute for Studies
   in American Music, Conservatory of Music, Brooklyn
   College of the City University of New York, 1990. Pp. 88–
   144. First published in 1976.
Oja, Carol J., ed. *American Music Recordings: A Discography of
   20th-Century U.S. Composers.* A Project of the Institute for

Studies in American Music for the Koussevitzky Music
Foundation. Brooklyn: Institute for Studies in American
Music, Conservatory of Music, Brooklyn College of the
City University of New York, 1982.

Conductors

Holmes, John L. *Conductors: A Record Collector's Guide, Includ-
ing Compact Discs.* London: Victor Gollancz, 1988.
————. *Conductors on Record.* Westport, Conn.: Greenwood
Press, 1982.
Musiker, Reuben, et al. *Conductors and Composers of Popular
Orchestral Music: A Biographical and Discographical
Sourcebook.* Westport, Conn.: Greenwood Press, 1998.

Women Composers

Cohen, Aaron I., comp. *International Discography of Women
Composers.* Discographies, no. 10. Westport, Conn.:
Greenwood Press, 1984.
Frasier, Jane. *Women Composers: A Discography.* Detroit Studies
in Music Bibliography, no. 50. Detroit: Information Coordi-
nators, 1983.
Mitchell, Charles, ed. *Discography of Works by Women Com-
posers.* Paterson, N.J.: Paterson Free Public Library, 1975.

Ethnomusicology and World Music

Gombert, Greg. *A Guide to Native American Music Recordings.*
Fort Collins, Colo.: Multi Cultural Publishing, 1994.
Keefer, Jane. *Folk Music: An Index to Recorded Sources.* Online
index to tunes and songs from more than twenty-two
hundred recordings supported by Johns Hopkins University. Internet address: http://milton.mse.jhu.edu:8001/
research/folkindex/index.htm
Keeling, Richard. *North American Indian Music: A Guide to
Published Sources and Selected Recordings.* Garland Library of Music Ethnology, vol. 5. New York: Garland, 1997.
*The Rough Guide to World Music. Volume 1: Africa, Europe and
the Middle East.* London: Rough Guides, Ltd., 1999. (Also
available at
http://www.roughguides.com/music/world.html)
*The Rough Guide to World Music. Volume 2: Latin and North
America, Caribbean, India, Asia and Pacific.* London:
Rough Guides, Ltd., 2000. (Also available at http://www
.roughguides.com/music/world.html)
The Rough Guide to World Music: 100 Essential CDs. London:
Rough Guides, Ltd., 2000.

Spottswood, Richard K. *Ethnic Music on Records: A Discography of Ethnic Recordings Produced in the United States, 1893–1942.* 7 vols. Urbana: University of Illinois Press, 1990.

    1. *Western Europe.*
    2. *Slavic.*
    3. *Eastern Europe.*
    4. *Spanish, Portuguese, Philippine, Basque.*
    5. *Mid-East, Far East, Scandinavian, English Language, American Indian, International.*
    6. Indexes.
    7. Indexes.

Vernon, Paul. *Ethnic and Vernacular Music, 1898–1960: A Resource and Guide to Recordings.* Westport, Conn.: Greenwood Press, 1995.

Jazz, Blues, and Popular Music

Bielefelder Katalog Schallplatten, Compact Discs, MusiCassetten. Jazz. (Formerly *Bielefelder Katalog Jazz.*) Published annually. Stuttgart: Vereinigte Motor-Verlage, 1986–.

Bogdanov, Vladimir, Chris Woodstra, and Stephen Thomas Erlewine. *All Music Guide: The Definitive Guide to Popular Music.* 4th ed. San Francisco: Backbeat Books, 2001. First published in 1994.

Cook, Richard, and Brian Morton. *Penguin Guide to Jazz on CD.* 6th ed. New York: Penguin Books, 2002. First published in 1992.

Erlewine, Michael, ed. *All Music Guide to Jazz: The Experts' Guide to the Best Jazz Recordings.* 3rd ed. San Francisco: Miller Freeman, 1998. First published in 1994.

———. *All Music Guide to the Blues: The Experts' Guide to the Best Blues Recordings.* 2nd ed. San Francisco: Miller Freeman, 1999. First published in 1996.

Erlewine, Michael, et al., eds. *All Music Guide: The Experts' Guide to the Best Recordings from Thousands of Artists in All Types of Music.* 3rd ed. San Francisco: Miller Freeman, 1997. First published in 1992.

Harrison, Max, et al. *The Essential Jazz Records.* London: Mansell Publishing, 2000–.

    1. *Ragtime to Swing.* 2nd ed. 2000. First published in 1984.
    2. *Modernism to Postmodernism.* 2000.

Lord, Tom. *The Jazz Discography.* CD-ROM: West Vancouver, Canada: Lord Music Reference, Inc., 2002.

Piazza, Tom. *The Guide to Classic Recorded Jazz.* CD-ROM:

Iowa City: University of Iowa Press, 1995. Electronic book:
Boulder, Colo.: NetLibrary, 2000.

The Rough Guide to Blues: 100 Essential CDs. London: Rough
Guides, Ltd., 2000.

The Rough Guide to Jazz. London: Rough Guides, Ltd., 2000.

The Rough Guide to Jazz: 100 Essential CDs. London: Rough
Guides, Ltd., 2001.

SELECTED GENERAL BIBLIOGRAPHIES

Music research is often cross-disciplinary, necessitating work in
other fields. The sources listed here are among the most widely
known and comprehensive listings of general sources. Balay and
Walford are both standard guides to reference works in all fields.
Haggerty's work is an annotated bibliography of resources on popular music. Mixter introduces the music researcher to general reference works outside the field of music, and the *Bibliographic Index* is
a serial publication that lists current bibliographies that are either
published separately or appear in books or periodicals.

The four remaining sources represent what are probably the
most important current book-trade publications in the English-
speaking world. *Books in Print* and *Subject Guide to Books in Print*
cover American publishers, and *British National Bibliography,* British
publishers; the *Cumulative Book Index* lists all English-language
publications.

Balay, Robert, et al., eds. *Guide to Reference Books.* 11th ed. Chicago: American Library Association, 1996. First published
in 1902.

*Bibliographic Index: A Cumulative Bibliography of Bibliogra-
phies, 1937–.* New York: H. W. Wilson, 1938–.

**Books in Print: An Author-Title-Series Index to the Publishers'
Trade List Annual.** New York: Bowker, 1948–. (Also
available on CD-ROM as *Books in Print with Book Reviews
Plus.*)

British National Bibliography. London: Council of the British
National Bibliography, British Museum, 1950–. (Also
available on CD-ROM.)

Cumulative Book Index. New York: Wilson, 1898–. Also available as an online database to OhioLINK (Ohio Library
and Information Network) member libraries.

Haggerty, Gary. *A Guide to Popular Music Reference Books:
An Annotated Bibliography.* Westport, Conn.: Greenwood
Press, 1995.

Mixter, Keith E. *General Bibliography for Music Research.* 3rd
        ed. Detroit Studies in Music Bibliography, no. 75. Warren,
        Mich.: Harmonie Park Press, 1996. First published in 1962.
*Subject Guide to Books in Print: An Index to the Publishers'
        Trade List Annual, 1957–.* New York: Bowker, 1957–. (Also
        available on CD-ROM as *Books in Print Plus.*)
Walford, Albert John, et al. *Walford's Guide to Reference Mate-
        rial.* 8th ed. London: Library Association, 1999. First
        published in 1959.

Area Bibliographies and Other Reference Sources

This chapter includes lists of basic sources in six fundamental areas of music research—general musicology, ethnomusicology, performance practice, music theory, music education, and music therapy. Then follow short lists of bibliographies, guides, and indexes of reference value for researching certain other selected topic areas.

MUSICOLOGY

Musicology, since its early recognition and definition in the late 1800s, has produced an extensive literature concerned with itself as a discipline. The following bibliography is a list of basic discussions of the theory and practice of musicology, intended to serve as an introduction to its content, organization, and history. The emphasis is largely on more recent sources but selected older classics also have been included.

Listed in the first category, "The History of Musicology," are two standard accounts of the history of the discipline. Sources that are primarily systematic presentations of the field and its philosophy and methodology are listed under "Comprehensive Overviews." Some of the most significant and influential early treatments are included, most notably the one by Adler, whose division into systematic and historical musicology largely has been observed ever since.

"Selected Discussions of the Discipline in Chronological Order" begins with Chrysander's preface in 1863 in which the word "Musikwissenschaft" was first presented, proceeds to Adler's pioneering article on the subject and Pratt's introduction of it to American readers, and continues with various writings that treat matters of definition, philosophical interpretation, trends, problems, challenges, and so on, in musicology up to 2003. "Selected Gender and Sexuality Studies in Chronological Order" presents a selection of the most significant sources representing the newest methodologies in the discipline. "Discussions of Musicology in the United States" brings together varied sources that deal with the history and practice of musicology in this country, including Crawford's history of the American Musicological Society and Steinzor's bibliography of the writings of the leading earlier American musicologists. The sources listed under "Music Historiography" are concerned with the techniques, theories, and principles of historical research and presentation.

"Miscellaneous Sources" includes the conference papers published as *Musicology and the Computer,* and the introductions to musicological materials and applications by Davies, Spiess, and Stevens (the first two now mostly of historical value); presentations by Foley, Lasker, Leman, Spencer, Wallin, and Zon of newly conceived aspects of the discipline; three guides to Internet resources in musicology; and several collections of essays: Seeger's, many of which are discussions of musicological theory and practice; and Wiora's, which amount to a virtual overview of the field.

Monographs on musicological subjects are often published in series, such as the substantial Musicological Studies and Documents series of the American Institute of Musicology, and the many German series, such as Beiträge zur rheinischen Musikgeschichte. Apart from Steinzor's *American Musicologists,* no bibliographies are listed here, but virtually all the bibliographies appearing in chapter 2 and the present chapter are applicable to the field of musicology in its broadest sense. There also are series of bibliographies that pertain to musicology, such as the Detroit Studies in Music Bibliography. For a list of standard musicological journals, see chapter 6, "Current Research Journals in Music," pp. 236–38 below.

The History of Musicology

Harrison, Frank Ll., Mantle Hood, and Claude V. Palisca. *Musicology* (Harrison: "American Musicology and the European Tradition," pp. 1–85; Palisca: "American Scholarship in Western Music," pp. 87–213). Englewood Cliffs, N.J.: Prentice Hall, 1963; reprint, Westport, Conn.: Greenwood Press, 1974.

Krohn, Ernst C. "The Development of Modern Musicology." In *Historical Musicology: A Reference Manual for Research in Music,* by Lincoln Bunce Spiess. Musicological Studies, no. 4. Brooklyn, N.Y.: Institute of Mediaeval Music, [1963];

reprint, Westport, Conn.: Greenwood Press, 1980. Pp. 153–72.

Comprehensive Overviews

Adler, Guido. *Methode der Musikgeschichte.* Leipzig: Breitkopf & Härtel, 1919; reprint, Farnborough: Gregg, 1971.

Chailley, Jacques, ed. *Précis de musicologie.* New ed., rev. Paris: Presses Universitaires de France, 1984. First published in 1958.

Dahlhaus, Carl, and Helga de la Motte-Haber, eds. *Systematische Musikwissenschaft.* Neues Handbuch der Musikwissenschaft, vol. 10. Laaber, Germany: Laaber-Verlag, 1982; reprint, Laaber, Germany: Laaber-Verlag, 1997.

Duckles, Vincent, et al. "Musicology." In *The New Grove Dictionary of Music and Musicians.* 2nd ed. Vol. 17, pp. 488–533.

Fellerer, Karl G. *Einführung in die Musikwissenschaft.* 2nd rev. and enl. ed. Münchberg, Germany: B. Hahnefeld, 1953. First published in 1942.

Haydon, Glen. *Introduction to Musicology: A Survey of the Fields, Systematic and Historical, of Musical Knowledge and Research.* Rev. ed. Chapel Hill: University of North Carolina Press, 1959; reprint, New York: Prentice Hall, 1980. First published in 1941.

Husmann, Heinrich. *Einführung in die Musikwissenschaft.* 3rd ed. Taschenbücher zur Musikwissenschaft, no. 40. Wilhelmshaven: Heinrichshofen's Verlag, 1980. First published in 1958.

Kimmey, John A., Jr. *A Critique of Musicology: Clarifying the Scope, Limits, and Purposes of Musicology.* Studies in the History and Interpretation of Music, vol. 12. Lewiston, N.Y.: Edwin Mellen Press, 1988.

Mielke-Gerdes, Dorothea, et al. "Musikwissenschaft." In *Die Musik in Geschichte und Gegenwart.* 2nd rev. and exp. ed. Vol. 6, cols. 1789–1834.

"Musicology." In *The New Harvard Dictionary of Music.* Pp. 520–22.

Riemann, Hugo. *Grundriss der Musikwissenschaft.* 4th ed. Revised by Johannes Wolff. Musikwissenschaft und Bildung, Einzeldarstellungen aus allen Gebieten des Wissens, no. 34. Leipzig: Quelle & Meyer, 1928. First published in 1908.

Weber, Edith. *Recherche musicologique: Objet, méthodologie, normes de présentation.* Guides musicologiques, no. 1. Paris: Beauchesne, 1980.

Selected Discussions of the Discipline in Chronological Order

Chrysander, Friedrich. "Vorwort und Einleitung." *Jahrbücher für musikalische Wissenschaft* 1 (1863): 9–16.

Adler, Guido. "Umfang, Methode und Ziel der Musikwissenschaft." *Vierteljahrsschrift für Musikwissenschaft* 1, no. 1 (1885): 5–20.

Pratt, Waldo S. "On Behalf of Musicology." *The Musical Quarterly* 1 (January 1915): 1–16.

Harap, Louis. "On the Nature of Musicology." *The Musical Quarterly* 23 (January 1937): 18–25.

Seeger, Charles L. "Systematic and Historical Orientations in Musicology." *Acta Musicologica* 11 (September–December 1939): 121–28.

———. "Systematic Musicology: Viewpoints, Orientations, and Methods." *Journal of the American Musicological Society* 4 (Fall 1951): 240–48.

Mendel, Arthur, Curt Sachs, and Carroll C. Pratt. *Some Aspects of Musicology: Three Essays* (Mendel: "The Services of Musicology to the Practical Musician"; Sachs: "The Lore of Non-Western Music"; Pratt: "Musicology and Related Disciplines"). New York: Liberal Arts Press, 1957.

Hibberd, Lloyd. "Musicology Reconsidered." *Acta Musicologica* 31 (January–March 1959): 25–31.

Lippman, Edward A. "What Should Musicology Be?" *Current Musicology*, no. 1 (1965): 55–60.

Ernst, Viet. "Über die Einheit von historischer und systematischer Musikwissenschaft." *Beiträge zur Musikwissenschaft* 9, no. 2 (1967): 91–97.

Tischler, Hans. "And What Is Musicology?" *Music Review* 30 (November 1969): 253–60.

Brook, Barry S., Edward O. D. Downes, and Sherman Van Solkema, eds. *Perspectives in Musicology*. New York: W. W. Norton, 1972.

Chase, Gilbert. "Musicology, History, and Anthropology: Current Thoughts." In *Current Thought in Musicology*, ed. John W. Grubbs et al. Symposia in the Arts and Humanities, no. 4. Austin: University of Texas Press, 1976. Pp. 231–46.

Holoman, D. Kern, and Claude V. Palisca, eds. *Musicology in the 1980s: Methods, Goals, Opportunities*. Da Capo Press Music Series. New York: Da Capo Press, 1982.

Kerman, Joseph. *Contemplating Music: Challenges to Musicology*. Cambridge, Mass.: Harvard University Press, 1985.

———. *Musicology*. London: Fontana Press, 1985.

Newman, William S. "Musicology among the Humanities." In

Essays in Musicology: A Tribute to Alvin Johnson, ed.
    Lewis Lockwood and Edward Roesner. N.p.: American
    Musicological Society, 1990. Pp. 292–302.
Bergeron, Katherine, and Philip V. Bohlman, eds. *Disciplining
    Music: Musicology and Its Canons.* Chicago: University
    of Chicago Press, 1992.
Kramer, Lawrence. "The Musicology of the Future." *repercus-
    sions* 1 (Spring 1992): 5–18.
Tomlinson, Gary. "Musical Pasts and Postmodern Musicologies:
    A Response to Lawrence Kramer." *Current Musicology,*
    no. 53 (1993): 411–36.
Kramer, Lawrence. "Music Criticism and the Postmodernist
    Turn: In Contrary Motion with Gary Tomlinson." *Current
    Musicology,* no. 53 (1993): 25–40.
Williams, Christopher A. "Of Canons & Context: Toward a
    Historiography of Twentieth-Century Music." *repercus-
    sions* 2 (Spring 1993): 31–74.
Helm, E. Eugene. *The Canon and the Curricula: A Study of
    Musicology and Ethnomusicology Programs in America.*
    Stuyvesant, N.Y.: Pendragon Press, 1994.
Treitler, Leo. "History and Music." In *History and—: Histories
    within the Human Sciences,* ed. Ralph Cohen and Michael
    S. Roth. Charlottesville: University Press of Virginia, 1995.
Greer, David Clive, Ian Rumbold, and Jonathan King. *Musicol-
    ogy and Sister Disciplines, Past, Present, Future: Proceed-
    ings of the 16th International Congress of the Interna-
    tional Musicological Society (London 1997).* Oxford:
    Oxford University Press, 2000.
Cook, Nicholas, and Mark Everist, eds. *Rethinking Music.* Ox-
    ford: Oxford University Press, 2001.
Williams, Alastair. *Constructing Musicology.* Aldershot, England:
    Ashgate, 2001.
Austern, Linda Phyllis, ed. *Music, Sensation, and Sensuality.*
    New York: Routledge, 2002.
Scott, Derek B. *From the Erotic to the Demonic: On Critical
    Musicology.* Oxford: Oxford University Press, 2003.
Clarke, Eric, and Nicholas Cook, eds. *Empirical Musicology:
    Aims, Methods, Prospects.* Oxford: Oxford University
    Press, 2004.

Selected Gender and Sexuality Studies in Chronological Order

Koskoff, Ellen. *Women and Music in Cross-Cultural Perspective.*
    Urbana: University of Illinois Press, 1989.
Austern, Linda Phyllis. "'Sing Againe Syren': The Female
    Musician and Sexual Enchantment in Elizabethan Life

and Literature." *Renaissance Quarterly* 42 (Fall 1989): 420–48.

Herndon, Marcia, and Susanne Ziegler, guest eds.; International Council for Traditional Music, ICTM Study Group on Music and Gender. *Music, Gender, and Culture.* Intercultural Music Studies, no. 1. Wilhelmshaven: Florian Noetzel, 1990.

McClary, Susan. *Feminine Endings: Music, Gender, and Sexuality.* Minneapolis: University of Minnesota Press, 1991.

Kallberg, Jeffrey. "The Harmony of the Tea Table: Gender and Ideology in the Piano Nocturne." *Representations* 39 (Summer 1992): 102–33.

Brett, Philip. "Britten's Bad Boys: Male Relations in *The Turn of the Screw.*" *repercussions* 1 (Fall 1992): 5–25.

Lewin, David. "Women's Voices and the Fundamental Bass." *The Journal of Musicology* 10 (Fall 1992): 464–82.

McClary, Susan. *Georges Bizet, Carmen.* Cambridge: Cambridge University Press, 1992.

Fink, Robert. "Desire, Repression and Brahms's First Symphony." *repercussions* 2 (Spring 1993): 75–103.

Citron, Marcia. *Gender and the Musical Canon.* Cambridge: Cambridge University Press, 1993.

Solie, Ruth A., ed. *Musicology and Difference: Gender and Sexuality in Music Scholarship.* Berkeley: University of California Press, 1993. Also available as an electronic book at http://www.netLibrary.com.

"Schubert: Music, Sexuality, Culture." Ed. Lawrence Kramer. *19th Century Music* 17, no. 1 (Summer 1993): 1–105.

Higgins, Paula. "Women in Music, Feminist Criticism, and Guerrilla Musicology: Reflections on Recent Polemics." *19th Century Music* 17, no. 2 (Fall 1993): 174–92.

Marshall, Kimberly, ed. *Rediscovering the Muses: Women's Musical Traditions.* Boston: Northeastern University Press, 1993.

Rycenga, Jennifer. "The Uncovering of Ontology in Music: Speculative and Conceptual Feminist Music." *repercussions* 3 (Spring 1994): 22–46.

Cusick, Suzanne G. "Gender and the Cultural Work of a Classical Music Performance." *repercussions* 3 (Spring 1994): 77–110.

Kielian-Gilbert, Marianne. "Of Poetics and Poiesis, Pleasure, and Politics: Music Theory and Modes of the Feminine." *Perspectives of New Music* 32 (Winter 1994): 44–67.

McClary, Susan. "Paradigm Dissonances: Music Theory, Cultural Studies, Feminist Criticism." *Perspectives of New Music* 32 (Winter 1994): 68–85.

Cook, Susan C., and Judy S. Tsou, eds. *Cecilia Reclaimed: Feminist Perspectives on Gender and Music.* Urbana: University of Illinois Press, 1994.

Brett, Philip, et al., eds. *Queering the Pitch: The New Gay and Lesbian Musicology.* New York: Routledge, 1994.

Jezic, Diane Peacock. *Women Composers: The Lost Tradition Found.* 2nd ed. New York: Feminist Press at the City University of New York, 1994. First published in 1988. Accompanying CD, New York: Leonarda, 2001.

Blackmer, Corinne, and Patricia Juliana Smith, eds. *En travesti: Women, Gender Subversion, Opera.* New York: Columbia University Press, 1995.

Head, Matthew. "'Like Beauty Spots on the Face of a Man': Gender in 18th-Century North-German Discourse on Genre." *The Journal of Musicology* 12 (Summer 1995): 143–67.

Clement, Catherine. *Opera, or, the Undoing of Women.* London: Tauris, 1997.

Dellamora, Richard, and Daniel Fischlin, eds. *The Work of Opera: Genre, Nationhood, and Sexual Difference.* New York: Columbia University Press, 1997.

Halstead, Jill. *The Woman Composer: Creativity and the Gendered Politics of Musical Composition.* Brookfield, Vt.: Ashgate, 1997.

Mender, Mona. *Extraordinary Women in Support of Music.* London: Scarecrow Press, 1997.

Fragner, Stefan, Jan Hemming, and Beate Kutschke, eds. *Gender Studies & Musik: Geschlechterrollen und ihre Bedeutung für die Musikwissenschaft.* Forum Musik Wissenschaft series, vol. 5. Regensburg, Germany: ConBrio, 1998.

Kramer, Lawrence. *Franz Schubert: Sexuality, Subjectivity, Song.* Cambridge: Cambridge University Press, 1998.

Barkin, Elaine, Lydia Hamessley, and Benjamin Boretz, eds. *Audible Traces: Gender, Identity, and Music.* Los Angeles: Carciofoli, 1999.

Grassl, Markus, and Cornelia Szabo-Knotik. *Frauen in der Musikwissenschaft / Women in Musicology: Dokumentation des internationalen Workshops, Wien 1998.* Vienna: n.p., 1999.

Baumer, Matthew Richard. "Aesthetic Theory and the Representation of the Feminine in Orchestral Program Music of the Mid-Nineteenth Century." Ph.D. diss., University of North Carolina at Chapel Hill, 2002.

Borgerding, Todd Michael, ed. *Gender, Sexuality, and Early Music.* New York: Routledge, 2002.

Bernstein, Jane A. *Women's Voices across Musical Worlds.* Boston: Northeastern University Press, 2003.

Discussions of Musicology
in the United States in Chronological Order

Bukofzer, Manfred. *The Place of Musicology in American Institutions of Higher Learning.* New York: Liberal Arts Press, 1957; reprint, New York: Da Capo Press, 1977.

Goldthwaite, Scott. "The Growth and Influence of Musicology in the United States." *Acta Musicologica* 33 (April–December 1961): 72–79.

Kerman, Joseph. "A Profile for American Musicology." *Journal of the American Musicological Society* 18 (Spring 1965): 60–69; reprinted in *Write All These Down: Essays on Music.* Berkeley: University of California Press, 1994.

Lowinsky, Edward E. "Character and Purposes of American Musicology: A Reply to Joseph Kerman." *Journal of the American Musicological Society* 18 (Summer 1965): 222–34.

McPeek, Gwynn. "Musicology in the United States: A Survey of Recent Trends." In *Studies in Musicology: Essays in the History, Style, and Bibliography of Music, in Memory of Glen Haydon,* ed. James W. Pruett. Chapel Hill: University of North Carolina Press, 1969. Pp. 260–75.

Crawford, Richard. *The American Musicological Society, 1934–1984: An Anniversary Essay.* Philadelphia: American Musicological Society, 1984.

Pruett, James W., and Thomas P. Slavens. *Research Guide to Musicology.* Sources of Information in the Humanities, no. 4. Chicago: American Library Association, 1985.

Steinzor, Curt Efram, comp. *American Musicologists, c. 1890–1945: A Bio-Bibliographical Sourcebook to the Formative Period.* Music Reference Collection, no. 17. Westport, Conn.: Greenwood Press, 1989.

Kerman, Joseph. "American Musicology in the 1990s." *The Journal of Musicology* 9 (Spring 1991): 131–44.

Bohlman, Philip V. "Musicology as a Political Act." *The Journal of Musicology* 11 (Fall 1993): 174–92.

Grunzweig, Werner. "Constructing Musical Sexuality: Anmerkungen zur amerikanischen Musikforschung der 90er Jahre." In *Aus der neuen Welt: Streifzuge durch die amerikanische Musik des 20. Jahrhunderts.* Hamburg: Lit, 1997. Pp. 211–22.

Music Historiography

Adler, Guido. *Methode der Musikgeschichte.* Leipzig: Breitkopf & Härtel, 1919; reprint, Farnborough, England: Gregg, 1971.

Allen, Warren Dwight. *Philosophies of Music: A Study of*

General Histories of Music, 1600–1960. New York: Dover
Publications, 1962. First published in 1939. Ph.D. diss.,
Columbia University, 193?.

Chase, Gilbert. "The Musicologist as Historian: A Matter of Dis-
tinction." *Notes* 29 (September 1972): 10–16.

Dahlhaus, Carl. *Foundations of Music History.* Trans. J. B. Robinson. Cambridge: Cambridge University Press, 1983. First
published in 1967.

Grout, Donald J. "Current Historiography and Music History."
In *Studies in Music History: Essays for Oliver Strunk,*
ed. Harold Powers. Princeton, N.J.: Princeton University
Press, 1968. Pp. 23–40.

———. *Western Concepts of Music History.* Ithaca, N.Y.: Cornell
University Press, 1981.

Huttunen, Matti. "The 'Canon' of Music History: Historical and
Critical Aspects." *The Maynooth International Musico-
logical Conference 1995: Selected Proceedings.* Portland,
Ore.: Four Courts Press, 1996. Pp. 110–18.

Lenneberg, Hans. *Witnesses and Scholars: Studies in Musical
Biography.* Musicology Book Series, vol. 5. New York:
Gordon and Breach, 1988.

Potter, Maxine. "Trends in German Musicology, 1918–1945: The
Effects of Methodological, Ideological, and Institutional
Change on the Writing of Music History." Ph.D. disserta-
tion, Yale University, 1991.

Stanley, Glenn. "Historiography." In *The New Grove Dictionary
of Music and Musicians.* 2nd ed. Vol. 11, pp. 546–61.

Tomlinson, Gary. *Music in Renaissance Magic: Toward a Historiography of Others.* Chicago: University of Chicago Press,
1993.

Treitler, Leo. "On Historical Criticism." *The Musical Quarterly*
53 (April 1967): 188–205.

Westrup, J. A. *An Introduction to Musical History.* 2nd ed.
London: Hutchinson University Library, 1973. First
published in 1955.

Wiora, Walter, ed. *Die Ausbreitung des Historismus über die
Musik.* Studien zur Musikgeschichte des 19. Jahrhunderts,
vol. 14. Regensburg: Gustav Bosse, 1969.

Miscellaneous Sources

Brook, Barry S., ed. *Musicology and the Computer: Musicology
1966–2000: A Practical Program—Three Symposia.* American Musicological Society, Greater New York Chapter,
Publications, no. 2. New York: City University of New
York Press, 1970.

Davies, J. H. *Musicalia: Sources of Information in Music.* 2nd
rev. and enl. ed. Oxford: Pergamon Press, 1969. First
published in 1966.

Ehn, Hope. *On-line Resources for Classical and Academic
Musicians: A Guide through the Wilds of the Internet.*
Newton Centre, Mass.: H. Ehn, 1994.

Foley, Edward. *Ritual Music: Studies in Liturgical Musicology.*
Beltsville, Md.: Pastoral Press, 1995.

Internet Resources for Music Scholars (maintained by the Edna
Kuhn Loeb Music Library of Harvard University). Internet
address: http://hcl.harvard.edu/loebmusic/online-ir-intro
.html.

Lang, Paul Henry, Alfred Mann, and George J. Buelow. *Musicology and Performance.* New Haven, Conn.: Yale University
Press, 1997.

Lasker, G. E., and James Rhodes. *Systems Research in Arts: Musicology.* Windsor, Ont.: International Institute for Advanced
Studies in Systems Research and Cybernetics, 1999.

Leman, Marc. *Music and Schema Theory: Cognitive Foundations
of Systematic Musicology.* New York: Springer, 1995.

———. *Music, Gestalt, and Computing: Studies in Cognitive
and Systematic Musicology.* New York: Springer, 1997.

Seeger, Charles. *Studies in Musicology 1935–1975.* Ed. Ann M.
Pescatello. Berkeley: University of California Press, 1977.

———. *Studies in Musicology II, 1929–1979.* Ed. Ann M.
Pescatello. Berkeley: University of California Press, 1994.

Spencer, Jon Michael. *Theological Music: Introduction to
Theomusicology.* Contributions to the Study of Music and
Dance, no. 23. Westport, Conn.: Greenwood Press, 1991.

Spiess, Lincoln Bunce. *Historical Musicology: A Reference
Manual for Research in Music.* Brooklyn, N.Y.: Institute
of Mediaeval Music, 1963; reprint, Westport, Conn.:
Greenwood Press, 1980.

Stevens, Denis. *Musicology: A Practical Guide.* Yehudi Menuhin
Music Guides. New York: Schirmer Books, 1980.

Stevens, Denis, and Thomas P. Lewis. *Musicology in Practice:
Selected Essays.* White Plains, N.Y.: Pro/AM Music
Resources, 1987.

Wallin, Nils L. *Biomusicology: Neurophysiological, Neuro-
psychological, and Evolutionary Perspectives on the
Origins and Purposes of Music.* Stuyvesant, N.Y.: Pendragon Press, 1991.

Wiora, Walter. *Historische und systematische Musikwissenschaft:
Ausgewählte Aufsätze.* Ed. Hellmut Kühn and Christoph-
Hellmut Mahling. Tutzing: Hans Schneider, 1972.

WWW Sites of Interest to Musicologists (maintained by the

American Musicological Society). Internet address: http://
www.ams-net.org/musicology_www.html. Provides
access to a large number of Internet resources about music
in general and for musicologists in particular.

Zon, Bennett. *Music and Metaphor in Nineteenth-Century
British Musicology.* Burlington, Vt.: Ashgate, 2000.

ETHNOMUSICOLOGY

The relative newness of what has come to be known as ethnomusicology is indicated by the fact that the term was coined, by
Jaap Kunst, only in 1950, although the study of non-Western and
folk music predates it by centuries and the origins of the field as it
is now understood go back to the 1880s. The English-language
sources listed below, dating with few exceptions from more recent
decades, have been selected from this vast and multifaceted field
not only to present some of its basic texts, overviews, and surveys,
but to give some notion of its scope and extent by listing examples
of more specific studies.

Thus, under "General Sources" are four "Classic Presentations
of the Field," beginning with Kunst's in 1950; several "Works
about Ethnomusicology as a Field of Research," comprising ré-
sumés of the discipline or discussions of areas within it; some "Surveys of World Music," basic coverages of the music of the world
or large regions of it, of which the twelve-volume *Universe of Music* will be by far the most comprehensive when completed; and
seven important representative sources on world instruments.
Then, under "Selected Monographs and Studies," are two highly
selective lists, each of a few representative studies from an extensive literature of such sources: "Examplars of Ethnomusicological
Method," works demonstrating some of the varied analytical approaches or methodologies employed in the field; and a selection
from the numerous "General Works about Individual Cultures or
Cultural Areas" that exist.

"Bibliographies and Other Reference Guides" constitutes the
final category. The regularly featured "Current Bibliography, Discography, and Filmography" sections in *Ethnomusicology* cumula-
tively form the most complete list of sources in the field. Nettl's,
Briegleb's, and Schuursma's bibliographies are also generalized in
their coverage, as is the latter author's *Directory* of sound recording archives in North America. All the remaining sources relate to
particular regions of the world.

For other bibliographies related to ethnomusicology, see under
"Bibliographies and Research Guides in Other Selected Areas" in
"African-American Music," pp. 137–38 below. For further cover-

age of the field, see *The Garland Encyclopedia of World Music,* listed on p. 98 below and in chapter 4; further coverage of instruments may be found in the dictionaries listed under "Specialized Dictionaries, Encyclopedias, and Guides" in "Musical Instruments and Makers," chapter 4 below. Standard ethnomusicological research journals are listed in chapter 6, "Current Research Journals in Music," p. 240 below. See also articles on individual countries, instruments, etc., in *The New Grove Dictionary.*

General Sources

Classic Presentations of the Field

Hood, Mantle. *The Ethnomusicologist.* New ed. Kent, Ohio: Kent State University Press, 1982; reprint, Ann Arbor, Mich.: UMI, 1998. First published in 1971.

Kunst, Jaap. *Ethnomusicology: A Study of Its Nature, Its Problems, Methods, and Representative Personalities, to Which Is Added a Bibliography.* 3rd ed., enl. The Hague: Martinus Nijhoff, 1959; reprint (including 2nd ed. of the supplement), The Hague: Martinus Nijhoff, 1974. Suppl., 1960. First published in 1950.

Merriam, Alan P. *The Anthropology of Music.* Evanston, Ill.: Northwestern University Press, 1964; reprint, Evanston, Ill.: Northwestern University Press, 1980.

Nettl, Bruno. *Theory and Method in Ethnomusicology.* New York: Schirmer, 1964.

Works about Ethnomusicology as a Field of Research

Baily, John. "Music Performance, Motor Structure, and Cognitive Models." In *European Studies in Ethnomusicology: Historical Developments and Recent Trends.* Wilhelmshaven, Germany: Florian Noetzel, 1992. Pp. 142–58.

Barz, Gregory F., and Timothy J. Cooley. *Shadows in the Field: New Perspectives for Fieldwork in Ethnomusicology.* New York: Oxford University Press, 1997.

Blum, Stephen, et al. *Ethnomusicology and Modern Music History.* Urbana: University of Illinois Press, 1991; Urbana: University of Illinois Press Illini Books Edition, 1993.

Bohlman, Philip V. "Ethnomusicology's Challenge to the Canon; the Canon's Challenge to Ethnomusicology." In *Disciplining Music: Musicology and Its Canons,* ed. Katherine Bergeron and Philip V. Bohlman. Chicago: University of Chicago Press, 1992. Pp. 116–36.

Born, Georgina, and David Hesmondhalgh, eds. *Western Music and Its Others: Difference, Representation, and Appropriation in Music.* Berkeley: University of California Press, 2000.

Clayton, Martin, Richard Middleton, and Trevor Herbert, eds. *The Cultural Study of Music.* New York: Routledge, 2003.

Emoff, Ron, and David Henderson, eds. *Mementos, Artifacts and Hallucinations from the Ethnographer's Tent.* New York: Routledge, 2002.

The Garland Library of Readings in Ethnomusicology: A Core Collection of Important Ethnomusicological Articles. 7 vols. Comp. Kay Kaufman Shelemay. New York: Garland Publishing, 1990.

Helm, E. Eugene. *The Canon and the Curricula: A Study of Musicology and Ethnomusicology Programs in America.* Stuyvesant, N.Y.: Pendragon Press, 1994.

Hood, Mantle. "Music, the Unknown." In *Musicology,* by Frank Ll. Harrison, Mantle Hood, and Claude V. Palisca. Englewood Cliffs, N.J.: Prentice Hall, 1963; reprint, Westport, Conn.: Greenwood Press, 1974. Pp. 215–326.

A Manual for Documentation, Fieldwork, and Preservation for Ethnomusicologists. 2nd ed. Bloomington, Ind.: Society for Ethnomusicology, 2001. First published in 1994.

McAllester, David P., comp. *Readings in Ethnomusicology.* Landmarks in Anthropology. New York: Johnson Reprint, 1971.

Merriam, Alan P. "Definitions of 'Comparative Musicology' and 'Ethnomusicology': An Historical-Theoretical Perspective." *Ethnomusicology* 21 (May 1977): 189–204.

Myers, Helen, ed. *Ethnomusicology: An Introduction.* The Norton/Grove Handbooks in Music. New York: W. W. Norton, 1992.

Nercessian, Andy H. *Postmodernism and Globalization in Ethnomusicology: An Epistemological Problem.* Lanham, Md.: Scarecrow Press, 2002.

Nettl, Bruno. "Ethnomusicology." In *The New Harvard Dictionary of Music.* Pp. 291–93.

———. *Heartland Excursions: Ethnomusicological Reflections on Schools of Music.* Urbana: University of Illinois Press, 1995.

———. *The Study of Ethnomusicology: Twenty-Nine Issues and Concepts.* Urbana: University of Illinois Press, 1983.

Nettl, Bruno, and Philip V. Bohlman, eds. *Comparative Musicology and Anthropology of Music: Essays on the History of Ethnomusicology.* Chicago Studies in Ethnomusicology. Chicago: University of Chicago Press, 1991.

Pegg, Carole, Helen Myers, Philip Bohlman, and Martin Stokes.

"Ethnomusicology." In *The New Grove Dictionary of Music and Musicians.* 2nd ed. Vol. 8, pp. 367–403.

Radano, Ronald Michael, and Houston A. Baker, Jr., eds. *Music and the Racial Imagination.* Chicago Studies in Ethnomusicology. Chicago: University of Chicago Press, 2000.

Rice, Timothy. "Toward the Remodeling of Ethnomusicology." *Ethnomusicology* 31 (Fall 1987): 469–88.

Shelemay, Kay Kaufman, ed. *Ethnomusicological Theory and Method.* Garland Library of Readings in Ethnomusicology, no. 2. New York: Garland, 1990.

———, ed. *Ethnomusicology: History, Definitions, and Scope: A Core Collection of Scholarly Articles.* New York: Garland Publishing, 1992.

Turkka, S. A. K. *Ethnomusicology: A Study of Intercultural Musicology.* Madras, India: Center for Ethnomusicology, 1996.

Surveys of World Music

Bohlman, Philip V. *World Music: A Very Short Introduction.* Oxford: Oxford University Press, 2002.

Fletcher, Peter. *World Musics in Context: A Comprehensive Survey of the World's Major Musical Cultures.* Oxford: Oxford University Press, 2001.

Hast, Dorothea, et al. *Exploring the World of Music: An Introduction to Music from a World Music Perspective.* Dubuque, Iowa: Kendall/Hunt, 1999.

Malm, William P. *Music Cultures of the Pacific, the Near East, and Asia.* 3rd ed. The Prentice Hall History of Music Series. Upper Saddle River, N.J.: Prentice Hall, 2000. First published in 1967.

May, Elizabeth, ed. *Musics of Many Cultures: An Introduction.* Berkeley: University of California Press, 1980. Also available on CD-ROM.

Nettl, Bruno, with Gerard Béhague. *Folk and Traditional Music of the Western Continents.* 3rd ed. Rev. and ed. Valerie Woodring Goertzen. The Prentice Hall History of Music Series. Englewood Cliffs, N.J.: Prentice Hall, 1990. First published in 1965.

Nettl, Bruno, et al. *Excursions in World Music.* 4th ed. Upper Saddle River, N.J.: Prentice Hall, 2004. First published in 1992.

Reck, David. *Music of the Whole Earth.* New York: Charles Scribner's Sons, 1997. First published in 1977.

Schneider, Marius. *Non-European Folklore and Art Music.* Anthology of Music, vol. 44. Cologne: Arno Volk Verlag, 1972.

Shelemay, Kay Kaufman. *Soundscapes: Exploring Music in a Changing World.* New York: W. W. Norton, 2001.

Titon, Jeff Todd, gen. ed. *Worlds of Music: An Introduction to the Music of the World's Peoples.* 4th ed. Belmont, Calif.: Schirmer/Thomson Learning, 2002. First published in 1984.

The Universe of Music: A History. A UNESCO/International Music Council Project. 12 vols. projected. Washington, D.C.: Smithsonian Institution Press, 1993–.

INSTRUMENTS

Buchner, Alexander. *Folk Music Instruments.* Trans. Alzbeta Nováková. New York: Crown Publishers, 1972. First published in 1968.

Devale, Sue Carole, ed. *Issues in Organology.* Selected Reports in Ethnomusicology, no. 8. Los Angeles: University of California Department of Ethnomusicology and Systematic Musicology, Ethnomusicology Publications, 1990.

Hornbostel, Erich M. von, and Curt Sachs. "Classification of Musical Instruments." Trans. Anthony Baines and Klaus P. Wachsmann. *Galpin Society Journal* (March 1961): 3–29. First published in 1914.

Kartomi, Margaret J. *On Concepts and Classifications of Musical Instruments.* Chicago Studies in Ethnomusicology. Chicago: University of Chicago Press, 1990.

Lysloff, René, and Jim Matson. "A New Approach to the Classification of Sound-Producing Instruments." In *Musical Processes, Resources, and Technologies.* New York: Garland, 1990. Pp. 315–38.

Musical Instruments of the World: An Illustrated Encyclopedia. New York: Stirling Publications, 1997.

Wachsmann, Klaus, Margaret J. Kartomi, Erich M. Hornbostel, and Curt Sachs. "Instruments, Classification of." In *The New Grove Dictionary of Music and Musicians.* 2nd ed. Vol. 12, pp. 418–28.

Selected Monographs and Studies

EXAMPLARS OF ETHNOMUSICOLOGICAL METHOD

Ames, David W., and Anthony V. King. *Glossary of Hausa Music and Its Social Contexts.* Evanston, Ill.: Northwestern University Press, 1971.

Blacking, John. *Music, Culture, and Experience: Selected Papers of John Blacking.* Chicago: University of Chicago Press, 1995.

————. *Venda Children's Songs: A Study in Ethnomusicological Analysis.* Johannesburg: Witwatersrand University Press, 1967; reprint, Chicago: University of Chicago Press, 1995.

Feld, Steven. *Sound and Sentiment: Birds, Weeping, Poetics and Song in Kaluli Expression.* 2nd ed. Publications of the American Folklore Society, new ser., vol. 5. Philadelphia: University of Pennsylvania Press, 1990. First published in 1982. Also available as an electronic book at http://www.netLibrary.com

Kaufmann, Walter. *Musical Notations of the Orient: Notational Systems of Continental, East, South, and Central Asia.* Indiana University Humanities Series, no. 60. Bloomington: Indiana University Press, 1967.

Lomax, Alan. *Folk Song Style and Culture.* Publication no. 88. Washington, D.C.: American Association for the Advancement of Science, 1968; reprint, New Brunswick, N.J.: Transaction Books, 1978.

Lord, Albert B. *The Singer of Tales.* 2nd ed. Cambridge, Mass.: Harvard University Press, 2000. First published in 1960.

Manuel, Peter. *Popular Musics of the Non-Western World: An Introductory Survey.* New York: Oxford University Press, 1988.

Powers, Harold. "An Historical and Comparative Approach to the Classification of Ragas (with an Appendix on Ancient Indian Tunings)." *Selected Reports: Publication of the Institute of Ethnomusicology of the University of California at Los Angeles* 1, no. 3 (1970): 1–78.

GENERAL WORKS ABOUT INDIVIDUAL CULTURES OR CULTURAL AREAS

Collections

Fujii, Tomoaki. *Music Culture in West Asia.* Suita, Japan: National Museum of Ethnology, 1980.

The Global Music Series. Bonnie C. Wade and Patricia Shehan Campbell, gen. eds. Oxford: Oxford University Press, 2003–.

    Carnival Music in Trinidad. By Shannon Dudley. 2003.
    Music in Bulgaria. By Timothy Rice. 2003.
    Music in North India. By George E. Ruckert. 2003.
    Music in South India. By Tanjore Viswanathan and Matthew Harp Allen. 2003.

Teaching Music Globally. By Patricia Shehan Campbell
and Bonnie C. Wade. 2003.

*Thinking Musically: Experiencing Music, Expressing
Culture.* By Bonnie C. Wade. 2003.

Hartigan, Royal James. *Cross-Cultural Performance and Analy-
sis of West African, African American, Native American,
Central Javanese, and South Indian Drumming.* Lewiston,
N.Y.: Edwin Mellen Press, 1998.

Herndon, Marcia, and Susanne Ziegler, guest eds.; International
Council for Traditional Music, ICTM Study Group on
Music and Gender. *Music, Gender, and Culture.* Inter-
cultural Music Studies, no. 1. Wilhelmshaven, Germany:
Florian Noetzel, 1990.

Koskoff, Ellen, ed. *Women and Music in Cross-Cultural Perspec-
tive.* Contributions in Women's Studies, no. 79. New York:
Greenwood Press, 1987; reprint, Urbana: University of
Illinois Press, 1989.

Myers, Helen, ed. *Ethnomusicology: Historical and Regional
Studies.* 1st American ed. The Norton/Grove Handbooks
in Music. New York: W. W. Norton, 1993.

Stokes, Martin, ed. *Ethnicity, Identity, and Music: The Musical
Construction of Place.* Oxford: Berg, 1994.

Afghanistan

Baily, John. *Music of Afghanistan: Professional Musicians
in the City of Herat.* Cambridge Studies in Ethnomusicology. Cambridge: Cambridge University Press,
1988.

Sakata, Hiromi. *Music in the Mind: The Concepts of Music and
Musician in Afghanistan.* Washington, D.C.: Smithsonian
Institution Press, 2003.

Slobin, Mark. *Music in the Culture of Northern Afghanistan.*
Viking Fund Publications in Anthropology, no. 54. Tucson:
University of Arizona Press, 1976.

Africa

Agawu, Victor Kofi. *African Rhythm: A Northern Ewe Perspective.* New York: Cambridge University Press, 1995.

———. *Representing African Music: Postcolonial Notes,
Queries, Positions.* New York: Routledge, 2003.

Ampene, Kwasi. *Female Song Tradition and the Akan of Ghana:
The Creative Process in Nnwonkoro.* Burlington, Vt.:
Ashgate, 2004.

Arom, Simha. *African Polyphony and Polyrhythm: Musical
Structure and Methodology.* Trans. Martin Thom et al.

Cambridge: Cambridge University Press, 1991. First published in 1985.

Barz, Gregory. *Music in East Africa: Experiencing Music, Expressing Culture.* New York: Oxford University Press, 2004.

Bender, Wolfgang, and Wolfgang Preis. *"Sweet Mother": Modern African Music.* Chicago Studies in Ethnomusicology. Chicago: University of Chicago Press, 1991.

Brandel, Rose. *The Music of Central Africa: An Ethnomusicological Study.* 2nd ed. New York: Da Capo Press, 1984. First published in 1973.

Charry, Eric S. *Mande Music: Traditional and Modern Music of the Maninka and Mandinka of Western Africa.* Chicago Studies in Ethnomusicology. Chicago: University of Chicago Press, 2000.

Chernoff, John Miller. *African Rhythm and African Sensibility: Aesthetics and Social Action in African Musical Idioms.* Chicago: University of Chicago Press, 1979.

Coplan, David B. *In the Time of Cannibals: The Word Music of South Africa's Basotho Migrants.* Chicago Studies in Ethnomusicology. Chicago: University of Chicago Press, 1994.

D'Amico, Leonardo, and Francesco Mizzau. *Africa Folk Music Atlas.* Florence, Italy: Amharsi, 1996.

Danielson, Virginia. *The Voice of Egypt: Umm Kulthum, Arabic Song, and Egyptian Society in the Twentieth Century.* Chicago Studies in Ethnomusicology. Chicago: University of Chicago Press, 1997.

Davis, Ruth Frances. "Traditional Arab Music Ensembles in Tunis: Modernizing Al-Turath in the Shadow of Egypt." *Asian Music* 28 (Spring–Summer 1997): 73–108.

El-Shawan, Salwa. "Traditional Arab Music Ensembles in Egypt since 1967: 'The Continuity of Traditions within a Contemporary Framework'?" *Ethnomusicology* 28 (May 1984): 271–88.

Erlmann, Veit. *African Stars: Studies in Black South African Performance.* Chicago Studies in Ethnomusicology. Chicago: University of Chicago Press, 1991.

———. *The Early Social History of Zulu Migrant Workers' Choral Music in South Africa.* Berlin: Das Arabische Buch, 1990.

———. *Music, Modernity, and the Global Imagination: South Africa and the West.* New York: Oxford University Press, 1999.

Ewens, Graeme. *Africa O-Ye!: A Celebration of African Music.* New York: Da Capo Press, 1992.

Floyd, Malcolm. *Composing the Music of Africa: Composition,*

Interpretation, and Realisation. Aldershot, England:
Ashgate, 1999.

Friedson, Steven M. *Dancing Prophets: Musical Experience in
Tumbuka Healing.* Chicago Studies in Ethnomusicology.
Chicago: University of Chicago Press, 1996.

Gunderson, Frank, and Gregory F. Barz. *Mashindano!: Competi-
tive Music Performance in East Africa.* Dar es Salaam and
Oxford: Mkuki na Nyota Publishers, 2000.

Kebede, Ashenafi. *Roots of Black Music: The Vocal, Instrumental, and Dance Heritage of Africa and Black America.* 2nd
ed. Trenton, N.J.: Africa World Press, 1995. First published
in 1982.

Monson, Ingrid, ed. *African Diaspora: A Musical Perspective.*
New York: Routledge, 2003.

Muller, Carol Ann. *Rituals of Fertility and the Sacrifice of
Desire: Nazarite Women's Performance in South Africa.*
Chicago Studies in Ethnomusicology. Chicago: University
of Chicago Press, 1999.

Nannyonga-Tamusuza, Sylvia. *Baakisimba: Gender in the Music
and Dance of the Baganda People of Uganda.* Current
Research in Ethnomusicology: Outstanding Dissertations,
no. 9. New York: Routledge, 2003.

Nketia, Joseph H. Kwabena. *The Music of Africa.* 3rd ed. London:
Gollancz, 1986. First published in 1974.

Palmberg, Mai, and Annemette Kirkegaard. *Playing with Iden-
tities in Contemporary Music in Africa.* Uppsala, Finland:
Nordiska Afrikainstitutet in cooperation with the Sibelius
Museum/Department of Musicology, Abo Akademi
University, 2002.

Selimovic, Johanna Mannergren. *Music, Power, and Diversity:
Encountering South Africa.* Göteborg: Musikhögskolan,
2002.

Turino, Thomas. *Nationalists, Cosmopolitans, and Popular
Music in Zimbabwe.* Chicago Studies in Ethnomusicology.
Chicago: University of Chicago Press, 2000.

Waterman, Christopher A. *Jùjú: A Social History and Ethnog-
raphy of an African Popular Music.* Chicago Studies in
Ethnomusicology. Chicago: University of Chicago Press,
1990.

Wiggins, Trevor. *Music of West Africa.* Oxford: Heinemann
Educational, 1993.

Bali and Java

Arps, Bernard. *Performance in Java and Bali: Studies of Narrative, Theatre, Music, and Dance.* London: School of

Oriental and African Studies, University of London, 1993.

Bakan, Michael B. *Music of Death and New Creation: Experiences in the World of Balinese Gamelan Beleganjur.* Chicago Studies in Ethnomusicology. Chicago: University of Chicago Press, 1999.

Becker, Judith. *Karawitan: Source Readings in Javanese Gamelan and Vocal Music.* Ann Arbor: Center for South and Southeast Asian Studies, University of Michigan, 1984.

———. *Traditional Music in Modern Java: Gamelan in a Changing Society.* Honolulu: University Press of Hawaii, 1980.

Brinner, Benjamin. "Cultural Matrices and the Shaping of Innovation in Central Javanese Performing Arts." *Ethnomusicology* 39 (Fall 1995): 433–56.

———. *Knowing Music, Making Music: Javanese Gamelan and the Theory of Musical Competence and Interaction.* Chicago Studies in Ethnomusicology. Chicago: University of Chicago Press, 1995.

Ferdinandus, Pieter. *The Role of Musicians during the Old Javanese and Balinese Period.* Jakarta: Pusat Penelitian Arkeologi Nasional, 2000.

Heimarck, Brita Renée. *Balinese Discourses on Music and Modernization: Village Voices and Urban Views.* New York: Routledge, 2003.

Herbst, Edward. *Voices in Bali: Energies and Perceptions in Vocal Music and Dance Theater.* Hanover, N.H.: University Press of New England, 1997.

Hood, Mantle. *The Enduring Tradition: Music and Theater in Java and Bali.* New Haven, Conn.: Yale University Southeast Asia Studies, 1963.

———. *The Evolution of Javanese Gamelan.* Wilhelmshaven, Germany: Heinrichshofen, n.d.

———. *Legacy of the Roaring Sea.* Wilhelmshaven, Germany: Heinrichshofen, 1984.

Kunst, Jaap. *Music in Java, Its History, Its Theory and Its Technique.* 3rd, enl. ed. 2 vols. Ed. E. L. Heins. The Hague: Martinus Nijhoff, 1973.

Lindsay, Jennifer. *Javanese Gamelan: Traditional Orchestra of Indonesia.* 2nd ed. New York: Oxford University Press, 1992.

Lysloff, René T. A. *The Gong-Chime Bonang Barung in the Central Javanese Gamelan: Aspects of Musical Function and Idiom in Contemporary Practice.* Lebanon, N.H.: American Gamelan Institute, 1990s.

McPhee, Colin. *The Balinese Wajang Koelit and Its Music.* New York: A.M.S. Press, 1981. First published in 1936.

————. *The Five-Tone Gamelan Music of Bali.* New York: Schirmer Books, 1949.

————. *Music in Bali: A Study in Form and Instrumental Organization in Balinese Orchestral Music.* New Haven, Conn.: Yale University Press, 1966; reprint, New York: Da Capo Press, 1976.

Perlman, Marc. *Unplayed Melodies: Javanese Gamelan and the Genesis of Music Theory.* Berkeley: University of California Press, 2004.

Schaareman, Danker H., ed. *Balinese Music in Context: A Sixty-Fifth Birthday Tribute to Hans Oesch.* Winterthur, Switzerland: Amadeus, 1992.

Sorrell, Neil, Martin Fellows Hatch, and Jody Diamond. *A Guide to the Gamelan.* 2nd ed. Ithaca, N.Y.: Cornell University Society for Asian Music, 2000. First published in 1990.

Sumarsam. *Gamelan: Cultural Interaction and Musical Development in Central Java.* Chicago Studies in Ethnomusicology. Chicago: University of Chicago Press, 1995.

Suryabrata. *The Island of Music: An Essay in Social Musicology.* Jakarta: Balai Pustaka, 1987.

Sutton, Richard Anderson. *The Javanese Gambang and Its Music.* Lebanon, N.H.: American Gamelan Institute, 1990s.

————. *Traditions of Gamelan Music in Java: Musical Pluralism and Regional Identity.* Cambridge Studies in Ethnomusicology. New York: Cambridge University Press, 1991.

————. *Variation in Central Javanese Gamelan Music: Dynamics of a Steady State.* Monograph Series on Southeast Asia, no. 28. DeKalb: Northern Illinois University, 1993.

Tenzer, Michael. *Balinese Music.* Rev. and updated ed. North Clarendon, Vt.: Periplus Editions, 1998. First published in 1991.

————. *Gamelan Gong Kebyar: The Art of Twentieth-Century Balinese Music.* Chicago Studies in Ethnomusicology. Chicago: University of Chicago Press, 2000.

Vetter, Roger R. *Formal Aspects of Performance Practice in Central Javanese Gamelan Music.* Lebanon, N.H.: American Gamelan Institute, 1990s.

Vickers, Adrian. *The Realm of the Senses: Images of the Court Music of Pre-Colonial Bali.* Sydney, Australia: University of Sydney, 1985.

Walton, Susan Pratt. *Mode in Javanese Music.* Athens: Ohio University Center for International Studies, 1987.

Zanten, Wim van. *Sundanese Music in the Cianjuran Style: Anthropological and Musicological Aspects of Tembang Sunda.* Providence, R.I.: Foris Publications, 1989.

China and Tibet

Chao, Mei-po. *A Guide to Chinese Music.* Iowa City: [n.p.], 1969.

Ellingson, Terry Jay. "The Mandala of Sound: Concepts and Sound Structures in Tibetan Ritual Music." Ph.D. diss., University of Wisconsin–Madison, 1979; reprint, Ann Arbor, Mich.: University Microfilms International, 1989.

Hatch, Martin, ed. *Views of Music in China Today.* Ithaca, N.Y.: Society for Asian Music, 1991.

Jones, Stephen. *Folk Music of China: Living Instrumental Traditions.* New York: Oxford University Press, 1995.

Kuttner, Fritz A. *The Archaeology of Music in Ancient China: 2000 Years of Acoustical Experimentation, 1400 B.C.–A.D. 750.* New York: Paragon House, 1990.

Liang, Ming Yueh. *Music of the Billion: An Introduction to Chinese Musical Culture.* New York: Heinrichshofen, 1985.

Norbu, Jamyang. *Zlos-Gar: Performing Traditions of Tibet.* Dharamsala, India: Library of Tibetan Works and Archives, 1986.

Pian, Rulan Chao. *Song Dynasty Musical Sources and Their Interpretation.* Hong Kong: Chinese University Press, 2003 (reprint of the Harvard University Press 1967 ed.).

Picken, Lawrence, Ernest Rowland, and Noel Nickson. *Music from the Tang Court.* Cambridge: Cambridge University Press, 2000.

Scheidegger, Daniel A. *Tibetan Ritual Music: A General Survey with Special Reference to the Mindroling Tradition.* Opuscula Tibetana, no. 19. Rikon, Tibet: Tibet Institute, 1988.

Shen, Sin-yan. *China: A Journey into Its Musical Art.* Chicago: Chinese Music Society of North America, 2000.

———. *Chinese Music in the Twentieth Century.* Chicago: Chinese Music Society of North America, 2001.

Stock, Jonathan. *Musical Creativity in Twentieth-Century China: Abing, His Music, and Its Changing Meanings.* Eastman Studies in Music, no. 6. Rochester, N.Y.: University of Rochester, 1996.

Thrasher, Alan R., ed. *Chinese Music Theory.* Ithaca, N.Y.: Society for Asian Music, 1989.

Wiant, Bliss. *The Music of China.* Hong Kong: Chung Chi Publications, Chung Chi College, Chinese University of Hong Kong, 1965.

Wu, Ben. "Ritual Music in the Court and Rulership of the Qing Dynasty (1644–1911)." Ph.D. diss., University of Pittsburgh, 1998.

Yung, Bell. *Cantonese Opera: Performance as Creative Process.*

Cambridge Studies in Ethnomusicology. Cambridge: Cambridge University Press, 1989.

Yung, Bell, Evelyn Sakakida Rawski, and Rubie S. Watson. *Harmony and Counterpoint: Ritual Music in Chinese Context.* Stanford, Calif.: Stanford University Press, 1996.

India

Chakravarty, Arati. *An Introduction to Hindustani Music.* New Delhi, India: Har-Anand Publications, 1999.

Clayton, Mark. *Time in Indian Music: Rhythm, Metre, and Form in North Indian Rag Performance.* Oxford: Oxford University Press, 2000.

Daniélou, Alain. *The Ragas of Northern Indian Music.* New Delhi, India: Munshiram Manoharlal, 1997.

Davies, Sandra. *The Music of India: Musical Forms, Instruments, Dance, and Folk Traditions.* Vancouver: Pacific Educational Press, 1993.

Farrell, Gary. *Indian Music and the West.* Oxford: Oxford University Press, 1999.

Gautam, Reena. *Sources of Research in Indian Classical Music.* New Delhi, India: Kanishka Publishers Distributors, 2002.

Hamilton, James Sadler. *Sitar Music in Calcutta: An Ethnomusicological Study.* Calgary: University of Calgary Press, 1989.

Jairazbhoy, Nazir A. *The Rags of North Indian Music, Their Structure and Evolution.* Middletown, Conn.: Wesleyan University Press, 1971; rev. Indian ed., Bombay, India: Popular Prakashan, 1995.

Kaufmann, Walter. *The Ragas of North India.* Bloomington: Indiana University Press, 1968; 1st Indian ed., New Delhi, India. Oxford and I.B.H. Publishing, 1993.

―――. *The Ragas of South India: A Catalogue of Scalar Material.* Bloomington: Indiana University Press, 1976; 1st Indian ed., New Delhi, India: Oxford and I.B.H. Publishing, 1991.

Kippen, James. *The Tabla of Lucknow: A Cultural Analysis of a Musical Tradition.* Cambridge Studies in Ethnomusicology. Cambridge: Cambridge University Press, 1988.

Latha, Mukunda. *Transformation as Creation: Essays in the History, Theory, and Aesthetics of Indian Music, Dance, and Theatre.* New Delhi, India: Aditya Prakashan, 1998.

Massey, Reginald, and Jamilla Massey. *The Music of India.* London: Kahn and Averill, 1993.

Neuman, Daniel M. *The Life of Music in North India: The Organization of an Artistic Tradition.* Reprint, with a new preface. Chicago: University of Chicago Press, 1990. First published in 1980.

Pesch, Ludwig. *The Illustrated Companion to South Indian Classical Music.* New Delhi, India: Oxford University Press, 1999.

Ravikumar, Geetha. *The Concept and Evolution of Raga in Hindustani and Karnatic Music.* Mumbai, India: Bharatiya Vidya Bhavan, 2002.

Rowell, Lewis. *Music and Musical Thought in Early India.* Chicago Studies in Ethnomusicology. Chicago: University of Chicago Press, 1992.

Sanyal, Ritwick, and Richard Widdess. *Dhurupad: Tradition and Performance in Indian Music.* Burlington, Vt.: Ashgate, 2004.

Viswanathan, T., and Matthew Harp Allen. *Music in South India: Experiencing Music, Expressing Culture.* New York: Oxford University Press, 2003.

Wade, Bonnie C. *Imaging Sound: An Ethnomusicological Study of Music, Art, and Culture in Mughal India.* Chicago Studies in Ethnomusicology. Chicago: University of Chicago Press, 1999.

———. *Khyal: Creativity within North India's Classical Music Tradition.* Cambridge Studies in Ethnomusicology. Cambridge: Cambridge University Press, 1990.

———. *Music in India: The Classical Traditions.* The Prentice Hall History of Music Series. Englewood Cliffs, N.J.: Prentice Hall, 1978; reprint, London: Sangam Books, 1988.

Iran, Iraq, and Syria

Babiracki, Carol, and Bruno Nettl. "Internal Interrelationships in Persian Classical Music: The Dastgah of Shur in Eighteen Radifs." *Asian Music* (Fall–Winter 1987): 46–98.

During, Jean, Zia Mirabdolbaghi, and Dariush Safvat. *The Art of Persian Music.* Washington, D.C.: Mage Publishers, 1991.

Farhat, Hormoz. *The Dastgah Concept in Persian Music.* Cambridge Studies in Ethnomusicology. Cambridge: Cambridge University Press, 1990.

———. "The Evolution of Style and Content in Performance Practices of Persian Traditional Music." *Muzikoloski Zbornik (Musicological Annual)* 33 (1997): 81–89.

Miller, Lloyd. *Music and Song in Persia: The Art of Avaz.* Salt Lake City: University of Utah Press, 1999.

Nettl, Bruno. "Aspects of Form in the Instrumental Performance of the Persian Avaz." *Ethnomusicology* 18 (September 1974): 405–14.

————. *Daramad of Chahargah: A Study in the Performance Practice of Persian Music.* Detroit Monographs in Musicology, no. 2. Detroit: Information Coordinators, 1972.

Nettl, Bruno, and Carol M. Babiracki. *The Radif of Persian Music: Studies of Structure and Cultural Context in the Classical Music of Iran.* Rev. ed. Champaign, Ill.: Elephant and Cat, 1992.

Qassim Hassan, Scheherazade. "The Long Necked Lute in Iraq." *Asian Music U.S.A.* 13 (Spring/Summer 1982): 1–18.

Racy, A. J. *Making Music in the Arab World: The Culture and Artistry of Tarab.* Cambridge Middle East Studies, no. 17. Cambridge: Cambridge University Press, 2003.

Shelemay, Kay Kaufman. *Let Jasmine Rain Down: Song and Remembrance among Syrian Jews.* Chicago Studies in Ethnomusicology. Chicago: University of Chicago Press, 1998.

Simms, Rob. *The Repertoire of Iraqi Maqam.* Lanham, Md.: Scarecrow Press, 2004.

Weger, Ulrich. "Traditional Music on Stage: Two Case Studies from Iraq." In *Music in the Dialogue of Cultures: Traditional Music and Cultural Policy.* Wilhelmshaven, Germany: Florian Noetzel, 1991. Pp. 255–71.

Wright, Owen. *The Modal System of Arab and Persian Music* **A.D.** *1250–1300.* Oxford: Oxford University Press, 1978.

Zonis, Ella. *Classical Persian Music: An Introduction.* Cambridge, Mass.: Harvard University Press, 1973.

Japan

Adriaansz, Willem. *The Kumiuta and Danmono Traditions of Japanese Koto Music.* Berkeley: University of California Press, 1973.

Daijo, Kazuo, and Naoyuki Suda. *The Birth of Tsugaru Shamisen Music: The Origin and Development of a Japanese Folk Performing Art.* Aomori, Japan: Aomori University Press, 1998.

De Ferranti, Hugh, and Veronica Crowe. *Traditional Music of Japan.* Pymble, Australia: Australia's Multicultural Music, 1992.

Galliano, Luciana. *Yogaku: Japanese Music in the 20th Century.* Lanham, Md.: Scarecrow Press, 2003.

Garfias, Robert. *Music of a Thousand Autumns: The Togaku Style of Japanese Court Music.* Berkeley: University of California Press, 1975.

Hattori, Koh-ichi. *36,000 Days of Japanese Music: The Culture*

of Japan through a Look at Its Music. Southfield, Mich.:
Pacific Vision, 1996.

Keister, Jay Davis. *Shaped by Japanese Music: Kikuoka Hiroaki
and Nagauta Shamisen in Tokyo.* New York: Routledge,
2004.

Kishibe, Shigeo. *The Traditional Music of Japan.* 2nd ed. Tokyo:
Japan Foundation, 1982. First published in 1966.

Malm, William. *Japanese Music and Musical Instruments.*
Rutland, Vt.: C. E. Tuttle, 1959; reprint, New York: Simon
and Schuster, 1991.

———. *Nagauta: The Heart of Kabuki Music.* Westport, Conn.:
Greenwood Press, 1973.

———. *Six Hidden Views of Japanese Music.* Berkeley: University of California Press, 1986.

Picken, Laurence Ernest Rowland, and Noel Nickson. *Music
from the Tang Court: Some Ancient Connections Explored.*
Cambridge: Cambridge University Press, 2000.

Tokita, Alison McQueen. *Kiyomoto-bushi: Narrative Music of
the Kabuki Theatre.* Kassel: Bärenreiter, 1999.

Tokita, Alison McQueen, and David W. Hughes, eds. *Japanese
Music: History, Performance, Research.* Cambridge: Cambridge University Press, 2003.

Wade, Bonnie C. *Tegotomono: Music for the Japanese Koto.*
Westport, Conn.: Greenwood Press, 1976.

Latin America

Austerlitz, Paul. *Merengue: Dominican Music and Dominican
Identity.* Philadelphia: Temple University Press, 1997.

Basso, Ellen B. "A Musical View of the Universe: Kalapalo Myth
and Ritual as Religious Performance." *Journal of American Folklore* 44 (July–September 1981): 273–91.

Carvalho, Martha De Ulhôa. "Musical Style, Migration, and
Urbanization: Some Considerations of Brazilian *Música
Sertaneja.*" *Studies in Latin American Popular Culture* 12
(1993): 75–94.

Chernela, Janet. "Gender, Language and Placement in Uanano
Songs." *Journal of Latin American Lore* 14 (Winter 1988):
193–206.

Hill, Jonathan. "Wakuénai Ceremonial Exchange in the Venezue-
lan Northwest Amazon." *Journal of Latin American Lore*
13 (Winter 1987): 183–224.

Mendoza, Zoila S. *Shaping Society through Dance: Mestizo
Ritual Performance in the Peruvian Andes.* Chicago
Studies in Ethnomusicology. Chicago: University of
Chicago Press, 2000.

Olsen, Dale A. "Music-Induced Altered States of Consciousness among Warao Shamans." *Journal of Latin American Lore* 1 (Summer 1975): 19–33.

Pinzon Urrea, Jesús. "The Vernacular Music of the Plateau of Bogotá." *Inter-American Music Bulletin* 77 (May 1970): 15–30.

Schechter, John. "Quecha Sanjuán in Northern Highland Ecuador: Harp Music as Structural Metaphor on Purina." *Journal of Latin American Lore* 13 (Summer 1987): 27–46.

Seeger, Anthony. *Why Suyá Sing: A Musical Anthropology of an Amazonian People.* Cambridge Studies in Ethnomusicology. Cambridge: Cambridge University Press, 1987.

Turino, Thomas Robert. *Moving Away from Silence: Music of the Peruvian Altiplano and the Experiment of Urban Migration.* Chicago Studies in Ethnomusicology. Chicago: University of Chicago Press, 1993.

Valldeperes, Manuel. "Music in the Dominican Republic." *Inter-American Music Bulletin* 77 (May 1970): 31–44.

Wade, Peter. *Music, Race, and Nation: Música Tropical in Colombia.* Chicago Studies in Ethnomusicology. Chicago: University of Chicago Press, 2000.

North America

Black Bear, Ben, and R. D. Theisz. *Songs and Dances of the Lakota.* 2nd ed. Aberdeen, S.D.: North Plains Press, 1984. First published in 1976.

Burton, Bryan. *Moving within the Circle: Contemporary Native American Music and Dance.* Danbury, Conn.: World Music Press, 1993.

Diamond, Beverly, Michael Sam Cronk, and Franziska Von Rosen. *Visions of Sound: Musical Instruments of First Nations Communities in Northeastern America.* Chicago Studies in Ethnomusicology. Chicago: University of Chicago Press, 1994.

Herndon, Marcia. *Native American Music.* Norwood, Pa.: Norwood Editions, 1980.

Heth, Charlotte. *The Traditional Music of North American Indians.* Selected Reports in Ethnomusicology, no. 3. Los Angeles: Program in Ethnomusicology, Department of Music, University of California Los Angeles, 1980.

Howard, James. "Pan-Indianism in Native American Music and Dance." *Ethnomusicology* 27 (January 1983): 71–82.

Keeling, Richard. *North American Indian Music: A Guide to Published Sources and Selected Recordings.* Garland Library of Music Ethnology, no. 5. New York: Garland, 1997.

————. *Women in North American Indian Music: Six Essays.* Society for Ethnomusicology Special Series, no. 6. Bloomington, Ind.: Society for Ethnomusicology, 1989.

Kolstee, Anton Frederick. *Bella Coola Indian Music: A Study of the Interaction between Northwest Coast Indian Structures and Their Functional Context.* Canadian Ethnology Service, Mercury Series, no. 83. Ottawa: National Museums of Canada, 1982.

Lutz, Maija M. *Musical Traditions of the Labrador Coast Inuit.* Canadian Ethnology Service, Mercury Series, no. 79. Ottawa: National Museums of Canada, 1982.

McAllester, David P. "New Perspectives in Native American Music." *Perspectives of New Music* 20 (Fall–Winter 1981, Spring–Summer 1982): 433–46.

Merriam, Alan P. *Ethnomusicology of the Flathead Indians.* Viking Fund Publications in Anthropology, no. 44. Chicago: Aldine Publishing Company, 1967.

Nettl, Bruno. *Blackfoot Musical Thought: Comparative Perspectives.* Kent, Ohio: Kent State University Press, 1989.

————. *Folk Music in the United States: An Introduction.* 3rd ed., rev. and exp. by Helen Myers. Detroit: Wayne State University Press, 1976. First published in 1960.

Smyth, Willie, and Esmé Ryan. *Spirit of the First People: Native American Music Traditions of Washington State.* Seattle: University of Washington Press, 1999.

Spotted Eagle, Douglas. *Voices of Native America: Native American Instruments and Music.* Liberty, Utah: Eagle's View Publishing, 1997.

Underhill, Ruth Murray. *Singing for Power: The Song Magic of the Papago Indians of Southern Arizona.* Tucson: University of Arizona Press, 1938; reprint, Berkeley: University of California Press, 1968.

Vander, Judith. *Songprints: The Musical Experience of Five Shoshone Women.* Urbana: University of Illinois Press, 1988.

Witmer, Robert. *The Musical Life of the Blood Indians.* Canadian Ethnology Service, Mercury Series, no. 86. Ottawa: National Museums of Canada, 1982.

Thailand

Miller, Terry E. *Traditional Music of the Lao: Kaen Playing and Mawlum Singing in Northeast Thailand.* Contributions in Intercultural and Comparative Studies, no. 13. Westport, Conn.: Greenwood Press, 1985.

Morton, David. *The Traditional Music of Thailand.* Berkeley: University of California Press, 1976.

Myers-Moro, Pamela. *Thai Music and Musicians in Contemporary Bangkok.* Berkeley: Centers for South and Southeast Asia Studies, University of California at Berkeley, 1993.

Swangviboonpong, Dusadee. *Thai Classical Singing: Its History, Musical Characteristics and Transmission.* Burlington, Vt.: Ashgate, 2004.

Wong, Deborah. *Sounding the Center: History and Aesthetics in Thai Buddhist Performance.* Chicago Studies in Ethnomusicology. Chicago: University of Chicago Press, 2001.

Turkey

Popescu-Judetz, Eugenia. *Meanings in Turkish Musical Culture.* Istanbul: Pan, 1996.

Signell, Karl L. *Makam: Modal Practice in Turkish Art Music.* Seattle, Wash.: Asian Music Publications, 1977; reprint, New York: Da Capo Press, 1986.

Stokes, Martin. *The Arabesk Debate: Music and Musicians in Modern Turkey.* New York: Oxford University Press, 1992.

Vietnam

Arana, Miranda. *Neotraditional Music in Vietnam.* Kent, Ohio: Nhac Viêt, 1999.

Hùng, Lê Tuân. *Dàn Tranh Music of Vietnam: Traditions and Innovations.* Melbourne, Australia: Australia Asia Foundation, 1998.

Nguyên, Thuyêt Phong. *New Perspectives on Vietnamese Music.* New Haven, Conn.: Yale Center for International and Area Studies, 1991.

Nguyên, Thuyêt Phong, and Patricia Shehan Campbell. *From Rice Paddies and Temple Yards: Traditional Music of Vietnam.* Danbury, Conn.: World Music Press, 1990.

PERFORMANCE PRACTICE

Béhague, Gerard, ed. *Performance Practice: Ethnomusicological Perspectives.* Contributions to Intercultural and Comparative Studies, no. 12. Westport, Conn.: Greenwood Press, 1984.

Bibliographies and Other Reference Guides

Briegleb, Ann, ed. *Directory of Ethnomusicological Sound Recording Collections in the U.S. and Canada.* Special Series, no. 2. Ann Arbor, Mich.: Society for Ethnomusicology, 1971.

"Current Bibliography, Discography, and Filmography." Ed.
Joseph C. Hickerson et al. In *Ethnomusicology* 1– (1953–).
Garland Encyclopedia of World Music. Bruno Nettl, advisory
ed.; James Porter and Timothy Rice, founding eds. 10 vols.
New York: Garland (vols. 1–5 and 8–9) and Routledge
(vols. 6–7, 10), 1998–2002.

1. *Africa.* Ed. Ruth M. Stone. 1998.
2. *South America, Mexico, Central America, and the
Caribbean.* Ed. Dale A. Olsen and Daniel E. Sheehy.
1998.
3. *The United States and Canada.* Ed. Ellen Koskoff. 2001.
4. *Southeast Asia.* Ed. Terry E. Miller and Sean Williams.
1998.
5. *South Asia: The Indian Subcontinent.* Ed. Alison Arnold.
2000.
6. *The Middle East.* Ed. Virginia Danielson, Scott Marcus,
and Dwight Reynolds. 2002.
7. *East Asia: China, Japan, and Korea.* Ed. Robert C.
Provine, Yosihiko Tokumaru, and J. Lawrence
Witzleben. 2002.
8. *Europe.* Ed. Timothy Rice, James Porter, and Chris
Goertzen. 2000.
9. *Australia and the Pacific Islands.* Ed. Adrienne L.
Kaeppler and J. W. Love. 1998.
10. *The World's Music: General Perspectives and Reference Tools.* Ed. Ruth Stone. 2002.

Gray, John. *African Music: A Bibliographical Guide to the
Traditional, Popular, Art and Liturgical Musics of Sub-
Saharan Africa.* African Special Bibliographic Series, no.
14. New York: Greenwood Press, 1991.
Heins, Ernst. *Music in Java: Current Bibliography, 1973–1992.*
3rd enl. ed. Amsterdam: University of Amsterdam Insti-
tute of Musicology, Ethnomusicology Center "Jaap
Kunst," 1993.
Lems-Dworkin, Carol. *African Music: A Pan-African Annotated
Bibliography.* London: Hans Zell Publishers, 1991.
———. *Videos of African and African-Related Performance: An
Annotated Bibliography.* Evanston, Ill.: C. Lems-Dworkin
Publishers, 1996.
Lieberman, Fredric. *Chinese Music: An Annotated Bibliography.*
2nd ed., rev. and enl. Garland Bibliographies in Ethnomu-
sicology, vol. 1. New York: Garland Publishing, 1979. First
published in 1970.
McLean, Mervyn. *An Annotated Bibliography of Oceanic Music*

and Dance. Rev. and enl. 2nd ed. Warren, Mich.: Harmonie
   Park Press, 1995. First published in 1977.
*Musikethnologische Jahresbibliographie Europas/Annual
   Bibliography of European Ethnomusicology.* Ed. Oskár
   Elschek et al. 10 vols. Bratislava: Slovenské Národné
   Múzeum, 1967–76.
Nettl, Bruno. *Reference Materials in Ethnomusicology: A
   Bibliographic Essay on Primitive, Oriental and Folk
   Music.* 2nd ed., rev. Detroit Studies in Music Bibliography,
   no. 1. Detroit: Information Coordinators, 1967. First
   published in 1961.
Post, Jennifer C. *Ethnomusicology: A Guide to Research.* New
   York: Routledge, 2003.
Rahkonen, Carl. *Film and Video Resources in Ethnomusicology:
   An Annotated Filmography.* Garland Library of Music
   Ethnology, vol. 3. New York: Garland Publishing, 1994.
Schuursma, Ann Briegleb. *Ethnomusicology Research: A Select
   Annotated Bibliography.* Garland Library of Music
   Ethnology, vol. 1. New York: Garland Publishing, 1992.
Song, Bang-Song. *An Annotated Bibliography of Korean Music.*
   Asian Music Publications, ser. A, no. 2. Providence: Brown
   University Press, 1971.
Tsuge, Gen'ichi. *Japanese Music: An Annotated Bibliography.*
   Garland Bibliographies in Ethnomusicology, vol. 2. New
   York: Garland Publishing, 1986.

PERFORMANCE PRACTICE

Until about the mid-twentieth century, "performance practice"
was little more than the translation of an obscure German term,
Aufführungspraxis, that represented the few ground-breaking studies in the area written prior to that time. Since then, this field has
grown, especially in the last twenty years, into one of the most visible, influential, and controversial branches of music scholarship,
affecting live and recorded performances of music of every historical period.

The following bibliography includes basic general texts and a
representative selection of other important sources in the area. The
first list, "General Treatments," offers recent comprehensive coverages of the subject. The second list, "Studies Specific to an Era,"
brings together sources that apply to a single historical period.
Next comes a much longer but far more selective list, "Examples
of More Specialized Discussions," combining a sampling of monographs and *New Grove* articles, each on a specific subject, together

illustrating something of the wide scope and variety of interests in the field.

There then follow two lists that are more concerned with matters of performance itself. Under "Discussions of the Performance Practice Movement" are two treatments (Cohen/Snitzer and Haskell) of the history and evolution of the "authentic performance" revival, Kottick's practical guide to the setting up and running of a Collegium Musicum, the texts of papers read at a conference on performance practice (Kenyon), and other discussions of the movement. Under "Guides for Performers" are listed a number of examples of performance practice sources addressed directly to performers. These works range from multivolume series (the Cambridge Handbooks to the Historical Performance of Music and the Performer's Guides to Early Music) to individual performance practice discussions of specific genres, periods, and repertoires.

The next two lists are of older sources: "Studies of Historical Interest," presenting a few of the pioneering earlier-twentieth-century works, and "Editions of Selected Primary Sources," comprising some of the best-known treatises that are valuable for the information they contain about the performance of music of their time. The list of "Anthologies" contains two collections (Ferand and Schmitz) of musical works with contemporaneous written-out ornamentation or improvisation, and MacClintock's unique anthology of excerpts from primary-source writings that pertain to performance practice. The concluding list is of the two standard bibliographies in the field, Vinquist/Zaslaw and the more recent one by Jackson, which is updated annually.

For a list of journals in the area, see chapter 6, "Current Research Journals in Music," pp. 239–40 below.

General Treatments

Brown, Howard Mayer, et al. "Performing Practice." In *The New Grove Dictionary of Music and Musicians.* 2nd ed. Vol. 19, pp. 349–88.

Brown, Howard Mayer, and Stanley Sadie, eds. *Performance Practice.* 1st American ed. 2 vols. The Norton/Grove Handbooks in Music. New York: W. W. Norton, 1990. First published in 1989.

Butt, John. *Playing with History: The Historical Approach to Musical Performance.* Cambridge: Cambridge University Press, 2002. Also available as an electronic book at http://www.netLibrary.com

Donington, Robert. *The Interpretation of Early Music.* New rev. ed. New York: W. W. Norton, 1992. First published in 1963.

Krausz, Michael, ed. *The Interpretation of Music: Philosophical*

Essays. Oxford: Clarendon Press of Oxford University Press, 1993.

Lang, Paul Henry. "On Performance Practice." In *Musicology and Performance,* ed. Alfred Mann and George J. Buelow. New Haven, Conn.: Yale University Press, 1997. Pp. 169–242.

Lawson, Colin, and Robin Stowell. *The Historical Performance of Music: An Introduction.* Cambridge: Cambridge University Press, 1999. Also available as an electronic book at http://www.netLibrary.com

Taruskin, Richard. *Text and Act: Essays on Music and Performance.* Oxford: Oxford University Press, 1995.

Walls, Peter. *History, Imagination, and the Performance of Music.* Rochester, N.Y.: Boydell Press, 2003.

Studies Specific to an Era

Arnold, Denis. *Giovanni Gabrieli and the Music of the Venetian High Renaissance.* Oxford: Oxford University Press, 1979.

Boorman, Stanley, ed. *Studies in the Performance of Late Medieval Music.* Cambridge: Cambridge University Press, 1983.

Bowles, Edmund A. *Musical Performance in the Late Middle Ages.* Paris: Minkoff, 1983.

Brown, Clive. *Classic and Romantic Performing Practice 1750– 1900.* Oxford: Oxford University Press, 2000.

Donington, Robert. *Baroque Music: Style and Performance.* New York: W. W. Norton, 1982.

Leech-Wilkinson, Daniel. *The Modern Invention of Medieval Music: Scholarship, Ideology, Performance.* Cambridge: Cambridge University Press, 2002.

Page, Christopher. *Music and Instruments of the Middle Ages: Studies on Texts and Performance.* Aldershot, England: Variorum, 1997.

———. *Voices and Instruments of the Middle Ages: Instrumental Practice and Songs in France, 1100–1300.* Berkeley: University of California Press, 1986.

Polk, Keith. *German Instrumental Music of the Late Middle Ages: Players, Patrons, and Performance Practice.* Cambridge: Cambridge University Press, 1992.

Saint-Arroman, Jean. *L'interprétation de la musique française, 1661–1789.* Vol. 1: *Dictionnaire d'interprétation (initiation);* Vol. 2: *L'interprétation de la musique pour orgue.* 6 vols. projected. Paris: Honoré Champion, 1983–.

Saint-Arroman, Jean, and Stephen Zachary Cook. "A Translation of Jean Saint-Arroman's L'interprétation de la musique française, 1661–1789, I. Dictionnaire d'interprétation (initiation)." D.M.A. thesis, University of Iowa, 1999.

Strohm, Reinhard, and Bonnie J. Blackburn, eds. *Music as Concept and Practice in the Late Middle Ages.* Oxford: Oxford University Press, 2001.

Examples of More Specialized Discussions

Arnold, Frank Thomas. *The Art of Accompaniment from a Thorough-Bass as Practised in the XVIIth and XVIIIth Centuries.* Reprint, with a new introduction by Denis Stevens. 2 vols. New York: Dover, 2003. First published in 1931.

Badura-Skoda, Eva, et al. "Cadenza." In *The New Grove Dictionary of Music and Musicians.* 2nd ed. Vol. 4, pp. 783–90.

Badura-Skoda, Eva, and Paul Badura-Skoda. *Interpreting Mozart on the Keyboard.* Trans. Leo Black. London: Barrie and Rockliff, 1962; reprint, New York: Da Capo Press, 1986.

Badura-Skoda, Paul. *Interpreting Bach at the Keyboard.* Oxford: Oxford University Press, 1995.

Barbour, J. Murray. *Tuning and Temperament: A Historical Survey.* East Lansing: Michigan State College Press, 1951; reprint, New York: Da Capo Press, 1972.

Bent, Margaret, and Alexander Silbiger. "Musica Ficta." In *The New Grove Dictionary of Music and Musicians.* 2nd ed. Vol. 17, pp. 441–53.

Berger, Anna Maria Busse. *Mensuration and Proportion Signs: Origins and Evolution.* Oxford: Oxford University Press, 1993.

Berger, Karol. *Musica Ficta: Theories of Accidental Inflections in Vocal Polyphony from Marchetto da Padova to Gioseffo Zarlino.* Cambridge: Cambridge University Press, 2003.

Borgir, Tharald. *The Performance of the Basso Continuo in Italian Baroque Music.* Studies in Musicology, no. 90. Ann Arbor, Mich.: UMI Research Press, 1987.

Bowles, Edmund A. *Haut and Bas: The Grouping of Musical Instruments in the Middle Ages.* Publications in the Humanities, no. 13. Cambridge, Mass.: Massachusetts Institute of Technology, 1955.

Boyden, David D. *The History of Violin Playing from Its Origins to 1761 and Its Relationship to the Violin and Violin Music.* London: Oxford University Press, 1965; reprint, Oxford: Clarendon Press, 1990.

Brown, Howard Mayer. *Sixteenth-Century Instrumentation: The Music for the Florentine Intermedii.* Musicological Studies and Documents, no. 30. First published by American

Institute of Musicology, 1973; now available from Middleton, Wisc.: A-R Editions.

Buelow, George J. *Thorough-Bass Accompaniment According to Johann David Heinichen.* Rev. ed. Lincoln: University of Nebraska Press, 1992. First published in 1966.

Burden, Michael. *Performing the Music of Henry Purcell.* Oxford: Oxford University Press, 1996.

Butt, John. *Music Education and the Art of Performance in the German Baroque.* Cambridge Musical Texts and Monographs. Cambridge: Cambridge University Press, 1994.

Byrt, John. *Notes inégales: A European Style.* Tiverton: Lowman Books, 1997.

Eppelsheim, Jürgen. *Das Orchester in den Werken Jean-Baptiste Lullys.* Münchner Veröffentlichungen zur Musikgeschichte, vol. 7. Tutzing: Hans Schneider, 1961.

Epstein, David. *Shaping Time: Music, the Brain, and Performance.* New York: Schirmer Books, 1994.

Fallows, David. "Tempo and Expression Marks." In *The New Grove Dictionary of Music and Musicians.* 2nd ed. Vol. 25, pp. 270–79.

Fuller, David. "Notes inégales." In *The New Grove Dictionary of Music and Musicians.* 2nd ed. Vol. 18, pp. 190–200.

———. "Ornamentation." In *The New Harvard Dictionary of Music.* Pp. 594–99.

Haines, John, and Randall Rosenfeld. *Music and Medieval Manuscripts: Paleography and Performance.* Aldershot, England: Ashgate, 2004.

Harrison, Bernard. *Haydn's Keyboard Music: Studies in Performance Practice.* Oxford: Oxford University Press, 1997.

Haynes, Bruce, and Peter R. Cooke. "Pitch." In *The New Grove Dictionary of Music and Musicians.* 2nd ed. Vol. 19, pp. 793–804.

Hefling, Stephen E. *Rhythmic Alteration in Seventeenth-and Eighteenth-Century Music:* Notes inégales *and Overdotting.* New York: Schirmer Books, 1993.

Houle, George. *Meter in Music, 1600–1800: Performance, Perception, and Notation.* Bloomington: Indiana University Press, 1987; reprint, Bloomington: Indiana University Press, 2000.

Hudson, Richard. *Stolen Time: The History of Tempo Rubato.* Oxford: Clarendon Press, 1994.

"The Interpretation of Music." Part 4 of *Companion to Contemporary Musical Thought,* ed. John Paynter et al., vol. 2. London: Routledge, 1992.

Kelly, Thomas Forrest, ed. *Plainsong in the Age of Polyphony.*

Cambridge Studies in Performance Practice, no. 2. Cambridge: Cambridge University Press, 1992.

Koury, Daniel J. *Orchestral Performance Practices in the Nineteenth Century: Size, Proportions, and Seating.* Studies in Musicology, no. 85. Ann Arbor, Mich.: UMI Research Press, 1986.

Kreitner, Kenneth, et al. "Ornaments." In *The New Grove Dictionary of Music and Musicians.* 2nd ed. Vol. 18, pp. 708–46.

Le Huray, Peter. *Authenticity in Performance: Eighteenth-Century Case Studies.* Cambridge: Cambridge University Press, 1990.

Lindley, Mark. *Lutes, Viols and Temperaments.* Cambridge: Cambridge University Press, 1984.

———. "Temperaments." In *The New Grove Dictionary of Music and Musicians.* 2nd ed. Vol. 25, pp. 248–68.

Marty, Jean-Pierre. *The Tempo Indications of Mozart.* New Haven, Conn.: Yale University Press, 1988.

Nettl, Bruno, et al. "Improvisation." In *The New Grove Dictionary of Music and Musicians.* 2nd ed. Vol. 12, pp. 94–133.

Neumann, Frederick. *Essays in Performance Practice.* Studies in Musicology, no. 58. Ann Arbor, Mich.: UMI Research Press, 1982.

———. *New Essays in Performance Practice.* Studies in Music, no. 108. Ann Arbor, Mich.: UMI Research Press, 1992. First published in 1989.

———. *Ornamentation and Improvisation in Mozart.* Princeton, N.J.: Princeton University Press, 1986.

———. *Ornamentation in Baroque and Post-Baroque Music with Special Emphasis on J. S. Bach.* 3rd printing with corrections. Princeton, N.J.: Princeton University Press, 1983. First published in 1978.

Newman, William S. *Beethoven on Beethoven: Playing His Piano Music His Way.* New York: W. W. Norton, 1991.

Renwick, William. *The Langloz Manuscript: Fugal Improvisation through Figured Bass.* Oxford: Oxford University Press, 2001.

Spitzer, John, and Neal Zaslaw. "Orchestra." In *The New Grove Dictionary of Music and Musicians.* 2nd ed. Vol. 18, pp. 530–48.

Spring, Matthew. *The Lute in Britain: A History of the Instrument and Its Music.* Oxford: Oxford University Press, 2001.

Stauffer, George, and Ernest May, eds. *J. S. Bach as Organist: His Instruments, Music, and Performance Practices.* Bloomington: Indiana University Press, 1986.

Stowell, Robin, ed. *Performing Beethoven.* Cambridge Studies in Performance Practice. Cambridge: Cambridge University Press, 1994.

Tyler, James, and Paul Sparks. *The Guitar and Its Music.* Oxford: Oxford University Press, 2002.

Whitmore, Philip J. *Unpremeditated Art: The Cadenza in the Classical Keyboard Concerto.* Oxford Monographs on Music. New York: Oxford University Press, 1991.

Williams, Peter. *The Organ Music of J. S. Bach.* 2nd ed. Cambridge: Cambridge University Press, 2003. First published in 1986.

Williams, Peter, ed. *Bach, Handel, Scarlatti: Tercentenary Essays.* Cambridge: Cambridge University Press, 1985.

Williams, Peter, and David Ledbetter. "Continuo [Basso continuo]." In *The New Grove Dictionary of Music and Musicians.* 2nd ed. Vol. 6, pp. 345–67.

Zaslaw, Neal. *Mozart's Symphonies: Context, Performance Practice, Reception.* Oxford: Oxford University Press, 1990.

Discussions of the Performance Practice Movement

Cohen, Joel, and Herb Snitzer. *Reprise: The Extraordinary Revival of Early Music.* Boston: Little, Brown, 1985.

Dreyfus, Laurence. "Early Music Defended against Its Devotees: A Theory of Historical Performance in the Twentieth Century." *The Musical Quarterly* 59 (Summer 1983): 297–322.

Dulak, Michelle. "The Quiet Metamorphosis of 'Early Music.'" *repercussions* 2 (Fall 1993): 31–61.

Fabian, Dorottya. "The Meaning of Authenticity and the Early Music Movement: A Historical Review." *International Review of the Aesthetics and Sociology of Music* 32 (December 2001): 153–67.

Haskell, Harry. *The Early Music Revival: A History.* London: Thames and Hudson, 1988; reprint, Mineola, N.Y.: Dover, 1996.

Kenyon, Nicholas, ed. *Authenticity and Early Music: A Symposium.* London: Oxford University Press, 1988.

Kerman, Joseph. "The Historical Performance Movement." In *Contemplating Music: Challenges to Musicology.* Cambridge, Mass.: Harvard University Press, 1985. Pp. 182–217.

Kivy, Peter. *Authenticities: Philosophical Reflections on Musical Performance.* Ithaca, N.Y.: Cornell University Press, 1995.

Kottick, Edward. *The Collegium: A Handbook.* Stonington, Conn.: October House, 1977.

Taruskin, Richard. "The Musicologist and the Performer." In *Musicology in the 1980s: Methods, Goals, Opportunities.* New York: Da Capo Press, 1982. Pp. 101–17.

Guides for Performers

Brown, A. Peter. *Joseph Haydn's Keyboard Music: Sources and Style.* Bloomington: Indiana University Press, 1986.

Brown, Howard Mayer. *Embellishing 16th-Century Music.* Early Music Series, no. 1. London: Oxford University Press, 1976.

Burton, Anthony. *A Performer's Guide to Music of the Classical Period.* London: Associated Board of the Royal Schools of Music, 2002.

Carroll, Paul. *Baroque Woodwind Instruments: A Guide to Their History, Repertoire and Basic Technique.* Brookfield, Vt.: Ashgate, 1999.

Collins, Fletcher, Jr. *The Production of Medieval Church Music-Drama.* Charlottesville: University Press of Virginia, 1972.

Cyr, Mary. *Performing Baroque Music.* Portland, Ore.: Amadeus Press, 1992; reprint, Portland, Ore.: Amadeus Press, 1998.

Davidson, Audrey Ekdahl, and Clifford Davidson. *Performing Medieval Music Drama.* Kalamazoo, Mich.: Medieval Institute Publications, 1998.

Donington, Robert. *A Performer's Guide to Baroque Music.* New York: Charles Scribner's Sons, 1973.

———. *String Playing in Baroque Music.* London: Faber and Faber, 1977.

Hochreither, Karl, and Melvin P. Unger. *Performance Practice of the Instrumental-Vocal Works of Johann Sebastian Bach.* Lanham, Md.: Scarecrow Press, 2002.

Jorgensen, Owen H. *The Equal-Beating Temperaments: A Handbook for Tuning Harpsichords and Fortepianos, with Tuning Techniques and Tables of Fifteen Historical Temperaments.* 2nd ed. Hendersonville, N.C.: Sunbury Press, 2000. First published in 1981.

———. *Tuning, Containing the Perfection of Eighteenth-Century Temperament, the Lost Art of Nineteenth-Century Temperament, and the Science of Equal Temperament, Complete with Instructions for Aural and Electronic Tuning.* East Lansing: Michigan State University Press, 1991.

———. *Tuning the Historical Temperaments by Ear: A Manual of Eighty-nine Methods of Tuning Fifty-one Scales on the Harpsichord, Piano, and Other Keyboard Instruments.* Marquette: Northern Michigan University Press, 1977.

Knighton, Tess, and David Fallows, eds. *Companion to Medieval and Renaissance Music.* 1st American ed. New York: Schirmer Books, 1992; reprint, New York: Oxford University Press, 1997.

Krausz, Michael. *The Interpretation of Music: Philosophical Essays.* New York: Oxford University Press, 1993.

Lasocki, David, and Betty Bang Mather. *The Classical Woodwind Cadenza: A Workbook.* New York: McGinnis & Marx, 1978.

Lawson, Colin, and Robin Stowell, gen. eds. *Cambridge Handbooks to the Historical Performance of Music.* Cambridge: Cambridge University Press, 2000–.

> *The Early Clarinet: A Practical Guide.* By Colin Lawson. 2000.
> *The Early Flute: A Practical Guide.* By Rachel Brown. 2002.
> *The Early Horn: A Practical Guide.* By John Humphries. 2000.
> *Early Keyboard Instruments: A Practical Guide.* By David Rowland. 2001.
> *The Early Violin and Viola: A Practical Guide.* By Robin Stowell. 2001.

Ledbetter, David. *Continuo Playing According to Handel: His Figured Bass Exercises.* Oxford: Oxford University Press, 1990.

Lester, Joel. *Bach's Works for Solo Violin: Style, Structure, Performance.* Oxford: Oxford University Press, 1999.

Little, Meredith, and Natalie Jenne. *Dance and the Music of J. S. Bach.* Bloomington: Indiana University Press, 2002.

Loft, Abram. *Ensemble! A Rehearsal Guide to Thirty Great Works of Chamber Music.* Portland, Ore.: Amadeus Press, 1992.

Marvin, Jameson Neil. *Perfection and Naturalness: A Practical Guide to the Performance of Renaissance Choral Music.* Oxford: Oxford University Press, 2001.

Mather, Betty Bang. *Interpretation of French Music from 1675 to 1775 for Woodwind and Other Performers.* New York: McGinnis & Marx, 1973.

Mather, Betty Bang, and David Lasocki. *The Art of Preluding, 1700–1830, for Flutists, Oboists, Clarinettists and Other Performers.* New York: McGinnis & Marx, 1984.

Mather, Betty Bang, with the assistance of Dean M. Karns. *Dance Rhythms of the French Baroque: A Handbook for Performance.* Bloomington: Indiana University Press, 1988.

McGee, Timothy J. *Medieval and Renaissance Music: A Per-*

former's Guide. Toronto: University of Toronto Press, 1985; reprint, Aldershot, England: Scholar Press, 1990.

————. *The Sound of Medieval Song: Ornamentation and Vocal Style According to the Treatises.* Oxford: Oxford University Press, 1998.

————, ed. *Singing Early Music: The Pronunciation of European Languages in the Late Middle Ages and Renaissance.* Bloomington: Indiana University Press, 1996.

Moens-Haenen, Greta. *Das Vibrato in der Musik des Barock: Ein Handbuch zur Aufführungspraxis für Vokalisten und Instrumentalisten.* Graz: Akademische Druck- und Verlagsanstalt, 1988.

Morehen, John. *English Choral Practice 1400–1650.* Cambridge Studies in Performance Practice, no. 5. Cambridge: Cambridge University Press, 2003.

Neumann, Frederick. *Performance Practices of the Seventeenth and Eighteenth Centuries.* New York: Schirmer Books, 1993.

Newman, Anthony. *Bach and the Baroque: A Performing Guide to Baroque Music with Special Emphasis on the Music of J. S. Bach.* Stuyvesant, N.Y.: Pendragon Press, 1985.

North, Nigel. *Continuo Playing on the Lute, Archlute and Theorbo: A Comprehensive Guide for Performers.* Bloomington: Indiana University Press, 1987.

Owen, Barbara. *The Registration of Baroque Organ Music.* Bloomington: Indiana University Press, 1997.

Page, Christopher. *Music and Instruments of the Middle Ages: Studies on Texts and Performance.* Brookfield, Vt.: Ashgate, 1997.

Parrott, Andrew. *The Essential Bach Choir.* Rochester, N.Y.: Boydell Press, 2000.

Performer's Guides to Early Music. Jeffery T. Kite-Powell, ser. ed. Various publishers, 1989–.

   A Performer's Guide to Medieval Music. Ed. Ross W. Duffin. 2nd ed. Bloomington: Indiana University Press, 2004. First published in 2000.

   A Performer's Guide to Renaissance Music. Ed. Jeffery T. Kite-Powell. 2nd ed. Bloomington: Indiana University Press, 2004. (Earlier edition published as *Practical Guide to Historical Performance: The Renaissance.* New York: Early Music America, 1989.)

   A Performer's Guide to Seventeenth-Century Music. Ed. Stewart Carter. New York: Schirmer Books, 1997.

Phillips, Elizabeth V., and John-Paul Christopher Jackson. *Performing Medieval and Renaissance Music: An Introductory Guide.* New York: Schirmer Books, 1986.

Poe, Frances R. *Teaching and Performing Renaissance Choral Music: A Guide for Conductors and Performers.* Metuchen, N.J.: Scarecrow Press, 1994.

Potter, John. *The Cambridge Companion to Singing.* Cambridge: Cambridge University Press, 2000.

Poulin, Pamela L. *J. S. Bach's Precepts and Principles for Playing the Thorough-Bass or Accompanying in Four Parts.* Oxford: Oxford University Press, 1995.

Rice, Albert R. *The Baroque Clarinet.* Oxford: Oxford University Press, 1992.

———. *The Clarinet in the Classical Period.* Oxford: Oxford University Press, 2003.

Rosenblum, Sandra P. *Performance Practices in Classic Piano Music: Their Principles and Applications.* Bloomington: Indiana University Press, 1988.

Rowland-Jones, Anthony. *Playing Recorder Sonatas: Interpretation and Technique.* New York: Oxford University Press, 1992.

Schultz, Timothy. *Performing French Classical Music: Sources and Applications.* Hillsdale, N.Y.: Pendragon Press, 2001.

Solum, John. *The Early Flute.* Oxford: Oxford University Press, 1993.

Stevens, Denis. "Applied Musicology." Part 3 of *Musicology: A Practical Guide.* New York: Schirmer Books, 1980.

Stowell, Robin. *Violin Technique and Performance Practice in the Late-Eighteenth and Early-Nineteenth Centuries.* Cambridge: Cambridge University Press, 1990.

Walden, Valerie. *One Hundred Years of Violoncello: A History of Technique and Performance Practice 1740–1840.* New York: Cambridge University Press, 1998.

Weisberg, Arthur. *Performing Twentieth-Century Music: A Handbook for Conductors and Instrumentalists.* New Haven, Conn.: Yale University Press, 1993.

Williams, Peter. *Figured Bass Accompaniment.* 2 vols. Edinburgh: Edinburgh University Press, 1970; reprint, Edinburgh: Edinburgh University Press, 1982.

Studies of Historical Interest

Aldrich, Putnam C. "The Principal Agréments of the Seventeenth and Eighteenth Centuries: A Study in Musical Ornamentation." Ph.D. thesis, Harvard University, 1942.

Arger, Jane. *Les agréments et le rythme: leur représentation graphique dans la musique vocale française du XVIIIe siècle.* Paris: Rouart, Lerolle, [1921].

Borrel, Eugène. *L'interprétation de la musique française (de Lully à la Révolution).* Les maîtres de la musique, new ser. Paris: Félix Alcan, 1934; reprint, New York: A.M.S. Press, 1978.

Dart, Thurston. *The Interpretation of Music.* 4th ed., rev. reimpression. London: Hutchinson's University Library, 1960. First published in 1954.

Dolmetsch, Arnold. *The Interpretation of the Music of the XVIIth and XVIIIth Centuries Revealed by Contemporary Evidence.* New ed. London: Novello, 1969; reprint, Seattle: University of Washington Press, 1977. First published in 1915.

Haas, Robert. *Aufführungspraxis der Musik.* 2nd ed. Wiesbaden: Akademische Verlagsgesellschaft Athenaion, 1979. First published in 1931.

Schering, Arnold. *Aufführungspraxis alter Musik.* 2nd ed. Wilhelmshaven, Germany: Heinrichshofen, 1983. First published in 1931.

Editions of Selected Primary Sources

Arbeau, Thoinot. *Orchesography* [1589]. Trans. Mary Stewart Evans. With a new introduction and notes by Julia Sutton. New York: Dover Publications, 1967. First published in 1948.

Bach, Carl Philipp Emanuel. *Essay on the True Art of Playing Keyboard Instruments* [original and rev. eds., 1753–97]. 2nd ed. Trans. and ed. William John Mitchell. London: Cassell and Company, 1951. First published in 1949.

Beicken, Suzanne J. *Treatise on Vocal Performance and Ornamentation by Johann Adam Hiller.* Cambridge: Cambridge University Press, 2001.

Caccini, Giulio. *Le nuove musiche* [1602]. Trans. and ed. H. Wiley Hitchcock. Recent Researches in the Music of the Baroque Era, vol. 9. 2nd printing with corrections. Madison, Wisc.: A-R Editions, 1982. First published in 1970.

Couperin, François. *L'art de toucher le clavecin/Die Kunst das Klavier zu spielen/The Art of Playing the Harpsichord* [1716]. English trans. Mevanwy Roberts; German trans. Anna Linde. Leipzig: Breitkopf & Härtel, 1933; reprint, Wiesbaden: Breitkopf und Härtel, 1990.

Gásser, Luis. *Luis Milán on Sixteenth-Century Performance Practice.* Bloomington: Indiana University Press, 1996.

Hotteterre, Jacques. *Principles of the Flute, Recorder & Oboe*

[1707]. Trans. and ed. David Lasocki. New York: Frede
rick A. Praeger, 1968; reprint, London: Barrie and Jenkins,
1978.

Mace, Thomas. *Musick's Monument; or, a Remembrancer of
the Best Practical Musick Both Divine and Civil, That
Has Ever Been Known, to Have Been in the World* [1676].
Facs. ed. New York: Broude Brothers, 1966.

Mersenne, Marin. *Harmonie universelle: The Books on Instruments* [1636]. Trans. Roger E. Chapman. The Hague:
Martinus Nijhoff, 1957.

Morley, Thomas. *A Plain and Easy Introduction to Practical Mu-
sic* [1597]. 2nd ed. Ed. R. Alec Harman, with a foreword by
Thurston Dart. London: J. M. Dent & Sons, 1963; reprint,
New York: W. W. Norton, 1973. First published in 1952.

Muffat, Georg. *Georg Muffat on Performance Practice: The Texts
from Florilegium primum, Florilegium secundum, and
Auserlesene Instrumentalmusik: A New Translation with
Commentary.* Trans. David Wilson. Bloomington: Indiana
University Press, 2001.

Praetorius, Michael. *Syntagma Musicum II* [1618]: *De Organographia, Parts I and II.* Trans. and ed. David Z. Crookes.
Early Music Series, no. 7. Oxford: Clarendon Press, 1986;
reprint, Oxford: Clarendon Press, 1991.

————. *Syntagma Musicum III* [1619]. Trans. Jeffery T. Kite-
Powell. Oxford: Oxford University Press, 2004.

Quantz, Johann Joachim. *On Playing the Flute* [1752]. Translated,
with an introduction and notes, by Edward R. Reilly. 2nd
ed. with new introduction. Boston: Northeastern University Press, 2001. First published in 1966.

Anthologies

Ferand, Ernst Thomas. *Improvisation in Nine Centuries of Western Music: An Anthology with a Historical Introduction.*
Anthology of Music, vol. 12. Cologne: Arno Volk Verlag,
1961.

MacClintock, Carol. *Readings in the History of Music in Performance.* Bloomington: Indiana University Press, 1979.

Mather, Betty Bang, and David Lasocki. *Free Ornamentation in
Woodwind Music, 1700–1775: An Anthology with Intro-
duction.* New York: McGinnis & Marx, 1976; reprint, New
York: McGinnis & Marx, 1987.

Schmitz, Hans-Peter. *Die Kunst der Verzierung im 18. Jahrhundert: Instrumentale und vokale Musizierpraxis in Beispielen.* 4th ed. Kassel: Bärenreiter, 1983. First published
in 1955.

Bibliographies of the Literature

Jackson, Roland John. *Performance Practice, Medieval to Contemporary: A Bibliographic Guide.* Music Research and Information Guides, vol. 9. New York: Garland Publishing, 1988. Annual suppl. in Fall issue of *Performance Practice Review* (see chapter 6).

Vinquist, Mary, and Neal Zaslaw, eds. *Performance Practice: A Bibliography.* New York: W. W. Norton, 1971. Suppls.: *Current Musicology* no. 12 (1971): 129–49, no. 15 (1973): 126–33.

MUSIC THEORY

In the past fifty years, especially in America, music theory has become a discipline with its own separate identity, rather than being considered an aspect of musicology. Furthermore, this period has seen the development of more specialized fields within the discipline, such as set theory, methodologies for explaining tonal music (Schenker's being generally regarded as the most important), and specific studies in the history of theory. The following bibliography of basic sources reflects within its seven main divisions some of the principal emphases in the field. Books designed specifically as course texts have been excluded, and more recent sources have been emphasized.

Of the sources listed under "The History of Theory," Christiansen's book is the most comprehensive, and Palisca and Bent's *New Grove* article is also substantial; Riemann and Shirlaw are included because both are classic early studies. Crocker, Herissone, Lester, and Mathiesen are examples of more specialized discussions of the history of theory.

With regard to "General Issues of Style and Analysis," the studies by Bent (*Analysis*), Cook, and Dunsby/Whittall may be singled out as surveys of the field of analysis, Bent's being the most complete. De la Motte's *Study of Harmony* is unique in its historical approach to the topic.

In "Twentieth-Century Theories of Tonal Music," the sources listed under "Theories of Tonality and Tonal Music" run from the early studies by Schoenberg, Hindemith, and Kurth (as discussed by Rothfarb) to the more current cognitive studies, the most notable new approach being that of Lerdahl and Jackendoff; the sources under "Schenkerian Analysis" similarly range from Schenker's chief treatises through the earliest explanation of *Der freie Satz* by Jonas, and Forte's later treatment of it, to the most recent Schenkerian studies.

Under "Twentieth-Century Theories of Nontonal Music," "Atonality, Serialism, and Set Theory" brings together a variety of treatments and viewpoints, including Hanson, now superseded by other points of view; Perle, one of the earliest studies in the field; the pioneering works of Forte and Rahn; and what are perhaps the most important current studies, those by Lewin, Morris, Moravec, and Schoffman. Under "Modality and Octatonicism," van den Toorn's *The Music of Igor Stravinsky* is probably the most significant item. Only older sources treat "Microtonality," a field that has failed to attract more recent scholarly attention.

"Musical Time: Theories of Rhythm and Meter" includes the classic study by Sachs, the pioneering modern treatment by Cooper/ Meyer, and the particularly significant recent studies by Hasty, London, Marsden, Reiner, and Swain. The "Theories of Musical Timbre" list is necessarily brief because the entire field is new. "Aesthetics and Semiotics of Music" is at present the fastest-growing area in music theory. The sources listed here range from the early works by Hanslick and Busoni through various standard twentieth-century studies to the most recent ones, reflecting the increased interest in the field in the past fifteen years. "Texts of Theoretical Treatises" (represented by the pioneering work of Indiana University) and "Bibliographies and Guides to the Literature" complete this section.

For a list of journals specializing in theory, see chapter 6, "Current Research Journals in Music," pp. 240–41 below.

The History of Theory

Balensuela, C. Matthew. "Anonymous Theoretical Writings." In *The New Grove Dictionary of Music and Musicians.* 2nd ed. Vol. 1, pp. 693–707.

Bent, Ian D. *Analysis.* With a glossary by William Drabkin. 1st American ed. The Norton/Grove Handbooks in Music. New York: W. W. Norton, 1987.

———. *Music Theory in the Age of Romanticism.* Cambridge: Cambridge University Press, 1996.

Bent, Ian D., and Anthony Pople. "Analysis." In *The New Grove Dictionary of Music and Musicians.* 2nd ed. Vol. 1, pp. 526–89.

Brown, Matthew. "Theory." In *The New Harvard Dictionary of Music.* Pp. 844–54.

Christiansen, Thomas. *Rameau and Musical Thought in the Enlightenment.* Cambridge: Cambridge University Press, 1995.

———, ed. *The Cambridge History of Western Music Theory.* Cambridge: Cambridge University Press, 2002.

Clark, Suzannah, and Alexander Rehding, eds. *Music Theory and Natural Order from the Renaissance to the Early Twentieth Century.* Cambridge: Cambridge University Press, 2001.

Crocker, Richard L. *Studies in Medieval Music Theory and the Early Sequence.* Brookfield, Vt.: Variorum, 1997.

Dahlhaus, Carl. *Die Musiktheorie im 18. und 19. Jahrhundert: Grundzuge einer Systematik.* Geschichte der Musiktheorie, vol. 10. Darmstadt: Wissenschaftliche Buchgesellschaft, 1984.

———. *Untersuchungen über die Entstehung der harmonischen Tonalität.* Saarbrücker Studien zur Musikwissenschaft, vol. 2. Kassel: Bärenreiter, 1968; unchanged 2nd ed., Kassel: Bärenreiter, 1988. English transl.: *Studies on the Origin of Harmonic Tonality.* Princeton, N.J.: Princeton University Press, 1990.

Forte, Allen. "Theory." In *Dictionary of Contemporary Music,* ed. John Vinton. New York: E. P. Dutton, 1974. Pp. 753–61.

Giger, Andreas, and Thomas J. Mathiesen. *Music in the Mirror: Reflections on the History of Music Theory and Literature for the Twenty-First Century.* Lincoln: University of Nebraska Press, 2003.

Herissone, Rebecca. *Music Theory in Seventeenth-Century England.* New York: Oxford University Press, 2000.

Lester, Joel. *Between Modes and Keys: German Theory, 1592–1802.* Stuyvesant, N.Y.: Pendragon Press, 1992.

———. *Compositional Theory in the Eighteenth Century.* Cambridge, Mass.: Harvard University Press, 1992.

Mathiesen, Thomas J. *Apollo's Lyre: Greek Music and Music Theory in Antiquity and the Middle Ages.* Lincoln: University of Nebraska Press, 1999.

Palisca, Claude V., and Ian D. Bent. "Theory, Theorists." In *The New Grove Dictionary of Music and Musicians.* 2nd ed. Vol. 25, pp. 359–85.

Riemann, Hugo. *Geschichte der Musiktheorie im IX.–XIX. Jahrhundert.* 2nd ed. Berlin: Max Hesse, 1921. First published in 1898. English transl.: (1) *History of Music Theory, Books I and II: Polyphonic Theory to the Sixteenth Century.* Translated, with preface, commentary, and notes, by Raymond H. Haggh. Lincoln: University of Nebraska Press, 1962. (2) *Hugo Riemann's Theory of Harmony: A Study . . . , and History of Music Theory, Book III.* Trans. and ed. William C. Mickelsen. Lincoln: University of Nebraska Press, 1977.

Rummenhöller, Peter. *Musiktheoretisches Denken im 19. Jahrhundert: Versuch einer Interpretation erkenntnistheoretis-*

cher Zeugnisse in der Musiktheorie. Regensburg: Gustav Bosse, 1967.

Shirlaw, Matthew. *The Theory of Harmony: An Inquiry into the Natural Principles of Harmony, with an Examination of the Chief Systems of Harmony from Rameau to the Present Day.* 2nd ed. De Kalb, Ill.: Dr. Birchard Coar, 1955. First published in 1917. Reprint of 1st ed., New York: Da Capo Press, 1969.

Thompson, David M. *A History of Harmonic Theory in the United States.* Kent, Ohio: Kent State University Press, 1980.

Wason, Robert. *Viennese Harmonic Theory from Albrechtsberger to Schenker and Schoenberg.* Ann Arbor, Mich.: UMI Research Press, 1984.

General Issues of Style and Analysis

Ayrey, Craig, and Mark Everist. *Analytical Strategies and Musical Interpretation: Essays on Nineteenth-and Twentieth-Century Music.* Cambridge: Cambridge University Press, 1996.

Bent, Ian D. *Analysis.* With a glossary by William Drabkin. 1st American ed. The Norton/Grove Handbooks in Music. New York: W. W. Norton, 1987.

Bent, Ian, ed. *Music Analysis in the Nineteenth Century I: Fugue, Form and Style.* Cambridge Readings in the Literature of Music. Cambridge: Cambridge University Press, 1994.

———, ed. *Music Analysis in the Nineteenth Century II: Hermeneutic Approaches.* Cambridge Readings in the Literature of Music. Cambridge: Cambridge University Press, 1994.

Bonds, Mark Evan. *Wordless Rhetoric: Musical Form and the Metaphor of the Oration.* Cambridge, Mass.: Harvard University Press, 1991.

Caplin, William E. *Classical Form: A Theory of Formal Functions for the Instrumental Music of Haydn, Mozart, and Beethoven.* Oxford: Oxford University Press, 1998.

Cone, Edward T. *Musical Form and Musical Performance.* New York: W. W. Norton, 1968.

Cook, Nicholas. *A Guide to Musical Analysis.* New York: W. W. Norton, 1992. First published in 1987.

Dunsby, Jonathan, and Arnold Whittall. *Music Analysis in Theory and Practice.* New Haven, Conn.: Yale University Press, 1988.

Ferrara, Lawrence. *Philosophy and the Analysis of Music: Bridges to Musical Sound, Form, and Reference.* Contri-

butions to the Study of Music and Dance, no. 24. New
York: Greenwood Press, 1991.

LaRue, Jan. *Guidelines for Style Analysis.* 2nd ed. Detroit
Monographs in Musicology, 12. Warren, Mich.: Harmonie
Park Press, 1992. First published in 1970.

Motte, Diether de la. *The Study of Harmony: An Historical Perspective.* Trans. Jeffrey L. Prater. Dubuque, Iowa: Wm. C.
Brown, 1991.

Sessions, Roger. *Questions about Music.* Cambridge, Mass.:
Harvard University Press, 1970.

Stein, Erwin. *Form and Performance.* New York: Alfred A.
Knopf, 1962; reprint, New York: Limelight Editions, 1989.

White, John D. *Comprehensive Musical Analysis.* Metuchen,
N.J.: Scarecrow Press, 1994.

Twentieth-Century Theories of Tonal Music

THEORIES OF TONALITY AND TONAL MUSIC

Browne, Richmond. *Music Theory: Special Topics.* New York:
Academic Press, 1981.

Carpenter, Patricia, and Severine Neff, eds. and trans. *The Musical Idea and the Logic, Technique, and Art of Its Presentation by Arnold Schoenberg.* New York: Columbia University Press, 1995.

Dahlhaus, Carl. *Studies on the Origin of Harmonic Tonality.*
Trans. Robert D. Gjerdingen. Princeton, N.J.: Princeton
University Press, 1990.

Dunsby, Jonathan, ed. *Early Twentieth-Century Music.* Models
of Musical Analysis. Oxford: Blackwell Publishers, 1993.

Epstein, David. *Beyond Orpheus: Studies in Musical Structure.*
Cambridge, Mass.: MIT Press, 1979; reprint, Oxford:
Oxford University Press, 1987.

Everist, Mark, ed. *Music before 1600.* Models of Musical Analysis. Oxford: Blackwell Publishers, 1992.

Harrison, Daniel. *The Analysis and Cognition of Melodic
Complexity: The Implication-Realization Model.* Chicago:
University of Chicago Press, 1992.

———. *Harmonic Function in Chromatic Music: A Renewed
Dualist Theory and an Account of Its Precedents.* Chicago:
University of Chicago Press, 1994.

Hindemith, Paul. *The Craft of Musical Composition.* 4th ed.
Trans. Arthur Mendel. London: B. Schott, 1968. First
published in 1937.

Hyer, Brian. "Tonality." In *The New Grove Dictionary of Music
and Musicians.* 2nd ed. Vol. 25, pp. 583–94.

Komar, Arthur. *Theory of Suspensions.* Princeton, N.J.: Princeton
University Press, 1971.
Lerdahl, Fred. *Tonal Pitch Space.* Oxford: Oxford University
Press, 2001.
Lerdahl, Fred, and Ray Jackendoff. *A Generative Theory of Tonal
Music.* Cambridge, Mass.: MIT Press, 1983.
Narmour, Eugene. *The Analysis and Cognition of Basic Melodic
Structures: The Implication-Realization Model.* Chicago:
University of Chicago Press, 1990.
———. *Beyond Schenkerism: The Need for Alternatives in Music
Analysis.* Chicago: University of Chicago Press, 1977.
Neff, Severine, ed. *Coherence, Counterpoint, Instrumentation,
Instruction in Form by Arnold Schoenberg.* Trans. Char-
lotte M. Cross and Severine Neff. Lincoln: University of
Nebraska Press, 1993.
Neumeyer, David. *The Music of Paul Hindemith.* New Haven,
Conn.: Yale University Press, 1986.
Norton, Richard. *Tonality in Western Culture: A Critical and
Historical Perspective.* University Park: Pennsylvania
State University Press, 1984.
Réti, Rudolph. *The Thematic Process in Music.* London: Faber
and Faber, 1961; reprint, Westport, Conn.: Greenwood
Press, 1978.
Rothfarb, Lee. *Ernst Kurth as Theorist and Analyst.* Philadel-
phia: University of Pennsylvania Press, 1988.
Serafine, Mary Louise. *Music as Cognition: The Development
of Thought in Sound.* New York: Columbia University
Press, 1988.
Straus, Joseph N. *Remaking the Past: Musical Modernism and
the Influence of the Tonal Tradition.* Cambridge, Mass.:
Harvard University Press, 1990.
Swain, Joseph P. *Harmonic Rhythm: Analysis and Interpreta-
tion.* Oxford: Oxford University Press, 2002.

Schenkerian Analysis

Beach, David, ed. *Aspects of Schenkerian Theory.* New Haven,
Conn.: Yale University Press, 1983.
Berry, David Carson. *A Topical Guide to Schenkerian Literature.*
Harmonologia Series, no. 11. Hillsdale, N.Y.: Pendragon
Press, 2004.
Blasius, Leslie David. *Schenker's Argument and the Claims of
Music Theory.* Cambridge: Cambridge University Press,
1996.
Cadwallader, Allen, ed. *Trends in Schenkerian Research.* New
York: Schirmer Books, 1990.

Cadwallader, Allen, and David Gagné. *Analysis of Tonal Music: A Schenkerian Approach.* New York: Oxford University Press, 1998.

Forte, Allen, and Steven E. Gilbert. *An Introduction to Schenkerian Analysis.* New York: W. W. Norton, 1982.

Jonas, Oswald. *Introduction to the Theory of Heinrich Schenker: The Nature of the Musical Work of Art.* Trans. and ed. John Rothgeb. New York: Schirmer Books, 1989. First published in 1934.

Neumeyer, David, and Susan Tepping. *A Guide to Schenkerian Analysis.* Englewood Cliffs, N.J.: Prentice Hall, 1992.

Renwick, William. *Analyzing Fugue: A Schenkerian Approach.* Stuyvesant, N.Y.: Pendragon Press, 1995.

Salzer, Felix. *Structural Hearing: Tonal Coherence in Music.* 2 vols. New York: Dover Publications, 1962. First published in 1952.

Salzer, Felix, and Carl Schachter. *Counterpoint in Composition: The Study of Voice Leading.* Morningside Edition, with new preface. New York: Columbia University Press, 1989. First published in 1969.

Salzer, Felix, and Carl Schachter, eds. *The Music Forum.* 6 vols. New York: Columbia University Press, 1967–82.

Schachter, Carl, and Joseph Nathan Straus. *Unfoldings: Essays in Schenkerian Theory and Analysis.* New York: Oxford University Press, 1999.

Schenker, Heinrich. *Counterpoint: A Translation of Kontrapunkt by Heinrich Schenker.* Ed. John Rothgeb. Trans. John Rothgeb and Jürgen Thym. 2 vols. New York: Schirmer Books, 1987. First published in 1922.

———. *Free Composition [Der freie Satz].* Trans. and ed. Ernst Oster. New York: Longman, 1979; reprint, Hillsdale, N.Y.: Pendragon Press, 2001. First published in 1935.

———. *Harmony [Harmonielehre].* Edited and annotated by Oswald Jonas. Translated by Elisabeth Mann Borgese. Chicago: University of Chicago Press, 1973. First published in 1906.

———. *Der Tonwille: Pamphlets in Witness of the Immutable Laws of Music.* Ed. William Drabkin. Oxford: Oxford University Press, 2003.

Siegel, Hedi, ed. *Schenker Studies.* Cambridge: Cambridge University Press, 1990.

Siegel, Hedi, and Carl Schachter, eds. *Schenker Studies 2.* Cambridge: Cambridge University Press, 1999.

Snarrenberg, Robert. *Schenker's Interpretive Practice.* New York: Cambridge University Press, 1997.

Yeston, Maury, ed. *Readings in Schenker Analysis and Other Approaches.* New Haven, Conn.: Yale University Press, 1977.

Twentieth-Century Theories of Nontonal Music

ATONALITY, SERIALISM, AND SET THEORY

Boretz, Benjamin, and Edward T. Cone, eds. *Perspectives on Contemporary Music Theory.* New York: W. W. Norton, 1972.

Forte, Allen. *The Structure of Atonal Music.* New Haven, Conn.: Yale University Press, 1973.

Grant, M. J. *Serial Music, Serial Aesthetics: Compositional Theory in Post-War Europe.* New York: Cambridge University Press, 2002.

Griffiths, Paul. "Serialism." In *The New Grove Dictionary of Music and Musicians.* 2nd ed. Vol. 23, pp. 116–23.

Hanson, Howard. *Harmonic Materials of Modern Music.* New York: Appleton-Century Crofts, 1960.

Lansky, Paul, George Perle, and Dave Headlam. "Atonality." In *The New Grove Dictionary of Music and Musicians.* 2nd ed. Vol. 2, pp. 138–45.

———. "Twelve-note composition." In *The New Grove Dictionary of Music and Musicians.* 2nd ed. Vol. 26, pp. 1–11.

Lewin, David. *Generalized Musical Intervals and Transformations.* New Haven, Conn.: Yale University Press, 1987.

Moravec, Paul. *New Tonality.* New York: Harwood Academic Publishers, 1992.

Morris, Robert. *Composition with Pitch-Classes: A Theory of Compositional Design.* New Haven, Conn.: Yale University Press, 1987.

Perle, George. *Serial Composition and Atonality: An Introduction to the Music of Schoenberg, Berg, and Webern.* 6th ed., rev. Berkeley: University of California Press, 1991. First published in 1962.

Rahn, John. *Basic Atonal Theory.* New York: Longman, 1980; reprint, New York: Schirmer Books, 1987.

Rufer, Josef. *Composition with Twelve Notes Related Only to One Another.* Rev. ed. Trans. Humphrey Searle. London: Barrie and Rockliff, Cresset Press, 1969; reprint, Westport, Conn.: Greenwood Press, 1979. First published in 1952.

Samson, Jim. *Music in Transition: A Study of Tonal Expansion and Atonality, 1900–1920.* London: Dent, 1993.

Schoenberg, Arnold. *Style and Idea: Selected Writings of Arnold Schoenberg.* Ed. Leonard Stein. New York: St. Martin's Press, 1975; reprint, Berkeley: University of California Press, 1985.

Schoffman, Nachum. *From Chords to Simultaneities: Chordal Indeterminacy and the Failure of Serialism.* New York: Greenwood Press, 1990.

Straus, Joseph N. *Introduction to Post-Tonal Theory.* 3rd ed. Upper Saddle River, N.J.: Prentice Hall, 2005.

Webern, Anton. *The Path to New Music.* Trans. Leo Black. Bryn Mawr, Pa.: Theodore Presser, 1963. First published in 1960.

Williams, J. Kent. *Theories and Analyses of Twentieth-Century Music.* New York: Schirmer Books, 1997.

Wittlich, Gary, ed. *Aspects of Twentieth-Century Music.* Englewood Cliffs, N.J.: Prentice Hall, 1975.

Wuorinen, Charles. *Simple Composition.* New York: Longman, 1979; reprint, New York: C. F. Peters, 1994.

MODALITY AND OCTATONICISM

Bacon, Ernst. *Our Musical Idiom.* Chicago: Open Court Press, 1917; reprint, Chicago: Open Court Publishing Company, 1986.

Lendvai, Ernö. *Béla Bartók: An Analysis of His Music.* London: Kahn and Averill, 1971; revised reprint, London: Kohn & Averill, 1990.

Mawer, Deborah. *Darius Milhaud: Modality and Structure in Music of the 1920s.* Aldershot, England: Ashgate Publishing Company, 1997.

Messiaen, Oliver. *Technique of My Musical Language.* Trans. John Satterfield. Paris: A. Leduc, 1956; reprint, Irvine, Calif.: American Reprint Service, 1987.

van den Toorn, Pieter C. *The Music of Igor Stravinsky.* New Haven, Conn.: Yale University Press, 1983.

MICROTONALITY

Hába, Alois. *Neue Harmonielehre des diatonischen, chromatischen Viertel-, Drittel-, Sechstel-und Zwölftel-Tonsystems.* Revised by Erich Steinhard. Leipzig: Fr. Kistner & C. F. W. Siegel, 1927; reprint, Vienna: Universal Edition, 1978.

Partch, Harry. *Genesis of a Music.* 2nd ed., enl. New York: Da Capo Press, 1974. First published in 1949.

Yasser, Joseph. *A Theory of Evolving Tonality.* New York: Amer-

ican Library of Musicology, 1932; reprint, New York: Da
Capo Press, 1975.

Musical Time: Theories of Rhythm and Meter

Barry, Barbara. *The Sense of Order: Perceptual and Analytical
  Studies in Musical Time.* Harmonologia Series, no. 5.
  Stuyvesant, N.Y.: Pendragon Press, 1990.
Cooper, Grosvenor, and Leonard B. Meyer. *The Rhythmic
  Structure of Music.* Chicago: University of Chicago Press,
  1960.
Epstein, David. *Shaping Time: Music, the Brain, and Perfor-
  mance.* New York: Schirmer Books, 1994.
Hasty, Christopher Francis. *Meter as Rhythm.* New York: Oxford
  University Press, 1997.
Kramer, Jonathan D. *The Time of Music: New Meanings, New
  Temporalities, New Listening Strategies.* New York:
  Schirmer Books, 1988.
Lester, Joel. *The Rhythms of Tonal Music.* Carbondale: Southern
  Illinois University Press, 1986.
London, Justin. *Hearing in Time: Psychological Aspects of Musi-
  cal Meter.* New York: Oxford University Press, 2004.
Marsden, A. *Representing Musical Time: A Temporal-Logical
  Approach.* Exton, Pa.: Swets & Zeitlinger Publishers, 2000.
Reiner, Thomas. *Semiotics of Musical Time.* New York: Peter
  Lang, 2000.
Rothstein, William Nathan. *Phrase Rhythm in Tonal Music.* New
  York: Schirmer Books, 1989.
Sachs, Curt. *Rhythm and Tempo: A Study in Music History.*
  New York: W. W. Norton, 1953; reprint, New York: Colum-
  bia University Press, 1988.
Yeston, Maury. *The Stratification of Musical Rhythm.* New
  Haven, Conn.: Yale University Press, 1976.

Theories of Musical Timbre

Cogan, Robert. *New Images of Musical Sound.* Cambridge, Mass.:
  Harvard University Press, 1984.
Fineberg, Joshua. *Spectral Music: Aesthetics and Music.* Con-
  temporary Music Review, vol. 19, part 1. New York:
  Harwood Academic Publishers, 2000.
———. *Spectral Music: History and Techniques.* Contemporary
  Music Review, vol. 19, part 2. New York: Harwood Acade-
  mic Publishers, 2000.
Slawson, Wayne. *Sound Color.* Berkeley: University of California
  Press, 1985.

Aesthetics and Semiotics of Music

Agawu, V. Kofi. *Playing with Signs: A Semiotic Interpretation of Classic Music.* Princeton, N.J.: Princeton University Press, 1991.

Bandur, Markus. *Aesthetics of Total Serialism: Contemporary Research from Music to Architecture.* Basel: Birkhäuser, 2001.

Boykan, Martin. *Silence and Slow Time: Studies in Musical Narrative.* Lanham, Md.: Scarecrow Press, 2003.

Bruhn, Siglind, ed. *Signs in Musical Hermeneutics.* Pensacola, Fla.: Semiotic Society of America, 1998.

Bucknell, Brad. *Literary Modernism and Musical Aesthetics: Pater, Pound, Joyce, and Stein.* Cambridge: Cambridge University Press, 2001.

Burrows, David. *Sound, Speech, and Music.* Amherst: University of Massachusetts Press, 1990.

Busoni, Ferruccio. *Sketch of a New Esthetic of Music.* Trans. Thomas Baker. New York: Schirmer Books, 1978. First published in 1907.

Clifton, Thomas. *Music as Heard: A Study in Applied Phenomenology.* New Haven, Conn.: Yale University Press, 1983.

Coker, Wilson. *Music and Meaning: A Theoretical Introduction to Musical Aesthetics.* New York: Free Press, 1972.

Cone, Edward. *The Composer's Voice.* Berkeley: University of California Press, 1974.

Cumming, Naomi. *The Sonic Self: Musical Subjectivity and Signification.* Bloomington: Indiana University Press, 2001.

Dahlhaus, Carl. *Esthetics of Music.* Trans. William W. Austin. Cambridge: Cambridge University Press, 1982. First published in 1967.

Davies, Stephen. *Musical Meaning and Expression.* Ithaca, N.Y.: Cornell University Press, 1994.

———. *Themes in the Philosophy of Music.* Oxford: Oxford University Press, 2003.

Goehr, Lydia, et al. "Philosophy of Music." In *The New Grove Dictionary of Music and Musicians.* 2nd ed. Vol. 19, pp. 601–31.

Hanrahan, Nancy Weiss. *Difference in Time: A Critical Theory of Culture.* Westport, Conn.: Praeger, 2000.

Hanslick, Eduard. *On the Musically Beautiful: A Contribution towards the Revision of the Aesthetics of Music.* Trans. and ed. Geoffrey Poyzant. Indianapolis: Hackett Publishing, 1986. First published in 1854.

Jankélévitch, Vladimir. *Music and the Ineffable.* Trans. Carolyn Abbate. Princeton, N.J.: Princeton University Press, 2003.

Johnson, Julian. *Who Needs Classical Music? Cultural Choice and Musical Value.* Oxford: Oxford University Press, 2002.

Kelly, Michael, ed. *Encyclopedia of Aesthetics.* 4 vols. Oxford: Oxford University Press, 1998.

Kivy, Peter. *The Corded Shell: Reflections on Musical Expression.* Princeton, N.J.: Princeton University Press, 1980.

———. *Introduction to a Philosophy of Music.* Oxford: Oxford University Press, 2002.

———. *New Essays on Musical Understanding.* Oxford: Oxford University Press, 2001.

———. *Osmin's Rage: Philosophical Reflections on Opera, Drama, and Text.* Princeton, N.J.: Princeton University Press, 1988; reprint, Ithaca, N.Y.: Cornell University Press, 1999.

———. *Sound and Semblance: Reflections on Music Representation.* Princeton, N.J.: Princeton University Press, 1984; reprint, Ithaca, N.Y.: Cornell University Press, 1991.

Korsyn, Kevin. *Decentering Music: A Critique of Contemporary Musical Research.* Oxford: Oxford University Press, 2002.

Kramer, Lawrence. *Classical Music and Postmodern Knowledge.* Berkeley: University of California Press, 1996.

———. *Musical Meaning: Toward a Critical History.* Berkeley: University of California Press, 2001.

Langer, Susanne. *Feeling and Form: A Theory of Art.* New York: Charles Scribner's Sons, 1953.

———. *Philosophy in a New Key: A Study in the Symbolism of Reason, Rite, and Art.* 3rd ed. Cambridge, Mass.: Harvard University Press, 1976. First published in 1942.

Lippman, Edward A. *A History of Western Musical Aesthetics.* Lincoln: University of Nebraska Press, 1992.

Lorraine, Rene Cox. *Music, Tendencies, and Inhibitions: Reflections on a Theory of Leonard Meyer.* Lanham, Md.: Scarecrow Press, 2001.

Meyer, Leonard B. *Emotion and Meaning in Music.* Chicago: University of Chicago Press, 1956.

———. *Music, the Arts, and Ideas: Patterns and Predictions in Twentieth-Century Culture.* With a new postlude. Chicago: University of Chicago Press, 1994. First published in 1967.

———. *Style and Music: Theory, History, and Ideology.* Philadelphia: University of Pennsylvania Press, 1989; reprint, Chicago: University of Chicago Press, 1996.

Monelle, Raymond. *Linguistics and Semiotics in Music.* Contemporary Music Studies, vol. 5. New York: Gordon and Breach Publishers, 1992.

———. *The Sense of Music: Semiotic Essays.* Princeton, N.J.: Princeton University Press, 2000.

Monelle, Raymond, and Catherine T. Gray. *Song and Significa-
    tion: Studies in Music Semiotics.* Edinburgh: University
    of Edinburgh Faculty of Music, 1995.
Nattiez, Jean-Jacques. *The Battle of Chronos and Orpheus:
    Essays in Applied Musical Semiology.* Trans. Jonathan
    Dunsby. Oxford: Oxford University Press, 2004.
————. *Music and Discourse: Toward a Semiology of Music.*
    Translated and revised by Carolyn Abbate. Princeton, N.J.:
    Princeton University Press, 1990. First published in 1987.
Paddison, Max. *Adorno's Aesthetics of Music.* Cambridge:
    Cambridge University Press, 1993.
Reiner, Thomas. *Semiotics of Musical Time.* New York: Peter
    Lang Publishers, 2000.
Rowell, Lewis. *Thinking about Music: An Introduction to the
    Philosophy of Music.* Amherst: University of Massachu-
    setts Press, 1983.
Rahn, John, ed. *Perspectives on Musical Aesthetics.* New York:
    W. W. Norton, 1994.
Savage, Roger W. H. *Structure and Sorcery: The Aesthetics of
    Post-War Serial Composition and Indeterminacy.* New
    York: Garland, 1989.
Scruton, Roger. *The Aesthetics of Music.* Oxford: Oxford Univer-
    sity Press, 1997.
Tarasti, Eero. *Musical Signification: Essays in the Semiotic
    Theory and Analysis of Music.* Approaches to Semiotics,
    no. 121. New York: Mouton de Gruyter, 1995.
————. *Signs of Music: A Guide to Musical Semiotics.* Haw-
    thorne, N.Y.: Mouton de Gruyter, 2002.
————. *A Theory of Musical Semiotics.* Advances in Semiotics.
    Bloomington: Indiana University Press, 1994.
Tarasti, Eero, Paul Forsell, and Richard Littlefield. *Musical
    Semiotics in Growth.* Bloomington: Indiana University
    Press, 1996.
————. *Musical Semiotics Revisited.* Approaches to Musical
    Semiotics, no. 4. Imatra, Finland: International Semiotics
    Institute, 2003.
van Baest, Arjan. *A Semiotics of Opera.* Delft, Netherlands:
    Eburon, 2000.
Van Leeuwen, Theo. *Speech, Music, Sound.* New York: St.
    Martin's Press, 1999.
Williams, Alastair. *New Music and the Claims of Modernity.*
    Aldershot, England: Ashgate, 1997.
Zannos, Ioannis, ed. *Music and Signs: Semiotic and Cognitive
    Studies in Music.* Bratislava: ASCO Art and Science,
    1999.
Zbikowski, Lawrence M. *Conceptualizing Music: Cognitive*

    Structure, Theory, and Analysis. Oxford: Oxford University Press, 2002.

Zuckerkandl, Victor. *The Sense of Music.* Corrected ed. with index. Princeton, N.J.: Princeton University Press, 1971. First published in 1959.

————. *Sound and Symbol.* 2 vols. Trans. Willard R. Trask and Norbert Guterman. New York: Pantheon Books, 1956–73.

Texts of Theoretical Treatises

Saggi musicali italiani: A Database for Texts on Music Theory and Aesthetics (SMI). Andreas Giger, project director. Bloomington: Indiana University, 2003–. Internet address: http://www.music.indiana.edu/smi. An evolving database for texts of Italian music theory and aesthetics from the Renaissance to the present; the joint effort of a consortium of universities.

Texts on Music in English from the Medieval and Early Modern Eras (TME). Peter M. Lefferts, project director. Bloomington: Indiana University, 2003–. Internet address: http://www.music.indiana.edu/tme. An evolving database for texts of music theory in English from the Middle Ages to the seventeenth century; the joint effort of a consortium of universities.

Thesaurus Musicarum Latinarum: A Comprehensive Database of Latin Music Theory of the Middle Ages and the Renaissance (TML). Thomas J. Mathiesen, project director. Bloomington: Indiana University, 1990–. Internet address: http://www.music.indiana.edu/tml. "An evolving database that will eventually contain the entire corpus of Latin music theory written during the Middle Ages and the early Renaissance"; the joint effort of a consortium of universities.

Traités français sur la musique (TFM). Peter Slemon, project director. Bloomington: Indiana University, 2003–. Internet address: http://www.music.indiana.edu/tfm. An evolving database that will eventually contain all manuscript and printed materials on music theory and aesthetics in French from the Middle Ages through the nineteenth century.

Bibliographies and Guides to the Literature

Basart, Ann Phillips. *Serial Music: A Classified Bibliography of Writings on Twelve-Tone and Electronic Music.* Berkeley: University of California Press, 1961; reprint, Westport, Conn.: Greenwood Press, 1976.

Beach, David, ed. "A Schenker Bibliography." *Journal of Music Theory* 13 (Spring 1969): 2–37.

———. "A Schenker Bibliography: 1969–1979." *Journal of Music Theory* 23 (Spring 1979): 275–86.

Burkholder, J. Peter, Andreas Giger, and David C. Birchler, eds. *Musical Borrowing: An Annotated Bibliography.* Bloomington: Indiana University, 1999–. Internet address: http://www.music.indiana.edu/borrowing. An online bibliography of published materials and theses relating to the uses of existing music in the tradition of Western music.

Coover, James. "Music Theory in Translation: A Bibliography." *Journal of Music Theory* 3 (April 1959): 70–96; 13 (Spring 1969): 230–48.

Damschroeder, David A., and David Russell Williams. *Music Theory from Zarlino to Schenker: A Bibliography and Guide.* Harmonologia Series, no. 4. Stuyvesant, N.Y.: Pendragon Press, 1990. First published in 1970.

Diamond, Harold J. *Music Analyses: An Annotated Guide to the Literature.* New York: Schirmer Books, 1991.

"Index of Music Theory in the United States, 1955–1970." Richmond Browne, supervising ed. *In Theory Only* 3, nos. 7–11 (October 1977–February 1978): entire issue.

Kramer, Jonathan D. "Studies of Time and Music: A Bibliography." *Music Theory Spectrum* 7 (1985): 72–106.

Laskowski, Larry, comp. and annot. *Heinrich Schenker: An Annotated Index to His Analyses of Musical Works.* New York: Pendragon Press, 1978.

Mathiesen, Thomas J. *Ancient Greek Music Theory: A Catalogue Raisonné of Manuscripts.* Munich: G. Henle, 1988.

Perone, James E., comp. *Form and Analysis Theory: A Bibliography.* Westport, Conn.: Greenwood Press, 1998.

———. *Harmony Theory: A Bibliography.* Westport, Conn.: Greenwood Press, 1997.

———. *Musical Anthologies for Analytical Study: A Bibliography.* Westport, Conn.: Greenwood Press, 1995.

Reese, Gustave. *Fourscore Classics of Music Literature: A Guide to Selected Original Sources on Theory and Other Writings on Music Not Available in English, with Descriptive Sketches and Bibliographical References.* New York: Liberal Arts Press, 1957; reprint, New York: Da Capo Press, 1970.

Répertoire international des sources musicales/Internationales Quellen-lexikon der Musik/International Inventory of Musical Sources (RISM). Historical treatises contained in ser. B. Munich: G. Henle, 1961–.

Rolf, Marie. *The State of Research in Music Theory: A Collection of Selective Bibliographies.* Rochester, N.Y.: Society for Music Theory, 1987.

"The Society for Music Theory: The First Decade," Special Issue, *Music Theory Spectrum* 11, no. 1 (Spring 1989).

Vander Weg, John Dean. "An Annotated Bibliography of Articles on Serialism: 1955–1980." *In Theory Only* 5, no. 1 (April 1979): entire issue.

————. *Serial Music and Serialism: A Research and Information Guide.* New York: Routledge, 2001.

Wenk, Arthur B., comp. *Analyses of Nineteenth-and Twentieth-Century Music: 1940–1985.* MLA Index and Bibliography Series, no. 25. Boston: Music Library Association, 1987. First published as separate vols. in 1975–76.

Winick, Steven D. *Rhythm: An Annotated Bibliography.* Metuchen, N.J.: Scarecrow Press, 1974.

MUSIC EDUCATION

The following sources are largely, but not exclusively, concerned with the field of music education in the United States. In the first category, "The History of Music Education," for example, the articles by Anderson, Page, Plummeridge, and Weber in *The New Grove* cover the entire history of the field from ancient Greece on; the other sources contain general overviews of music education in the United States and Canada. Under "Research Methodology," Borg and Gall is a comprehensive overview of what research in the social sciences entails, drawing examples from the many disciplines involved in the broad field of education. The remaining sources are focused primarily on how research has and can be conducted specifically in music education—Barnes contains actual examples of different types of such research.

"General Reference Sources" brings together works that constitute a general orientation to the field of music education, paying some attention to the past as well as assessing current issues and directions. Nelson is a classic reference work in its pioneering attempt to examine the field. Although Leonhard and House remains a significant historical contribution in its comprehensive attention to the philosophy and curriculum of public school music, more recent studies (such as Barrett et al., Hoffer, Jorgensen, Philpott, Reimer, Spruce, and Volk) address current issues at the turn of the twenty-first century. Mark is an excellent summary and bibliographic resource on the main people, ideas, and literature of the field.

The sources listed under "Research Overviews" are evaluative reflections on the results of research efforts in both general and mu-

sic education; each is based on the review of a substantial number
of research projects and offers direction for future efforts. The four
handbooks sponsored by AERA (Gage, Travers, Wittrock, Richardson) are monumental attempts to examine the current status of
the field of educational research and illustrate how it has changed
drastically over a period of forty years. The MENC *Handbooks* are
devoted specifically to music, containing essays on topics pertaining to all age levels and related to all areas of music teaching and
learning.

The final list, "Bibliographies, Directories, and Indexes," is of important bibliographic tools in music education, including the major
sources from the Educational Resources Information Center (ERIC),
located in Washington, D.C., and those available on CD-ROM and
the Internet.

For a list of research journals in the field, see chapter 6, "Current Research Journals in Music," pp. 243–44 below.

The History of Music Education

Anderson, Warren. "Music education." In *The New Grove
    Dictionary of Music and Musicians.* 2nd ed. Vol. 17, pp.
    480–83.
Birge, Edward Bailey. *History of Public School Music in the
    United States.* New and augm. ed. Bryn Mawr, Pa.: Oliver
    Ditson, 1937; reprint, Reston, Va.: Music Educators Na-
    tional Conference, 1988. First published in 1928.
Colwell, Richard, et al. "Education in Music." In *The New Grove
    Dictionary of American Music.* Ed. H. Wiley Hitchcock
    and Stanley Sadie. 4 vols. New York: Grove's Dictionaries
    of Music, 1986. Vol. 2, pp. 11–21.
"Education in the United States." In *The New Harvard Dictio-
    nary of Music.* Pp. 276–78.
Goodman, A. Harold. *Music Education: Perspectives and Per-
    ceptions.* Dubuque, Iowa: Kendall-Hunt, 1982.
Green, J. Paul, and Nancy F. Vogan. *Music Education in Canada:
    A Historical Account.* Toronto: University of Toronto
    Press, 1991.
Keene, James A. *A History of Music Education in the United
    States.* Hanover, N.H.: University Press of New England,
    1982.
Labuta, Joseph A., and Deborah A. Smith. *Music Education:
    Historical Contexts and Perspectives.* Upper Saddle River,
    N.J.: Prentice Hall, 1997.
Mark, Michael L. *Source Readings in Music Education History.*
    New York: Schirmer Books, 1982.
Mark, Michael L., and Charles L. Gary. *A History of American*

Music Education. 2nd ed. Reston, Va.: Music Educators National Conference, 1999. First published in 1992.

Page, Christopher, et al. "Universities." In *The New Grove Dictionary of Music and Musicians.* 2nd ed. Vol. 26, pp. 135–47.

Plummeridge, Charles. "Schools." In *The New Grove Dictionary of Music and Musicians.* 2nd ed. Vol. 22, pp. 614–29.

Tellstrom, A. Theodore. *Music in American Education: Past and Present.* New York: Holt, Rinehart and Winston, 1971.

Weber, William, et al. "Conservatories." In *The New Grove Dictionary of Music and Musicians.* 2nd ed. Vol. 6, pp. 311–24.

Wilson, Bruce Dunbar, and Marie McCarthy. *Music in American Schools, 1838–1988: Proceedings of a Symposium at the University of Maryland at College Park, August 26–28, 1988 Celebrating the Sesquicentennial of Music in American Public Education.* College Park, Md.: Music Library, University of Maryland at College Park, 1998.

Research Methodology

Barnes, Stephen H., ed. *A Cross Section of Research in Music Education.* Washington, D.C.: University Press of America, 1982.

Borg, Walter R., and Meredith Damien Gall. *Educational Research: An Introduction.* 7th ed. Boston: Allyn and Bacon, 2003. First published in 1963.

Kemp, Anthony. *Some Approaches to Research in Music Education.* Reading, England: International Society for Music Education, 1992.

Phelps, Roger P., et al. *Guide to Research in Music Education.* 4th ed. Metuchen, N.J.: Scarecrow Press, 1993. First published in 1969.

Rainbow, Edward L., and Hildegard C. Froehlich. *Research in Music Education: An Introduction to Systematic Inquiry.* New York: Schirmer Books, 1987.

Weimer, George William. "Trends in Topics, Methods, and Statistical Techniques Employed in Dissertations Completed for Doctor's Degrees in Music Education 1963–1978." Ed.D. diss., University of Illinois at Urbana-Champaign, 1980.

General Reference Sources

Abeles, Harold F., et al. *Foundations of Music Education.* 2nd ed. New York: Schirmer Books, 1994. First published in 1984.

Barrett, Janet R., Claire W. McCoy, and Kari K. Veblen. *Sound*

Ways of Knowing: Music in the Interdisciplinary Curriculum. New York: Schirmer Books, 1997.

Campbell, Patricia Shehan. *Lessons from the World: A Cross-Cultural Guide to Music Teaching and Learning.* New York: Schirmer Books, 1991.

Colwell, Richard J., ed. *Basic Concepts of Music Education, II.* Niwot: University Press of Colorado, 1991.

Elliott, David J. *Music Matters: A New Philosophy of Music Education.* New York: Oxford University Press, 1995.

Fletcher, Peter. *Education and Music.* New York: Oxford University Press, 1987.

Gates, J. Terry, ed. *Music Education in the United States: Contemporary Issues.* Tuscaloosa: University of Alabama Press, 1988.

Hodges, Donald A. *Handbook of Music Psychology.* 2nd ed. San Antonio, Tex.: IMR Press, 1996. First published in 1980.

Hoffer, Charles R. *Introduction to Music Education.* New York: Schirmer Books, 1993.

Jorgensen, Estelle R. *Transforming Music Education.* Bloomington: Indiana University Press, 2002.

Leonhard, Charles, and Robert W. House. *Foundations and Principles of Music Education.* 2nd ed. New York: McGraw-Hill, 1972. First published in 1959.

Mark, Michael L. *Contemporary Music Education.* 3rd ed. New York: Schirmer Books, 1996. First published in 1978.

Nelson, Henry, ed. *Basic Concepts in Music Education.* Fifty-seventh Yearbook of the National Society for the Study of Education, part 1. Chicago: The National Society for the Study of Education, 1958.

Parncutt, Richard, and Gary McPherson, eds. *The Science and Psychology of Music Performance: Creative Strategies for Teaching and Learning.* Oxford: Oxford University Press, 2002.

Philpott, Chris, ed. *Learning to Teach Music in the Secondary School.* New York: Routledge, 2001.

Philpott, Chris, and Charles Plummeridge, eds. *Issues in Music Teaching.* New York: Routledge, 2001.

Reese, Sam, Kimberly McCord, and Kimberly C. Walls. *Strategies for Teaching: Technology.* Reston, Va.: Music Educators National Conference, 2001.

Reimer, Bennett. *A Philosophy of Music Education: Advancing the Vision.* 3rd ed. Upper Saddle River, N.J.: Prentice Hall, 2003. First published in 1970.

———. *World Musics and Music Education: Facing the Issues.* Reston, Va.: Music Educators National Conference, 2002.

Religious Music in the Schools. Reston, Va.: Music Educators
    National Conference, 1996.
Spruce, Gary. *Teaching Music in Secondary Schools: A Reader.*
    New York: Routledge, 2002.
———, ed. *Aspects of Teaching Secondary Music: Perspectives
    on Practice.* New York: Routledge, 2002.
Volk, Terese M. *Music, Education, and Multiculturalism: Foun-
    dations and Principles.* Oxford: Oxford University Press,
    1998.

Research Overviews

Berz, William L., and Judith Bowman. *Applications of Research
    in Music Technology.* Reston, Va.: Music Educators
    National Conference, 1994.
Brittin, Ruth V., and Jayne M. Standley. "Researchers in Music
    Education/Therapy: Analysis of Publications, Citations,
    and Retrievability of Work." *Journal of Research in Music
    Education* 45 (Spring 1997): 145–60.
Colwell, Richard, ed. "Symposium on K-12 Music Education."
    Design for Arts in Education 91 (May/June 1990):
    14–52.
Encyclopedia of Educational Research. 6th ed. Ed. Marvin Alkin.
    4 vols. A Project of the American Educational Research
    Association. New York: Macmillan, 1992. First published
    in 1941.
Fowler, Charles, ed. *The Crane Symposium: Toward an Under-
    standing of the Teaching and Learning of Musical Perfor-
    mance.* Potsdam: Potsdam College of the State University
    of New York, 1988.
Handbook of Research on Curriculum. Ed. Philip Jackson. New
    York: Macmillan, 1992.
Handbook of Research on Music Teaching and Learning.
    Ed. Richard Colwell. A Project of the Music Educators
    National Conference. New York: Schirmer Books, 1992.
*The New Handbook of Research on Music Teaching and
    Learning.* Ed. Richard Colwell and Carol Richardson.
    A Project of the Music Educators National Conference.
    Oxford: Oxford University Press, 2002.
Handbook of Research on Teaching. Ed. Nathaniel Lees Gage.
    A Project of the American Educational Research Associa-
    tion. Chicago: Rand McNally, 1963.
Second Handbook of Research on Teaching. Ed. Robert M. W.
    Travers. A Project of the American Educational Research
    Association. Chicago: Rand McNally, 1973.
Handbook of Research on Teaching. 3rd ed. Ed. Merlin C.

Wittrock. A Project of the American Educational Research Association. New York: Macmillan, 1986.

Handbook of Research on Teaching. 4th ed. Ed. Virginia Richardson. Washington, D.C.: American Educational Research Association, 2001.

Leonhard, Charles, and Richard Colwell. "Research in Music Education." In *Arts and Aesthetics: An Agenda for the Future Based on a Conference Held at Aspen, Colorado, June 22–25, 1976.* Ed. Stanley Madeja. St. Louis: CEMREL, 1977.

Madson, Clifford K., and Carol A. Prickett, eds. *Applications of Research in Music Behavior.* Tuscaloosa: University of Alabama Press, 1987.

Schneider, Erwin H., and Henry L. Cady. *Evaluation and Synthesis of Research Studies Related to Music Education.* Columbus: Ohio State University, 1965.

Sloboda, John A. *The Musical Mind: The Cognitive Psychology of Music.* New York: Oxford University Press, 1985; reprint with corrections, New York: Oxford University Press, 1999.

Bibliographies, Directories, and Indexes

Bibliography of Research Studies in Music Education, 1932–1948. Rev. ed. Prepared by William S. Larson and presented by The Music Education Research Council. Washington, D.C.: Music Educators National Conference, 1949. First published in 1944.

Bibliography of Research Studies in Music Education, 1949–1956. By William S. Larson. Washington, D.C.: Music Educators National Conference, 1957.

Brookhart, Edward. *Music in American Higher Education: An Annotated Bibliography.* Bibliographies in American Music, no. 10. Warren, Mich.: Harmonie Park Press, 1988.

CAIRSS for MUSIC. Charles T. Eagle, Jr., ed. San Antonio: Institute for Music Research (Donald A. Hodges, director), University of Texas at San Antonio, 1993–. Internet address: http://imr.utsa.edu/cairss.html. This "Computer-Assisted Information Retrieval Service System" is a bibliographic database of music research literature that emphasizes music education, music therapy, music psychology, and medicine. Currently there are eighteen "primary" journals in these areas that are completely indexed, with selected articles from more than twelve hundred "secondary" journals that are also in the database.

Complete Guide and Index to ERIC Reports through December

1969. Comp. the Prentice Hall Editorial Staff. Englewood Cliffs, N.J.: Prentice Hall, 1970.

Current Index to Journals in Education (CIJE). Phoenix: Oryx Press for Educational Resources Information Center (ERIC) of the National Institute of Education, U.S. Department of Education, 1969–. (Also available on CD-ROM as *ERIC.*)

Education Index: A Cumulative Author-Subject Index to a Selected List of Educational Periodicals and Yearbooks. New York: H. W. Wilson, 1929–.

Gordon, Roderick D. "Doctoral Dissertations in Music and Music Education, 1957–1963." *Journal of Research in Music Education* 13 (Spring 1965): 45–55.

Harris, Ernest E., ed. *Music Education: A Guide to Information Sources.* Education Information Guide Series, vol. 1. Detroit: Gale Research, 1978.

Heller, George N. *Historical Research in Music Education: A Bibliography.* 4th ed. Silver Spring, Md.: The American Music Therapy Association, 2002. First published in 1988.

International Directory of Approved Music Education Doctoral Dissertations in Progress (DIP). Ed. Richard J. Colwell. Council for Research in Music Education, University of Illinois, in behalf of The Graduate Program in Music Education. Urbana: University of Illinois, 1989–99. Also available as an online, searchable database at http://reese2 .music.uiuc.edu:591/bulletin/dip/default2.htm

Kantorski, Vincent J. *A Bibliography of Source Readings in Music Education.* Detroit Studies in Music Bibliography, no. 78. Warren, Mich.: Harmonie Park Press, 1997.

Resources in Education (RIE). Washington, D.C.: Educational Resources Information Center (ERIC), U.S. Department of Health, Education, and Welfare, National Institute of Education, 1974–. (Formerly *Research in Education,* 1966–73.) (Also available on CD-ROM as *ERIC.*)

Thesaurus of ERIC Descriptors. 14th ed. Ed. James Houston. Phoenix: Oryx Press, 2001. First published in 1968. (See current issues of *Resources in Education* for "Thesaurus Additions and Changes.")

MUSIC THERAPY

Introductions to the Discipline

Alvin, Juliette. *Music Therapy.* Rev. ed. London: Stainer and Bell, 1991. First published in 1966.

Bunt, Leslie. "Music therapy." In *The New Grove Dictionary
of Music and Musicians.* 2nd ed. Vol. 17, pp. 535–40.
———. *Music Therapy: An Art beyond Words.* New York:
Routledge, 1994.
Darnley-Smith, Rachel, and Helen M. Patey. *Music Therapy.*
Thousand Oaks, Calif.: Sage Publications, 2003.
Darrow, Alice-Ann. *Introduction to Approaches in Music
Therapy.* Silver Spring, Md.: American Music Therapy
Association, 2004.
Gouk, Penelope, ed. *Musical Healing in Cultural Contexts.*
Burlington, Vt.: Ashgate Publishing, 2000.
Michel, Donald E. *Music Therapy: An Introduction, Including
Music in Special Education.* 2nd ed. Springfield, Ill.:
Charles C. Thomas, 1985. First published in 1976.
Michel, Donald E., and Joe Pinson. *Music Therapy in Principle
and Practice.* Springfield, Ill.: Charles C. Thomas, 2004.
Warren, Bernie. *Using the Creative Arts in Therapy: A Practical
Introduction.* 2nd ed. New York: Routledge, 2000. First
published in 1993.

**Various Guides and Discussions
of History, Theory, and Practice**

Aldridge, David. *Case Study Designs in Music Therapy.* London:
Jessica Kingsley Publications, 2004.
———. *Music Therapy in Dementia Care.* London: Jessica Kings-
ley Publishers, 2000.
———. *Music Therapy in Palliative Care: New Voices.* London:
Jessica Kingsley Publishers, 1999.
———. *Music Therapy Research and Practice in Medicine: From
Out of the Silence.* London: Jessica Kingsley Publications,
1996.
Barksdale, Alicia L. *Music Therapy and Leisure for Persons with
Disabilities.* Champaign, Ill.: Sagamore Publications, 2003.
Bean, John, and Amelia Oldfield. *Pied Piper: Musical Activities
to Develop Basic Skills.* New York: Routledge, 2001.
Benenzon, Rolando O. *Music Therapy Theory and Manual:
Contributions to the Knowledge of Nonverbal Contexts.*
2nd ed. Springfield, Ill.: Charles C. Thomas, 1997. First
published in 1981.
Berger, Dorita S. *Music Therapy, Sensory Integration, and the Au-
tistic Child.* London: Jessica Kingsley Publications, 2002.
Boyce-Tillman, June. *Constructing Musical Healing: The Wounds
That Sing.* New York: Routledge, 2000.
Bruscia, Kenneth E. *Improvisational Models of Music Therapy.*
Springfield, Ill.: Charles C. Thomas, 1987.

Bunt, Leslie, and Sarah Hoskyns, eds. *The Handbook of Music Therapy.* New York: Routledge, 2002.

Corke, Margaret. *Approaches to Communication through Music.* New York: Routledge, 2002.

Crowe, Barbara J. *Music and Soul-Making: Music Therapy and Complexity Science.* Lanham, Md.: Scarecrow Press, 2004.

Davies, Alison, and Eleanor Richards, eds. *Music Therapy and Group Work.* New York: Routledge, 2002.

Dileo, Cheryl. *Music Therapy: International Perspectives.* Pipersville, Pa.: Jeffrey Books, 1993.

Effectiveness of Music Therapy Procedures: Documentation of Research and Clinical Practice. Rev. 3rd ed. Silver Spring, Md.: American Music Therapy Association, 2000. First published in 1988.

Eschen, Johannes, ed. *Analytical Music Therapy.* New York: Routledge, 2002.

Farbman, Andrea H., Ellen R. Griggs-Drane, and Tamara W. Zavislan. *Music Therapy and Medicine: Research Compendium.* Silver Spring, Md.: American Music Therapy Association, 2000.

Gilroy, Andrea, and Colin Lee, eds. *Art and Music: Therapy and Research.* New York: Routledge, 1994.

Hadley, Susan. *Psychodynamic Music Therapy: Case Studies.* Gilsum, N.H.: Barcelona Publishers, 2003.

Horden, Peregrine, ed. *Music as Medicine: The History of Music Therapy since Antiquity.* Burlington, Vt.: Ashgate Publishing, 2000.

Lathom, Wanda. *Pediatric Music Therapy.* Springfield, Ill.: Charles C. Thomas, 2002.

Nordoff, Paul, and Clive Robbins. *Creative Music Therapy.* New York: John Day Company, 1977.

Pavlicevic, Mercedes. *Groups in Music: Strategies from Music Therapy.* New York: Routledge, 2003.

Priestley, Mary. *Essays on Analytical Music Therapy.* Philadelphia: Barcelona Publishers, 1995.

Ruud, Evan. *Music Therapy and Its Relationship to Current Treatment Theories.* St. Louis, Mo.: Magnamusic-Baton, 1980.

Standley, Jayne M. *Music Therapy with Premature Infants: Research and Developmental Interventions.* Silver Spring, Md.: American Music Therapy Association, 2003.

Streeter, Elaine. *Making Music with the Young Child with Special Needs: A Guide for Parents.* Rev. ed. London: Jessica Kingsley Publishers, 2001. First published in 1993.

Sutton, Julie P. *Music, Music Therapy and Trauma: International Perspectives.* New York: Routledge, 2002.

Wigram, Tony. *Improvisation: Methods and Techniques for Music Therapy Clinicians, Educators, and Students.* London: Jessica Kingsley Publications, 2004.

Wigram, Tony, Inge Nygaard Pedersen, and Lars Ole Bonde. *A Comprehensive Guide to Music Therapy: Theory, Clinical Practice, Research, and Training.* New York: Routledge, 2002.

Wilson, Brian L. *Models of Music Therapy Interventions in School Settings.* 2nd ed. Silver Spring, Md.: American Music Therapy Association, 2002. First published in 1996.

Wong, Elizabeth H. *Clinical Guide to Music Therapy in Adult Physical Rehabilitation Settings.* Silver Spring, Md.: American Music Therapy Association, 2004.

Bibliographies and Other Guides to Research

Aigen, Kenneth. *A Guide to Writing and Presenting in Music Therapy.* Gilsum, N.H.: Barcelona Publishers, 2003.

Heller, George N. *Historical Research in Music Therapy: A Bibliography.* Lawrence: University of Kansas, Department of Art and Music Education and Music Therapy, 1988.

Parker, James N., and Philip M. Parker. *Music Therapy: A Medical Dictionary, Bibliography and Annotated Research Guide to Internet References.* San Diego, Calif.: ICON Health Publications, 2004.

Robarts, J. Z. *Music Therapy Research.* East Barnet, England: British Society for Music Therapy, 2000.

Wheeler, Barbara, ed. *Music Therapy Research: Quantitative and Qualitative Perspectives.* Philadelphia: Barcelona Publishers, 1995.

BIBLIOGRAPHIES AND RESEARCH GUIDES IN OTHER SELECTED AREAS

This section consists of important bibliographical and other sources of music literature through which to initiate research in other selected subject areas. Only five areas are given here; the number could be expanded to include separate countries, individual genres, popular and rock music, folk song, etc., bibliographies of which may be found in Duckles's *Music Reference and Research Materials* and in Marco's *Information on Music* (see p. 49 above). It should be noted that sources appearing in one category may also apply to another, most notably those pertaining to various aspects of American music, e.g., sources in the "African-American Music" section that concern "Jazz."

African-American Music

de Lerma, Dominique-René. *Bibliography of Black Music.*
4 vols. The Greenwood Encyclopedia of Black Music.
Westport, Conn.: Greenwood Press, 1981–84.

1. *Reference Materials.* 1981.
2. *Afro-American Idioms.* 1981.
3. *Geographical Studies.* 1981.
4. *Theory, Education, and Related Studies.* 1984.

de Lerma, Dominique-René, and Marsha J. Reisser. *Black Music and Musicians in The New Grove Dictionary of American Music and The New Harvard Dictionary of Music.* CBMR Monographs, no. 1. Chicago: Center for Black Music Research, Columbia College Chicago, 1989.

Floyd, Samuel A., Jr. "Books on Black Music by Black Authors: A Bibliography." *The Black Perspective in Music* 14 (Fall 1986): 215–32.

Floyd, Samuel A., Jr., and Marsha J. Reisser. *Black Music Biography: An Annotated Bibliography.* White Plains, N.Y.: Kraus International Publications, 1987.

———. *Black Music in the United States: An Annotated Bibliography of Selected Reference and Research Materials.* Millwood, N.Y.: Kraus International Publications, 1983.

Gray, John, comp. *Blacks in Classical Music: A Bibliographical Guide to Composers, Performers, and Ensembles.* Music Reference Collection, no. 15. Westport, Conn.: Greenwood Press, 1988.

Horne, Aaron. *Brass Music of Black Composers: A Bibliography.* Music Reference Collection, no. 51. Westport, Conn.: Greenwood Press, 1996.

———. *Keyboard Music of Black Composers: A Bibliography.* Music Reference Collection, no. 37. Westport, Conn.: Greenwood Press, 1992.

———. *Woodwind Music of Black Composers: A Bibliography.* Music Reference Collection, no. 24. Westport, Conn.: Greenwood Press, 1990.

Johnson, James Peter, comp. *Bibliographic Guide to the Study of Afro-American Music.* Washington, D.C.: Howard University Libraries, 1973.

Skowronski, JoAnn. *Black Music in America: A Bibliography.* Metuchen, N.J.: Scarecrow Press, 1981.

Southern, Eileen, and Josephine Wright, comps. *African-American Traditions in Song, Sermon, Tale, and Dance, 1600s–1920: An Annotated Bibliography of Literature, Collections, and Artworks.* The Greenwood Encyclopedia of Black Music. Westport, Conn.: Greenwood Press, 1990.

Szwed, John F., Roger D. Abrahams, et al. *Afro-American Folk Culture: An Annotated Bibliography of Materials from North, Central, and South America, and the West Indies.* Publications of the American Folklore Society, Bibliographical and Special Series, no. 31. Philadelphia: Institute for the Study of Human Issues, 1978.

Vann, Kimberly R., et al. *Black Music in* **Ebony:** *An Annotated Guide to the Articles on Music in* **Ebony** *Magazine, 1945–1985.* CBMR Monographs, no. 2. Chicago: Center for Black Music Research, Columbia College Chicago, 1990.

White, Evelyn Davidson. *Choral Music by African-American Composers: A Selected, Annotated Bibliography.* 2nd ed. Lanham, Md.: Scarecrow Press, 1999. First published in 1996.

Wright, Josephine. "Research in Afro-American Music, 1968–88: A Survey with Selected Bibliography of the Literature." In *New Perspectives on Music: Essays in Honor of Eileen Southern,* ed. Josephine Wright, with Samuel A. Floyd, Jr. Detroit Monographs in Musicology/Studies in Music, no. 11. Warren, Mich.: Harmonie Park Press, 1992. Pp. 481–515.

American Music

Bibliographies in American Music. Published for the College Music Society. Warren, Mich.: Harmonie Park Press, 1974–90.

Brookhart, Edward. *Music in American Higher Education: An Annotated Bibliography.* Bibliographies in American Music, no. 10. Warren, Mich.: Harmonie Park Press, 1988.

Carman, Judith E. *Art Song in the United States, 1759–1999: An Annotated Bibliography.* 3rd ed. Lanham, Md.: Scarecrow Press, 2002. First published in 1987.

District of Columbia Historical Records Survey. *Bio-Bibliographical Index of Musicians in the United States of America since Colonial Times/Indice bio-bibliográfico de músicos de los Estados Unidos de America desde la época de la colonia.* 2nd ed. Washington, D.C.: Music Section, Pan American Union, 1956; reprint, New York: Da Capo Press, 1971. First published in 1940.

Heintze, James R. *Early American Music: A Research and*

Information Guide. Music Research and Information
Guides, no. 13. New York: Garland Publishing, 1990.

Horn, David, and Guy A. Marco. *The Literature of American
Music in Books and Folk Music Collections: A Fully
Annotated Bibliography.* 4 vols. Metuchen, N.J.: Scare-
crow Press, 1977–96.

I.S.A.M. Monographs. Brooklyn: Institute for Studies in American Music, Department of Music, Brooklyn College of the
City University of New York, 1973–.

Jackson, Richard. *United States Music: Sources of Bibliography
and Collective Biography.* I.S.A.M. Monographs, no. 1.
Brooklyn: Institute for Studies in American Music, Department of Music, Brooklyn College of the City University
of New York, 1973; reprint with corrections and additions,
Brooklyn: Institute for Studies in American Music, Department of Music, Brooklyn College of the City University
of New York, 1976.

Krummel, D. W. *Bibliographical Handbook of American Music.*
Music in American Life Series. Urbana: University of
Illinois Press, 1987.

Krummel, D. W., et al. *Resources of American Music History:
A Directory of Source Materials from Colonial Times to
World War II.* Urbana: University of Illinois Press, 1981.

Marco, Guy A. *Literature of American Music and Checklist
of Writings on American Music, 1640–1992.* 2–vol. set.
Lanham, Md.: Scarecrow Press, 2000. *Checklist of Writings* first published in 1996.

McCarty, Frank. *American Music Resource.* Chapel Hill, N.C.:
The University of North Carolina, 1993–. Internet address:
http://www.uncg.edu/%7Eflmccart/amrhome.html. A
"multi-dimensional source of reference information about
all styles of music indigenous to the Western Hemisphere."

Mead, Rita H. *Doctoral Dissertations in American Music: A
Classified Bibliography.* I.S.A.M. Monographs, no. 3.
Brooklyn: Institute for Studies in American Music, De-
partment of Music, School of Performing Arts, Brooklyn
College of the City University of New York, 1974.

Warner, Thomas E. *Periodical Literature on American Music,
1620–1920: A Classified Bibliography with Annotations.*
Bibliographies in American Music, no. 12. Warren, Mich.:
Harmonie Park Press, 1988.

Dance

Adamczyk, Alice J. *Black Dance: An Annotated Bibliography.*
New York: Garland Publishing, 1989.

Bopp, Mary S. *Research in Dance: A Guide to Resources.* New York: G. K. Hall Reference, 1993.

Edsall, Mary E. *A Core Collection in Dance.* Chicago: The Association of College and Research Libraries Dance Librarians Committee, 2001.

Forbes, Fred R., Jr. *Dance: An Annotated Bibliography, 1965–1982.* Music Research and Information Guides, vol. 3. New York: Garland Publishing, 1986.

Hunt, Marilyn, and Sara Coffey. *Research Sources for Dance Writers.* New York: Dance Critics Association, 1995.

Johnson, Thomas J. *Review and Index to Research in Dance Relevant to Aesthetic Education, 1900–1968.* St. Ann, Mo.: CEMREL, 1970.

New York Public Library. Research Libraries. *Dictionary Catalog of the Dance Collection: A List of Authors, Titles, and Subjects of Multi-Media Materials in the Dance Collection of the Performing Arts Research Center of the New York Public Library.* 10 vols. + yearly suppls. (titled *Bibliographic Guide to Dance*). Boston: New York Public Library et al., 1974–98. (Also available on CD-ROM under the title *Dance on Disc.*)

Rust, Ezra Gardner. *The Music and Dance of the World's Religions: A Comprehensive, Annotated Bibliography of Materials in the English Language.* Westport, Conn.: Greenwood Press, 1996.

Schwartz, Judith L., and Christena L. Schlundt. *French Court Dance and Dance Music: A Guide to Primary Source Writings 1643–1789.* Dance and Music Series, no. 1. Stuyvesant, N.Y.: Pendragon Press, 1987.

Jazz, Blues, etc.

Carner, Gary, comp. *Jazz Performers: An Annotated Bibliography of Biographical Materials.* Music Reference Collection, no. 26. Westport, Conn.: Greenwood Press, 1990.

Gray, John, comp. *Fire Music: A Bibliography of the New Jazz, 1959–1990.* Music Reference Collection, no. 31. Westport, Conn.: Greenwood Press, 1991.

Gregor, Carl, Duke of Mecklenburg. *International Bibliography of Jazz Books.* Compiled with the assistance of Norbert Ruecker. 4 vols. projected. Collections d'études musicologiques/Sammlung musikwissenschaftlicher Abhandlungen. Baden-Baden: Valentin Koerner, 1983–.

1. *1921–1949.* No. 67 in series. 1983.
2. *1950–1959.* No. 76 in series. 1988.

————. *International Jazz Bibliography: Jazz Books from 1919 to 1968.* Strasbourg: P. H. Heitz, 1969. Suppls., Graz: Universal Edition, 1971–1975.

Hart, Mary L., et al. *The Blues: A Bibliographic Guide.* Music Research and Information Guides, vol. 4. Garland Reference Library of the Humanities, vol. 565. New York: Garland Publishing, 1989.

Hefele, Bernhard. *Jazz-Bibliography: International Literature on Jazz, Blues, Spirituals, Gospel and Ragtime Music. . . .* New York: K. G. Saur, 1981.

Jazz Index: Bibliographie unselbständiger Jazzliteratur/Bibliography of Jazz Literature in Periodicals and Collections. Comp. Norbert Ruecker and C. Reggentin-Scheidt. Frankfurt: N. Ruecker, 1977–83.

Kennington, Donald, and Danny Read. *The Literature of Jazz: A Critical Guide.* 2nd ed., rev. Chicago: American Library Association, 1980. First published in 1970.

Meadows, Eddie S. *Jazz Research and Performance Materials: A Select Annotated Bibliography.* 2nd ed. Garland Library of Music Ethnology, no. 4; Garland Reference Library of the Humanities, vol. 1471. New York: Garland Publishing, 1995. First published in 1981.

Merriam, Alan P., with the assistance of Robert J. Banford. *A Bibliography of Jazz.* Publications of the American Folklore Society, Bibliographical Series, vol. 4. Philadelphia: The American Folklore Society, 1954; reprint, New York: Da Capo Press, 1970.

Reisner, Robert G. *The Literature of Jazz: A Selective Bibliography.* 2nd ed., rev. and enl. New York: New York Public Library, 1959. First published in 1954.

Women in Music

Bibliography of Sources Related to Women's Studies, Gender Studies, Feminism, and Music. Internet address: http://home1.gte.net/esayrs68/CSWBibIndex.html. Society for Music Theory, 1999–.

Block, Adrienne Fried, and Carol Neuls-Bates, comps. and eds. *Women in American Music: A Bibliography of Music and Literature.* Westport, Conn.: Greenwood Press, 1979.

Ericson, Margaret D. *Women and Music: A Selective Bibliography on Women and Gender Issues in Music, 1987–1992.* New York: G. K. Hall, 1995.

Hixon, Don L., and Don A. Hennessee. *Women in Music: An Encyclopedic Biobibliography.* 2nd ed. Metuchen, N.J.: Scarecrow Press, 1993. First published in 1975.

LePage, Jane Weiner. *Women Composers, Conductors, and Musicians of the Twentieth Century: Selected Bibliographies.* 3 vols. Metuchen, N.J.: Scarecrow Press, 1980–88.

The Musical Woman: An International Perspective. Judith Lang Zaimont, editor-in-chief. 3 vols. New York: Greenwood Press, 1984–90.

Resource Guide on Women in Music. Ed. Judith Cody. Materials comp. Laura M. Gilliard. San Francisco: Bay Area Congress on Women in Music, 1981.

Rieger, Eva, Ruth Heckmann, and Jeanne Rosenstein. *Frau und Musik: Bibliographie 1970–1996.* Hildesheim: Georg Olms, 1999.

Skowronski, JoAnn. *Women in American Music: A Bibliography.* Metuchen, N.J.: Scarecrow Press, 1978.

Stern, Susan. *Women Composers: A Handbook.* Metuchen, N.J.: Scarecrow Press, 1978.

Women's Early Music Web-Ring Index. Internet address: http://music.acu.edu/www/iawm/pages/webring.html. Indiana, Pa.: International Alliance for Women in Music.

Women's Studies/Women's Status. By the Committee on the Status of Women in Music (1984–1986). CMS Report no. 5. Boulder, Colo.: College Music Society, 1988.

Miscellaneous Sources

Fasman, Mark J. *Brass Bibliography: Sources on the History, Literature, Pedagogy, Performance, and Acoustics of Brass Instruments.* Bloomington: Indiana University Press, 1990.

Wolcott, Michiko Ishiyama. *Piano, the Instrument: An Annotated Bibliography.* Lanham, Md.: Scarecrow Press, 2001.

CHAPTER FOUR

Dictionaries and Encyclopedias of Music

The dictionaries and encyclopedias of music listed in this chapter have been divided by type into (1) the recent large sources and selected concise ones that contain articles on people as well as on terms, (2) selected sources, international and North American, that contain only biographical articles, (3) the chief sources that contain only articles on terms, and (4) selected specialized dictionaries—those treating specific areas or subjects, regardless of approach. In all but one category, the names of certain older sources of historical interest are also included. For comprehensive lists of such sources, see under "Music Dictionaries and Encyclopedias" in chapter 2 above. As an addendum to this chapter, a representative list of articles in what is probably the most common single-volume dictionary of terms, *The New Harvard Dictionary of Music,* has been added as an indication of the variety of information that it contains. Similar articles can be found in *The New Grove Dictionary* and other such sources.

GENERAL DICTIONARIES AND ENCYCLOPEDIAS

These sources are "general" dictionaries and encyclopedias of music in that all of them (with the exception of the *Encyclopedia of World Music*) include articles on both biographical and non-biographical subjects, on people as well as terms, forms, genres, countries, etc. Beyond that, however, there are considerable differences among them in size, comprehensiveness, and recentness. There are sometimes specified limitations (e.g., *Dictionary of Contemporary Music, Encyclopedia of Music in Canada,* The Garland Encyclopedia of World Music, and *New Grove Dictionary of American Music*). Less obvious in the international sources is that there are often differences of emphasis, e.g., more detailed coverage of subjects pertaining to the country in which the work originated.

By far the most comprehensive sources in any language in this category are the well-known *Die Musik in Geschichte und Gegenwart* [*MGG*] and *New Grove Dictionary. Das grosse Lexikon der Musik*, the greatly enlarged translation into German of Honegger's four-volume French original, and the *Dizionario enciclopedico* should also be mentioned as quite lengthy and thorough works.

The Lavignac/La Laurencie *Encyclopédie*, though dating back to earlier in the twentieth century, still holds a place of importance; not in alphabetical order, it consists of a series of book-length articles on a wide variety of musical subjects. The *Brockhaus Riemann Musik-Lexikon* (formerly *Riemann Musik-Lexikon*, which went through twelve editions), *New Oxford Companion to Music* (the continuation of Percy Scholes's *Oxford Companion to Music*, which went through eleven editions), and *International Cyclopedia* are especially worthy of mention as standard sources of medium length. The Westrup/Harrison *New College Encyclopedia, The Norton/Grove Concise Encyclopedia, The Oxford Dictionaries of Music*, the *Hutchinson Dictionaries*, and the *Random House Dictionary* are all short one-volume works. Also listed are several recent and more specialized dictionaries, such as *A Dictionary of the Avant-Gardes, The Companion to 20th-Century Music*, and the nineteenth-century volume of the *Dictionnaire de la musique en France*.

Under "Of Historical Interest" are two of the many earlier dictionaries of music, each an important first: Walther's venerable *Musicalisches Lexicon* (1732), the earliest example of the genre, and Moore's *Encyclopedia* (1854), the earliest major American one.

Bennet, Roy. *Music Dictionary.* Cambridge: Cambridge University Press, 1995.

Brockhaus Riemann Musik-Lexikon. 3rd ed. Ed. Carl Dahlhaus, Hans Heinrich Eggebrecht, and Kurt Oehl. 5 vols. Serie Musik Atlantis-Schott. Mainz: Atlantis Musikbuch-Verlag, 2001. First published in 1978.

Dictionary of Contemporary Music. Ed. John Vinton. New York: E. P. Dutton, 1974.

Dictionnaire de la musique en France aux XVIIe et XVIIIe siècles. Marcelle Benoit, gen. ed. Paris: Fayard, 1992.

Dictionnaire de la musique en France aux XIXe siècle. Joël-Marie Fauquet, gen. ed. Paris: Fayard, 2003.

Dizionario enciclopedico universale della musica e dei musicisti. Ed. Alberto Basso. 16 vols. Turin: Unione Tipografico-Editrice Torinese, 1983–99.

[Part 1, vols. 1–4.] *Il lessico.* 1983–84.
[Part 2, vols. 1–8.] *Le biografie.* 1985–88.

[Part 3, vols. 1–3.] *I titoli e i personaggi,* 1999. *Appendice.* 1990.

Enciclopedia della musica. New ed. Ed. Claudio Sartori. 4 vols. Milan: Ricordi, 1972–74. First published in 1963–64.

Enciclopedia della musica. Ed. Jean-Jacques Nattiez, Margaret Bent, Rossana Dalmonte, and Mario Baroni. Torino: G. Einaudi, 2001–.

Encyclopedia of Music in Canada. 2nd ed. Ed. Helmut Kallman et al. Toronto: University of Toronto Press, 1992. First published in 1981.

Encyclopedia of Music in the Twentieth Century. Ed. Lee Stacy and Lol Henderson. London: Fitzroy Dearborn Publishers, 1999.

Encyclopédie de la musique. Ed. Marc Honegger. 2 vols. Paris: Bordas, 1995–96.

Encyclopédie de la musique et dictionnaire du Conservatoire. Founded by Albert Lavignac. Ed. Lionel de La Laurencie. 11 vols. Paris: Delagrave, 1913–31.

Garland Encyclopedia of World Music. Bruno Nettl, advisory ed. James Porter and Timothy Rice, founding eds. 10 vols. New York: Garland (vols. 1–5 and 8–9) and Routledge (vols. 6–7, 10), 1998–2002.

1. *Africa.* Ed. Ruth M. Stone. 1998.
2. *South America, Mexico, Central America, and the Carib-bean.* Ed. Dale A. Olsen and Daniel E. Sheehy. 1998.
3. *The United States and Canada.* Ed. Ellen Koskoff. 2001.
4. *Southeast Asia.* Ed. Terry E. Miller and Sean Williams. 1998.
5. *South Asia: The Indian Subcontinent.* Ed. Alison Arnold. 2000.
6. *The Middle East.* Ed. Virginia Danielson, Scott Marcus, and Dwight Reynolds. 2002.
7. *East Asia: China, Japan, and Korea.* Ed. Robert C. Provine, Yosihiko Tokumaru, and J. Lawrence Witzleben. 2002.
8. *Europe.* Ed. Timothy Rice, James Porter, and Chris Goertzen. 2000.
9. *Australia and the Pacific Islands.* Ed. Adrienne L. Kaeppler and J. W. Love. 1998.
10. *The World's Music: General Perspectives and Refer-ence Tools.* Ed. Ruth Stone. 2002.

Griffiths, Paul. *The Thames and Hudson Encyclopaedia of 20th-Century Music.* London: Thames and Hudson, 1986.

Das grosse Lexikon der Musik. Ed. Marc Honegger and Günther Massenkeil. Translated into German from the original

French, and enl. 8 vols. Freiburg: Herder, 1978–82. First published in 1970–76.

The Hutchinson Dictionary of Classical Music. London: Brockhampton Press, 1994.

The Hutchinson Encyclopedia of Music. Ed. David Cummings and Tallis Barker. Oxford: Helicon, 1995.

The International Cyclopedia of Music and Musicians. Oscar Thompson, gen. ed. 11th ed. Ed. Bruce Bohle. New York: Dodd, Mead, 1985. First published in 1939.

Jablonski, Edward. *The Encyclopedia of American Music.* Garden City, N.Y.: Doubleday, 1981.

Jones, Barrie. *The Hutchinson Concise Dictionary of Music.* Chicago: Fitzroy Dearborn Publishers, 1999.

Kennedy, Michael. *The Concise Oxford Dictionary of Music.* 4th ed. Oxford: Oxford University Press, 1996. First published in 1980.

———. *The Oxford Dictionary of Music.* 2nd ed. London: Oxford University Press, 1994. First published in 1985.

Kostelanetz, Richard. *A Dictionary of the Avant-Gardes.* 2nd ed. New York: Routledge, 2001. First published in 1993.

Latham, Alison. *The Oxford Companion to Music.* Oxford: Oxford University Press, 2002.

Lebrecht, Norman. *The Companion to 20th-Century Music.* London: Simon & Schuster, 1992; reprint, New York: Da Capo Press, 1996.

Morehead, Philip D., with Anne MacNeal. *The New International Dictionary of Music.* New York: Penguin Books, 1992. First published in 1991 as *The New American Dictionary of Music.*

Die Musik in Geschichte und Gegenwart: Allgemeine Enzyklopädie der Musik. 2nd ed. Ed. Ludwig Finscher. Kassel: Bärenreiter, 1994–2004. First published in 1949–68.

[Part 1, 10 vols.] **Sachteil.** 1998–2004.
[Part 2, 17 vols.] **Personenteil.** 1998–2004.

The New Grove Dictionary of American Music. Ed. H. Wiley Hitchcock and Stanley Sadie. 4 vols. New York: Grove's Dictionaries of Music, 1986.

The New Grove Dictionary of Music and Musicians. 2nd ed. Ed. Stanley Sadie. 29 vols. London: Macmillan, 2001. First published in 1980.

The New Oxford Companion to Music. Reprint with corrections. Ed. Denis Arnold. 2 vols. Oxford: Oxford University Press, 1994. First published in 1983.

The Norton/Grove Concise Encyclopedia of Music. Ed. Stanley

Sadie. Rev. and enl. New York: W. W. Norton, 1994. First published in 1986.

Pickering, David. *Cassell Companion to 20th-Century Music.* Rev. and updated ed. London: Cassell, 1998. First published in 1994.

Random House Encyclopedic Dictionary of Classical Music. Ed. David Cummings. New York: Random House, 1997.

Roche, Jerome, and Elizabeth Roche. *A Dictionary of Early Music: From the Troubadours to Monteverdi.* London: Oxford University Press, 1981.

Westrup, Jack A., and Frank L. Harrison. *The New College Encyclopedia of Music.* Rev. ed. Ed. Conrad Wilson. New York: W. W. Norton, 1976. First published in 1959.

Of Historical Interest

Moore, John. *Complete Encyclopaedia of Music, Elementary, Technical, Historical, Biographical, Vocal and Instrumental.* New York: Sheldon, Lamport and Blakeman, 1854; reprint, New York: A.M.S. Press, 1973.

Walther, Johann Gottfried. *Musicalisches Lexicon oder musicalische Bibliothec.* Leipzig: Wolffgang Deer, 1732; study edition, ed. Friederike Ramm, Kassel: Bärenreiter, 2001.

BIOGRAPHICAL DICTIONARIES AND ENCYCLOPEDIAS

The first of the following lists, "International," includes the most comprehensive international dictionaries devoted exclusively to biographies of musicians: *Baker's Biographical Dictionary,* the recent *Baker's Biographical Dictionary of Twentieth-Century Classical Musicians,* and the expanded *International Who's Who in Music* volumes. The remaining sources are specialized biographical works, representative of many such sources that have some specific delimitation such as period (*Companion to Baroque Music*), style of music (the *Who's Who of Jazz* volumes), gender or race (*Women Composers and Songwriters, Komponistinnen von A-Z,* and *International Directory of Black Composers*), or type of musical figure (composer, performer, music educator, etc.).

The works in the next list, "North American," are fairly recent and each is slightly different in scope; under "English," although Poulton's work is the most recent, Pulver's work is given because it is still of value in researching pre-eighteenth-century English music.

The several sources listed under "Of Historical Interest" include two monuments of nineteenth-century single-author scholarship, Fétis and Eitner, neither completely out-of-date although their biographical portions are now largely superseded by more recent sources. The remaining works by Mattheson and Gerber represent the beginnings of purely biographical dictionaries in music, dating back to the mid- and late eighteenth century, respectively.

For further information, see chapter 2 under "Biographies of Musicians," pp. 42–43 above. See also the sections "Biographies of Composers in English," pp. 203–24, and "Series of Composers' Biographies in English," pp. 224–28, in chapter 5 below. (Other national biographical dictionaries, including American, are listed in Duckles, *Music Reference and Research Materials;* see p. 49 above.)

International

Baker's Biographical Dictionary of Musicians. Centennial ed. Ed. Nicolas Slonimsky and Laura Diane Kuhn. New York: Schirmer Books, 2001. First published in 1900.

Berry, Lemuel, Jr. *Biographical Dictionary of Black Musicians and Music Educators.* Vol. 1. N.p.: Educational Book Publishers, 1978.

Carlson, Effie B. *A Bio-Bibliographical Dictionary of Twelve-Tone and Serial Composers.* Metuchen, N.J.: Scarecrow Press, 1970.

Chilton, John. *Who's Who of Jazz: Storyville to Swing Street.* 4th ed. New York: Da Capo Press and London: Macmillan, 1985. First published in 1970.

Claghorn, Charles Eugene. *Biographical Dictionary of Jazz.* Englewood Cliffs, N.J.: Prentice Hall, 1982.

———. *Women Composers and Hymnists: A Concise Biographical Dictionary.* Metuchen, N.J.: Scarecrow Press, 1984.

———. *Women Composers and Songwriters: A Concise Biographical Dictionary.* London: Scarecrow Press, 1996.

Cohen, Aaron I. *International Encyclopedia of Women Composers.* 2nd ed., rev. and enl. 2 vols. New York: Books & Music, 1987. First published in 1981.

Companion to Baroque Music. Comp. and ed. Julie Anne Sadie. New York: Schirmer Books, 1990; reprint, New York: Oxford University Press, 1998.

Contemporary Composers. Ed. Brian Morton and Pamela Collins. Detroit: St. James Press, 1992.

Floyd, Samuel. *International Directory of Black Composers.* Chicago: Fitzroy Dearborn, 1999.

Grattan, Virginia L. *American Women Songwriters: A Biograph-*

ical Dictionary. Westport, Conn.: Greenwood Press, 1993.

Harvard Biographical Dictionary of Music. Ed. Don Michael Randel. Cambridge, Mass.: Belknap Press of Harvard University Press, 1996.

Harvard Concise Dictionary of Music and Musicians. Ed. Don Michael Randel. Cambridge, Mass.: Belknap Press of Harvard University Press, 1999.

International Who's Who in Classical Music 2003. 19th ed. New York: Routledge, 2003. First published in 1984.

International Who's Who in Music and Musicians' Directory. 17th ed. Cambridge, England: Melrose Press, 2000–2001. First published in 1935.

International Who's Who in Music. Volume 2: Popular Music. Ed. Sean Tyler. 3rd ed. Cambridge, England: Melrose Press, 2000–2001. First published in 1996–97.

Larkin, Colin. *The Guinness Who's Who of Jazz.* 2nd ed. Enfield, England: Guinness Publications, 1995. First published in 1992.

Latin American Classical Composers: A Bibliographical Dictionary. 2nd ed. Ed. Miguel Ficher, Martha Furman Schleifer, and John M. Furman. Lanham, Md.: Scarecrow Press, 2002. First published in 1996.

LePage, Jane Weiner. *Women Composers, Conductors, and Musicians of the Twentieth Century: Selected Biographies.* 3 vols. Metuchen, N.J.: Scarecrow Press, 1980–88.

Morris, Mark. *The Pimlico Dictionary of 20th-Century Composers.* London: Pimlico, 1999.

The Norton/Grove Dictionary of Women Composers. Ed. Julie Anne Sadie and Rhian Samuel. New York: W. W. Norton, 1995.

Olivier, Antje, and Karin Weingartz-Perschel. *Komponistinnen von A–Z.* Düsseldorf: Tokkata, 1988.

Sitsky, Larry. *Music of the Twentieth-Century Avant-Garde: A Biocritical Sourcebook.* Westport, Conn.: Greenwood Press, 2002.

Slonimsky, Nicolas. *Baker's Biographical Dictionary of Twentieth-Century Classical Musicians.* Ed. Laura Kuhn. Westport, Conn.: Greenwood Press, 2002.

Smith, Eric Ledell. *Blacks in Opera: An Encyclopedia of People and Companies 1873–1993.* Jefferson, N.C.: McFarland, 1995.

Southern, Eileen. *Biographical Dictionary of Afro-American and African Musicians.* The Greenwood Encyclopedia of Black Music. Westport, Conn.: Greenwood Press, 1982.

Stern, Susan. *Women Composers: A Handbook.* Metuchen, N.J.:
     Scarecrow Press, 1978.
Thompson, Clifford. *Contemporary World Musicians.* Chicago:
     Fitzroy Dearborn, 1999.
Thompson, Kenneth. *A Dictionary of Twentieth-Century Com-
     posers, 1911–1971.* London: Faber and Faber, 1973.
Who's Who in Black Music. Ed. Robert E. Rosenthal and Portia
     K. Maultsby. New Orleans: Edwards Printing, 1985.
*Who's Who in Opera: An International Biographical Dictionary
     of Singers, Conductors, Directors, Designers, and Adminis-
     trators, also Including Profiles of 101 Opera Companies.*
     Ed. Maria F. Rich. New York: Arno Press, 1976.

North American

American Society of Composers, Authors, and Publishers.
     ASCAP Biographical Dictionary. 4th ed. Compiled for
     the American Society of Composers, Authors, and Pub-
     lishers by Jaques Cattell Press. New York: R. R. Bowker,
     1980. First published in 1948.
Bomberger, E. Douglas. *Brainerd's Biographies of American
     Musicians.* Westport, Conn.: Greenwood Press, 1999.
Butterworth, Neil. *A Dictionary of American Composers.*
     Garland Reference Library of the Humanities, vol. 296.
     New York: Garland Publishing, 1984.
Claghorn, Charles Eugene. *Biographical Dictionary of American
     Music.* West Nyack, N.Y.: Parker Publishing, 1973.
Contemporary American Composers: A Biographical Dictionary.
     2nd ed. Comp. E. Ruth Anderson. Boston: G. K. Hall, 1982.
     First published in 1976.
Contemporary Canadian Composers. Ed. Keith MacMillan
     and John Beckwith. London: Oxford University Press,
     1975.
DuPree, Mary Herron. *Musical Americans: A Biographical
     Dictionary 1918–1926.* Berkeley: Fallen Leaf Press, 1997.
Ewen, David. *American Composers: A Biographical Dictionary.*
     New York: G. P. Putnam's Sons, 1982.
Who's Who in American Music: Classical. 2nd ed. Ed. Jaques
     Cattell Press. New York: R. R. Bowker, 1985. First pub-
     lished in 1983.

English

Poulton, Alan. *A Dictionary-Catalog of Modern British Com-
     posers.* 3 vols. Westport, Conn.: Greenwood Press, 2000.
Pulver, Jeffrey. *A Biographical Dictionary of Old English Music.*

Reprint, with an introduction by Gilbert Blount. New
York: Da Capo Press, 1973. First published in 1927.

Of Historical Interest

Eitner, Robert. *Biographisch-bibliographisches Quellen-Lexikon
der Musiker und Musikgelehrten christlicher Zeitrechnung
bis zur Mitte des neunzehnten Jahrhunderts.* 2nd ed.,
improved and enl. 11 vols. Graz: Akademische Druck-
und Verlagsanstalt, 1959. First published in 1898–1904.
Fétis, François-Joseph. *Biographie universelle des musiciens
et bibliographie générale de la musique.* 2nd ed. 8 vols.
Paris: Firmin-Didot, 1866–70. First published in 1835–44.
Gerber, Ernst Ludwig. *Historisch-biographisches Lexikon der
Tonkünstler, welches Nachrichten von dem Leben und
Werken musikalischer Schriftsteller, berühmter Compon-
isten, Sänger, usw. . . . enthält.* 2 vols. Leipzig: J. G. I.
Breitkopf, 1790–92.
————. *Neues historisch-biographisches Lexikon der Tonkün-
stler. . . .* 4 vols. Leipzig: A. Kühnel, 1812–14.
Mattheson, Johann. *Grundlage einer Ehren-Pforte, woran der
tüchtigsten Capellmeister, Componisten, Musikgelehrten,
Tonkünstler, usw., erscheinen sollen.* Rev. and enl. ed. Ed.
Max Schneider. Kassel: Bärenreiter, 1969. First published in
1740.

DICTIONARIES OF TERMS

In this list of dictionaries of musical terms—tempo markings,
forms, genres, even names of compositions, instruments, countries, etc., the diversity and quantity of terms varying from one
source to the next—the key word is variety. The most detailed and
elaborate is Eggebrecht's *Handwörterbuch,* still unfinished and
growing in its unique looseleaf format, to which additional pages
continue to be added (the projected completion date is 2005 with
a total of forty volumes). *The New Harvard Dictionary of Music* is
perhaps the most widely used one-volume general dictionary of
terms; Slonimsky's *Lectionary,* although similar in scope, bears the
unmistakable stamp of its author. Ammer's *A to Z,* equally recent,
gives definitions in English of terms from French, German, Italian, Latin, Portuguese, and Spanish musical scores, as well as pronunciation guides to Italian, German, and French. Boccagna's
Compendium contains a brief history of agogic terms and Italian,
German, and French equivalents of the most commonly used English musical terms. Schaal's *Abkürzungen* consists entirely of

abbreviations commonly used in music, emphasizing German terms.

The remaining items are all concerned with the equivalence of terms in various languages and thus include no definitions, except for an occasional one in the *Terminorum Musicae.* The works listed under "Individual Subject Areas" are each limited to a particular area, but in Levarie and Levy there is a lengthy essay addressing matters of musical form and structure that precedes the dictionary of terms concerning formal principles.

Under "Of Historical Interest" appear three very important older dictionaries of musical terms, those by Tinctoris (the first self-contained dictionary, which predates all others by centuries), Brossard (the model for all subsequent works of the type), and the celebrated Jean-Jacques Rousseau (whose initial efforts in this form appeared in Diderot's and d'Alembert's *Encyclopédie,* 1751–72).

Ammer, Christine. *The A to Z of Foreign Musical Terms from Adagio to Zierlich: A Dictionary for Performers and Students.* Boston: E. C. Schirmer, 1989. Rev. and exp. ed. of *Musician's Handbook of Foreign Terms,* 1971.

Boccagna, David L. *Musical Terminology: A Practical Compendium in Four Languages.* Stuyvesant, N.Y.: Pendragon Press, 1999.

Eggebrecht, Hans Heinrich, and Albrecht Riethmüller. *Handwörterbuch der musikalischen Terminologie.* 40 vols. projected. (35 vols. as of 2004.) Wiesbaden: Franz Steiner, 1972–.

Music Translation Dictionary: An English-Czech-Danish-Dutch-French-German-Hungarian-Italian-Polish-Portuguese-Russian-Spanish-Swedish Vocabulary of Music Terms. Comp. Carolyn Doub Grigg. Westport, Conn.: Greenwood Press, 1978.

The New Harvard Dictionary of Music. Ed. Don Michael Randel. 4th ed. Cambridge, Mass.: Belknap Press of Harvard University Press, 2003. First published in 1986.

Schaal, Richard. *Abkürzungen in der Musik-Terminologie: Eine Übersicht.* Taschenbücher zur Musikwissenschaft, vol. 1. Wilhelmshaven: Heinrichshofen's Verlag, 1969.

Slonimsky, Nicolas. *Lectionary of Music.* New York: McGraw-Hill, 1989.

Smith, W. J. *A Dictionary of Musical Terms in Four Languages.* London: Hutchinson, 1961.

Terminorum Musicae Index Septem Linguis Redactus: Polyglottes Wörterbuch der musikalischen Terminologie. Ed. Horst Leuchtmann et al. Kassel: Bärenreiter, 1978.

Wörterbuch Musik: Englisch-Deutsch, Deutsch-Englisch/ Dictionary of Terms in Music: English-German, German-

English. Ed. Horst Leuchtmann. 5th ed., enl. Stuttgart: J. B. Metzler, 1998. First published in 1964.

Individual Subject Areas

Carter, Henry Holland. *A Dictionary of Middle English Musical Terms.* Ed. George B. Gerhard. Indiana University Humanities Series, no. 45. Bloomington: Indiana University Press, 1961.

Cary, Tristram. *Dictionary of Musical Technology.* New York: Greenwood Press, 1992.

————. *Illustrated Compendium of Musical Technology.* Boston: Faber and Faber, 1992.

Dobson, Richard. *A Dictionary of Electronic and Computer Music Technology: Instruments, Terms, Techniques.* Oxford: Oxford University Press, 1992.

Enders, Bernd. *Lexikon Musik-Elektronik.* Rev. ed. Zurich: Atlantis Musikbuch-Verlag, 1997. First published in 1985.

Fink, Robert, and Robert Ricci. *The Language of Twentieth Century Music: A Dictionary of Terms.* New York: Schirmer Books, 1975.

Hinson, Maurice. *The Pianist's Dictionary.* Bloomington: Indiana University Press, 2004.

Kaufmann, Walter. *Selected Musical Terms of Non-Western Cultures: A Notebook-Glossary.* Warren, Mich.: Harmonie Park Press, 1990.

Lee, William F. *Music in the 21st Century: The New Language.* Miami: CPP/Belwin, 1994.

Levarie, Siegmund, and Ernst Levy. *Musical Morphology: A Discourse and a Dictionary.* Kent, Ohio: Kent State University Press, 1983.

Reid, Cornelius. *A Dictionary of Vocal Terminology: An Analysis.* New York: Joseph Patelson Music House, 1983; reprint, Huntsville, Tex.: Recital Publications, 1995.

Strahle, Graham. *An Early Music Dictionary: Musical Terms from British Sources, 1500–1740.* Cambridge: Cambridge University Press, 1995.

Tomlyn, Bo, and Steve Leonard. *Electronic Music Dictionary: A Glossary of the Specialized Terms Relating to the Music and Sound Technology of Today.* Milwaukee: Hall Leonard Books, 1988.

Of Historical Interest

Brossard, Sébastien de. *Dictionaire de musique, contenant une explication des termes grecs, latins, italiens & françois les*

plus usitez dans la musique. . . . 2nd ed. Paris: Christophe
Ballard, 1705. First published in 1703. English transla-
tions: (1) *Dictionary of Music*. . . . Trans. and ed. Albion
Gruber. Musical Theorists in Translation, vol. 12. Ottawa:
Institut de Musique Médiévale, 1982. (2) *A Musical Dic-
tionary*. . . . Trans. James Grassineau. Briston: Thoemmes
Press, 2003.

Rousseau, Jean-Jacques. *Dictionnaire de musique.* Paris: Duchesne,
1768. English trans.: *A Complete Dictionary of Music*. . . .
2nd ed. Trans. William Waring. London: J. Murray, 1779;
reprint, New York: AMS Press, 1975. First published in
1771.

Tinctoris, Johannes. *Terminorum Musicae Diffinitorium* [ca.
1494]; reprint, New York: Broude Brothers, 1966. English
trans.: *Dictionary of Musical Terms . . . Together with
the Latin Text.* Translated and annotated by Carl Parrish.
Da Capo Press Music Reprint Series. New York: Da Capo
Press, 1978.

SPECIALIZED DICTIONARIES,
ENCYCLOPEDIAS, AND GUIDES

Many music dictionaries and encyclopedias are organized
around a single subject or interest. Some of the most significant and
well known of these are listed here, divided into eleven groups according to whether they concern instruments, jazz, sacred music,
etc. The opera and dance sections reflect the recent growth of interest, both popular and scholarly, in those fields. Some include
terms only (e.g., Marcuse's *Musical Instruments*), some are exclusively biographical (e.g., Vannes's *Dictionnaire universel des luthiers*
[violin makers]), some combine the two (e.g., Julian's *Dictionary of
Hymnology* and the *New Grove Dictionary of Opera*), and some de-
part completely from the usual alphabetical arrangement in favor
of some other organization, but are encyclopedic in their treatment
of the subject (e.g., Michel's *Historical Pianos,* which is a kind of dictionary of pictures; Loewenberg's *Annals of Opera,* a chronological
list by date of first performance, with indexes; and the various companions and guides to individual instruments, which include essays on history and development, literature and repertoire, performance practice and technique, lists of instrument makers, and
glossaries of specific terms).

Under "Musical Themes and Compositional Devices" are dictionaries of musical themes by Barlow/Morgenstern, Burrows/
Redmond, and Parsons; Read's *Thesaurus,* a "lexicon of instrumentation"; Slonimsky's *Thesaurus of Scales* (almost one thousand of

them); and the first volume of LaRue's unfinished *Catalogue*, unique in listing the incipits in letter notation of 16,558 symphonies from ca. 1720 to ca. 1810. The "Miscellaneous Sources" section contains a sampling of other works in lexicon form, including dictionaries and encyclopedias of quotations and Slonimsky's *Lexicon of Musical Invective* (an anthology of negative reviews of music from Beethoven to Webern).

Musical Instruments and Makers

GENERAL

Baines, Anthony N. *The Oxford Companion to Musical Instruments.* New York: Oxford University Press, 1993. German version: *Lexikon der Musikinstrumente.* Kassel: Bärenreiter, 1996.

Bragard, Roger, and Ferdinand J. de Hen. *Musical Instruments in Art and History.* Trans. Bill Hopkins. New York: Viking Press, 1968. First published in 1967.

Groce, Nancy. *Musical Instrument Makers of New York: A Directory of Eighteenth-and Nineteenth-Century Urban Craftsmen.* Stuyvesant, N.Y.: Pendragon Press, 1991.

Hornbostel, Erich M. von, and Curt Sachs. "Classification of Musical Instruments." Trans. Anthony Baines and Klaus P. Wachsmann. *Galpin Society Journal,* no. 14 (March 1961): 2–19. First published in 1914.

Kartomi, Margaret J., et al. "Instruments, Classification of." In *The New Grove Dictionary of Music and Musicians.* 2nd ed. Vol. 12, pp. 418–28.

Marcuse, Sibyl. *Musical Instruments: A Comprehensive Dictionary.* Rev. ed. Garden City, N.Y.: Doubleday, 1975. First published in 1964.

Musical Instruments of the World: An Illustrated Encyclopedia. New York: Sterling Publishing Company, 1997. First published in 1976 by Facts on File Publications.

The New Grove Dictionary of Musical Instruments. Ed. Stanley Sadie. 3 vols. London: Macmillan, 1984. Reprint with minor corrections, London: Macmillan, 1997.

Sachs, Curt. *Handbuch der Musikinstrumentenkunde.* 5th ed. Kleine Handbücher der Musikgeschichte nach Gattungen, no. 12. Leipzig: Breitkopf & Härtel, 1977. First published in 1920.

————. *Real-Lexikon der Musikinstrumente, zugleich ein Polyglossar für das gesamte Instrumentengebiet.* (Rev. and enl. ed.) New York: Dover, 1964. First published in 1913.

Of Historical Interest

Mersenne, Marin. *Harmonie universelle: The Books on Instruments* [1636]. Trans. Roger E. Chapman. The Hague: Martinus Nijhoff, 1957.

Praetorius, Michael. *Syntagma Musicum II* [1618]*: De Organographia, Parts I and II.* Trans. and ed. David Z. Crookes. Early Music Series, no. 7. Oxford: Clarendon Press, 1986.

Strings

Bachman, Alberto. *An Encyclopedia of the Violin.* Ed. Albert E. Wier. Trans. Frederick H. Martens. New York: D. Appleton, 1925; reprint, New York: Da Capo Press, 1966.

Jalovec, Karel. *Encyclopedia of Violin-Makers.* Trans. J. B. Kozak. Ed. Patrick Hanks. 2 vols. London: Paul Hamlyn, 1968. First published in 1965.

Rensch, Roslyn. *Harps and Harpists.* Bloomington: Indiana University Press, 1989.

Stowell, Robin, ed. *The Cambridge Companion to the Cello.* Cambridge: Cambridge University Press, 1999.

Straeten, Edmund van der. *The History of the Violin, Its Ancestors, and Collateral Instruments from the Earliest Times to the Present Day.* London: Cassell, 1933; reprint, New York: Da Capo Press, 1968.

Vannes, René. *Dictionnaire universel des luthiers.* 3rd ed., rev. and enl. 2 vols. in 1. Brussels: Les Amis de la Musique, 1993. First published in 1932.

Winds

Burgess, Geoffrey, and Bruce Haynes. *The Oboe.* New Haven, Conn.: Yale University Press, 2003.

Griscom, Richard, and David Lasocki. *The Recorder: A Research and Information Guide.* 2nd ed. New York: Routledge, 2003. First published in 1994.

Herbert, Trevor, and John Wallace, eds. *The Cambridge Companion to Brass Instruments.* Cambridge: Cambridge University Press, 1997.

Ingham, Richard, ed. *The Cambridge Companion to the Saxophone.* Cambridge: Cambridge University Press, 1999.

The New Langwill Index: A Dictionary of Musical Wind-Instrument Makers and Inventors. Ed. William Waterhouse. London: Tony Bingham, 1993.

Powell, Ardal. *The Flute.* New Haven, Conn.: Yale University
    Press, 2002.

PERCUSSION

Encyclopedia of Percussion. Ed. John H. Beck. Garland Refer-
    ence Library of the Humanities, vol. 947. New York:
    Garland Publishing, 1995.
Holland, James. *Practical Percussion: A Guide to the Instru-
    ments and Their Sources.* Lanham, Md.: Scarecrow Press,
    2003.
Montagu, Jeremy. *Timpani and Percussion.* New Haven, Conn.:
    Yale University Press, 2002.
*The Percussionists's Dictionary: Translations, Descriptions
    and Photographs of Percussion Instruments from around
    the World.* Comp. and ed. Joseph Adato and George Judy.
    Miami: Belwin Mills, 1984.

KEYBOARD

Brauchli, Bernard. *The Clavichord.* Cambridge: Cambridge
    University Press, 1998.
Encyclopedia of Keyboard Instruments. 2nd ed. Ed. Robert
    Palmieri. 3 vols. New York: Routledge, 2003. First pub-
    lished in 1994.

> 1. *The Piano.* Ed. Robert Palmieri and Margaret W.
>   Palmieri.
> 2. *The Harpsichord and Clavichord.* Ed. Igor Kipnis
>   and Robert Zappulla.
> 3. *The Organ.* Ed. Douglas E. Bush.

Hinson, Maurice. *The Pianist's Dictionary.* Bloomington:
    Indiana University Press, 2004.
Irwin, Stevens. *Dictionary of Pipe Organ Stops.* 2nd ed. New
    York: Schirmer Books, 1983. First published in 1962.
Michel, Norman Elwood. *Historical Pianos, Harpsichords and
    Clavichords.* Pico Rivera, Calif.: By the author, 1963.
Rowland, David, ed. *The Cambridge Companion to the Piano.*
    Cambridge: Cambridge University Press, 1999.
Russell, Raymond. *The Harpsichord and Clavichord: An Intro-
    ductory Study.* 2nd ed. Rev. Howard Schott. New York:
    Norton, 1973. First published in 1959.
Thistlethwaite, Nicholas, and Geoffrey Webber, eds. *The Cam-
    bridge Companion to the Organ.* Cambridge: Cambridge
    University Press, 1999.

Dramatic Music

Adam, Nicky. *Who's Who in British Opera.* Aldershot: Ashgate Press, 1993.

Anderson, James, and Nick Kimberly. *Dictionary of Opera.* 3rd ed. London: Bloomsbury, 1998. First published in 1995 as *Dictionary of Opera and Operetta.*

Batta, András, and Sigrid Neef. *Opera: Composers, Works, Performers.* Cologne: Könemann, 2000.

Bloomsbury Dictionary of Opera and Operetta. Ed. James Anderson. London: Bloomsbury, 1992.

Der Brockhaus Oper: Werke, Personen, Sachbegriffe. Ed. Marianna Strzysch-Siebeck and Jan Brachmann. Mannhein: F. A. Brockhaus, 2003.

Dictionary-Catalogue of Operas and Operettas Which Have Been Performed on the Public Stage. Comp. John Towers. 2 vols. Morgantown, W.Va.: Acme Publishing, 1910; reprint, New York: Da Capo Press, 1967.

The Encyclopedia of Opera. Ed. Leslie Orrey. New York: Charles Scribner's Sons, 1976.

Everett, William. *The Musical: A Research Guide to Musical Theater and Film.* New York: Routledge, 2004.

Ewen, David. *The New Encyclopedia of the Opera.* New York: Hill and Wang, 1971. First published in 1955 as *Encyclopedia of the Opera.*

Griffel, Margaret Ross, and Adrienne Fried Block. *Operas in English: A Dictionary.* Westport, Conn.: Greenwood Press, 1999.

International Dictionary of Opera. Ed. C. Steven LaRue. 2 vols. Detroit: St. James Press, 1993.

Kuhn, Laura. *Baker's Dictionary of Opera.* New York: Schirmer Books, 2000.

The La Scala Encyclopedia of Opera. Ed. Giorgio Bagnoli. New York: Simon and Schuster, 1993.

Loewenberg, Alfred. *Annals of Opera, 1597–1940, Compiled from the Original Sources.* 3rd ed., rev. and corrected. Totowa, N.J.: Rowman and Littlefield, 1978. First published in 1943.

Marco, Guy A. *Opera: A Research and Information Guide.* 2nd ed. New York: Routledge, 2000. First published in 1984.

Martin, Nicholas Ivor. *The Da Capo Opera Manual.* New York: Da Capo Press, 1997.

Moore, Frank L. *Crowell's Handbook of World Opera.* New York: Thomas Y. Crowell, 1961; reprint, Westport, Conn.: Greenwood Press, 1974.

The New Grove Book of Operas. Ed. Stanley Sadie. New York: St. Martin's Press, 2000.

The New Grove Dictionary of Opera. Ed. Stanley Sadie. 4 vols. London: Macmillan, 1992.

The New Penguin Opera Guide. Ed. Amanda Holden. London: Penguin, 2001.

Opera: The Rough Guide. 2nd ed., exp. and completely rev. Ed. Matthew Boyden, et al. New York: Rough Guides, 1999.

Osborne, Charles. *The Dictionary of the Opera.* Rev. and updated ed. New York: Welcome Rain Publishers, 2001. First published in 1983.

Parsons, Charles H. *The Mellen Opera Reference Index.* 26 vols. projected. Lewiston, N.Y.: Edwin Mellen Press, 1986–.

> 1–4. *Opera Composers and Their Works.* 1986–87.
> 5–6. *Opera Librettists and Their Works.* 1990.
> 7–8. *Opera Premieres: A Geographical Index.* 1990.
> 9. *Opera Subjects.* 1990.
> 10–12. *An Opera Discography.* 1990.
> 13–14. *Opera Premieres.* 1992.
> 15–16. *Opera Premieres: An Index of Casts/Performers.* 1993.
> 17–18. *An Opera Bibliography.* 1996.
> 19A–19B. *Opera Premiere Reviews and Reassessments.* 1997–2002.
> 20. *An Opera Videography.* 1997.
> 21A–21C. *Printed Editions of Opera Scores in American Libraries.* 1998.
> 22A–22D. *Recent International Opera Discography.* 2003.

Pipers Enzyklopädie des Musiktheaters: Oper, Operette, Musical, Ballet. Ed. Carl Dahlhaus and Sieghart Döhring. 7 vols. Munich: Piper, 1986–97.

Rosenthal, Harold, and John Warrack. *The Concise Oxford Dictionary of Opera.* 3rd ed. New York: Oxford University Press, 1996. First published in 1964.

Schmierer, Elisabeth. *Lexikon der Oper: Komponisten, Werke, Interpreten, Sachbegriffe.* Laaber: Laaber Verlag, 2002.

Smith, Eric Ledell. *Blacks in Opera: An Encyclopedia of People and Companies, 1873–1993.* Jefferson, N.C.: McFarland, 1995.

Stieger, Franz. *Opernlexikon/Opera Catalogue/Lexique des opéras/Dizionario operistico.* 4 parts in 11 vols. Tutzing: Hans Schneider, 1975–83.

The Viking Opera Guide. Ed. Amanda Holden et al. London: Viking/Penguin Books, 1993.

Wagner, Heinz. *Das grosse Operettenbuch: 120 Komponisten und 430 Werke.* Berlin: Parthas, 1997.

Warrack, John, and Ewan West. *The Oxford Dictionary of Opera.* New York: Oxford University Press, 1992.

White, Michael, and Elaine Henderson. *Opera and Operetta.* Glasgow: HarperCollins, 1997.

The Wordsworth A-Z of Opera. Ed. Mary Hamilton. Ware, England: Wordsworth, 1996.

Sacred Music

Davidson, James Robert. *A Dictionary of Protestant Church Music.* Metuchen, N.J.: Scarecrow Press, 1975.

Encylopédie des musiques sacrées. Ed. Jacques Porte. 3 vols. and 16 phonodiscs. Paris: Editions Labergerie, 1968–70.

Julian, John. *A Dictionary of Hymnology, Setting Forth the Origin and History of Christian Hymns of All Ages and Nations.* Rev. ed., with new suppl. 2 vols. London: J. Murray, 1907; reprint, Grand Rapids, Mich.: Kregel Publications, 1985. First published in 1892.

Nulman, Macy. *Concise Encyclopedia of Jewish Music.* New York: McGraw-Hill, 1975.

Poultney, David. *Dictionary of Western Church Music.* Chicago: American Library Association, 1991.

Schneider, Tina M. *Hymnal Collections of North America.* Studies in Liturgical Musicology, no. 10. Lanham, Md.: Scarecrow Press, 2003.

Wasson, D. DeWitt, comp. *Hymntune Index and Related Hymn Materials.* Studies in Liturgical Musicology, no. 6. Lanham, Md.: Scarecrow Press, 1998. Also available on CD-ROM.

Zahn, Johannes. *Die Melodien der deutschen evangelischen Kirchenlieder aus den Quellen geschöpft und mitgeteilt. . . .* 6 vols. Gütersloh, Germany: C. Bertelsmann, 1889–93; reprint, Hildesheim: G. Olms, 1997.

Jazz and Popular Music

Carr, Ian, et al. *Jazz: The Rough Guide.* 2nd ed., exp. and completely rev. New York: Rough Guides, 2000. First published in 1995.

Feather, Leonard G., and Ira Gitler. *The Biographical Encyclopedia of Jazz.* Oxford: Oxford University Press, 1999.

Gold, Robert S. *Jazz Talk.* Indianapolis: Bobbs-Merrill, 1975; reprint, New York: Da Capo Press, 1982.

Kinkle, Roger D. *Leading Musical Performers (Popular Music* and Jazz) *1900–1950: 2150 Biographies Updated to 1996 with Additions and Corrections.* Mt. Vernon, Ill.: Windmill Publications, 1999.

Larkin, Colin. *The Guinness Who's Who of Jazz.* 2nd ed. Enfield: Guinness Publications, 1995. First published in 1992.

Miller, Mark. *The Miller Companion to Jazz in Canada and Canadians in Jazz.* Toronto: Mercury Press, 2003.

The New Grove Dictionary of Jazz. 2nd ed. Ed. Barry Kernfeld. 3 vols. London: Macmillan, 2002. First published in 1988.

Dance

The Concise Oxford Dictionary of Ballet. 2nd ed. Comp. Horst Koegler. London: Oxford University Press, 1982. First published in 1977.

Craine, Debra, and Judith Mackrell. *The Oxford Dictionary of Dance.* Oxford: Oxford University Press, 2000.

International Dictionary of Ballet. Ed. Martha Bremser. 2 vols. Detroit: St. James Press, 1992.

International Encyclopedia of Dance. 6 vols. Oxford: Oxford University Press, 1998.

Kersley, Leo, and Janet Sinclair. *A Dictionary of Ballet Terms.* 4th ed. London: A. & C. Black, 1997. First published in 1953.

Macpherson, Susan. *Dictionary of Dance: Words, Terms and Phrases.* Toronto: Dance Collection Danse Press, 1996.

Pitou, Spire. *The Paris Opéra: An Encyclopedia of Operas, Ballets, Composers, and Performers.* 3 vols. Westport, Conn.: Greenwood Press, 1983.

Musical Themes and Compositional Devices

Barlow, Harold, and Sam Morgenstern. *A Dictionary of Musical Themes.* Rev. ed. New York: Crown Publishers, 1975. First published in 1948.

———. *A Dictionary of Opera and Song Themes, Including Cantatas, Oratorios, Lieder and Art Songs.* Rev. ed. New York: Crown Publishers, 1976. First published in 1950.

Burrows, Raymond M., and Bessie C. Redmond. *Concerto Themes.* New York: Simon and Schuster, 1951.

———. *Symphony Themes.* New York: Simon and Schuster, 1942.

LaRue, Jan. *A Catalogue of 18th-Century Symphonies.* 3 vols. projected. Vol. 1: Thematic Identifier. Bloomington: Indiana University Press, 1988.

Parsons, Denys. *The Directory of Tunes and Musical Themes.* Cambridge, England: Spencer Brown, 1975.

Read, Gardner. *Thesaurus of Orchestral Devices.* New York:
    Pitman, 1953; reprint, New York: Greenwood Press, 1969.
Slonimsky, Nicolas. *Thesaurus of Scales and Melodic Patterns.*
    New York: Coleman-Ross, 1947; reprint, New York:
    Coleman-Ross Company, 1993.

Miscellaneous Sources

A Dictionary of Musical Quotations. Comp. Ian Crofton and
    Donald Fraser. 1st American ed. New York: Schirmer
    Books, 1985.
Encyclopedia of National Anthems. Comp. Xing Hang. Lanham,
    Md.: Scarecrow Press, 2003.
An Encyclopedia of Quotations about Music. Comp. and ed.
    Nat Shapiro. Garden City, N.Y.: Doubleday, 1978; reprint,
    New York: Da Capo Press, 1981.
Kelly, Michael, ed. *Encyclopedia of Aesthetics.* 4 vols. Oxford:
    Oxford University Press, 1998.
Kibler, William W., ed. *Medieval France: An Encyclopedia.*
    Garland Reference Library of the Humanities, vol. 932.
    Garland Encyclopedias of the Middle Ages, vol. 2. New
    York: Garland Publishing, 1995.
Reid, Jane Davidson, assisted by Chris Rohmann. *The Oxford
    Guide to Classical Mythology in the Arts, 1300–1990s.*
    2 vols. New York: Oxford University Press, 1993.
Room, Adrian. *A Dictionary of Music Titles: The Origins of the
    Names and Titles of 3,500 Musical Compositions.* London:
    McFarland and Company, 2000.
Slonimsky, Nicolas. *Lexicon of Musical Invective: Critical
    Assaults on Composers since Beethoven's Time.* Seattle:
    University of Washington Press, 1953; reprint, New York:
    W. W. Norton, 2000.
Watson, Derek. *The Wordsworth Dictionary of Musical Quota-
    tions.* Edinburgh: W. & R. Chambers, 1991.

THE NEW HARVARD DICTIONARY OF MUSIC:
ARTICLES OF GENERAL INTEREST

Many of the music dictionaries and encyclopedias listed in the
present chapter can be useful in researching almost any topic.
Among these, *The New Harvard Dictionary of Music* may well be
the one most often found in personal libraries. As a practical guide
it, or similar sources, can introduce, organize, summarize, and provide an initial bibliography for various areas of study, such as
courses, term papers, and examinations. Many entries in such

sources, however, might be overlooked. Examples from *The New Harvard Dictionary* are listed below, with related terms grouped together.

Research in Music

Aesthetics
Authenticity
Autograph; Sketch
Bibliography
Computers, Musical Applications of
Dictionaries and Encyclopedias
Editions, Historical
Festschrift
Iconography of Music
Libraries
Liturgical Books
Musicology; Ethnomusicology
Notation; Paleography; Textual Criticism; Transcription;
        Transmission; Watermark
Organology
Periodicals
Printing of Music
Publishing of Music
Societies, Musical; Academy; Collegium Musicum
Sociology of Music
Sources (Pre-1500)

Music History, Style Periods, and Trends

History of Music
Ars Antiqua, Ars Vetus; Ars Nova; Mannerism
Middle Ages, Music of the; Renaissance, Music of the; Baroque;
        Rococo; Classical; Romantic
Galant Style; Empfindsam Style
Nationalism; Verismo; Impressionism; Expressionism
Aleatory Music; Neoclassical; Twelve-Tone Music
Twentieth Century, Western Art Music of the

Countries, Cities, and Musical Centers

Berlin School; Bologna School; Mannheim School; Neapolitan
        School; Venetian School; New German School; Viennese
        Classical School; Viennese School, Second
Canada; England; France; Germany; Italy; Netherlands; Spain;
        Union of Soviet Socialist Republics; United States; etc.
East Asia; South Asia; Southeast Asia; Latin America; Near and
        Middle East; Africa; Oceania and Australia

General Music Theory

Acoustics
Analysis; Harmonic Analysis
Composition
Counterpoint; Invertible Counterpoint
Harmonics
Interval
Isorhythm
Key; Mode
Melody; Harmony; Rhythm; Form; Texture
Modes, Rhythmic
Modulation
Orchestration; Instrumentation
Pitch; Pitch Class; Pitch Names
Polyphony; Homophony
Scale
Schenker Analysis
Serial Music
Solfège; Solmization
Twelve-Tone Music

Musical Forms and Genres

Bar Form; Formes fixes; Rondeau; Ballata; Caccia; etc.
Dance; Ballet; Basse danse; Gagliarda; Minuet; Polonaise; etc.
Folk Music; Jazz; Blues; etc.
Fugue; Double Fugue; Fuging Tune; Canon
Estampie; Canzona; Ricercar; Concerto; Concerto grosso;
       Program Music; Rondo; Symphony; Suite; Sonata;
       Toccata; etc.
Mass; Motet; Madrigal; Chanson; Opera; Cantata; Oratorio; Pas-
       sion; Seven (Last) Words, The; Lied; Song; Song Cycle; etc.

Performance and Performance Practice

Affections (Affects), Doctrine of; Rhetoric
Chamber Music; Chamber Orchestra; String Quartet
Choirbook; Partbook; Chansonnier
Chorus; Choral Music; Schola (Cantorum)
Church Music; Chapel; Kapelle; Capella
Concert; Concert Hall
Conducting; Ensemble; Consort; Kantor; Kantorei
Copyright and Performance Right
Expression; Performance Marks
Fingering
Gregorian Chant; Liturgy
Interpretation; Phrasing; Style

Musica Ficta
Notation; Mensural Notation
Orchestra; Instrument (also see under individual instruments);
      Bowing; etc.
Ornamentation (also see under individual ornaments); Improvi-
      sation; Extemporization
Performance Practice
Piano; Organ; Harpsichord; etc.
Proportion
Psalmody, British and North American
Score; Tablature
Sight-Reading
Singing; Voice; Cantor
Temperament
Tempo; Tempus
Text and Music; Libretto
Thoroughbass; Figured Bass

The Music Profession

Conservatory
Criticism
Education in the United States; Music Appreciation
Music Therapy
Psychology of Music
Radio and Television Broadcasting
Recording

CHAPTER FIVE

Sources Treating
the History of Music

The present chapter classifies many of the myriad sources in the field of music history into eleven lists with varying degrees of selectivity and a distinct emphasis on sources in English. "Historical Surveys of Western Music" is one of the most selective, with only thirteen coverages of Western music in English—most quite recent and intended as course texts—followed by three of the most prominent older sources and some miscellaneous ones. "Histories in Series" lists the contents of the eight most recent series of books on periods of music history, followed by the titles of three of the most important earlier twentieth-century series.

Next are found selective lists of "Studies in English of Individual Historical Periods," "Histories of American Music," "English-Language Sources on Musical Genres and Forms," and "Chronologies and Outlines" of music history.

"Biographies of Composers in English," the longest bibliography in the chapter, is highly selective—only a representative selection of works on prominent composers has been included; next are listed the contents of three of the most important "Series of Composers' Biographies in English."

The final lists are of the major "Collections of Excerpts from Primary Sources on Music," "Histories of Musical Instruments," and significant "Pictorial Sources on Music History."

HISTORICAL SURVEYS OF WESTERN MUSIC

The oldest of these modern single-volume histories of music in English is Lang's staple, *Music in Western Civilization*, published in 1941; the most recent are Bonds's and Seaton's generalized histories and Pendle's history of women in music.

Under "Miscellaneous Sources" are five special works: *The Garland Library* (plus Basart's index to the series) and Hays's *Twentieth-Century Views*, both anthologies of reprinted significant English-language articles and excerpts arranged in chronological order (the former also includes volumes devoted to opera and to music criticism and analysis); Bowers and Tick's collection of essays on women in music, in chronological order; Poultney's *Studying Music History*, which is more of a study guide to the subject; and Raynor's specialized approach. Finally, Burney, Forkel, and Hawkins, listed under "Of Historical Interest," are three of the most important early histories.

For historical perspective on published histories, see Eggebrecht's *New Grove* article, "Historiography," and Allen's *Philosophies of Music* (see pp. 76–77 above); an exhaustive chronological list of music histories from Calvisius (1600) to Schering (1931) may be seen on pp. 343–65 in the latter source.

Abraham, Gerald. *The Concise Oxford History of Music.* London: Oxford University Press, 1979.

Bonds, Mark Evan. *A History of Music in Western Culture.* Upper Saddle River, N.J.: Prentice Hall, 2003.

Borroff, Edith. *Music in Europe and the United States: A History.* 2nd ed. New York: Ardsley House, 1990. First published in 1971.

Crocker, Richard L. *A History of Musical Style.* New York: McGraw-Hill, 1966; reprinted and slightly corrected, New York: Dover, 1986.

Fuller, Sarah. *The European Musical Heritage 800–1750.* New York: McGraw Hill, 1986; reprint, New York: McGraw-Hill, 1993.

Grout, Donald Jay, and Claude V. Palisca. *A History of Western Music.* 6th ed. New York: W. W. Norton, 2001. First published in 1960.

Harman, Alec, Wilfrid Mellers, and Anthony Miller. *Man and His Music: The Story of Musical Experience in the West.* Rev. ed. London: Barrie & Jenkins, 1988. First published in 1962.

Lang, Paul Henry. *Music in Western Civilization.* New York: W. W. Norton, 1941; reprint, New York: W. W. Norton, 1997.

Olivier, Antje, and Sevgi Braun. *Komponistinnen aus 800 Jahren.* Kamen, Germany: Sequentia, 1996.

Pendle, Karin, ed. *Women and Music: A History.* 2nd ed. Bloomington: Indiana University Press, 2001. First published in 1991.

Schirmer History of Music. Léonie Rosenstiel, gen. ed. New York: Schirmer Books, 1982.

Seaton, Douglass. *Ideas and Styles in the Western Musical Tradition.* 2nd ed. New York: McGraw-Hill, 2005. First published in 1991.

Stolba, K. Marie. *The Development of Western Music: A History.* 3rd ed. Dubuque, Iowa: William C. Brown Publishers, 1998. First published in 1990.

Ulrich, Homer, and Paul Pisk. *A History of Music and Musical Style.* New York: Harcourt, Brace & World, 1963.

Miscellaneous Sources

Bowers, Jane, and Judith Tick, eds. *Women Making Music: The Western Art Tradition, 1150–1950.* Urbana: University of Illinois Press, 1986.

The Garland Library of the History of Western Music. Ellen Rosand, gen. ed. 14 vols. New York: Garland Publishing, 1985.

    1. *Medieval Music: Monophony.*

    2. *Medieval Music: Polyphony.*

    3. *Renaissance Music: 15th Century.*

    4. *Renaissance Music: 16th Century.*

    5. *Baroque Music: 17th Century.*

    6. *Baroque Music: 18th Century.*

    7. *Classic Music.*

    8. *Eighteenth- and Nineteenth-Century Source Studies.*

    9. *Nineteenth-Century Music.*

    10. *Twentieth-Century Music.*

    11. *Opera: Up to Mozart.*

    12. *Opera: Mozart and After.*

    13. *Criticism and Analysis.*

    14. *Approaches to Tonal Analysis.*

Basart, Ann Phillips. *The Garland Library of the History of Western Music: An Index.* Berkeley: Cum Notis Variorum, 1987.

Hays, William, ed. *Twentieth-Century Views of Music History.* New York: Charles Scribner's Sons, 1972.

Poultney, David. *Studying Music History: Learning, Reasoning, and Writing about Music History and Literature.* 2nd ed. Upper Saddle River, N.J.: Prentice Hall, 1996. First published in 1983.

Raynor, Henry. *A Social History of Music from the Middle Ages to Beethoven/Music and Society since 1815.* 2 vols. in one. New York: Taplinger Publishing, 1978. First published as single volumes in 1972 and 1976, respectively.

Of Historical Interest

Burney, Charles. *A General History of Music, from the Earliest Ages to the Present Period* [1776–89]. Ed. Frank Mercer. 4 vols. in 2. London: G. T. Foulis, 1935; reprint, New York: Dover Publications, 1957.

Forkel, Johann Nikolaus. *Allgemeine Geschichte der Musik.* . . . 2 vols. Leipzig: Schwikertschen Verlag, 1788–1801; reprint: Graz, Austria, Akademische Druck und Verlagsanstalt, 1967.

Hawkins, Sir John. *A General History of the Science and Practice of Music* [1776], with a new introduction by Charles Cudworth. 2 vols. American Musicological Society, Music Library Association Reprint Series. New York: Dover Publications, 1963.

HISTORIES IN SERIES

This bibliography lists the most important recent multivolume histories of music (two of which, the Neues Handbuch der Musikwissenschaft and The Prentice Hall History of Music Series, also include volumes organized in some other way—by country, for example; The Universe of Music is unique in being organized exclusively by major geographical region). Of special value in such histories is the bringing together of the contributions of various specialists in different fields, although sometimes the result is criticized for lacking a totally unified approach.

The three oldest series are The Norton History of Music Series, The New Oxford History of Music, and The Prentice Hall History of Music Series, but only the New Oxford History appears to be complete, and Prentice Hall continues to bring out revised versions or replacements of its original volumes. The remaining series were begun more recently and are now complete (although some volumes of the Storia della musica have not yet been published in English translations). The Oxford History of Western Music will in all likelihood supersede the New Oxford History of Music series.

Under "Of Historical Interest" are the titles of three major earlier series. Ambros's monumental work was not conceived as a multivolume set to be written in collaboration with other authors, like the other sources listed here, but it is virtually that because of its period-by-period breakdown into volumes and its having been completed and/or revised by others. Bücken's Handbuch der Musikwissenschaft series is historically important, but it has been superseded by the Neues Handbuch series. The Kleine Handbücher series is different from the others in that it is organized by subject rather than by period, e.g., histories of the oratorio, of the cantata, of conducting; some volumes are still quite useful while others are outdated.

Heritage of Music Series. Michael Raeburn and Alan Kendall, gen. eds. 4 vols. Oxford: Oxford University Press, 1989.

> 1. *Classical Music and Its Origins.* Ed. Roger Blanchard, Denis Arnold, and H. C. Robbins Landon.
> 2. *The Romantic Era.* Ed. Denis Matthews, Ludwig Finscher, and Robert Donington.
> 3. *The Nineteenth-Century Legacy.* Ed. Martin Cooper and Heinz Becker.
> 4. *Music in the Twentieth Century.* Ed. Felix Aprahamian and Wilfrid Mellers.

Music and Society Series. Stanley Sadie, gen. ed. 8 vols. Englewood Cliffs, N.J.: Prentice Hall, 1989–94.

> *Antiquity and the Middle Ages: From Ancient Greece to the 15th Century.* Ed. James W. McKinnon. 1st North American ed. 1991. First published in 1990.
> *The Renaissance: From the 1470s to the End of the 16th Century.* Ed. Iain Fenlon. 1st North American ed. 1989.
> *The Early Baroque Era: From the Late 16th Century to the 1660s.* Ed. Curtis Price. 1st North American ed. 1994. First published in 1993.
> *The Late Baroque Era: From the 1680s to 1740.* Ed. George J. Buelow. 1st North American ed. 1994. First published in 1993.
> *The Classical Era: From the 1740s to the End of the 18th Century.* Ed. Neal Zaslaw. 1st North American ed. 1989.
> *The Early Romantic Era: Between Revolutions: 1789 and 1848.* Ed. Alexander Ringer. 1st North American ed. 1991. First published in 1990.
> *The Late Romantic Era: From the Mid-19th Century to World War I.* Ed. Jim Samson. 1st North American ed. 1991.
> *Modern Times: From World War I to the Present.* Ed. Robert P. Morgan. 1st North American ed. 1994. First published in 1993.

Neues Handbuch der Musikwissenschaft. Carl Dahlhaus, gen. ed. 12 vols. Laaber, Germany: Laaber-Verlag, 1980–92; special ed., 1996–97.

1. *Die Musik des Altertums.* Ed. Albrecht Riethmüller
and Frieder Zaminer, in collaboration with Ellen
Hickmann. 1989; special ed., 1996.
2. *Die Musik des Mittelalters.* Ed. Hartmut Möller and
Rudolf Stephan. 1991; special ed., 1996.
3. *Die Musik des 15. und 16. Jahrhunderts.* Ed. Ludwig
Finscher et al. 2 vols. 1989–90; special ed., 1996.
4. *Die Musik des 17. Jahrhunderts.* By Werner Braun. 1981;
special ed., 1996.
5. *Die Musik des 18. Jahrhunderts.* Ed. Carl Dahlhaus.
1985; special ed., 1996.
6. *Die Musik des 19. Jahrhunderts.* By Carl Dahlhaus.
1980; special ed., 1996. Trans. J. Bradford Robinson:
Nineteenth-Century Music. California Studies
in Nineteenth-Century Music, vol. 5. Berkeley:
University of California Press, 1989.
7. *Die Musik des 20. Jahrhunderts.* By Hermann Danuser.
1984; special ed., 1996.
8. *Aussereuropäische Musik. (Teil 1.)* By Hans Oesch et al.
1984; special ed., 1997.
9. *Aussereuropäische Musik. (Teil 2.)* By Hans Oesch et al.
1987; special ed., 1997.
10. *Systematische Musikwissenschaft.* Ed. Carl Dahlhaus
and Helga de la Motte-Haber. 1982; special ed., 1997.
11. *Musikalische Interpretation.* 1992; special ed., 1997.
12. *Volks-und Popularmusik in Europa.* Ed. Doris Stock-
mann et al. 1992; special ed., 1997.

The New Oxford History of Music. 10 vols. London: Oxford
University Press, 1954–90.

1. *Ancient and Oriental Music.* Ed. Egon Wellesz. 1957.
2. *The Early Middle Ages to 1300.* 2nd ed. Ed. Richard
Crocker and David Hiley. 1990. First published
in 1954.
3. *Ars Nova and the Renaissance, 1300–1450.* Ed. Anselm
Hughes and Gerald Abraham. Reprint with corrections, 1986. First published in 1960.
4. *The Age of Humanism, 1540–1630.* Ed. Gerald Abraham.
1968.
5. *Opera and Church Music, 1630–1750.* Ed. Anthony
Lewis and Nigel Fortune. 1975.
6. *Concert Music, 1630–1750.* Ed. Gerald Abraham. 1986.
7. *The Age of Enlightenment, 1745–1790.* Ed. Egon Wellesz
and Frederick Sternfeld. 1973.
8. *The Age of Beethoven, 1790–1830.* Ed. Gerald Abraham.
1982.

    9. *Romanticism, 1830–1890.* Ed. Gerald Abraham. 1990.
   10. *The Modern Age, 1890–1960.* Ed. Martin Cooper. 1974.

The Norton History of Music Series. New York: W. W. Norton, 1940–66. (The Classical era volume was never published.)

> *The Rise of Music in the Ancient World.* By Curt Sachs. 1943.
> *Music in the Middle Ages.* By Gustave Reese. 1940.
> *Music in the Renaissance.* By Gustave Reese. Rev. ed. 1959. First published in 1954.
> *Music in the Baroque Era, from Monteverdi to Bach.* By Manfred Bukofzer. 1947.
> *Music in the Romantic Era.* By Alfred Einstein. 1947.
> *Music in the 20th Century.* By William W. Austin. 1966.

The Norton Introduction to Music History Series. Paul Henry Lang, gen. ed. 6 vols. New York: W. W. Norton, 1978–2004.

> *Medieval Music.* By Richard H. Hoppin. 1978.
> *Renaissance Music: Music in Western Europe, 1400–1600.* By Allan W. Atlas. 1998.
> *Baroque Music.* By John Walter Hill. 2004.
> *Classical Music: The Era of Haydn, Mozart, and Beethoven.* By Philip G. Downs. 1992.
> *Romantic Music.* By Leon Plantinga. 1985.
> *Twentieth-Century Music: A History of Musical Style in Modern Europe and America.* By Robert P. Morgan. 1991.

The Oxford History of Western Music. 6 vols. Richard Taruskin, ed. Oxford: Oxford University Press, 2005.

> 1. *Origins to the Sixteenth Century.*
> 2. *The Seventeenth and Eighteenth Centuries.*
> 3. *The Nineteenth Century.*
> 4. *The Early Twentieth Century.*
> 5. *The Late Twentieth Century.*
> 6. *Chronology, Bibliography, Master Index.*

The Prentice Hall History of Music Series. Ed. H. Wiley Hitchcock. 11 vols. Englewood Cliffs, N.J.: Prentice Hall, 1965–2002.

> *Music in Medieval Europe.* By Jeremy Yudkin. 1989.
> *Music in the Renaissance.* By Howard M. Brown and Louise Stein. 2nd ed. 1999. First published in 1976.
> *Baroque Music.* By Claude V. Palisca. 3rd ed. 1991. First published in 1968.

Music in the Classic Period. By Reinhard G. Pauly. 4th ed. 2000. First published in 1973.

Nineteenth-Century Romanticism in Music. By Rey M. Longyear. 3rd ed. 1988. First published in 1969.

Twentieth-Century Music: An Introduction. By Eric Salzman. 4th ed. 2002. First published in 1967.

Folk and Traditional Music of the Western Continents. By Bruno Nettl, with Gerard Béhague. 3rd ed. Rev. and ed. Valerie Woodring Goertzen. 1990. First published in 1965.

Music Cultures of the Pacific, the Near East, and Asia. By William P. Malm. 3rd ed. 1996. First published in 1967.

Music in the United States: A Historical Introduction. By H. Wiley Hitchcock. 4th ed. 2000. First published in 1969.

Music in India: The Classical Traditions. By Bonnie C. Wade. 1979.

Music in Latin America: An Introduction. By Gerard Béhague. 1979.

Storia della musica. 12 vols. Turin: Edizioni di Torino, 1976–82.

1/i. *La musica nella cultura greca e romana.* By Giovanni Comotti. 1979. Trans. Rosaria V. Munson: *Music in Greek and Roman Culture.* Baltimore: Johns Hopkins University Press, 1989.

1/ii. *Il medioevo I.* By Giulio Cattin. 1979. Trans. Steven Botterill: *Music of the Middle Ages I.* Cambridge: Cambridge University Press, 1984.

2. *Il medioevo II.* By F. Alberto Gallo. 1977. Trans. Karen Eales: *Music of the Middle Ages II.* Cambridge: Cambridge University Press, 1985.

3. *L'età dell'umanesimo e del rinascimento.* By Claudio Gallico. Rev. and corr. ed. 1991. First published in 1978.

4. *Il seicento.* By Lorenzo Bianconi. Rev. and corr. ed. 1991. First published in 1982. Trans. David Bryant: *Music in the Seventeenth Century.* Cambridge: Cambridge University Press, 1987.

5. *L'età di Bach e di Haendel.* By Alberto Basso. Rev. and corr. ed. 1991. First published in 1976.

6. *L'età di Mozart e di Beethoven.* By Giorgio Pestelli. Rev. and corr. ed. 1991. First published in 1979. Trans. Eric Cross: *The Age of Mozart and Beethoven.* Cambridge: Cambridge University Press, 1984.

7. *L'ottocento I.* By Renato Di Benedetto. 1982.

8. *L'ottocento II.* By Claudio Casini. 1978.
9. *Il novecento I.* By Guido Salvetti. 1977.
10/i. *Il novecento II.* By Gianfranco Vinay. 1978.
10/ii. *Il novecento III.* By Andrea Lanza. 1980.

Of Historical Interest

Ambros, August Wilhelm. *Geschichte der Musik.* . . . 5 vols.
     Leipzig: Leuckart, 1887–1911. Continued by Wilhelm
     Langhans as *Die Geschichte der Musik des 17. 18. und
     19. Jahrhunderts in chronologischen Anschlusse an die
     Musikgeschichte von A. W. Ambros.* 2 vols. Leipzig:
     Leuckart, 1884.
Handbuch der Musikwissenschaft. Ed. Ernst Bücken. 13 vols. in
     10. Potsdam: Akademische Verlagsgesellschaft Athenaion,
     [1927–31]; reprint, Wiesbaden, Germany: Laaber Verlag,
     1979.
Kleine Handbücher der Musikgeschichte nach Gattungen. Ed.
     Hermann Kretzschmar. 14 vols. in 15. Leipzig: Breitkopf &
     Härtel, 1905–22.

STUDIES IN ENGLISH
OF INDIVIDUAL HISTORICAL PERIODS

This list completes the previous one with mostly recent histories of periods in English or English translation that do not belong
to multivolume sets (except for the two volumes edited by Sternfeld, which were originally intended to form part of a series that
was later abandoned). Useful supplementary period studies are
Blume's excellent comprehensive monographs on four historical
periods, listed here in the "Miscellaneous Sources" section.

Classical Antiquity

Landels, John G. *Music in Ancient Greece and Rome.* New York:
     Routledge, 2001.
Murray, Penelope, and Peter Wilson, eds. *Music and the Muses:
     The Culture of Mousike in the Classical Athenian City.*
     Oxford: Oxford University Press, 2004.

Medieval, Renaissance

Caldwell, John. *Medieval Music.* Bloomington: Indiana Univer-
     sity Press, 1978.
Knighton, Tess, and David Fallows, eds. *Companion to Medieval*

and Renaissance Music. 1st American ed. New York: Schirmer Books, 1992.

Perkins, Leeman. *Music in the Age of the Renaissance.* New York: W. W. Norton, 1999.

Sternfeld, F. W., ed. *Music from the Middle Ages to the Renaissance.* London: Weidenfeld & Nicholson, 1973.

Stevens, John. *Words and Music in the Middle Ages: Song, Narrative, Dance and Drama, 1050–1350.* Cambridge Studies in Music. Cambridge: Cambridge University Press, 1986.

Strohm, Reinhard. *The Rise of European Music, 1380–1500.* Cambridge: Cambridge University Press, 1993.

Treitler, Leo. *With Voice and Pen: Coming to Know Medieval Song and How It Was Made.* Oxford: Oxford University Press, 2003.

Wilson, David Fenwick. *Music of the Middle Ages: Style and Structure.* New York: Schirmer Books, 1990.

Baroque, Classic, Romantic

Abraham, Gerald. *A Hundred Years of Music* [1830s–1930s]. 4th ed. London: Duckworth, 1974. First published in 1938.

Anderson, Nicholas. *Baroque Music: From Monteverdi to Handel.* London: Thames and Hudson, 1994.

Buelow, George J. *A History of Baroque Music.* Bloomington: Indiana University Press, 2004.

Heartz, Daniel. *Haydn, Mozart, and the Viennese School, 1740–1780.* New York: W. W. Norton, 1995.

———. *Music in European Capitals: The Galant Style, 1720–1780.* New York: W. W. Norton, 2003.

Klaus, Kenneth B. *The Romantic Period in Music.* Boston: Allyn and Bacon, 1970.

Ratner, Leonard G. *Classic Music: Expression, Form, and Style.* New York: Schirmer Books, 1980.

———. *Romantic Music: Sound and Syntax.* New York: Schirmer Books, 1992.

Rosen, Charles. *The Classical Style: Haydn, Mozart, Beethoven.* Exp. ed. New York: W. W. Norton, 1997. First published in 1971.

———. *The Romantic Generation.* Cambridge, Mass.: Harvard University Press, 1995.

Rushton, Julian. *Classical Music: A Concise History from Gluck to Beethoven.* World of Art Series. New York: Thames and Hudson, 1986.

Sadie, Julie Anne, comp. and ed. *Companion to Baroque Music.* New York: Schirmer Books, 1990.

Samson, Jim, ed. *The Cambridge History of Nineteenth-Century Music.* Cambridge: Cambridge University Press, 2002.

Schulenberg, David. *Music of the Baroque.* Oxford: Oxford University Press, 2001.

Whittall, Arnold. *Romantic Music: A Concise History from Schubert to Sibelius.* World of Art Series. New York: Thames and Hudson, 1987.

Twentieth Century

Antokoletz, Elliott. *Twentieth-Century Music.* Englewood Cliffs, N.J.: Prentice Hall, 1992.

Brindle, Reginald Smith. *The New Music: The Avant-Garde since 1945.* 2nd ed. Oxford: Oxford University Press, 1987. First published in 1975.

Carroll, Mark. *Music and Ideology in Cold War Europe.* Music in the Twentieth Century, no. 18. Cambridge: Cambridge University Press, 2003.

Cope, David. *New Directions in Music.* 7th ed. Prospect Heights, Ill.: Waveland Press, 2001. First published in 1971.

Davies, Laurence. *Paths to Modern Music: Aspects of Music from Wagner to the Present Day.* New York: Charles Scribner's Sons, 1971.

Griffiths, Paul. *Modern Music: A Concise History.* Rev. ed. World of Art Series. London: Thames and Hudson, 1994. First published in 1978 as *A Concise History of Avant-Garde Music from Debussy to Boulez.*

Martin, William R., and Julius Drossin. *Music of the Twentieth Century.* Englewood Cliffs, N.J.: Prentice Hall, 1980.

Metzer, David. *Quotation and Cultural Meaning in Twentieth-Century Music.* New Perspectives in Music History and Criticism, no. 12. Cambridge: Cambridge University Press, 2003.

Schwartz, Elliott, and Daniel Godfrey. *Music since 1945: Issues, Materials, and Literature.* New York: Schirmer Books, 1993.

Simms, Bryan R. *Music of the Twentieth Century: Style and Structure.* 2nd ed. New York: Schirmer Books, 1996. First published in 1986.

Sternfeld, F. W., ed. *Music in the Modern Age.* London: Weidenfeld & Nicholson, 1973.

Stuckenschmidt, H. H. *Twentieth Century Music.* Trans. Richard Deveson. World University Library. New York: McGraw-Hill, 1969.

Watkins, Glenn. *Soundings: Music in the Twentieth Century.* New York: Schirmer Books, 1988.

Whittall, Arnold. *Exploring Twentieth-Century Music: Tradition and Innovation.* Cambridge: Cambridge University Press, 2003.

Miscellaneous Sources

Blume, Friedrich. *Renaissance and Baroque Music: A Comprehensive Survey.* Trans. M. D. Herter Norton. New York: W. W. Norton, 1967. First published in 1949 and 1963 in *Die Musik in Geschichte und Gegenwart.*
———. *Classic and Romantic Music: A Comprehensive Survey.* Trans. M. D. Herter Norton. New York: W. W. Norton, 1970. First published in 1958 and 1963 in *Die Musik in Geschichte und Gegenwart.*
Graf, Max. *Composer and Critic: Two Hundred Years of Musical Criticism.* Westport, Conn.: Greenwood Press, 1969.
Haskell, Harry. *The Attentive Listener: Three Centuries of Music Criticism.* Princeton, N.J.: Princeton University Press, 1996.

HISTORIES OF AMERICAN MUSIC

The major recent histories of music in the United States, all in English, are listed here, including some that have a specific focus as well as those that are more general or comprehensive.

Alexander, J. Heywood. *To Stretch Our Ears: A Documentary History of America's Music.* New York: W. W. Norton, 2002.
Ammer, Christine. *Unsung: A History of Women in American Music.* Century ed. Portland, Ore.: Amadeus Press, 2001. First published in 1980.
Brooks, Tilford. *America's Black Musical Heritage.* Englewood Cliffs, N.J.: Prentice Hall, 1984.
Broyles, Michael. *Mavericks and Other Traditions in American Music.* New Haven, Conn.: Yale University Press, 2004.
Chase, Gilbert. *America's Music from the Pilgrims to the Present.* Rev. 3rd ed. Music in American Life. Urbana: University of Illinois Press, 1987. First published in 1955.
Crawford: Richard. *The American Musical Landscape: The Business of Musicianship from Billings to Gershwin.* Berkeley: University of California Press, 2000.
———. *America's Musical Life: A History.* New York: W. W. Norton, 2001.
Crawford, Richard, et al. "United States of America." In *The New*

Grove Dictionary of Music and Musicians. 2nd ed. Vol. 26, pp. 76–133.

Davis, Ronald L. *A History of Music in American Life.* 3 vols. Huntington, N.Y.: R. E. Krieger Publishing, 1980–81.

Ferris, Jean. *America's Musical Landscape.* 4th ed. Boston: McGraw-Hill, 2002. First published in 1990.

Gann, Kyle. *American Music in the Twentieth Century.* Belmont, Calif.: Wadsworth/Thomson Learning, 1997.

Grant, Mark N., and Eric Friedheim. *Maestros of the Pen: A History of Classical Music Criticism in America.* Boston: Northeastern University Press, 1998.

Gridley, Mark. *Jazz Styles: History & Analysis.* 8th ed. Upper Saddle River, N.J.: Prentice Hall, 2003. First published in 1978.

Griffin, Clive D. *Afro-American Music.* London: Dryad Press, 1987.

Hamm, Charles. *Music in the New World.* New York: W. W. Norton, 1983.

Harrelson, John W. "Theme and Variation, Call and Response: A Critical History of America's Music." Ph.D. diss, Claremont Graduate University, 2001.

Hitchcock, H. Wiley. *Music in the United States: A Historical Introduction.* 4th ed. The Prentice Hall History of Music Series. Upper Saddle River, N.J.: Prentice Hall, 2000. First published in 1969.

Kempton, Arthur. *Boogaloo: The Quintessence of American Popular Music.* New York: Pantheon Books, 2003.

Kingman, Daniel. *American Music: A Panorama.* 2nd ed. New York: Schirmer Books, 1990. First published in 1979.

Lowens, Irving. *Music and Musicians in Early America.* New York: W. W. Norton, 1964.

Marini, Stephen A. *Sacred Song in America: Religion, Music, and Public Culture.* Urbana: University of Illinois Press, 2003.

Mellers, Wilfrid. *Music in a New Found Land.* Rev. ed. New York: Oxford University Press, 1987. First published in 1964.

Nicholls, David. *The Cambridge History of American Music.* Cambridge: Cambridge University Press, 1998.

Peretti, Burton W. *Jazz in American Culture.* Chicago: Ivan R. Dee, 1997.

Porter, Lewis. *Jazz: A Century of Change.* New York: Schirmer Books, 1997.

Porter, Lewis, and Michael Ullman, with Ed Hazell. *Jazz: From Its Origins to the Present.* Englewood Cliffs, N.J.: Prentice Hall, 1993. (Also available on CD-ROM.)

Radano, Ronald Michael. *Lying Up a Nation: Race and Black Music.* Chicago: University of Chicago Press, 2003.

Ramsey, Guthrie P. *Race Music: Black Cultures from Behop to Hip-Hop.* Berkeley: University of California Press, 2003.

Roach, Hildred. *Black American Music: Past and Present.* 2nd ed., reissued with corrections. Malabar, Fla.: R. E. Krieger Publishing, 1994. First published in 1973.

Roberts, John S. *Black Music of Two Worlds: African, Caribbean, Latin, and African-American Traditions.* 2nd ed. New York: Schirmer Books, 1998. First published in 1972.

Rublowsky, John. *Black Music in America.* New York: Basic Books, 1971.

Schuller, Gunther. *The History of Jazz.* 2 vols. to date. New York: Oxford University Press, 1968–.

1. *Early Jazz: Its Roots and Musical Development.* 1968.
2. *The Swing Era: The Development of Jazz, 1930–1945.* 1989.

Southern, Eileen. *The Music of Black Americans: A History.* 3rd ed. New York: W. W. Norton, 1997. First published in 1971.

Stowe, David W. *How Sweet the Sound: Music in the Spiritual Lives of Americans.* Cambridge, Mass.: Harvard University Press, 2004.

Struble, John Warthen. *The History of American Classical Music: MacDowell through Minimalism.* New York: Facts on File Publications, 1995.

Sullivan, Jack. *New World Symphonies: How American Culture Changed European Music.* New Haven, Conn.: Yale University Press, 1999.

Tirro, Frank. *Jazz: A History.* 2nd ed. New York: W. W. Norton, 1993. First published in 1977.

Von Glahn, Denise. *The Sounds of Place: Music and the American Cultural Landscape.* Boston: Northeastern University Press, 2003.

Waller Hill, Helen. *From Spirituals to Symphonies: African-American Women Composers and Their Music.* Westport, Conn.: Greenwood Press, 2002.

ENGLISH-LANGUAGE SOURCES ON MUSICAL GENRES AND FORMS

A great many sources deal with a single category of music, often loosely termed a genre or form. The scope of such studies may be the entire history of the category or only a century, stylistic period, or other portion of its evolution, and/or a limitation by country or region may also be imposed. As might be expected, the treatment in such discussions varies from fairly concise to extremely detailed.

Moreover, the approach may be oriented more to music history, literature, or theory.

In the lists that follow, divided overall into "Vocal" and "Instrumental" sections, with each subdivided by form or genre, an attempt has been made to present a good selection from more recent studies of this sort in English or English translation. The only exception to this grouping is the inclusion of the *Handbuch der musikalischen Gattungen* series, an update of the earlier *Handbücher der Musikgeschichte nach Gattungen* volumes. Relevant volumes of the *Anthology of Music* (complete contents listed on pp. 280–81 below) are included here because each consists of excerpts that illustrate the form or genre in question and a preface, often extensive, in which it is discussed.

The art song, chamber music, opera, the piano and its music, and the symphony are the subjects of four volumes in Garland Publishing's series entitled *Music Research and Information Guides*, a set of extensive area bibliographies, which should be consulted for further information in these categories.

A wealth of additional information on such subjects can be found in period histories and in the many published studies about specific works or genres of individual composers, too numerous to be listed here. In the field of opera, studies of individual works may be found in series such as *Cambridge Opera Handbooks* and *English National Opera Guides*.

Vocal

SOLO SONG

Aubrey, Elizabeth. *The Music of the Troubadours.* Bloomington: Indiana University Press, 1996.

Böker-Heil, Norbert, et al. "Lied." In *The New Grove Dictionary of Music and Musicians,* 2nd ed. Vol. 14, pp. 662–81.

Brody, Elaine, and Robert A. Fowkes. *The German Lied and Its Poetry.* New York: New York University Press, 1971.

Brown, Howard Mayer, et al. "Chanson." In *The New Grove Dictionary of Music and Musicians,* 2nd ed. Vol. 5, pp. 472–84.

Bruckner, Matilda Tomaryn, Laurie Shepard, and Sarah Melhado White. *Songs of the Women Troubadours.* New York: Garland Publishing, 2000.

Chew, Geoffrey, et al. "Song." In *The New Grove Dictionary of Music and Musicians,* 2nd ed. Vol. 23, pp. 704–16.

Fellerer, Karl Gustav. *The Monody.* Anthology of Music, vol. 31 (1968).

Fortune, Nigel, and Tim Carter. "Monody." In *The New Grove Dictionary of Music and Musicians,* 2nd ed. Vol. 17, pp. 5–6.

Friedberg, Ruth C. *American Art Song and American Poetry.* 3 vols. Metuchen, N.J.: Scarecrow Press, 1981–87.

Gorrell, Lorraine. *The Nineteenth-Century German Lied.* Portland, Ore.: Amadeus Press, 1993.

Haines, John. *Eight Centuries of Troubadours and Trouvères: The Changing Identity of Medieval Music.* Cambridge: Cambridge University Press, 2004.

Hall, Michael. *Schubert's Song Sets.* Burlington, Vt.: Ashgate, 2003.

Hallmark, Rufus, ed. *German Lieder in the Nineteenth Century.* Studies in Musical Genres and Repertories. New York: Schirmer Books, 1995.

Hold, Trevor. *Parry to Finzi: Twenty English Song-Composers.* Rochester, N.Y.: Boydell Press, 2002.

Johnson, Graham, and Richard Stokes. *A French Song Companion.* New York: Oxford University Press, 2000.

Kravitt, Edward F. *The Lied: Mirror of Late Romanticism.* New Haven, Conn.: Yale University Press, 1996.

Lakeway, Ruth C., and Robert C. White, Jr. *Italian Art Song.* Bloomington: Indiana University Press, 1989.

Meister, Barbara. *Nineteenth-Century French Song: Fauré, Chausson, Duparc, and Debussy.* Bloomington: Indiana University Press, 1980.

Moser, Hans Joachim. *The German Solo Song and the Ballad.* Anthology of Music, vol. 14 (1958).

Noske, Frits. *French Song from Berlioz to Duparc: The Origin and Development of the Mélodie.* 2nd ed. Rev. Rita Benton and Frits Noske. Trans. Rita Benton. New York: Dover Publications, 1970. First published in 1954.

———. *The Solo Song outside German Speaking Countries.* Anthology of Music, vol. 16 (1958).

Osborne, Charles. *The Concert Song Companion: A Guide to the Classical Repertoire.* London: Victor Gollancz, 1974; reprint, New York: Da Capo Press, 1985.

Spink, Ian. *English Song: Dowland to Purcell.* London: Batsford, 1974.

Stein, Jack M. *Poem and Music in the German Lied from Gluck to Hugo Wolf.* Cambridge, Mass.: Harvard University Press, 1971.

Stevens, Denis, ed. *A History of Song.* Rev. ed. New York: W. W. Norton, 1970; reprint, Westport, Conn.: Greenwood Press, 1982. First published in 1960.

Tunley, David. *Salons, Singers and Songs: A Background to Romantic French Song 1830–1870.* Burlington, Vt.: Ashgate, 2002.

Tunley, David, and Frits Noske. "Mélodie." In *The New Grove Dictionary of Music and Musicians,* 2nd ed. Vol. 16, pp. 356–60.

Youens, Susan. *Schubert's Poets and the Making of Lieder.* Cambridge: Cambridge University Press, 1996.

CANTATA

Chafe, Eric. *Analyzing Bach Cantatas.* Oxford: Oxford University Press, 2000.

Dürr, Alfred, and Richard Jones. *Bach's Cantatas.* Oxford: Oxford University Press, 2003.

Jacoby, Richard. *The Cantata.* Anthology of Music, vol. 32 (1968).

Timms, Colin, et al. "Cantata." In *The New Grove Dictionary of Music and Musicians,* 2nd ed. Vol. 5, pp. 8–41.

Tunley, David. *The Eighteenth-Century French Cantata.* 2nd ed. Oxford: Clarendon Press, 1997. First published in 1974.

Vollen, Gene E. *The French Cantata: A Survey and Thematic Catalog.* Studies in Musicology, no. 51. Ann Arbor, Mich.: UMI Research Press, 1982. Revision of Ph.D. diss., North Texas State University, 1970.

DRAMATIC MUSIC

Surveys and General Studies

Abbate, Carolyn. *In Search of Opera.* Princeton, N.J.: Princeton University Press, 2003.

Abert, Anna Amalie. *The Opera from Its Beginnings until the Early 19th Century.* Anthology of Music, vol. 5 (1962).

Brown, Howard Mayer, et al. "Opera." In *The New Grove Dictionary of Music and Musicians,* 2nd ed. Vol. 18, pp. 416–71.

Charlton, David, ed. *The Cambridge Companion to Grand Opera.* Cambridge: Cambridge University Press, 2003.

Dent, Edward J. *The Rise of Romantic Opera.* Ed. Winton Dean. Cambridge: Cambridge University Press, 1976. Lectures originally delivered at Cornell University, 1937–38.

Donington, Robert. *The Rise of Opera.* New York: Charles Scribner's Sons, 1981.

Fanelli, Jean Grundy. *Opera for Everyone: A Historical, Social, Artistic, Literary, and Musical Study.* Lanham, Md.: Scarecrow Press, 2003.

Fisher, Burton. *A History of Opera: Milestones and Metamor-*

phoses. Coral Gables, Fla.: Opera Journeys Publishers, 2003.

Grout, Donald J., with Hermine Weigel Williams. *A Short History of Opera.* 4th ed. New York: Columbia University Press, 2003. First published in 1947.

Headington, Christopher, et al. *Opera: A History.* 1st U.S. ed. New York: St. Martin's Press, 1987.

Kerman, Joseph. *Opera as Drama.* New and rev. ed. Berkeley: University of California Press, 1988. First published in 1956.

Lindenberger, Herbert Samuel. *Opera in History: From Monteverdi to Cage.* Stanford: Stanford University Press, 1998.

Mordden, Ethan. *Opera in the Twentieth Century: Sacred, Profane, Godot.* Oxford: Oxford University Press, 1978.

———. *The Splendid Art of Opera: A Concise History.* New York: Methuen, 1980.

Orrey, Leslie. *Opera: A Concise History.* Rev. and updated ed. by Rodney Milnes. World of Art Series. New York: Thames and Hudson, 1987. First published in 1972.

Parker, Roger, ed. *The Oxford Illustrated History of Opera.* Oxford Illustrated Histories. Oxford: Oxford University Press, 1994.

Robinson, Michael F. *Opera before Mozart.* 3rd ed. London: Hutchinson, 1978. First published in 1966.

Sadie, Stanley, ed. *History of Opera.* 1st American ed. The Norton/Grove Handbooks in Music. New York: W. W. Norton, 1990. First published in 1989.

———. *The New Grove Book of Operas.* New York: St. Martin's Press, 2002.

Smoldon, William L. *The Music of the Medieval Church Dramas.* Ed. Cynthia Bourgeault. London: Oxford University Press, 1980.

Sutcliffe, Tom. *The Faber Book of Opera.* London: Faber and Faber, 2002.

Traubner, Richard. *Operetta: A Theatrical History.* Rev. ed. New York: Routledge, 2003. First published in 1983.

Wolff, Hellmuth Christian. *The Opera: I: 17th Century; II: 18th Century; III: 19th Century.* Anthology of Music, vols. 38 (1971), 39 (1971), 40 (1975).

Studies by Country

UNITED STATES OF AMERICA

DiGaetani, John Louis, and Josef P. Sirefman. *Opera and the Golden West: The Past, Present, and Future of Opera in the U.S.A.* London: Associated University Presses, 1994.

Dizikes, John. *Opera in America: A Cultural History.* New Haven, Conn.: Yale University Press, 1993.

Kirk, Elise K. *American Opera.* Urbana: University of Illinois Press, 2001.

Ottenberg, June C. *Opera Odyssey: Toward a History of Opera in Nineteenth-Century America.* Westport, Conn.: Greenwood Press, 1994.

CZECH REPUBLIC

Tyrrell, John. *Czech Opera.* National Traditions of Opera. Cambridge: Cambridge University Press, 1988.

ENGLAND

Biddlecombe, George. *English Opera from 1834 to 1864 with Particular Reference to the Works of Michael Balfe.* New York: Garland Publishing, 1994.

Dent, Edward J. *Foundations of English Opera: A Study of Musical Drama in England during the Seventeenth Century.* With a new introduction by Michael M. Winesanker. New York: Da Capo Press, 1965. First published in 1928.

Fiske, Roger. *English Theatre Music in the Eighteenth Century.* 2nd ed. Oxford: Oxford University Press, 1986. First published in 1973.

Gagey, Edmond McAdoo. *Ballad Opera.* New York: Columbia University Press, 1937.

Girdham, Jane. *English Opera in Late Eighteenth-Century London: Stephen Storace at Drury Lane.* Oxford: Oxford University Press, 1997.

LaRue, C. Steven. *Handel and His Singers: The Creation of the Royal Academy Operas, 1720–1728.* Oxford: Oxford University Press, 1995.

Lefkowitz, Murray. "Masque." In *The New Grove Dictionary of Music and Musicians,* 2nd ed. Vol. 16, pp. 42–58.

Milhous, Judith, Gabriela Dideriksen, and Robert D. Hume. *Italian Opera in Late Eighteenth-Century London.* 2 vols. Oxford: Oxford University Press, 1995–2001.

> Vol. 1. *The King's Theatre, Haymarket, 1778–1791.* 1995.
> Vol. 2. *The Pantheon Opera and Its Aftermath.* 2001.

Price, Curtis A. *Music in the Restoration Theatre, with a Catalogue of Instrumental Music in the Plays 1665–1713.* Studies in Musicology, no. 4. Ann Arbor, Mich.: UMI Research Press, 1979. Revision of Ph.D. diss., Harvard University, 1974.

White, Eric Walter. *A History of English Opera.* London: Faber and Faber, 1983.

Woodfield, Ian. *Opera and Drama in Eighteenth-Century London.* Cambridge: Cambridge University Press, 2001.

FRANCE

Barbier, Patrick, and Robert Gust Luoma. *Opera in Paris, 1800–1850: A Lively History.* Portland, Ore.: Amadeus Press, 1995.

Brown, Howard Mayer. *Music in the French Secular Theater, 1400–1550.* Cambridge, Mass.: Harvard University Press, 1963.

Crosten, William L. *French Grand Opera: An Art and a Business.* New York: Da Capo Press, 1972. Ph.D. diss., Columbia University, 1948.

Demuth, Norman. *French Opera: Its Development to the Revolution.* [Horsham], Sussex, England: Artemis Press, 1963; reprint, New York: Da Capo Press, 1978.

Dill, Charles William. *Monstrous Opera: Rameau and the Tragic Tradition.* Princeton, N.J.: Princeton University Press, 1998.

Fulcher, Jane F. *The Nation's Image: French Grand Opera as Politics and Politicized Art.* Cambridge: Cambridge University Press, 1987.

Gerhard, Anselm. *The Urbanization of Opera: Music Theater in Paris in the Nineteenth Century.* Chicago: University of Chicago Press, 1998.

Hensen, Karen. "Of Men, Women and Others: Exotic Opera in Late Nineteenth-Century France." D. Phil. diss., University of Oxford, 1999.

Huebner, Steven. *French Opera at the Fin de Siècle: Wagnerism, Nationalism, and Style.* Oxford: Oxford University Press, 1999.

Kennedy, Emmet. *Theatre, Opera, and Audiences in Revolutionary Paris: Analysis and Repertory.* Westport, Conn.: Greenwood Press, 1996.

Lacombe, Hervé. *The Keys to French Opera in the Nineteenth Century.* Trans. Edward Schneider. Berkeley: University of California Press, 2001.

Rice, Paul F. *Fontainebleau Operas for the Court of Louis XV of France by Jean-Philippe Rameau (1683–1764).* Lewiston, N.Y.: Edwin Mellen Press, 2004.

Smith, Marian Elizabeth. *Ballet and Opera in the Age of Giselle.* Princeton, N.J.: Princeton University Press, 2000.

Thomas, Downing A. *Aesthetics of Opera in the Ancien Régime, 1647–1785.* Cambridge: Cambridge University Press, 2002.

Wood, Caroline. *Music and Drama in the Tragédie en Musique,*

1673–1715: Jean-Baptiste Lully and His Successors. New York: Garland Publications, 1996.

GERMANY AND AUSTRIA

Baker, Nicole Edwina Ivy. "Italian Opera at the Court of Mannheim, 1758–1770." Ph.D. diss., University of California–Los Angeles, 1994.

Bauman, Thomas. *North German Opera in the Age of Goethe.* Cambridge: Cambridge University Press, 1985.

Brown, Bruce Alan. *Gluck and the French Theatre in Vienna.* Oxford: Clarendon Press, 1991.

Meyer, Stephen C. *Carl Maria von Weber and the Search for a German Opera.* Bloomington: Indiana University Press, 2003.

Tambling, Jeremy. *Opera and the Culture of Fascism.* Oxford: Oxford University Press, 1996.

Warrack, John. *German Opera: From the Beginnings to Wagner.* Cambridge: Cambridge University Press, 2001.

———. *German Romantic Opera.* Cambridge: Cambridge University Press, 2001.

ITALY

Bianconi, Lorenzo, and Giorgio Pestelli. *Opera in Theory and Practice, Image and Myth.* Chicago: University of Chicago Press, 2003.

Carter, Tim. *Monteverdi's Musical Theatre.* New Haven, Conn.: Yale University Press, 2002.

Celletti, Rodolfo, and Frederick Fuller. *A History of Bel Canto.* Oxford: Oxford University Press, 1991.

Fearn, Raymond. *Italian Opera since 1945.* Amsterdam: Harwood Academic Publishers, 1997.

Heller, Wendy Beth. *Emblems of Eloquence: Opera and Women's Voices in Seventeenth-Century Venice.* Berkeley: University of California Press, 2003.

Kimbell, David R. B. *Italian Opera.* National Traditions of Opera. Cambridge: Cambridge University Press, 1991.

Osborne, Charles. *The Bel Canto Operas of Rossini, Donizetti, and Bellini.* Portland, Ore.: Amadeus Press, 1994.

Pirrotta, Nino, and Elena Povoledo. *Music and Theatre from Poliziano to Monteverdi.* Trans. Karen Eales. Cambridge Studies in Music. Cambridge: Cambridge University Press, 1982. First published in 1969.

Pistone, Danièle. *Nineteenth-Century Italian Opera from Rossini to Puccini.* Portland, Ore.: Amadeus Press, 1995.

Robinson, Michael F. *Naples and Neapolitan Opera.* Oxford

Monographs on Music. Oxford: Clarendon Press, 1972; reprint, New York: Da Capo Press, 1984.

Rosand, Ellen. *Opera in Seventeenth-Century Venice: The Creation of a Genre.* Berkeley: University of California Press, 1991.

Rosselli, John. *The Opera Industry in Italy from Cimarosa to Verdi: The Role of the Impresario.* Cambridge: Cambridge University Press, 1984.

Sternfield, Frederick William. *The Birth of Opera.* New York: Clarendon Press, 1995.

Strohm, Reinhard. *Dramma per Musica: Italian Opera Seria of the Eighteenth Century.* New Haven, Conn.: Yale University Press, 1997.

Troy, Charles E. *The Comic Intermezzo: A Study in the History of Eighteenth-Century Italian Opera.* Studies in Musicology, no. 9. Ann Arbor, Mich.: UMI Research Press, 1979. Ph.D. diss., Harvard University, 1972.

Weaver, William. *The Golden Century of Italian Opera from Rossini to Puccini.* New York: Thames and Hudson, 1980.

Weimer, Eric. **Opera seria** *and the Evolution of Classical Style, 1755–1772.* Studies in Musicology, no. 78. Ann Arbor, Mich.: UMI Research Press, 1984. Revision of Ph.D. diss., University of Chicago, 1982.

Worsthorne, Simon Towneley. *Venetian Opera in the Seventeenth Century.* Oxford: Clarendon Press, 1954; reprint, New York: Da Capo Press, 1984.

Libretto Studies

Aikin, Judith Popovich. *A Language for German Opera: The Development of Forms and Formulas for Recitative and Aria in Seventeenth-Century German Libretti.* Wiesbaden, Germany: Harrassowitz, 2002.

Dace, Wallace. *Opera as Dramatic Poetry.* New York: Vantage Press, 1993.

Groos, Arthur, and Roger Parker, eds. *Reading Opera.* Princeton, N.J.: Princeton University Press, 1988.

Macnutt, Richard. "Libretto." In *The New Grove Dictionary of Music and Musicians,* 2nd ed. Vol. 14, pp. 645–49.

O'Grady, Deirdre. *The Last Troubadours: Poetic Drama in Italian Opera 1597–1887.* London: Routledge, 1991.

Schmidgall, Gary. *Literature as Opera.* New York: Oxford University Press, 1977.

Smith, Patrick J. *The Tenth Muse: A Historical Study of the Opera Libretto.* New York: Alfred A. Knopf, 1970.

SECULAR PART SONG

Brown, Howard Mayer, et al. "Chanson." In *The New Grove Dictionary of Music and Musicians,* 2nd ed. Vol. 5, pp. 472–84.

Einstein, Alfred. *The Italian Madrigal.* Rev. ed. Trans. Alexander H. Krappe et al. 3 vols. Princeton, N.J.: Princeton University Press, 1971. First published in 1949.

Everist, Mark. *French Motets in the Thirteenth Century: Music, Poetry and Genre.* Cambridge Studies in Medieval and Renaissance Music. Cambridge: Cambridge University Press, 1994.

Feldman, Martha. *City Culture and the Madrigal at Venice.* Berkeley: University of California Press, 1995.

Fellowes, Edmund H. *The English Madrigal Composers.* 2nd ed. London: Oxford University Press, 1948. First published in 1921.

Fischer, Kurt von, et al. "Madrigal." In *The New Grove Dictionary of Music and Musicians,* 2nd ed. Vol. 15, pp. 545–71.

Haar, James, ed. *Chanson and Madrigal 1480–1530: Studies in Comparison and Contrast.* A Conference at Isham Memorial Library September 13–14, 1961. Cambridge, Mass.: Harvard University Press, 1964.

Kerman, Joseph. *The Elizabethan Madrigal: A Comparative Study.* Studies and Documents, no. 4. New York: American Musicological Society, 1962.

Roche, Jerome. *The Madrigal.* 2nd ed. Early Music Series, no. 11. Oxford: Oxford University Press, 1991. First published in 1972.

Werf, Hendrik van der. *The Chansons of the Troubadours and Trouvères: A Study of the Melodies and Their Relation to the Poems.* Utrecht: Oosthoek, 1972.

SACRED MUSIC

Adler, Samuel. *American Sacred Choral Music: Overview and Handbook.* Brewster, Mass.: Paraclete Press, 2001.

Apel, Willi. *Gregorian Chant.* Bloomington: Indiana University Press, 1958.

Bergeron, Katherine. *Decadent Enchantments: The Revival of Gregorian Chant at Solesmes.* Berkeley: University of California Press, 1998.

Blume, Friedrich, et al. *Protestant Church Music: A History.* Trans. and enl. from the 2nd ed., 1965. New York: W. W. Norton, 1974. First published in 1931.

Combe, Pierre. *The Restoration of Gregorian Chant: Solesmes and the Vatican Edition.* Washington, D.C.: Catholic University of America Press, 2003.

Crocker, Richard L. *An Introduction to Gregorian Chant.* New Haven, Conn.: Yale University Press, 2000.

Dearnley, Christopher. *English Church Music, 1650–1750, in Royal Chapel, Cathedral and Parish Church.* London: Oxford University Press, 1970.

Ellinwood, Leonard. *The History of American Church Music.* Rev. ed. New York: Da Capo Press, 1970. First published in 1953.

Fellerer, Karl Gustav. *The History of Catholic Church Music.* Trans. Francis A. Brunner. Baltimore: Helicon Press, 1961; reprint, Westport, Conn.: Greenwood Press, 1979.

Fellowes, Edmund H. *English Cathedral Music from Edward VI to Edward VII.* 5th ed., rev. J. A. Westrup. London: Methuen, 1969. First published in 1941.

Gallagher, Sean, James Haar, John Nádas, and Timothy Striplin, eds. *Western Plainchant in the First Millennium: Studies in the Medieval Liturgy and Its Music.* Burlington, Vt.: Ashgate, 2003.

Gatens, William J. *Victorian Cathedral Music in Theory and Practice.* Cambridge. Cambridge University Press, 1986.

Heskes, Irene. *Passport to Jewish Music: Its History, Traditions, and Culture.* Contributions to the Study of Music and Dance, no. 33. Westport, Conn.: Greenwood Press, 1994; reprint, Milwaukee, Wisc.: Hal Leonard, 2002.

Hiley, David. *Western Plainchant: A Handbook.* Oxford: Clarendon Press, 1993.

Hoffman, Lawrence A., and Janet Roland Walton. *Sacred Sound and Social Change: Liturgical Music in Jewish and Christian Experience.* South Bend, Ind.: University of Notre Dame Press, 1992.

Hüschen, Heinrich. *The Motet.* Anthology of Music, vol. 47 (1975).

Hutchings, Arthur. *Church Music in the Nineteenth Century.* London: Herbert Jenkins, 1967; reprint, Westport, Conn.: Greenwood Press, 1977.

Idelsohn, Abraham Z. *Jewish Music in Its Historical Development.* New York: Henry Holt, 1929; reprint, New York: Dover Publications, 1992.

Jeffery, Peter. *Re-Envisioning Past Musical Cultures: Ethnomusicology in the Study of Gregorian Chant.* Chicago: University of Chicago Press, 1992.

Jeffery, Peter, ed. *The Study of Medieval Chant: Paths and Bridges, East and West.* Rochester, N.Y.: Boydell Press, 2001.

Karp, Theodore. *Aspects of Orality and Formularity in Gregorian Chant.* Evanston: Northwestern University Press, 1998.

Le Huray, Peter. *Music and the Reformation in England, 1549–1660.* 2nd ed., rev. London: Oxford University Press, 1978. First published in 1967.

Levy, Kenneth. *Gregorian Chant and the Carolingians.* Princeton, N.J.: Princeton University Press, 1998.

Long, Kenneth R. *The Music of the English Church.* New York: St. Martin's Press, 1972; reprint, London: Hodder and Stoughton, 1991.

MacIntyre, Bruce C. *The Viennese Concerted Mass of the Classic Period.* Studies in Musicology, no. 89. Ann Arbor, Mich.: UMI Research Press, 1986. Ph.D. diss., City University of New York, 1984.

Marini, Stephen A. *Sacred Song in America: Religion, Music, and Public Culture.* Urbana: University of Illinois Press, 2003.

McKinnon, James W. *The Advent Project: The Later-Seventh-Century Creation of the Roman Mass Proper.* Berkeley: University of California Press, 2000.

———. *The Temple, the Church Fathers, and Early Western Chant.* Brookfield, Vt.: Ashgate, 1998.

McKinnon, James W., et al. "Mass." In *The New Grove Dictionary of Music and Musicians,* 2nd ed. Vol. 16, pp. 58–85.

Rainbow, Bernarr. *The Choral Revival in the Anglican Church, 1839–1872.* Oxford: Oxford University Press, 1970; reprint, Rochester, N.Y.: Boydell Press, 2001.

Rastall, Richard. *Heaven Singing: Music in Early English Religious Drama I.* Rochester, N.Y.: Boydell and Brewer, 1999.

———. *Minstrels Playing: Music in Early English Religious Drama II.* Rochester, N.Y.: Boydell and Brewer, 2001.

Routley, Eric. *Twentieth Century Church Music.* New York: Oxford University Press, 1964; reprint, Carol Stream, Ill.: Agape Press, 1984.

Routley, Eric, and Lionel Dakers. *A Short History of English Church Music.* New ed. London: Mowbray, 2000. First published in 1996.

Sanders, Ernest H., et al. "Motet." In *The New Grove Dictionary of Music and Musicians,* 2nd ed. Vol. 17, pp. 190–227.

Schmidt-Görg, Joseph. *History of the Mass.* Anthology of Music, vol. 30 (1968).

Seroussi, Edwin, et al. "Jewish Music." In *The New Grove Dictionary of Music and Musicians,* 2nd ed. Vol. 13, pp. 24–112.

Shiloah, Amnon. *The Dimension of Music in Islamic and Jewish Culture.* Burlington, Vt.: Ashgate Variorum, 2000.

————. *Jewish Musical Traditions.* Jewish Folklore and Anthropology Series. Detroit: Wayne State University Press, 1992.

Spink, Ian. *Restoration Cathedral Music: 1660–1714.* Oxford: Oxford University Press, 1995.

Steiner, Ruth. *Studies in Gregorian Chant.* Brookfield, Vt.: Ashgate, 1999.

Stevens, Denis. *Tudor Church Music.* Rev. ed. New York: W. W. Norton, 1961. First published in 1955.

Stevenson, Robert. *Spanish Cathedral Music in the Golden Age.* Berkeley: University of California Press, 1961; reprint, Westport, Conn.: Greenwood Press, 1976.

Summit, Jeffrey A. *The Lord's Song in a Strange Land: Music and Identity in Contemporary Jewish Worship.* Oxford: Oxford University Press, 2003.

Tack, Franz. *Gregorian Chant.* Anthology of Music, vol. 18 (1960).

Temperley, Nicholas. *The Music of the English Parish Church.* 2 vols. Cambridge: Cambridge University Press, 1979.

Wellesz, Egon. *A History of Byzantine Music and Hymnography.* 2nd ed., rev. and enl. Oxford: Clarendon Press, 1998. First published in 1961.

————. *The Music of the Byzantine Church.* Anthology of Music, vol. 13 (1959).

Werner, Eric. *Hebrew Music.* Anthology of Music, vol. 20 (1961).

Wienandt, Elwyn Arthur. *Choral Music of the Church.* New York: Free Press, 1965; reprint, New York: Da Capo Press, 1980.

Wienandt, Elwyn Arthur, and Robert H. Young. *The Anthem in England and America.* New York: Free Press, 1970.

Wilson, Ruth Mack. *Anglican Chant and Chanting in England, Scotland, and America, 1660 to 1820.* Oxford: Oxford University Press, 1996.

Zon, Bennett. *The English Plainchant Revival.* Oxford: Oxford University Press, 1998.

ORATORIO, PASSION, AND REQUIEM

Arnold, Denis, and Elsie Arnold. *The Oratorio in Venice.* Royal Musical Association Monographs, no. 2. London: Royal Musical Association, 1986.

Chase, Robert. *Dies Irae: A Guide to Requiem Music.* Lanham, Md.: Scarecrow Press, 2003.

Fischer, Kurt von, and Werner Braun. "Passion." In *The New Grove Dictionary of Music and Musicians,* 2nd ed. Vol. 19, pp. 200–11.

Harleben, John. "A Critical Survey of the North German Oratorio

Passion to 1700." D.M.A. thesis, University of Illinois, 1974.

Karp, Theodore, et al. "Requiem mass." In *The New Grove Dictionary of Music and Musicians,* 2nd ed. Vol. 21, pp. 203–208.

Kovalenko, Susan Chaffins. "The Twentieth-Century Requiem: An Emerging Concept." Ph.D. diss., Washington University, 1971.

Luce, Harold Talmadge. "The Requiem Mass from Its Plainsong Beginnings to 1600." 2 vols. Ph.D. diss., Florida State University, 1958.

Massenkeil, Günther. *The Oratorio.* Anthology of Music, vol. 37 (1970).

Pahlen, Kurt, with the collaboration of Werner Pfister and Rosemarie König. *The World of the Oratorio: Oratorio, Mass, Requiem, Te Deum, Stabat Mater, and Large Cantatas.* Additional material for the English language edition by Thurston Dox. Portland, Ore.: Amadeus Press, 1990. First published in 1985.

Robertson, Alec. *Requiem: Music of Mourning and Consolation.* London: Cassell, 1967; reprint, Westport, Conn.: Greenwood Press, 1976.

Smallman, Basil. *The Background of Passion Music: J. S. Bach and His Predecessors.* 2nd rev. and enl. ed. New York: Dover Publications, 1970. First published in 1957.

Smither, Howard E. *A History of the Oratorio.* 4 vols. Chapel Hill: University of North Carolina Press, 1977–2000.

1. *The Oratorio in the Baroque Era: Italy, Vienna, Paris.* 1977.
2. *The Oratorio in the Baroque Era: Protestant Germany and England.* 1977.
3. *The Oratorio in the Classical Era.* 1987.
4. *The Oratorio in the Nineteenth and Twentieth Centuries.* 2000.

———. "Oratorio." In *The New Grove Dictionary of Music and Musicians,* 2nd ed. Vol. 18, pp. 503–28.

SURVEYS OF CHORAL MUSIC

Jacobs, Arthur, ed. *Choral Music: A Symposium.* Baltimore: Penguin Books, 1963.

Sharp, Avery T., and John Michael Floyd. *Choral Music: A Research and Information Guide.* New York: Routledge, 2001.

Ulrich, Homer. *A Survey of Choral Music.* The Harbrace History of Musical Forms. New York: Harcourt Brace Jovanovich, 1973.

Young, Percy M. *The Choral Tradition: An Historical and Analytical Survey from the Sixteenth Century to the Present Day.* Rev. ed. New York: W. W. Norton, 1981. First published in 1962.

Instrumental

SYMPHONIC MUSIC

Ballantine, Christopher. *Twentieth Century Symphony.* London: Dennis Dobson, 1983.

Brook, Barry S., and Jean Gribenski. "Symphonie concertante." In *The New Grove Dictionary of Music and Musicians,* 2nd ed. Vol. 24, pp. 807–12.

Brown, Carol, gen. ed. *The Symphonic Repertoire.* 5 vols. projected. Bloomington: Indiana University Press, 2002–.

    1. *The Eighteenth-Century Symphony.*
    2. *The First Golden Age of the Viennese Symphony.* By
       A. Peter Brown. 2002.
    3. *The European Symphony, ca. 1800–ca. 1930.*
    4. *The Second Golden Age of the Viennese Symphony.*
       By A. Peter Brown. 2003.
    5. *The Symphony in Europe and the Americas in the*
       Twentieth Century.

Cuyler, Louise. *The Symphony.* 2nd ed. Warren, Mich.: Harmonie Park Press, 1995. First published in 1973.

Daniels, David. *Orchestral Music: A Handbook.* 3rd ed. Lanham, Md.: Scarecrow Press, 1996. First published in 1982.

Downes, Edward. *Guide to Symphonic Music.* New York: Walker, 1976. Previously published in 1976 as *The New York Philharmonic Guide to the Symphony.*

Engel, Hans. *The Solo Concerto.* Anthology of Music, vol. 25 (1964).

Harris, John M. *A History of Music for Harpsichord or Piano and Orchestra.* Lanham, Md.: Scarecrow Press, 1997.

Hausswald, Günter. *The Serenade for Orchestra.* Anthology of Music, vol. 34 (1970).

Hill, Ralph, ed. *The Concerto.* New York: Penguin Books, 1952; reprint, Westport, Conn.: Greenwood Press, 1978.

Hoffmann-Erbrecht, Lothar. *The Symphony.* Anthology of Music, vol. 29 (1967).

Holoman, D. Kern. *The Nineteenth-Century Symphony.* New York: Schirmer Books, 1997.

Hutchings, Arthur. *The Baroque Concerto.* 3rd rev. ed. London: Faber and Faber, 1973. First published in 1959.

Hutchings, Arthur, et al. "Concerto." In *The New Grove Dictionary of Music and Musicians,* 2nd ed. Vol. 6, pp. 240–60.

Koshgarian, Richard. *American Orchestral Music: A Performance Catalog.* Lanham, Md.: Scarecrow Press, 1992.

Kramer, Jonathan D. *Listen to the Music: A Self-Guided Tour through the Orchestral Repertoire.* New York: Schirmer Books, 1988.

LaRue, Jan, et al. "Symphony." In *The New Grove Dictionary of Music and Musicians,* 2nd ed. Vol. 24, pp. 812–49.

Layton, Robert, ed. *A Guide to the Concerto.* Oxford: Oxford University Press, 1996. Previously published in 1988 as *A Companion to the Concerto.*

Lee, Douglas. *Masterworks of 20th-Century Music: The Modern Repertory of the Symphony Orchestra.* New York: Routledge, 2002.

Macdonald, Hugh. "Symphonic poem." In *The New Grove Dictionary of Music and Musicians,* 2nd ed. Vol. 24, pp. 802–807.

Moore, Earl V., and Theodore E. Heger. *The Symphony and the Symphonic Poem: Analytical and Descriptive Charts of the Standard Symphonic Repertory.* 6th ed., rev. Ann Arbor, Mich.: Ulrich Books, 1974. First published in 1949.

Roeder, Michael Thomas. *A History of the Concerto.* Portland, Ore.: Amadeus Press, 1994.

Simpson, Robert, ed. *The Symphony.* 2 vols. Baltimore: Penguin Books, 1966–67; reprint with revisions, New York: Penguin Books, 1977–78.

Spitzer, John, and Neal Zaslaw. *The Birth of the Orchestra: History of an Institution, 1650–1815.* Oxford: Oxford University Press, 2004.

Stedman, Preston. *The Symphony.* 2nd ed. Englewood Cliffs, N.J.: Prentice Hall, 1992. First published in 1979.

Steinberg, Michael. *The Concerto: A Listener's Guide.* New York: Oxford University Press, 1998.

———. *The Symphony: A Listener's Guide.* Oxford: Oxford University Press, 1995.

Ulrich, Homer. *Symphonic Music: Its Evolution since the Renaissance.* New York: Columbia University Press, 1952.

Veinus, Abraham. *The Concerto.* Rev. ed. New York: Dover Publications, 1964. First published in 1944.

Will, Richard. *The Characteristic Symphony in the Age of Haydn and Beethoven.* New Perspectives in Music History and Criticism, no. 7. Cambridge: Cambridge University Press, 2002.

Chamber Music

Ashbee, Andrew, and Peter Holman. *John Jenkins and His Time: Studies in English Consort Music.* Oxford: Oxford University Press, 1996.

Baron, John H. *Chamber Music: A Research and Information Guide.* 2nd ed. New York: Routledge, 2002. First published in 1987.

———. *Intimate Music: A History of the Idea of Chamber Music.* Stuyvesant, N.Y.: Pendragon Press, 1998.

Bashford, Christina. "Chamber music." In *The New Grove Dictionary of Music and Musicians,* 2nd ed. Vol. 5, pp. 434–48.

Berger, Melvin. *Guide to Chamber Music.* 3rd corr. ed. Mineola, N.Y.: Dover Publications, 2001. First published in 1985.

Cobbett, Walter Willson, comp. and ed., with Colin Mason, ed. *Cobbett's Cyclopedic Survey of Chamber Music.* 2nd ed. 3 vols. London: Oxford University Press, 1963. First published in 1929–30.

Druckner, Arno P. *American Piano Trios: A Resource Guide.* Lanham, Md.: Scarecrow Press, 1999.

Eisen, Cliff, et al. "String quartet." In *The New Grove Dictionary of Music and Musicians,* 2nd ed. Vol. 24, pp. 585–95.

Griffiths, Paul. *The String Quartet: A History.* New York: Thames and Hudson, 1983.

Hefling, Stephen. *19th-Century Chamber Music.* 2nd ed. New York: Routledge, 2003. First published in 1998.

Konold, Wulf. *The String Quartet: From Its Beginnings to Franz Schubert.* Trans. Susan Hellauer. Paperbacks in Musicology, no. 6. New York: Heinrichshofen Edition, 1983. First published in 1980.

Lawrence, Ian. *The Twentieth-Century String Quartet.* Lanham, Md.: Scarecrow Press, 2001.

Loft, Abram. *Violin and Keyboard: The Duo Repertoire.* 2 vols. New York: Grossman Publishers, 1973; reprint, Portland, Ore.: Amadeus Press, 1991.

McCalla, James. *20th-Century Chamber Music.* 2nd ed. New York: Routledge, 2003. First published in 1996.

Meyer, Ernst H. *Early English Chamber Music: From the Middle Ages to Purcell.* 2nd, rev. ed. Ed. the author and Diana Poulton. London: Lawrence and Wishart, 1982. First published as *English Chamber Music* in 1946.

Palkovic, Mark. *Harp Music Bibliography: Chamber Music and Concertos.* Lanham, Md.: Scarecrow Press, 2002.

———. *Harp Music Bibliography Supplement: Compositions for Solo Harp and Harp Ensemble.* Lanham, Md.: Scarecrow Press, 2002.

Robertson, Alec, ed. *Chamber Music.* Baltimore: Penguin Books, 1957.

Rowen, Ruth Halle. *Early Chamber Music.* With a new preface and supplementary bibliography. Da Capo Press Music Reprint Series. New York: Da Capo Press, 1974. First published in 1949.

Secrist-Schmedes, Barbara. *Wind Chamber Music: For Two to Sixteen Winds, an Annotated Guide.* Lanham, Md.: Scarecrow Press, 2002.

———. *Wind Chamber Music: Winds with Piano and Wood-wind Quintets, an Annotated Guide.* Lanham, Md.: Scarecrow Press, 1996.

Smallman, Basil. *The Piano Quartet and Quintet: Style, Structure, and Scoring.* Oxford: Clarendon Press, 1994.

———. *The Piano Trio: Its History, Technique, and Repertoire.* Oxford: Clarendon Press, 1989.

Ulrich, Homer. *Chamber Music.* 2nd ed. New York: Columbia University Press, 1966. First published in 1948.

Unverricht, Hubert. *Chamber Music.* Anthology of Music, vol. 46 (1975).

KEYBOARD MUSIC

Apel, Willi. *The History of Keyboard Music to 1700.* Trans. and rev. Hans Tischler. Bloomington: Indiana University Press, 1972. First published in 1967.

———. *Masters of the Keyboard: A Brief Survey of Pianoforte Music.* Cambridge, Mass.: Harvard University Press, 1947.

Archbold, Lawrence, and William Peterson, eds. *French Organ Music from the Revolution to Franck and Widor.* Rev. ed. Rochester, N.Y.: University of Rochester Press, 1999. First published in 1995.

Arnold, Corliss Richard. *Organ Literature: A Comprehensive Survey.* 3rd ed. 2 vols. Lanham, Md.: Scarecrow Press, 1995. First published in 1973.

Axford, Elizabeth C. *Traditional World Music Influences in Contemporary Solo Piano Literature: A Selected Bibliographic Survey and Review.* Lanham, Md.: Scarecrow Press, 1997.

Bedford, Frances. *Harpsichord and Clavichord Music of the Twentieth Century.* Fallen Leaf Reference Books in Music, no. 22. Lanham, Md.: Scarecrow Press, 1993.

Burge, David. *Twentieth-Century Piano Music.* Lanham, Md.: Scarecrow Press, 2003. First published in 1990 by Schirmer Books.

Caldwell, John. *English Keyboard Music before the Nineteenth*

Century. Blackwell's Music Series. Oxford: Basil Blackwell, 1973; reprint, New York: Dover Publications, 1985.

Caldwell, John, et al. "Keyboard music." In *The New Grove Dictionary of Music and Musicians,* 2nd ed. Vol. 13, pp. 513–48.

Clark, J. Bunker. *The Dawning of American Keyboard Music.* Contributions to the Study of Music and Dance, no. 12. New York: Greenwood Press, 1988.

Dale, Kathleen. *Nineteenth-Century Piano Music: A Handbook for Pianists.* London: Oxford University Press, 1954; reprint, New York: Da Capo Press, 1972.

Dees, Pamela Youngdahl. *A Guide to Piano Music by Women Composers. Volume 1: Composers Born before 1900.* Westport, Conn.: Greenwood Press, 2002.

Edel, Theodore. *Piano Music for One Hand.* Bloomington: Indiana University Press, 1994.

Georgii, Walter. *Four Hundred Years of European Keyboard Music.* Anthology of Music, vol. 1 (1959).

Gillespie, John. *Five Centuries of Keyboard Music: An Historical Survey of Music for Harpsichord and Piano.* Belmont, Calif.: Wadsworth Publishing, 1965; reprint, New York: Dover Publications, 1972.

Hardwick, Peter. *British Organ Music of the Twentieth Century.* Lanham, Md.: Scarecrow Press, 2002.

Hinson, Maurice. *Guide to the Pianist's Repertoire.* 3rd ed. Bloomington: Indiana University Press, 2001. First published in 1973.

———. *Music for More Than One Piano: An Annotated Guide.* Bloomington: Indiana University Press, 1983.

———. *The Pianist's Guide to Transcriptions, Arrangements, and Paraphrases.* Bloomington: Indiana University Press, 2001.

Kirby, F. E. *A Short History of Keyboard Music.* New York: Free Press, 1966.

Marshall, Robert L., ed. *Eighteenth-Century Keyboard Music.* Rev. ed. New York: Routledge, 2003. First published in 1994.

Maxwell, Grant L. *Music for Three or More Pianists: A Historical Survey and Catalogue.* Lanham, Md.: Scarecrow Press, 1993.

McGraw, Cameron. *Piano Duet Repertoire: Music Originally Written for One Piano, Four Hands.* Bloomington: Indiana University Press, 2001.

Ochse, Orpha. *Organists and Organ Playing in Nineteenth-Century France and Belgium.* Bloomington: Indiana University Press, 2000.

Silbiger, Alexander, ed. *Keyboard Music before 1700.* 2nd ed.
New York: Routledge, 2003. First published in 1995.

Sutcliffe, W. Dean. *The Keyboard Sonatas of Domenico Scarlatti
and Eighteenth-Century Musical Style.* Cambridge:
Cambridge University Press, 2003.

Todd, R. Larry, ed. *Nineteenth-Century Piano Music.* Rev. ed.
New York: Routledge, 2003. First published in 1990.

Wolff, Konrad. *Masters of the Keyboard: Individual Style
Elements in the Piano Music of Bach, Haydn, Mozart,
Beethoven, Schubert, Chopin, and Brahms.* Enl. ed.
Bloomington: Indiana University Press, 1990. First pub-
lished in 1983.

Sonata

Allsop, Peter. *The Italian "Trio" Sonata: From Its Origins until
Corelli.* Oxford Monographs on Music. New York: Oxford
University Press, 1992.

Berger, Melvin. *Guide to Sonatas: Music for One or Two Instruments.* New York: Anchor Books/Doubleday, 1991.

Giegling, Franz. *The Solo Sonata.* Anthology of Music, vol. 15
(1960).

Hogwood, Christopher. *The Trio Sonata.* BBC Music Guides.
London: British Broadcasting Corporation, 1979.

Mangsen, Sandra, et al. "Sonata." In *The New Grove Dictionary
of Music and Musicians,* 2nd ed. Vol. 23, pp. 671–87.

Newman, William S. *The Sonata in the Baroque Era.* 4th ed.
New York: W. W. Norton, 1983. First published in 1959.

———. *The Sonata in the Classic Era.* 3rd ed. New York: W. W.
Norton, 1983. First published in 1963.

———. *The Sonata since Beethoven.* 3rd ed. New York: W. W.
Norton, 1983. First published in 1969.

Schenk, Erich. *The Italian Trio Sonata.* Anthology of Music, vol.
7 (1955).

———. *The Trio Sonata outside Italy.* Anthology of Music, vol.
35 (1970).

Shedlock, John. *The Pianoforte Sonata: Its Origin and Develop-
ment.* With a new foreword by William S. Newman. Da
Capo Press Reprint Series. New York: Da Capo Press, 1964.
First published in 1926.

Fugue

Adrio, Adam. *The Fugue I: From the Beginnings to Johann
Sebastian Bach.* Anthology of Music, vol. 19 (1961).

Horsley, Imogene. *Fugue: History and Practice.* New York: Free Press, 1966.

Kirkendale, Warren. *Fugue and Fugato in Rococo and Classical Chamber Music.* Rev. and exp. 2nd ed. Trans. Margaret Bent and the author. Durham, N.C.: Duke University Press, 1979. First published in 1966.

Mann, Alfred. *The Study of Fugue.* Enl. and corr. version. New York: Dover Publications, 1987. First published in 1958.

Müller-Blattau, Josef. *The Fugue II: From Handel to the Twentieth Century.* Anthology of Music, vol. 33 (1968).

Oldroyd, George. *The Technique and Spirit of Fugue: An Historical Study.* London: Oxford University Press, 1948; reprint, Westport, Conn.: Greenwood Press, 1986.

Walker, Paul. "Fugue." In *The New Grove Dictionary of Music and Musicians,* 2nd ed. Vol. 9, pp. 318–32.

———. *Theories of Fugue from the Age of Josquin to the Age of Bach.* Rochester, N.Y.: University of Rochester Press, 2003.

ELECTRONIC AND COMPUTER MUSIC

Chadabe, Joel. *Electric Sound: The Past and Promise of Electronic Music.* Upper Saddle River, N.J.: Prentice Hall, 1997.

Davies, Hugh. "Electronic instruments." In *The New Grove Dictionary of Music and Musicians,* 2nd ed. Vol. 8, pp. 67–107.

Dodge, Charles, and Thomas A. Jerse. *Computer Music: Synthesis, Composition, and Performance.* 2nd ed. New York: Thomson/Schirmer, 1997. First published in 1985.

Emmerson, Simon. *The Language of Electroacoustic Music.* New York: Harwood Academic Publishers, 1986.

Emmerson, Simon, and Denis Smalley. "Electro-acoustic music." In *The New Grove Dictionary of Music and Musicians,* 2nd ed. Vol. 8, pp. 59–67.

Harris, Craig, ed. *Computer Music in Context.* New York: Routledge, 1996.

Holmes, Thomas B. *Electronic and Experimental Music: Pioneers in Technology and Composition.* 2nd ed. New York: Routledge, 2002. First published in 1985.

Judd, Frederick Charles. *Electronic Music and Musique Concrète.* London: N. Spearman, 1961.

Licata, Thomas. *Electroacoustic Music: Analytical Perspectives.* Westport, Conn.: Greenwood Press, 2002.

Manning, Peter D. *Electronic and Computer Music.* Rev. ed. Oxford: Oxford University Press, 2003. First published in 1985.

Manning, Peter, et al. "Computers and music." In *The New Grove Dictionary of Music and Musicians,* 2nd ed. Vol. 6, pp. 202–18.

Russcol, Herbert. *The Liberation of Sound: An Introduction to Electronic Music.* Englewood Cliffs, N.J.: Prentice Hall, 1972; reprint, New York: Da Capo Press, 1994.

Schwartz, Elliott. *Electronic Music: A Listener's Guide.* New York: Praeger, 1975; reprint, New York: Da Capo Press, 1989.

GERMAN MULTIVOLUME SERIES ON GENRES

Handbuch der musikalischen Gattungen. Ed. Siegfried Mauser. 15 vols. projected. Laaber, Germany: Laaber-Verlag, 1993–.

1. *Die Sinfonie im 18. Jahrhundert: Von der Opernsinfonie zur Konzertsinfonie.* By Stefan Kunze. 1993.

2. *Die Sinfonie der Wiener Klassik.* By Gernot Gruber.

3. *Symphonische Musik im 19. und 20. Jahrhundert.* By Christoph von Blumroeder and Wolfram Steinbeck. 2002.

4. *Das Konzert.* By Volker Scherliess. 2000.

5. *Die Sonate.* By Michael Zimmermann.

6. *Das Streichquartett.* By Friedheim Krummacher. 2001–2003.

7. *Musik für Tasteninstrumente.* By Arnfried Edler. 1997–2003.

8. *Musikalische Lyrik: Lied und vokale Ensemblekunst.* Ed. Hermann Danuser.

9. *Motette und Messe.* By Horst Leuchtmann. 1998.

10. *Oratorium und Passion.* By Günther Massenkeil. 1999.

11. *Die Oper im 17. Jahrhundert.* By Silke Leopold.

12. *Die Oper im 18. Jahrhundert.* By Herbert Schneider and Reinhard Wiesend. 2001.

13. *Oper und Musikdrama im 19. Jahrhundert.* By Siegfried Doehring and Sabine Henz-Doehring. 1997.

14. *Musiktheater im 20. Jahrhundert.* Ed. Siegfried Mauser. 2002.

15. *Gattungstheorie.* By Siegfried Mauser.

MISCELLANEOUS SOURCES

Tovey, Donald Francis. *Essays in Musical Analysis.* New ed. 3 vols. London: Oxford University Press, 1989. Originally published in 6 vols., 1935–44.

1. *Symphonies and Other Orchestral Works.*
2. *Concertos and Choral Works.*
3. *Chamber Music.*

CHRONOLOGIES AND OUTLINES

Treatments of music history in the form of chronological lists or outlines may be useful for study or reference. The following sources fall into four categories: "General," "Twentieth Century," "American Music," and "Opera." There is a good deal of diversity within the categories, with considerable difference in scope and amount of detail. Eisler's *World Chronology* (although apparently it will remain incomplete) is by far the most detailed, with the Gleason/Becker outlines and Slonimsky's *Music since 1900* not far behind. The arrangement of information is either chronological by historical period, by year, by day, by composer, etc. Some sources, like Eisler and Hall, include nonmusical information; others are concerned only with music. The chronologies listed here are mostly recent, but older sources like Lahee and Schering continue to be valid.

General and Comprehensive

Cullen, Marion Elizabeth, comp. *Memorable Days in Music.*
    Metuchen, N.J.: Scarecrow Press, 1970.
Dufourcq, Norbert, Marcelle Benoit, and Bernard Gangepain.
    Les grandes dates de l'histoire de la musique. 4th ed., corr.
    Que sais-je? no. 1333. Paris: Presses Universitaires de
    France, 1991. First published in 1969.
Eisler, Paul E., comp. and ed., vols. 1–5, and Neal Hatch, comp.
    and ed., vol. 6. *World Chronology of Music History.*
    Dobbs Ferry, N.Y.: Oceana Publications, 1972–80. 8 to 10
    vols. projected; apparently halted after vol. 6.

1. *30,000 B.C.–1594 A.D.* 1972.
2. *1594–1684.* 1973.
3. *1685–1735.* 1974.
4. *Name Index* (vols. 1–3). 1976.
5. *1736–1786.* 1978.
6. *1771–1796.* By Neal Hatch. 1980.

Gangwere, Blanche M. *Music History during the Renaissance
    Period, 1425–1520: A Documented Chronology.* Music
    Reference Collection, no. 28. Westport, Conn.: Greenwood
    Press, 1991.
———. *Music History from the Late Roman through the Gothic*

Periods, 313–1425: A Documented Chronology. Music
Reference Collection, no. 6. Westport, Conn.: Greenwood
Press, 1986.

Gleason, Harold, and Warren Becker. **Music Literature Outlines.**
5 series. 2nd/3rd ed. Bloomington, Ind.: Frangipani Press,
1980–81. First published in 1949–55.

> Series 1. *Music in the Middle Ages and the Renaissance.*
> 3rd ed., 1981.
> Series 2. *Music in the Baroque.* 3rd ed., 1980.
> Series 3. *Early American Music from 1620 to 1920.* 2nd ed.,
> 1981.
> Series 4. *20th-Century American Composers.* 2nd ed., 1980.
> Series 5. *Chamber Music from Haydn to Bartók.* 2nd ed.,
> 1980.

Hall, Charles John, comp. *Chronology of Western Classical
Music, 1751–2000.* 2 vols. New York: Routledge, 2002.

———. *An Eighteenth-Century Musical Chronicle: Events
1750–1799.* Music Reference Collection, no. 25. Westport,
Conn.: Greenwood Press, 1990.

———. *A Nineteenth-Century Musical Chronicle: Events
1800–1899.* Music Reference Collection, no. 21. Westport,
Conn.: Greenwood Press, 1989.

———. *A Twentieth-Century Musical Chronicle: Events
1900–1988.* Music Reference Collection, no. 20. Westport,
Conn.: Greenwood Press, 1989. An earlier version pub-
lished in 1980 as *Hall's Musical Years, the Twentieth
Century 1900–1979: A Comprehensive Year-by-Year
Survey of the Fine Arts.*

Kendall, Alan. *The Chronicle of Classical Music: An Intimate
Diary of the Lives and Music of the Great Composers.*
London: Thames and Hudson, 1994.

Manson, Adele P. *Calendar of Music and Musicians.* Metuchen,
N.J.: Scarecrow Press, 1981.

Michels, Ulrich. *DTV-Atlas zur Musik: Tafeln und Texte.* 2 vols.
Kassel: Bärenreiter, 1977–85.

> 1. *Systematischer Teil; Historischer Teil [1]: Von den
> Anfängen bis zur Renaissance.* 1977.
> 2. *Historischer Teil [2]: Vom Barock bis zur Gegenwart.*
> 1985.

Miller, Hugh M. *History of Music.* Barnes and Noble Outline
Series. 4th ed. New York: Barnes and Noble, 1972. First
published in 1947.

Schering, Arnold. *Tabellen zur Musikgeschichte: Ein Hilfsbuch
beim Studium der Musikgeschichte.* 5th ed., enl. Hans

Joachim Moser. Wiesbaden: Breitkopf & Härtel, 1962. First
published in 1914.

Wold, Milo, et al. *An Outline History of Western Music.* 9th ed.
Boston: WCB McGraw-Hill, 1997. First published in 1963.

Wörner, Karl H. *History of Music: A Book for Study and Reference.* 5th ed. Trans. and suppl. Willis Wager. New York:
Free Press, 1973. First published in 1954.

Twentieth Century

Burbank, Richard. *Twentieth Century Music.* Introduction by
Nicolas Slonimsky. New York: Facts on File, 1984.

Slonimsky, Nicolas, and Laura Diane Kuhn. *Music since 1900.*
6th ed. New York: Schirmer Reference, 2001. First published in 1937.

American

Caldwell, Hansonia L. *An Educator's Resource Manual for
African-American Music: A Chronology 1619–1995.*
Culver City, Calif.: Ikoro Communications, 1997.

Hall, Charles John, comp. *A Chronicle of American Music 1700–
1995.* New York: Schirmer Books, 1996.

Lahee, Henry C. *Annals of Music in America: A Chronological
Record of Significant Musical Events from 1640 to the
Present Day, with Comments on the Various Periods
into Which the Work Is Divided.* Boston: Marshall Jones,
1922; reprint, Freeport, N.Y.: Books for Libraries Press,
1970.

Sablosky, Irving. *What They Heard: Music in America, 1852–
1881, from the Pages of* Dwight's Journal of Music. Baton
Rouge: Louisiana State University Press, 1986.

Opera

Loewenberg, Alfred. *Annals of Opera, 1597–1940, Compiled
from the Original Sources.* 3rd ed., rev. and corr. Totowa,
N.J.: Rowman and Littlefield, 1978. First published in
1943.

BIOGRAPHIES OF COMPOSERS IN ENGLISH

From its beginnings in the mid-eighteenth century, the category
of composer biographies has steadily grown to its present enor-
mous size. Biographical writing has also passed through various
stylistic phases; in light of current rigorous scholarly standards, ac-

cumulated research, and availability of information, most earlier biographies must be viewed in their historical context rather than taken at face value.

The present bibliography lists reliable, serious, and for the most part recent biographies in English, or in English translation, of some of the best-known composers, listed in alphabetical order by composer. Only a few of the classic nineteenth-century or earlier-twentieth-century standards (e.g., Spitta/Bach, Thayer/Beethoven, Moser/Schütz) have been included. Those felt to be overly romanticized or popular in tone, even though still known and used, have been omitted, as have those that are essentially brief sketches or summaries. A few examples of the pictorial or documentary biography have been included.

The present list is one of the most selective in this book; for more comprehensive lists of biographies of composers and other musical figures, the section "Biographies of Musicians" in chapter 2, pp. 42–48 above, should be consulted. The composer biographies comprising three important publishers' series are enumerated separately following the present listing. See also the periodicals devoted to individual composers, such as those listed in chapter 6 under "Musicology," "Limited to a Single Composer," pp. 238–39 below.

Ottenberg, Hans-Günter. *C. P. E. Bach.* Trans. Philip Whitmore. London: Oxford University Press, 1987. First published in 1982.

Gärtner, Heinz. *John Christian Bach: Mozart's Friend and Mentor.* Trans. Reinhard G. Pauly. Portland, Ore.: Amadeus Press, 1994. First published in 1989.

David, Hans T., and Arthur Mendel, eds. *The New Bach Reader: A Life of Johann Sebastian Bach in Letters and Documents.* Rev. and enl. Christoph Wolff. New York: W. W. Norton, 1999. First published in 1945 as *The Bach Reader.*

Felix, Werner. *Johann Sebastian Bach.* 1st American ed. New York: W. W. Norton, 1985. First published in 1984.

Geiringer, Karl, in collaboration with Irene Geiringer. *Johann Sebastian Bach: The Culmination of an Era.* London: Oxford University Press, 1966.

Spitta, Philipp. *Johann Sebastian Bach: His Work and Influence on the Music of Germany, 1685–1750.* Trans. Clara Bell and J. A. Fuller-Maitland. 3 vols. London: Novello, 1884–85; reprint, New York: Dover Publications, 1992. First published in 1873–80.

Terry, Charles Sanford. *Bach: A Biography.* 2nd ed., rev. London: Oxford University Press, 1933; reprint, London: Oxford University Press, 1972. First published in 1928.
Wolff, Christoph. *Johann Sebastian Bach: The Learned Musician.* New York: W. W. Norton, 2000.

Antokoletz, Elliott, Victoria Fischer, and Benjamin Suchoff. *Bartók Perspectives: Man, Composer, and Ethnomusicologist.* Oxford: Oxford University Press, 2000.
Bartók, Peter. *My Father.* Homosassa, Fla.: Bartók Records, 2002.
Chalmers, Kenneth. *Béla Bartók.* London: Phaidon Press, 1995.
Gillies, Malcolm. *The Bartók Companion.* Portland, Ore.: Amadeus Press, 1994.
Stevens, Halsey. *The Life and Music of Béla Bartók.* 3rd ed. Ed. Malcolm Gillies. London: Oxford University Press, 1993. First published in 1953.
Suchoff, Benjamin. *Béla Bartók: Life and Work.* Lanham, Md.: Scarecrow Press, 2001.

Davies, Peter J. *Beethoven in Person: His Deafness, Illnesses, and Death.* Westport, Conn.: Greenwood Press, 2001.
———. *The Character of a Genius: Beethoven in Perspective.* Westport, Conn.: Greenwood Press, 2002.
Kindermann, William. *Beethoven.* Oxford: Oxford University Press, 1995.
Landon, H. C. Robbins. *Beethoven: His Life, Work and World.* New York: Thames and Hudson, 1993. Adapted from *Beethoven: A Documentary Study,* 1970.
Lockwood, Lewis. *Beethoven: The Music and the Life.* New York: W. W. Norton, 2003.
Marek, George R. *Beethoven: Biography of a Genius.* New York: Funk & Wagnalls, 1969.
Solomon, Maynard. *Beethoven.* 2nd rev. ed. New York: Schirmer Books, 1998. First published in 1977.
———. *Late Beethoven: Music, Thought, Imagination.* Berkeley: University of California Press, 2003.
Thayer, Alexander Wheelock. *Thayer's Life of Beethoven.* Trans. Henry Edward Krehbiel (1921). Rev. and ed. Elliot Forbes, Herman Deiters, and Hugo Riemann. Princeton, N.J.: Princeton University Press, 1991. First published in 1866–79 (vols. 1–3) and 1907–1908 (vols. 4–5).

Weinstock, Herbert. *Vincenzo Bellini: His Life and His Operas.* New York: Alfred A. Knopf, 1971.

Carner, Mosco. *Alban Berg: The Man and the Work.* 2nd rev. ed. New York: Holmes & Meier Publishers, 1983. First published in 1975.

Monson, Karen. *Alban Berg.* Boston: Houghton Mifflin, 1979.

Redlich, Hans. *Alban Berg: The Man and His Music.* New York: Abelard-Schuman, 1957.

Reich, Willi. *The Life and Work of Alban Berg.* Trans. Cornelius Cardew. New York: Harcourt, Brace & World, 1965; reprint, New York: Da Capo Press, 1981. First published in 1963.

Barzun, Jacques. *Berlioz and the Romantic Century.* 3rd ed. 2 vols. New York: Columbia University Press, 1969. First published in 1950. Rev. and abridged as *Berlioz and His Century: An Introduction to the Age of Romanticism.* Chicago: University of Chicago Press, 1982.

Berlioz, Hector. *The Memoirs of Hector Berlioz.* Trans. David Cairns. New York: Alfred A. Knopf, 2002. First published in 1870.

Bloom, Peter, ed. *Berlioz: Past, Present, Future: Bicentenary Essays.* Rochester, N.Y.: University of Rochester Press, 2003.

Cairns, David. *Berlioz. Volume 1: The Making of an Artist, 1803–1832. Volume 2: Servitude and Greatness.* Berkeley: University of California Press, 2000.

Holoman, D. Kern. *Berlioz: A Musical Biography of the Creative Genius of the Romantic Era.* Cambridge, Mass: Harvard University Press, 1989.

Macdonald, Hugh. *Berlioz.* Rev. ed. Oxford: Oxford University Press, 2000. First published in 1991.

Rose, Michael. *Berlioz Remembered.* New York: Faber, 2001.

McKay, David P., and Richard Crawford. *William Billings of Boston: Eighteenth-Century Composer.* Princeton, N.J.: Princeton University Press, 1975.

Kirkman, Andrew, and Dennis Slavin, eds. *Binchois Studies.* Oxford: Oxford University Press, 2001.

Curtiss, Mina Kirstein. *Bizet and His World.* Westport, Conn.: Greenwood Press, 1977.

Dean, Winton. *Georges Bizet: His Life and Work.* London: J. M. Dent, 1965.

Jameux, Dominique. *Pierre Boulez.* Cambridge, Mass.: Harvard University Press, 1991.

Peyser, Joan. *Boulez.* New York: Schirmer Books, 1976.

Avins, Styra, and Josef Eisinger. *Johannes Brahms: Life and Letters.* Oxford: Oxford University Press, 1998.

Beller-McKenna, Daniel. *Brahms and the German Spirit.* Cambridge, Mass.: Harvard University Press, 2004.

Brown, Jonathon. *Johannes Brahms: An Essential Guide to His Life and Works.* London: Pavilion, 1996.

Dietrich, Albert Hermann, Joseph Viktor Widmann, and Dora E. Hecht. *Recollections of Johannes Brahms.* Honolulu: University Press of the Pacific, 2000.

Gál, Hans. *Johannes Brahms: His Work and Personality.* Rev. ed. Trans. Joseph Stein. Westport, Conn.: Greenwood Press, 1975. First published in 1961.

Geiringer, Karl, in collaboration with Irene Geiringer. *Brahms: His Life and Work.* 3rd, enl. ed. New York: Da Capo Press, 1982. First published in 1934.

James, Burnett. *Brahms: A Critical Study.* London: J. M. Dent and Sons, 1972.

Keys, Ivor. *Johannes Brahms.* London: Christopher Helm, 1989.

May, Florence. *The Life of Johannes Brahms.* Rev. 2nd ed. 2 vols. London: William Reeves, Bookseller, 1988. First published in 1905.

Neunzig, Hans A. *Brahms.* Trans. Mike Mitchell. London: Haus, 2003. First published in 1997.

Swafford, Jan. *Johannes Brahms: A Biography.* New York: Vintage Books, 1999.

Britten, Beth. *My Brother Benjamin.* Abbotsbrook, Bourne End, Buckinghamshire, England: The Kensal Press, 1986.

Carpenter, Humphrey. *Benjamin Britten: A Biography.* London: Faber and Faber, 1992.

Headington, Christopher. *Britten.* London: Omnibus Press, 1996.

Matthews, David. *Britten.* London: Haus, 2003.

Oliver, Michael. *Benjamin Britten.* London: Phaidon, 1996.

White, Eric Walter. *Benjamin Britten: His Life and Operas.* 2nd ed. Ed. John Evans. Berkeley: University of California Press, 1983. First published in 1970.

Doernberg, Erwin. *The Life and Symphonies of Anton Bruckner.* London: Barrie & Rockliff, 1960; reprint, New York: Dover Publications, 1968.

Howie, Crawford. *Anton Bruckner: A Documentary Biography.* 2 vols. Lewiston, N.Y.: Edwin Mellen Press, 2002.

Howie, Crawford, Paul Hankshaw, and Timothy L. Jackson.

Perspectives on Anton Bruckner. Aldershot, England:
  Ashgate, 2001.
Jackson, Timothy L., and Paul Hankshaw. *Bruckner Studies.*
  Cambridge: Cambridge University Press, 1997.
Johnson, Stephen. *Bruckner Remembered.* London: Faber and
  Faber, 1998.
Watson, Derek. *Bruckner.* New York: Schirmer Books, 1997.

Snyder, Kerala J. *Dieterich Buxtehude: Organist in Lübeck.* New
  York: Schirmer Books, 1987.

Brown, Alan, and Richard Turbet. *Byrd Studies.* Cambridge:
  Cambridge University Press, 1992.
Harley, John. *William Byrd: Gentleman of the Chapel Royal.*
  Reprint with amendments. Aldershot, England: Ashgate
  Publishing, 1999. First published in 1997.
Howes, Frank Stewart. *William Byrd.* London: Trubner, 1928;
  reprint, Westport, Conn.: Greenwood Press, 1978.

Patterson, David. *John Cage: The Early Decades; Music, Philoso-*
  phy and Intention, 1933–1950. New York: Garland Publishing, 2000.
Revill, David. *The Roaring Silence: John Cage: A Life.* London:
  Bloomsbury, 1992.

Atwood, William G. *Fryderyk Chopin: Pianist from Warsaw.*
  New York: Columbia University Press, 1987.
Azoury, P. H. *Chopin through His Contemporaries: Friends,*
  Lovers, and Rivals. Westport, Conn.: Greenwood Press,
  1999.
Gavoty, Bernard. *Frederic Chopin.* Trans. Martin Sokolinsky. New
  York: Charles Scribner's Sons, 1977. First published in 1974.
Hadden, J. Cuthbert. *Chopin.* London: Cambridge Scholars,
  2002. First published in 1903.
Jordan, Ruth. *Nocturne: A Life of Chopin.* New York: Taplinger
  Publishing, 1978.
Marek, George R., and Maria Gordon-Smith. *Chopin.* New York:
  Harper & Row, 1978.
Samson, Jim. *Chopin.* New York: Oxford University Press, 1998.
Siepmann, Jeremy. *Chopin, the Reluctant Romantic.* Boston:
  Northeastern University Press, 1995.
Szulc, Tad. *Chopin in Paris: The Life and Times of the Romantic*
  Composer. New York: Scribner, 1998.
Zamoyski, Adam. *Chopin: A New Biography.* 1st American ed.
  Garden City, N.Y.: Doubleday, 1980. First published in
  1979.

Copland, Aaron, and Vivian Perlis. *Copland: 1900 through 1942.* New York: St. Martin's Press, 1984.

————. *Copland since 1943.* New York: St. Martin's Press, 1989.

Pollack, Howard. *Aaron Copland: The Life and Work of an Uncommon Man.* Urbana: University of Illinois Press, 2000.

Allsop, Peter. *Arcangelo Corelli: New Orpheus of Our Times.* Oxford: Oxford University Press, 1999.

Pincherle, Marc. *Corelli: His Life, His Work.* Trans. Hubert E. M. Russell. New York: W. W. Norton, 1956. First published in 1933.

Beaussant, Philippe. *François Couperin.* Trans. Alexandria Land. Portland, Ore.: Amadeus Press, 1990. First published in 1980.

Mellers, Wilfrid. *François Couperin and the French Classical Tradition.* New vers. London: Faber and Faber, 1987. First published in 1950.

Hicks, Michael. *Henry Cowell, Bohemian.* Urbana: University of Illinois Press, 2002.

Gillespie, Don C. *George Crumb.* New York: C. F. Peters, 1986.

Fearn, Raymond. *The Music of Luigi Dallapiccola.* Rochester, N.Y.: University of Rochester Press, 2004.

Lockspeiser, Edward. *Debussy: His Life and Mind.* 2 vols. New York: Macmillan, 1962–65; reprint, Cambridge: Cambridge University Press, 1978.

von Dohnányi, Ilona. *Ernst von Dohnányi: A Song of Life.* Ed. James A. Grymes. Bloomington: Indiana University Press, 2002.

Weinstock, Herbert. *Donizetti and the World of Opera in Italy, Paris and Vienna in the First half of the Nineteenth Century.* London: Methuen and Company, 1963.

Fallows, David. *Dufay.* Rev. ed. London: Dent, 1987. First published in 1982.

Beckerman, Michael Brim. *New Worlds of Dvořák: Searching in America for the Composer's Inner Life.* New York: W. W. Norton, 2003.

Clapham, John. *Dvořák.* 1st American ed. New York: W. W. Norton, 1979.

Dvořák, Otakar, and Paul J. Polansky. *Antonín Dvořák, My Father.* Spillville, Iowa: Czech Historical Research Center, 1993.

Hughes, Gervaise. *Dvořák: His Life and Music.* New York: Dodd, Mead, 1967.

Schönzeler, Hans-Hubert. *Dvořák.* London: Marion Boyars, 1984.

Kennedy, Michael. *Portrait of Elgar.* 3rd ed. Oxford: Clarendon Press, 1993. First published in 1968.

Moore, Jerrold Northrop. *Edward Elgar: A Creative Life.* Oxford: Oxford University Press, 1984.

Mundy, Simon. *Elgar.* Rev. ed. London: Omnibus Press, 2001. First published in 1980.

Piggott, Patrick. *The Life and Music of John Field, 1782–1837, Creator of the Nocturne.* Berkeley: University of California Press, 1973.

Hammond, Frederick. *Girolamo Frescobaldi.* Cambridge, Mass.: Harvard University Press, 1983.

Arnold, Denis. *Giovanni Gabrieli and the Music of the Venetian High Renaissance.* Reprint with corrections. Oxford: Oxford University Press, 1986. First published in 1979.

Kenton, Egon. *Life and Works of Giovanni Gabrieli.* Musicological Studies and Documents, no. 16. [Rome]: American Institute of Musicology, 1967.

Hyland, William. *George Gershwin: A New Biography.* Westport, Conn.: Greenwood Press, 2003.

Jablonski, Edward. *Gershwin.* New York: Doubleday, 1987.

———. *Gershwin Remembered.* Portland, Ore.: Amadeus Press, 1992.

Leon, Ruth. *Gershwin.* London: Haus, 2003.

Peyser, Joan. *The Memory of All That: The Life of George Gershwin.* New York: Simon and Schuster, 1993.

Wood, Ean. *George Gershwin: His Life and Music.* London: Sanctuary Publishing, 1996.

Watkins, Glenn. *Gesualdo: The Man and His Music.* 2nd ed. Oxford: Clarendon Press, 1979. First published in 1973.

Ainger, Michael. *Gilbert and Sullivan: A Dual Biography.* New York: Oxford University Press, 2002.

Maycock, Robert. *Glass: A Biography of Philip Glass.* London: Sanctuary, 2002.

Howard, Patricia. *Gluck: An Eighteenth-Century Portrait in Letters and Documents.* Oxford: Clarendon Press, 1995.

Harding, James. *Gounod.* New York: Stein and Day, 1973.

Benestad, Finn, and Dag Schjelderup-Ebbe. *Edvard Grieg: The Man and the Artist.* Lincoln: University of Nebraska Press, 1988.
Layton, Robert. *Grieg.* London: Omnibus Press, 1998.

Burrows, Donald. *Handel.* Oxford: Oxford University Press, 1996.
Deutsch, Otto Erich. *Handel: A Documentary Biography.* Rev. ed. New York: W. W. Norton, 1974. First published in 1955. An updated ed. based on this work with the documents in their original language, most of which are in English, is published as *Dokumente zu Leben und Schaffen: Auf der Grundlage von Otto Erich Deutsch, Handel: A Documentary Biography,* ed. the staff of the Hallischen Händel-Ausgabe (vol. 4 of *Händel-Handbuch*), Kassel: Bärenreiter, 1985.
Hogwood, Christopher. *Handel.* New York: Thames and Hudson, 1984.
Keates, Jonathan. *Handel: The Man and His Music.* New York: St. Martin's Press, 1985.
Landon, H. C. Robbins. *Handel and His World.* 1st American ed. Boston: Little, Brown, 1984.
Lang, Paul Henry. *George Frideric Handel.* Rev. ed. New York: W. W. Norton, 1977, reprint, Mineola, N.Y.: Dover Publications, 1996. First published in 1966.

Geiringer, Karl. *Haydn: A Creative Life in Music.* 3rd ed., rev. and enl. Berkeley: University of California Press, 1982. First published in 1946.
Landon, H. C. Robbins. *Haydn: A Documentary Study.* New York: Rizzoli, 1981.
———. *Haydn: Chronicle and Works.* 1st American ed. 5 vols. Bloomington: Indiana University Press, 1976–80; updated reprint, London: Thames and Hudson, 1984.
Landon, H. C. Robbins, and David Wyn Jones. *Haydn: His Life and Music.* Bloomington: Indiana University Press, 1988.

Bobko, Jane, Matthew Fox, and Barbara Newman. *Vision: The*

Life and Music of Hildegard von Bingen. New York: Penguin Studio, 1995.

Schipperges, Heinrich. *The World of Hildegard of Bingen: Her Life, Times, and Visions.* Trans. John Cumming. Collegeville, Minn.: Liturgical Press, 1998. First published in 1997.

Skelton, Geoffrey. *Paul Hindemith: The Man Behind the Music: A Biography.* London: Victor Gollancz, 1975.

Burkholder, J. Peter. *Charles Ives: The Ideas behind the Music.* New Haven, Conn.: Yale University Press, 1985.

Cowell, Henry, and Sidney Cowell. *Charles Ives and His Music.* 2nd ed., rev. with a new foreword, an updated list of works, bibliography, and discography. New York: Da Capo Press, 1983. First published in 1955.

Feder, Stuart. *Charles Ives, "My Father's Song": A Psychoanalytic Biography.* New Haven, Conn.: Yale University Press, 1992.

Rossiter, Frank R. *Charles Ives and His America.* New York: Liveright, 1975.

Swafford, Jan. *Charles Ives: A Life with Music.* New York: W. W. Norton, 1996.

Wooldridge, David. *From the Steeples and Mountains: A Study of Charles Ives.* New York: Alfred A. Knopf, 1974.

Vogel, Jaroslav. *Leos Janáček: A Biography.* 3rd rev. ed. Prague: Academia, 1997. First published in 1981.

Zemanová, Mirka. *Janáček: A Composer's Life.* London: John Murray, 2002.

Sherr, Richard, ed. *The Josquin Companion.* Oxford: Oxford University Press, 2000.

Eosze, László. *Zoltán Kodály: His Life and Work.* Boston: Crescendo Publishing Company, 1962.

Arnold, Ben. *The Liszt Companion.* Westport, Conn.: Greenwood Press, 2002.

Burger, Ernst. *Franz Liszt: A Chronicle of His Life in Pictures and Documents.* Trans. Stewart Spencer. Princeton, N.J.: Princeton University Press, 1989.

Gooley, Dana A. *The Virtuoso Liszt.* Cambridge: Cambridge University Press, 2004.

Perényi, Eleanor Spencer (Stone). *Liszt: The Artist as Romantic Hero.* Boston: Little, Brown, 1974.

Taylor, Ronald. *Franz Liszt: The Man and the Musician.* London: Grafton Books, 1986.

Walker, Alan. *Franz Liszt.* Rev. ed. 3 vols. Ithaca, N.Y.: Cornell University Press, 1987–96. First published in 1983.

Newman, Joyce. *Jean-Baptiste de Lully and His Tragédies lyriques.* Studies in Musicology, no. 1. Ann Arbor, Mich.: UMI Research Press, 1979.

Scott, R. H. F. *Jean-Baptiste Lully.* London: Owen, 1973.

Reaney, Gilbert. *Guillaume de Machaut.* London: Oxford University Press, 1971.

Blaukopf, Kurt. *Gustav Mahler.* Trans. Inge Goodwin. New York: Praeger and Praeger, 1973; reprint, New York: Limelight Editions, 1991. First published in 1969.

———, comp. and ed., with contributions by Zoltan Roman. *Mahler: A Documentary Study.* Trans. Paul Baker et al. London: Thames and Hudson, 1976.

Blaukopf, Kurt, Herta Blaukopf, and Zoltan Roman. *Mahler: His Life, Work and World.* London: Thames and Hudson, 2000.

Gartenberg, Egon. *Mahler: The Man and His Music.* New York: Schirmer Books, 1978.

Kennedy, Michael. *Mahler.* 2nd ed. Oxford: Oxford University Press, 2000. First published in 1974.

La Grange, Henri-Louis de. *Mahler. Vol. 1.* Garden City, N.Y.: Doubleday, 1973. First published in 1973.

———. *Mahler. Vol. 2: Vienna: The Years of Challenge (1897–1904).* Rev., enl., and updated trans. Oxford: Oxford University Press, 1995. First published in 1983.

———. *Mahler. Vol. 3: Vienna: Triumph and Disillusion (1904–1907).* Rev., enl., and updated trans. Oxford: Oxford University Press, 1995. First published in 1984.

Mitchell, Donald. *Gustav Mahler: Songs and Symphonies of Life and Death: Interpretations and Annotations.* Berkeley: University of California Press, 1986.

———. *Gustav Mahler: The Early Years.* New ed. Rev. and ed. Paul Banks and David Matthews. Rochester, N.Y.: Boydell Press, 2003. First published in 1980.

———. *Gustav Mahler: The Wunderhorn Years: Chronicles and Commentaries.* New ed. Rochester, N.Y.: Boydell Press, 2003. First published in 1975.

Brown, Clive. *A Portrait of Mendelssohn.* New Haven, Conn.: Yale University Press, 2003.

Cooper, John Michael, and Julie D. Prandi, eds. *The Mendels-sohns: Their Music in History.* New York: Oxford University Press, 2003.

Marek, George R. *Gentle Genius: The Story of Felix Mendels-sohn.* New York: Funk & Wagnalls, 1972.

Todd, R. Larry. *Mendelssohn: A Life in Music.* New York: Oxford University Press, 2003.

Werner, Eric. *Mendelssohn: A New Image of the Composer and His Age.* Trans. Dika Newlin. New York: Free Press of Glencoe, 1963. Rev. and enl. ed. in German, 1980.

Carter, Tim. *Monteverdi and His Contemporaries.* Aldershot, England: Ashgate Press, 2000.

Fabbri, Paolo. *Monteverdi.* Trans. Tim Carter. Cambridge: Cambridge University Press, 1994. First published in 1985.

Redlich, Hans. *Claudio Monteverdi: Life and Works.* Trans. Kathleen Dale. London: Oxford University Press, 1952; reprint, Westport, Conn.: Greenwood Press, 1970. First published in 1949.

Schrade, Leo. *Monteverdi: Creator of Modern Music.* New York: W. W. Norton, 1950; reprint, New York: Da Capo Press, 1979.

Stevens, Denis. *Monteverdi in Venice.* Madison, N.J.: Fairleigh Dickinson University Press, 2001.

Tomlinson, Gary. *Monteverdi and the End of the Renaissance.* Berkeley: University of California Press, 1987.

Deutsch, Otto Erich. *Mozart: A Documentary Biography.* Rev. ed. Trans. Eric Blom et al. Stanford: Stanford University Press, 1965. First published in 1961.

Einstein, Alfred. *Mozart: His Character, His Work.* Trans. Arthur Mendel and Nathan Broder. London: Oxford University Press, 1945; reprint, London: Oxford University Press, 1972. Original German version published in 1947.

Elias, Norbert. *Mozart: Portrait of a Genius.* Trans. Edmund Jephcott. Berkeley: University of California Press, 1993. First published in 1991.

Gutman, Robert W. *Mozart: A Cultural Biography.* New York: Harcourt Brace, 1999.

Hildesheimer, Wolfgang. *Mozart.* Trans. Marion Faber. New York: Farrar Straus Giroux, 1981; reprint, Norwalk, Conn.: Easton Press, 1992. First published in 1977.

Hutchings, Arthur. *Mozart: The Man, the Musician.* New York: Schirmer Books, 1976.

Keys, Ivor. *Mozart: His Music in His Life.* New York: Holmes & Meier Publishers, 1979.

Knepler, Georg. *Wolfgang Amadé Mozart.* Trans. J. Bradford Robinson. Cambridge: Cambridge University Press, 1993. First published in 1991.

Küster, Konrad. *Mozart: A Musical Biography.* Trans. Mary Whittall. Oxford: Clarendon Press, 1996. First published in 1990.

Landon, H. C. Robbins. *1791: Mozart's Last Year.* London: Thames and Hudson, 1999.

Solomon, Maynard. *Mozart: A Life.* New York: Harper/Collins, 1995.

Leyda, Jay, and Sergei Bertensson, eds. and transls. *The Musorgsky Reader: A Life of Modeste Petrovich Musorgsky in Letters and Documents.* Rev. ed. New York: W. W. Norton, 1970. First published in 1947.

Orlova, Alexandra. *Musorgsky's Days and Works: A Biography in Documents.* Trans. and ed. Roy J. Guenther. Russian Music Studies, no. 4. Ann Arbor, Mich.: UMI Research Press, 1983. First published in 1963.

———. *Musorgsky Remembered.* Trans. Véronique Zaytzeff and Frederick Morrison. Bloomington: Indiana University Press, 1991. First published in 1963.

Seroff, Victor. *Modeste Moussorgsky.* New York: Funk & Wagnalls, 1968.

Wegman, Rob C. *Born for the Muses: The Life and Masses of Jacob Obrecht.* Oxford: Clarendon Press, 1994.

Cametti, Alberto. *Palestrina.* 1st A.M.S. ed. New York: A.M.S. Press, 1979. First published in 1979.

Pyne, Zoë Kendrick. *Giovanni Pierluigi da Palestrina: His Life and Times.* London: Dodd Mead and Company, 1922; reprint, Temecula, Calif.: Reprint Services, 2003.

Schwinger, Wolfram. *Krzysztof Penderecki: His Life and Work: Encounters, Biography, and Musical Commentary.* Trans. William Mann. London: Schott, 1989. First published in 1979.

Carter, Tim. *Jacopo Peri, 1561–1633: His Life and Works.* New York: Garland Publications, 1989.

Buckland, Sidney, and Myriam Chimènes. *Francis Poulenc:*

Music, Art and Literature. Aldershot, England: Ashgate
Publishing, 1999.
Mellers, Wilfrid Howard. *Francis Poulenc.* Oxford: Oxford
University Press, 1993.
Schmidt, Carl B. *Entrancing Muse: A Documented Biography
of Francis Poulenc.* Hillsdale, N.Y.: Pendragon Press,
2001.

Gutman, David. *Prokofiev.* Alderman Music Makers. London:
Alderman, 1987.
Jaffé, Daniel. *Sergey Prokofiev.* London: Phaidon, 1998.
Nice, David. *Prokofiev: From Russia to the West, 1891–1935.*
New Haven, Conn.: Yale University Press, 2003.
Robinson, Harlow. *Sergei Prokofiev: A Biography.* New York:
Viking Press, 1987; reprint with a new introduction.
Boston: Northeastern University Press, 2002.
Samuel, Claude. *Prokofiev.* Trans. Miriam John. London: Marion
Boyars, 2000. First published in 1971.
Schipperges, Thomas. *Prokofiev.* Trans. J. M. Q. Davies. London:
Haus, 2003. First published in 1995.
Seroff, Victor. *Sergei Prokofiev: A Soviet Tragedy: The Case of
Sergei Prokofiev, His Life and Work, His Critics, and His
Executioners.* New York: Funk & Wagnalls, 1968.

Carner, Mosco. *Puccini: A Critical Biography.* 3rd ed. New York:
Holmes and Meier, 1992. First published in 1959.
Phillips-Matz, Mary Jane. *Puccini: A Biography.* Boston: North-
eastern University Press, 2002.
Ramsden, Timothy. *Puccini.* London: Omnibus, 1996.

Adams, Martin. *Henry Purcell: The Origins and Development
of His Musical Style.* Cambridge: Cambridge University
Press, 1995.
Campbell, Margaret. *Henry Purcell: Glory of His Age.* London:
Hutchinson, 1993.
Duffy, Maureen. *Henry Purcell.* London: Fourth Estate, 1994.
Holman, Peter. *Henry Purcell.* Oxford: Oxford University Press,
1994.
King, Robert. *Henry Purcell.* London: Thames and Hudson,
1994.
Zimmerman, Franklin B. *Henry Purcell, 1659–1695: His Life and
Times.* 2nd, rev. ed. Philadelphia: University of Pennsylva-
nia Press, 1983. First published in 1967.

Bertensson, Sergei, Jay Leyda, and Sophia Satina. *Sergei Rachmaninoff: A Lifetime in Music.* New York: New York

University Press, 1956; reprint with a new introduction, Bloomington: Indiana University Press, 2001.

Martyn, Barrie. *Rachmaninoff: Composer, Pianist, Conductor.* Aldershot, England: Scholar Press, 1990.

Norris, Geoffrey. *Rachmaninoff.* 2nd ed. Oxford: Oxford University Press, 2000. First published in 1993.

Wehrmeyer, Andreas. *Rakhmaninov.* Trans. Anne Wyburd. London: Haus, 2003. First published in 1999.

Girdlestone, Cuthbert. *Jean-Philippe Rameau: His Life and Work.* 2nd ed., rev. and enl. New York: Dover Publications, 1969. First published in 1957.

Larner, Gerald. *Maurice Ravel.* London: Phaidon, 1996.

Myers, Rollo H. *Maurice Ravel: Life and Works.* London: Gerald Duckworth, 1960.

Orenstein, Arbie. *Ravel: Man and Musician.* New York: Columbia University Press, 1975.

Iastrebtsev, V. V. *Reminiscences of Rimsky-Korsakov.* Trans. Florence Jonas. New York: Columbia University Press, 1985. First published in 1917.

Kendall, Alan. *Gioacchino Rossini.* London: Gollancz, 1992.

Osborne, Richard. *Rossini.* Boston: Northeastern University Press, 1990.

Servadio, Gaia. *Rossini.* New York: Carroll and Graf Publishers, 2003.

Weinstock, Herbert. *Rossini: A Biography.* New York: Alfred A. Knopf, 1968; reprint, New York: Limelight Editions, 1987.

Meconi, Honey. *Pierre de la Rue and Musical Life at the Habsburg-Burgundian Court.* Oxford: Oxford University Press, 2002.

Braunbehrens, Volkmar. *Maligned Master: The Real Story of Antonio Salieri.* 1st U.S. ed. Trans. Eveline L. Kanes. New York: Fromm International Publishing Corporation, 1992. First published in 1989.

Rice, John A. *Antonio Salieri and Viennese Opera.* Chicago: University of Chicago Press, 1998.

Gillmor, Alan M. *Erik Satie.* New York: W. W. Norton, 1992.

Myers, Rollo H. *Erik Satie.* London: D. Dobson, 1948; reprint, St. Clair Shores, Mich.: Scholarly Press, 1977.

Orledge, Robert. *Satie Remembered.* Portland, Ore.: Amadeus Press, 1995.

Volta, Ornella. *Erik Satie.* Trans. Simon Pleasance. Paris: Hazan, 1997. First published in 1979.

Whiting, Steven Moore. *Satie the Bohemian: From Cabaret to Concert Hall.* Oxford: Oxford University Press, 1999.

Dent, Edward Joseph. *Alessandro Scarlatti: His Life and Works.* London: E. Arnold, 1960.

Boyd, Malcolm. *Domenico Scarlatti—Master of Music.* 1st American ed. New York: Schirmer Books, 1987. First published in 1986.

Kirkpatrick, Ralph. *Domenico Scarlatti.* 3rd ed., rev. Princeton, N.J.: Princeton University Press, 1968. First published in 1953.

Auner, Joseph Henry. *A Schoenberg Reader: Documents of a Life.* New Haven, Conn.: Yale University Press, 2003.

Bailey, Walter. *The Arnold Schoenberg Companion.* Westport, Conn.: Greenwood Press, 1998.

Frisch, Walter. *Schoenberg and His World.* Princeton, N.J.: Princeton University Press, 1999.

Reich, Willi. *Schoenberg: A Critical Biography.* Trans. Leo Black. London: Longman, 1971; reprint, New York: Da Capo Press, 1981. First published in 1968.

Ringer, Alexander L. *Arnold Schoenberg: The Composer as Jew.* Oxford: Clarendon Press, 1990.

Rosen, Charles. *Arnold Schoenberg.* Chicago: University of Chicago Press, 1975; reprint with a new introduction, Chicago: University of Chicago Press, 1996.

Stuckenschmidt, H. H. *Schoenberg: His Life, World, and Work.* 1st American ed. Trans. Humphrey Searle. New York: Schirmer Books, 1977. First published in 1974.

Baker, Richard. *Schubert: A Life in Words and Pictures.* London: Little, Brown, 1997.

Black, Leo. *Franz Schubert: Music and Belief.* Woodbridge, England: Boydell Press, 2003.

Brown, Maurice J. E. *Schubert: A Critical Biography.* New York: St. Martin's Press, 1958; reprint, New York: Da Capo Press, 1988.

Deutsch, Otto Erich. *The Schubert Reader: A Life of Franz Schubert in Letters and Documents.* Rev. ed. Trans. Eric Blom. New York: W. W. Norton, 1977. First published in 1947.

Einstein, Alfred. *Schubert: A Musical Portrait.* London: Oxford University Press, 1951; reprint, New York: Da Capo Press, 1981.

Marek, George R. *Schubert.* New York: Viking Press, 1985.

McKay, Elizabeth Norman. *Franz Schubert: A Biography.* Oxford: Oxford University Press, 2001.

Osborne, Charles. *Schubert and His Vienna.* New York: Alfred A. Knopf, 1985.

Moser, Hans Joachim. *Heinrich Schütz: His Life and Work.* 2nd ed., rev. (1954). Trans. Carl F. Pfatteicher. St. Louis: Concordia Publishing House, 1959. First published in 1936.

Chissell, Joan. *Clara Schumann, a Dedicated Spirit: A Study of Her Life and Work.* New York: Taplinger Publishing Company, 1983.

Reich, Nancy B. *Clara Schumann: The Artist and the Woman.* Rev. ed. Ithaca, N.Y.: Cornell University Press, 2001. First published in 1985.

Daverio, John. *Robert Schumann: Herald of a "New Poetic Age."* New York: Oxford University Press, 1997.

Meier, Barbara. *Robert Schumann.* London: Haus, 2004.

Ostwald, Peter. *Schumann: The Inner Voices of a Musical Genius.* Boston: Northeastern University Press, 1985.

Taylor, Ronald. *Robert Schumann: His Life and Work.* New York: Universe Books, 1982.

Todd, R. Larry, ed. *Schumann and His World.* Princeton, N.J.: Princeton University Press, 1994.

Bowers, Faubion. *Scriabin: A Biography.* 2nd rev. ed. New York: Dover, 1996. First published in 1969.

Schloezer, Boris de. *Scriabin: Artist and Mystic.* Trans. Nicolas Slonimsky. Berkeley: University of California Press, 1987. First published in 1923.

Ardov, Mikhail. *Memories of Shostakovich: Interviews with the Composer's Children and Friends.* Trans. Rosanna Kelly and Michael Meylic. London: Short, 2004. First published in 2003.

Brown, Malcolm Hamrick. *A Shostakovich Casebook.* Bloomington: Indiana University Press, 2004.

Fay, Laurel E. *Shostakovich: A Life.* Oxford: Oxford University Press, 2000.

Ho, Allan Benedict, and Dmitry Feofanov. *Shostakovich Reconsidered.* London: Toccata Press, 1998.

MacDonald, Ian. *The New Shostakovich.* London: Fourth Estate, 1990.

Moshevich, Sofia. *Dmitri Shostakovich, Pianist.* Montreal, Canada: McGill-Queen's University Press, 2004.

Norris, Christopher, ed. *Shostakovich: The Man and His Music.* London: Lawrence and Wishart, 1982.

Volkov, Solomon. *Shostakovich and Stalin: The Extraordinary Relationship between the Great Composer and the Brutal Dictator.* Trans. Antonina W. Bovis. New York: Knopf, 2004.

Wilson, Elizabeth. *Shostakovich: A Life Remembered.* London: Faber and Faber, 1994.

Burnett-James, David. *Sibelius.* London: Omnibus Press, 1989.

Rickards, Guy. *Jean Sibelius.* London: Phaidon Press, 1997.

Tawaststjerna, Erik. *Sibelius.* Trans. Robert Layton. 3 vols. projected. Berkeley: University of California Press, 1976–. First published in 1965–67.

Large, Brian. *Smetana.* New York: Praeger, 1970.

Kurtz, Michael. *Stockhausen: A Biography.* London: Faber and Faber, 1991.

Wörner, Karl Heinrich. *Stockhausen: Life and Work.* Trans. Bill Hopkins. Berkeley: University of California Press, 1973. First published in 1963.

Mayer, Anton. *Johann Strauss: A Nineteenth-Century Pop-Idol.* Trans. Rita Steblin. Vienna: Böhlau, 1999.

Ashley, Tim. *Richard Strauss.* London: Phaidon, 1999.

Boyden, Matthew. *Richard Strauss.* London: Weidenfeld and Nicolson, 1999.

Del Mar, Norman. *Richard Strauss: A Critical Commentary on His Life and Works.* Corr. ed. 3 vols. London: Barrie and Jenkins, 1978; reprint, Ithaca, N.Y.: Cornell University Press, 1986. First published in 1962.

Gilliam, Bryan Randolph, ed. *Richard Strauss and His World.* Princeton, N.J.: Princeton University Press, 1992.

Jefferson, Alan. *The Life of Richard Strauss.* Newton Abbot, England: David & Charles, 1973.

Marek, George R. *Richard Strauss: The Life of a Non-Hero.* New York: Simon and Schuster, 1967.

Nice, David. *Richard Strauss.* London: Omnibus Press, 1993.

Schmid, Mark-Daniel, ed. *The Richard Strauss Companion.* Westport, Conn.: Praeger, 2003.

Wilhelm, Kurt. *Richard Strauss: An Intimate Portrait.* Trans. Mary Whittall. London: Thames and Hudson, 1989. First published in 1984.

Boucourechliev, André. *Stravinsky.* Trans. Martin Cooper. London: Victor Gollancz, 1987. First published in 1968.
Craft, Robert. *Stravinsky: Glimpses of a Life.* London: Lime Tree, 1991.
Stravinsky, Igor, and Robert Craft. *Memories and Commentaries.* London: Faber and Faber, 2002.
Stravinsky, Vera, and Robert Craft. *Stravinsky in Pictures and Documents.* New York: Simon and Schuster, 1978.
Taruskin, Richard. *Stravinsky and the Russian Traditions: A Biography of the Works through* Mavra. Berkeley: University of California Press, 1996.
Tierney, Neil. *The Unknown Country: A Life of Igor Stravinsky.* London: Robert Hale, 1977.
Vlad, Roman. *Stravinsky.* 3rd ed. Trans. Frederick Fuller. Oxford: Oxford University Press, 1985. First published in 1960.
Walsh, Stephen. *Stravinsky: A Creative Spring: Russia and France, 1882–1934.* Berkeley: University of California Press, 1999.
Wenborn, Neil. *Stravinsky.* London: Omnibus Press, 1999.
White, Eric Walter. *Stravinsky: The Composer and His Works.* 2nd ed. Berkeley: University of California Press, 1979. First published in 1966.

Wightman, Alistair. *Karol Szymanowski: His Life and Work.* Burlington, Vt.: Ashgate Publishing, 1999.

Brown, David. *Tchaikovsky.* 1st American ed. 4 vols. New York: W. W. Norton, 1978–92.
———. *Tchaikovsky: A Biographical and Critical Study: The Years of Fame, 1878–1893.* London: Victor Gollancz, 1992.
———. *Tchaikovsky Remembered.* Portland, Ore.: Amadeus Press, 1994.
Holden, Anthony. *Tchaikovsky.* Toronto: Viking, 1995.
Kearney, Leslie, ed. *Tchaikovsky and His World.* Princeton, N.J.: Princeton University Press, 1998.
Kendall, Alan. *Tchaikovsky: A Biography.* London: Bodley Head, 1988.
Orlova, Alexandra. *Tchaikovsky: A Self-Portrait.* Trans. R. M. Davison. Oxford: Oxford University Press, 1990.
Poznansky, Alexander. *Tchaikovsky: The Quest for the Inner Man.* New York: Schirmer Books, 1991.

————. *Tchaikovsky's Last Days: A Documentary Study.*
Oxford: Oxford University Press, 1996.
————, ed. *Tchaikovsky through Others' Eyes.* Bloomington:
Indiana University Press, 1999.
Warrack, John. *Tchaikovsky.* New York: Charles Scribner's Sons,
1973.

Petzoldt, Richard. *Georg Philipp Telemann.* Trans. Horace Fitz-
patrick. New York: Oxford University Press, 1974. First
published in 1967.

Ouellette, Fernand. *Edgard Varèse.* New York: Orion Press, 1968;
reprint, New York: Da Capo Press, 1981.

Frogley, Alain. *Vaughan Williams Studies.* Cambridge: Cam-
bridge University Press, 1996.
Heffer, Simon. *Vaughan Williams.* London: Weidenfeld and
Nicolson, 2000.
Holmes, Paul. *Vaughan Williams: His Life and Times.* London:
Onmibus Press, 1997.
Moore, Jerrold Northrop. *Vaughan Williams: A Life in Pho-
tographs.* Oxford: Oxford University Press, 1992.
Vaughan Williams, Ursula. *R. V. W.: A Biography of Ralph
Vaughan Williams.* London: Oxford University Press,
1964; reprint, Oxford: Clarendon Press, 1992.
Vaughan Williams, Ursula, Roger Buckley, and Joyce Kennedy.
Paradise Remembered. London: Albion Music Ltd.,
2002.

Berger, William. *Verdi with a Vengeance.* New York: Random
House, 2001.
Hardcastle, Robert. *Verdi.* London: Omnibus, 1996.
Kimbell, David R. B. *Verdi in the Age of Italian Romanticism.*
Cambridge: Cambridge University Press, 1981.
Martin, George Whitney. *Verdi: His Music, Life and Times.* 1st
Limelight ed. New York: Limelight Editions, 1992. First
published in 1963.
Meier, Barbara. *Verdi.* Trans. Rosemary Smith. London: Haus,
2003. First published in 2000.
Osborne, Charles. *Verdi: A Life in the Theatre.* New York: Alfred
A. Knopf, 1987.
Phillips-Matz, Mary Jane. *Verdi: A Biography.* Oxford: Oxford
University Press, 1994.
Sadie, Stanley, and Roger Parker. *Verdi and His Operas.* London:
Macmillan Reference, 2000.
Walker, Frank. *The Man Verdi.* Phoenix ed. With a new introduc-

tion by Philip Gossett. Chicago: University of Chicago Press, 1982. First published in 1962.

Weaver, William, comp., ed., and trans. *Verdi: A Documentary Study.* London: Thames and Hudson, [1977].

Appleby, David P. *Heitor Villa-Lobos: A Life (1887–1959).* Lanham, Md.: Scarecrow Press, 2002.

Heller, Karl. *Antonio Vivaldi: The Red Priest of Venice.* Trans. David Marinelli. Portland, Ore.: Amadeus Press, 1997.

Kolneder, Walter. *Antonio Vivaldi: His Life and Work.* Trans. Bill Hopkins. Berkeley: University of California Press, 1970. First published in 1965.

Landon, H. C. Robbins. *Vivaldi: Voice of the Baroque.* New York: Thames and Hudson, 1993.

Pincherle, Marc. *Vivaldi: Genius of the Baroque.* Trans. Christopher Hatch. New York: W. W. Norton, 1957. First published in 1955.

Cotterill, Rowland. *Wagner and His Operas.* London: Omnibus Press, 1996.

Falkayn, David. *The Life of Richard Wagner and the Wagnerian Drama.* Amsterdam: Fredonia Books, 2002.

Gregor-Dellin, Martin. *Richard Wagner: His Life, His Work, His Century.* Trans. J. Maxwell Brownjohn. San Diego: Harcourt Brace Jovanovich, 1983. First published in 1980.

Gutman, Robert W. *Richard Wagner: The Man, His Mind, and His Music.* New York: Harcourt, Brace & World, 1968.

Millington, Barry, ed. *The Wagner Compendium: A Guide to Wagner's Life and Music.* New York: Schirmer Books, 1992.

Newman, Ernest. *The Life of Richard Wagner.* 1st American ed. 4 vols. New York: Alfred A. Knopf, 1933–46; reprint, Cambridge: Cambridge University Press, 1976.

Sabor, Rudolph. *The Real Wagner.* London: André Deutsch, 1987.

Sadie, Stanley. *Wagner and His Operas.* London: Macmillan, 2000.

Spencer, Stewart. *Wagner Remembered.* London: Faber, 2000.

Tanner, Michael. *Wagner.* Princeton, N.J.: Princeton University Press, 1995.

Westernhagen, Curt von. *Wagner: A Biography.* 2 vols. Trans. Mary Whittall. Cambridge: Cambridge University Press, 1978. First published in 1968.

Lloyd, Stephen. *William Walton: Muse of Fire.* Rochester, N.Y.: Boydell and Brewer, 2002.

Friese-Greene, Anthony. *Weber.* London: Omnibus, 1991.
Warrack, John. *Carl Maria von Weber.* 2nd ed. Cambridge:
    Cambridge University Press, 1976. First published in 1968.

Hayes, Malcolm. *Anton von Webern.* London: Phaidon Press,
    1995.
Moldenhauer, Hans, and Rosaleen Moldenhauer. *Anton von
    Webern: A Chronicle of His Life and Works.* 1st American
    ed. New York: Alfred A. Knopf, 1979.

Newman, Ernest. *Hugo Wolf.* London: Methuen, 1907; reprint,
    Wilmington, Del.: International Academic Publishers, 1979.
Walker, Frank. *Hugo Wolf: A Biography.* 2nd, enl. ed. New York:
    Alfred A. Knopf, 1968; reprint, Princeton, N.J.: Princeton
    University Press, 1992. First published in 1951.

Beaumont, Antony. *Zemlinsky.* London: Faber, 2000.

SERIES OF COMPOSERS' BIOGRAPHIES IN ENGLISH

As a supplement to the previous bibliography, the present one
itemizes the contents of four of the best-known and most up-to-
date series of composer biographies (or, in the case of some of the
volumes in the New Grove series, groups of biographies) in English. The Master Musicians Series, whose initial volumes go back
to the 1930s, currently is being expanded and updated by Oxford
University Press. New works are being added to the series, as well
as new editions of many earlier ones, even replacing older studies
with totally new ones by other authors (in which case only the most
recent work on a given composer is listed below). The New Grove
Composer Biography Series was begun in the 1980s as a means of
updating composer articles in *The New Grove Dictionary* and of making them available in a practical format, but the degree of revision
from dictionary to separate volume varies considerably, from com-
paratively little to total rewriting by other authors. The Cambridge
Companions to Music Series composer volumes, written for students, performers, and music lovers, each contain collections of essays by leading authorities. The Cambridge Musical Lives volumes
are biographies written in narrative form, with a discussion of major works included in chronological order.

Cambridge Companions to Music Series. Cambridge: Cam-
    bridge University Press.

Bach. Ed. John Butt. 1997.
Bartók. Ed. Amanda Bayley. 2001.

Beethoven. Ed. Glenn Stanley. 2000.
Berg. Ed. Anthony Pople. 1997.
Britten. Ed. Mervyn Cooke. 1999.
Berlioz. Ed. Peter Bloom. 2000.
Brahms. Ed. Michael Musgrave. 1999.
Cage. Ed. David Nicholls. 2002.
Chopin. Ed. Jim Samson. 1995.
Debussy. Ed. Simon Trezise. 2003.
Handel. Ed. Donald Burrows. 1998.
Mozart. Ed. Simon P. Keefe. 2003.
Ravel. Ed. Deborah Mawer. 2000.
Rossini. Ed. Emanuele Senici. 2004.
Schubert. Ed. Christopher H. Gibbs. 1997.
Sibelius. Ed. Daniel M. Grimley. 2004.
Stravinsky. Ed. Jonathan Cross. 2003.

Cambridge Musical Lives Series. Cambridge: Cambridge
University Press.

The Life of Bach. By Peter Williams. 2004.
The Life of Beethoven. By David Wyn Jones. 1998.
The Life of Bellini. By John Rosselli. 1997.
The Life of Berlioz. By Peter Bloom. 1998.
The Life of Debussy. By Roger Nichols. 1998.
The Life of Elgar. By Michael Kennedy. 2004.
The Life of Charles Ives. By Stuart Feder. 1999.
The Life of Mahler. By Peter Franklin. 1997.
The Life of Mendelssohn. By Peter Mercer-Taylor. 2000.
The Life of Mozart. By John Rosselli.
The Life of Musorgsky. By Caryl Emerson. 1999.
The Life of Schubert. By Christopher H. Gibbs. 2000.
The Life of Richard Strauss. By Bryan Gilliam. 1999.
The Life of Verdi. By John Rosselli. 2000.
The Life of Webern. By Kathryn Bailey. 1998.

Master Musicians Series. Originally published in London by J.
M. Dent and Sons. Oxford University Press, New York,
now has exclusive rights to the series in the United States.
Although some older titles are no longer available, O.U.P.
currently is updating important editions and adding new
titles.

Bach. By Malcolm Boyd. 3rd ed. 2001. First published in
1983.
Bartók. By Paul Griffiths. 1984.
Beethoven. By Barry Cooper. O.U.P. ed., 2002. First pub-
lished in 1985.
Bellini. By Leslie Orrey. 1969.

Berlioz. By Hugh Macdonald. O.U.P. ed., 2001. First
    published in 1982.
Bizet. By Winton Dean. 3rd ed. 1975. First published in
    1948.
Brahms. By Malcolm MacDonald. 2002.
Britten. By Michael Kennedy. Rev. ed. 1994. First pub-
    lished in 1981.
Bruckner. By Derek Watson. 2nd ed. 2001. First published
    in 1975.
Chopin. By Jim Samson. O.U.P. ed., 1994. First published
    in 1947.
Debussy. By Edward Lockspeiser. 5th ed. 1980. First
    published in 1936.
Delius. By Alan Jefferson. 1972.
Dufay. By David Fallows. Rev. ed. 1987. First published in
    1982.
Dvořák. By Alec Robertson. Rev. ed. 1974. First published
    in 1945.
Elgar. By Robert Anderson. 1993.
Franck. By Laurence Davies. 1973.
Grieg. By John Horton. 1974.
Handel. By Donald Burrows. 1995.
Haydn. By Rosemary Hughes. Rev. ed. 1989. First pub-
    lished in 1950.
Liszt. By Derek Watson. O.U.P. ed., 1994. First published
    in 1988.
Mahler. By Michael Kennedy. 2nd ed. 1994. First pub-
    lished in 1974.
Mendelssohn. By Philip Radcliffe. 3rd ed. Rev. Peter Ward
    Jones. 2001. First published in 1954.
Monteverdi. By Denis Arnold. O.U.P. ed., 1994. First
    published in 1963.
Mozart. By Eric Blom. Rev. ed. 1974. First published in
    1935.
Musorgsky. By David Brown. O.U.P. ed., 2002. First
    published in 1946.
Puccini. By Julian Budden. O.U.P. ed., 2002. First pub-
    lished in 1958.
Purcell. By J. A. Westrup. O.U.P. ed., 2001. First published
    in 1937.
Rachmaninoff. By Geoffrey Norris. 2nd ed. First published
    in 1976.
Ravel. By Roger Nichols. 1977.
Rossini. By Richard Osborne. O.U.P. ed., 2002. First
    published in 1986.
Schoenberg. By Malcolm MacDonald. 1976.

Schubert. By John Reed. 2nd ed. 1997. First published in 1987.

Schumann. By Eric Frederick Jensen. O.U.P. ed., 2001. First published in 1948.

Schütz. By Basil Smallman. 2000.

Sibelius. By Robert Layton. 4th ed. 1993. First published in 1965.

Smetana. By John Clapham. 1972.

Richard Strauss. By Michael Kennedy. 2nd ed. 1995. First published in 1976.

Stravinsky. By Paul Griffiths. O.U.P. ed., 1993. First published in 1992.

Tchaikovsky. By Edward Garden. O.U.P. ed., 1994. First published in 1973.

Vaughan Williams. By James Day. 3rd ed. 1998. First published in 1961.

Verdi. By Julian Budden. 1985.

Vivaldi. By Michael Talbot. O.U.P. ed., 2001. First published in 1978.

Wagner. By Barry Millington. O.U.P. ed., 1992. First published in 1984.

The New Grove Composer Biography Series. London: Macmillan; New York: W. W. Norton. In 2001 Oxford University Press, New York, began issuing updated titles based on the second ed. of the *New Grove Dictionary.*

Bach Family. By Christoph Wolff et al. 1983.

Beethoven. By Joseph Kerman and Alan Tyson. 1983.

Early Romantic Masters 1: Chopin, Schumann, Liszt. By Nicholas Temperley et al. 1985.

Early Romantic Masters 2: Weber, Berlioz, Mendelssohn. By John Warrack et al. 1985.

French Baroque Masters: Lully, Charpentier, Lalande, Couperin, Rameau. By James R. Anthony et al. 1986.

Gospel, Blues and Jazz: With Spiritual and Ragtime. By Paul Oliver, Max Harrison, and William Bolcom. 1986.

Handel. By Winton Dean, with Anthony Hicks. 1983.

Haydn. By James Webster. O.U.P., 2001. First published in 1983.

High Renaissance Masters: Josquin, Palestrina, Lassus, Byrd, Victoria. By Gustave Reese et al. 1984.

Italian Baroque Masters: Monteverdi, Frescobaldi, Cavalli, Corelli, A. Scarlatti, Vivaldi, D. Scarlatti. By Denis Arnold et al. 1984.

Late Romantic Masters: Bruckner, Brahms, Dvořák, Wolf. By Deryck Cooke et al. 1985.

Masters of Italian Opera: Rossini, Donizetti, Bellini, Verdi, Puccini. By Philip Gossett et al. 1983.

Modern Masters: Bartók, Stravinsky, Hindemith. By Laszlo Somfai et al. 1984.

Mozart. By Stanley Sadie. O.U.P., 2001. First published in 1983.

North European Baroque Masters: Schütz, Froberger, Buxtehude, Purcell, Telemann. By Joshua Rifkin et al. 1985.

Russian Masters 1: Glinka, Borodin, Balakirev, Musorgsky, Tchaikovsky. By David Brown et al. 1986.

Russian Masters 2: Rimsky-Korsakov, Skryabin, Rakhmaninov, Prokofiev, Shostakovich. By Gerald Abraham et al. 1986.

Schubert. By Maurice J. E. Brown, with Eric Sams. 1983.

Second Viennese School: Schoenberg, Webern, Berg. By Oliver Neighbour et al. 1983.

Stravinsky. By Stanley Sadie. O.U.P., 2001.

Turn of the Century Masters: Janácek, Mahler, Strauss, Sibelius. By John Tyrrell et al. 1985.

Twentieth-Century American Masters: Ives, Thomson, Sessions, Cowell, Gershwin, Copland, Carter, Barber, Cage, Bernstein. By William Austin et al. 1988.

Twentieth-Century English Masters: Elgar, Delius, Vaughan Williams, Holst, Walton, Tippett, Britten. By Diana McVeagh et al. 1986.

Twentieth-Century French Masters: Fauré, Debussy, Satie, Ravel, Poulenc, Messiaen, Boulez. By Jean-Michel Nectoux et al. 1986.

Wagner. By John Deathridge. O.U.P., 2001. First published in 1984.

COLLECTIONS OF EXCERPTS
FROM PRIMARY SOURCES ON MUSIC

Strunk's *Source Readings* has long been known and used by music students and others as the source of excerpts from significant historical writings on music in English or English translation. Some of the other such anthologies of excerpts, like Strunk's, constitute a general history of writings on music (*Cambridge Readings,* Rowen, Weiss/Taruskin). Others focus on a particular aspect, either aesthetics (*Contemplating Music, Musical Aesthetics*), performance practice (MacClintock), women in music (Neuls-Bates), black American music (Southern), music education (Mark), opera (Weiss), jazz (Walser), or hymnology (Music).

A whole category of primary sources not included here comprises compilations of twentieth-century composer interviews, of which there are numerous examples.

Cambridge Readings in the Literature of Music. John Stevens and Peter Le Huray, gen. eds. Cambridge: Cambridge University Press, 1981–.

> *Greek Musical Writings I: The Musician and His Art.* Ed. Andrew Barker. 1984.
> *Greek Musical Writings II: Harmonic and Acoustic Theory.* Ed. Andrew Barker. 1984.
> *Music in Early Christian Literature.* Ed. James McKinnon. 1987.
> *Music and Aesthetics in the Eighteenth and Early-Nineteenth Centuries.* Ed. Peter Le Huray and James Day. 1981. Abridged ed., 1988.
> *Music in European Thought, 1851–1912.* Ed. Bojan Bujic. 1988.
> *Music Analysis in the Nineteenth Century I: Fugue, Form and Style.* Ed. Ian Bent. 1994.
> *Music Analysis in the Nineteenth Century II: Hermeneutic Approaches.* Ed. Ian Bent. 1994.

Contemplating Music: Source Readings in the Aesthetics of Music. Ed. Ruth Katz and Carl Dahlhaus. 4 vols. Aesthetics in Music, no. 5. New York: Pendragon Press, 1987–92.

> 1. *Substance.* 1987.
> 2. *Import.* 1989.
> 3. *Essence.* 1992.
> 4. *Community of Discourse.* 1992.

Downes, Olin, and Irene Downes. *Olin Downes on Music: A Selection from His Writings during the Half Century 1906 to 1955.* New York: Simon and Schuster, 1957; reprint, New York: Greenwood Press, 1968.

Fubini, Enrico, ed. *Music and Culture in Eighteenth-Century Europe: A Source Book.* Translations from the original sources by Wolfgang Freis, Lisa Gasbarrone, and Michael Louis Leone. Translation ed. Bonnie J. Blackburn. Chicago: University of Chicago Press, 1994. First published in 1986.

MacClintock, Carol, ed., trans., and comp. *Readings in the History of Music in Performance.* Bloomington: Indiana University Press, 1979.

Mark, Michael, ed. *Music Education: Source Readings from Ancient Greece to Today.* 2nd ed. New York: Routledge, 2002. First published in 1982.

Music, David W. *Hymnology: A Collection of Source Readings.* Studies in Liturgical Musicology, no. 4. Lanham, Md.: Scarecrow Press, 1996.

————. *Instruments in Church: A Collection of Source Documents.* Studies in Liturgical Musicology, no. 7. Lanham, Md.: Scarecrow Press, 1998.

Musical Aesthetics: A Historical Reader. Ed. Edward A. Lippman. 3 vols. Aesthetics in Music, no. 4. New York: Pendragon Press, 1986–91.

> 1. *From Antiquity to the 18th Century.* 1986.
> 2. *The Nineteenth Century.* 1988.
> 3. *The Twentieth Century.* 1991.

Neuls-Bates, Carol, ed. *Women in Music: An Anthology of Source Readings from the Middle Ages to the Present.* Rev. ed. Boston: Northeastern University Press, 1996. First published in 1982.

Pleasants, Henry. *The Agony of Modern Music.* New York: Simon and Schuster, 1955.

Rowen, Ruth Halle, ed. *Music through Sources and Documents.* Englewood Cliffs, N.J.: Prentice Hall, 1979.

Schonberg, Harold C. *Facing the Music.* New York: Summit Books, 1981.

Southern, Eileen, comp. and ed. *Readings in Black American Music.* 2nd ed. New York: W. W. Norton, 1983. First published in 1971.

Strunk, Oliver, comp. *Source Readings in Music History from Classical Antiquity through the Romantic Era.* Rev. ed. Ed. Leo Treitler. New York: W. W. Norton, 1998. First published in 1950. (Also published in seven separate paperback volumes.)

Sullivan, Jack. *Words on Music: From Addison to Barzun.* Athens: Ohio University Press, 1990.

Thomson, Virgil. *The State of Music.* New York: W. Morrow and Company, 1939; reprint, Westport, Conn.: Greenwood Press, 1974.

————. *A Virgil Thomson Reader.* Boston: Houghton Mifflin, 1981.

Walser, Robert. *Keeping Time: Readings in Jazz History.* New York: Oxford University Press, 1999.

Weiss, Piero. *Opera: A History in Documents.* New York: Oxford University Press, 2002.

Weiss, Piero, and Richard Taruskin, comps. and annots. *Music in the Western World: A History in Documents.* New York: Schirmer Books, 1984.

Wood, Caroline, and Graham Sadler. *French Baroque Opera: A Reader.* Burlington, Vt.: Ashgate Publishing, 2000.

HISTORIES OF MUSICAL INSTRUMENTS

The selected one-volume histories of musical instruments listed below span a sixty-year period, from Sachs's and Geiringer's classic treatments, first published in the 1940s, to Wade-Matthews's coverage of 2001. They also vary in length, geographic and historical comprehensiveness, and amount of detail (the most substantial being Sachs and Marcuse), as well as in number of illustrations (up to the profusely illustrated works by Bragard/de Hen and by Remnant). Baines, Galpin, Marcuse, and Remnant are organized by category of instruments; Bragard/de Hen, Geiringer, and Sachs by historical sequence.

Books on individual instruments are not included, although there is a large literature of such sources. Other specialized studies which exist include The New Grove Musical Instruments Series, published by W. W. Norton, consisting at present of the volumes *Early Keyboard Instruments, Organ, Piano,* and *Violin Family,* with *Brass* and *Woodwind* volumes in preparation.

Baines, Anthony, ed. *Musical Instruments through the Ages.* Baltimore: Penguin Books, 1961.

Bragard, Roger, and Ferdinand J. de Hen. *Musical Instruments in Art and History.* Trans. Bill Hopkins. New York: Viking Press, 1968. First published in 1967.

Campbell, Murray, Clive Greated, and Arnold Myers. *Musical Instruments: History, Technology and Performance of Instruments of Western Music.* Oxford: Oxford University Press, 2003.

Galpin, Francis William. *A Textbook of European Musical Instruments: Their Origin, History and Character.* Westport, Conn.: Greenwood Press, 1976. First published in 1956.

Geiringer, Karl. *Instruments in the History of Western Music.* 3rd ed. New York: Oxford University Press, 1978. First published as *Musical Instruments: Their History from the Stone Age to the Present Day* in 1943.

Kottick, Edward L. *A History of the Harpsichord.* Bloomington: Indiana University Press, 2003.

Marcuse, Sibyl. *A Survey of Musical Instruments.* New York: Harper & Row, 1975.

Montagu, Jeremy. *Musical Instruments of the Bible.* Lanham,
    Md.: Scarecrow Press, 2002.
Rault, Lucy. *Musical Instruments: A Worldwide Survey of
    Traditional Music-Making.* London: Thames and Hudson,
    2000.
Rault, Lucy, and Jane Brenton. *Musical Instruments: Craftsman-
    ship and Traditions from Prehistory to the Present.* New
    York: Harry N. Abrams, 2000.
Sachs, Curt. *The History of Musical Instruments.* New York: W.
    W. Norton, 1940.
Straeten, Edmund van der. *The History of the Violin, Its Ances-
    tors, and Collateral Instruments from the Earliest Times
    to the Present Day.* London: Cassell, 1933; reprint, New
    York: Da Capo Press, 1968.
Wade-Matthews, Max, and William Mival. *The World Guide to
    Musical Instruments.* London: Southwater, 2001.
Williams, Peter F. *A New History of the Organ from the Greeks
    to the Present Day.* Bloomington: Indiana University
    Press, 1980.
————. *The Organ in Western Culture 750–1250.* Cambridge:
    Cambridge University Press, 1993.

PICTORIAL SOURCES ON MUSIC HISTORY

Many sources on the history of music consist primarily of pictures, including pictorial biographies, a few of which appear above
in the lists of composer biographies. Other important types of
iconographical sources include catalogs of individual musical instrument collections and exhibitions. The following bibliography
is a selection of the more important comprehensive sources of this
sort, divided into works that concern music history in general and
those that concern musical instruments.

The "General" list includes the work, still in progress, that is already the last word on the subject, *Musikgeschichte in Bildern,* which
consists of four multivolume series, as well as the better-known
one-volume picture histories (Kinsky, Lang, Lesure, Pincherle).
Beck and Roth is a study of historic prints with musical subjects,
and Collaer and van der Linden is a unique musical atlas that also
contains many pictures.

In the "Instruments and Ensembles" list, all the sources are comprehensive treatments of the subject except the more specialized
studies by Bowles and Winternitz (*Musical Instruments and Their
Symbolism*) and the historic works by Buonanni and Praetorius. For
other discussions of the history of instruments that are not primarily pictorial, see "Histories of Musical Instruments," pp. 231–32

above. For further information, see Frederick Crane, *A Bibliography of the Iconography of Music* (Iowa City: University of Iowa, 1971); and Tilman Seebass's *New Grove* article "Iconography of Music."

General

Beck, Sydney, and Elizabeth E. Roth. *Music in Prints.* New York: New York Public Library, 1965.

Besseler, Heinrich, and Max Schneider, eds. **Musikgeschichte in Bildern.** Leipzig: Deutscher Verlag für Musik, 1961–.

> Series 1. *Musikethnologie.*
> Series 2. *Musik des Altertums.*
> Series 3. *Musik des Mittelalters und der Renaissance.*
> Series 4. *Oper, Konzert, Privates Musizieren, 1600–1900.*

Blackwood, Alan. *Music of the World.* New York: Facts on File, 1991.

Collaer, Paul, and Albert van der Linden. *Historical Atlas of Music: A Comprehensive Study of the World's Music, Past and Present.* Trans. Allan Miller. Cleveland: World Publishing, 1968. First published in 1960.

Kinsky, Georg, et al., eds. *A History of Music in Pictures.* New York: Dover, 1951. First published in 1930.

Lang, Paul Henry, and Otto Bettman. *A Pictorial History of Music.* New York: W. W. Norton, 1960.

Lesure, François. *Music and Art in Society.* Trans. Denis and Sheila Stevens. University Park: Pennsylvania State University Press, 1968. First published in 1966.

Pincherle, Marc. *An Illustrated History of Music.* Rev. ed. Ed. Georges and Rosamond Bernier. Trans. Rollo Myers. New York: Reynal, 1962. First published in 1959.

Instruments and Ensembles

Baines, Anthony. *European and American Musical Instruments.* New York: Viking Press, 1966.

Bowles, Edmund A. *Musical Ensembles in Festival Books, 1500–1800: An Iconographical and Documentary Survey.* Studies in Musicology, no. 103. Ann Arbor, Mich.: UMI Research Press, 1989.

Bragard, Roger, and Ferdinand J. de Hen. *Musical Instruments in Art and History.* Trans. Bill Hopkins. New York: Viking Press, 1968. First published in 1967.

Buchner, Alexander. *Folk Music Instruments.* Trans. Alzbeta Nováková. New York: Crown Publishers, 1972. First published in 1968.

———. *Musical Instruments: An Illustrated History.* Trans. Borek Vancurel. New York: Crown Publishers, 1973. First published in 1956. An earlier translation called *Musical Instruments through the Ages* was also first published in 1956; 4th ed., 1962. There is also an enlarged version in German: *Musikinstrumente von dem Anfängen bis zur Gegenwart.* Trans. Otto Guth. Prague: Artia, 1972.

Buonanni, Filippo. *Descrizione degli'stromenti armonici d'ogni genere del padre Bonanni.* [2nd ed., 1726.] First published in 1722. Reprint of the 1776 ed.: Kassel: Bärenreiter, 1974. The instrumental plates only are reprinted in *The Showcase of Musical Instruments by Filippo Bonanni.* New York: Dover Publications, 1964.

Harrison, Frank Ll., and Joan Rimmer. *European Musical Instruments.* New York: W. W. Norton, 1964.

Montagu, Jeremy. *The World of Baroque & Classical Musical Instruments.* Woodstock, N.Y.: Overlook Press, 1979.

———. *The World of Medieval & Renaissance Musical Instruments.* Woodstock, N.Y.: Overlook Press, 1976.

———. *The World of Romantic and Modern Musical Instruments.* Woodstock, N.Y.: Overlook Press, 1981.

Munrow, David. *Instruments of the Middle Ages and Renaissance.* London: Oxford University Press, 1976.

Praetorius, Michael. *Syntagma Musicum. De Organographia, Parts I and II.* Trans. and ed. David Z. Crookes. Early Music Series, no. 7. London: Oxford University Press, 1986.

Remnant, Mary. *Musical Instruments: An Illustrated History from Antiquity to the Present.* London: B. T. Batsford, 1989.

Winternitz, Emanuel. *Musical Instruments and Their Symbolism in Western Art.* 2nd ed. New Haven, Conn.: Yale University Press, 1979. First published in 1967.

———. *Musical Instruments of the Western World.* London: Thames and Hudson, 1966.

Specific Subjects

Parker, Roger, ed. *The Oxford Illustrated History of Opera.* Oxford Illustrated Histories. Oxford: Oxford University Press, 1994.

Southern, Eileen, and Josephine Wright. *Images: Iconography of Music in African-American Culture (1770s–1920s).* Music in African-American Culture, no. 1. New York: Garland Publishers, 2000.

Current Research
Journals in Music

This chapter consists of a representative listing of scholarly research journals in music that are currently being published. The oldest is the durable *Musical Times;* among the newest are several journals (e.g., *Journal of Music Teacher Education*) that began publication in the last few years. It is in journals of this sort that new research is most likely to be reported, rather than in the host of periodicals concerned with current musical events, individual instruments, the opera scene, etc.

The list is by no means complete, but a fairly broad selection has been made. The most thorough is in the area of musicology, but other types of research journals are included, as indicated by the subdivisions of this listing. These subdivisions, however, are not rigid; e.g., a general musicological journal may carry an article of a more theoretical or ethnomusicological nature. Furthermore, among the musicology journals listed as being of a general nature, some are more so than others, in which, for example, a period or national emphasis is apparent.

The information given about each periodical specifies country of publication, frequency of appearance, first year of publication, and whether the journal is the official organ of a society or issues from a university music department or research institute. Consult the key to abbreviations preceding the list. Internet addresses are given for websites that contain a description of a periodical and/or an index of issues. In addition, many individual periodical articles are available in online searchable databases such as J-STOR: The Scholarly Journal Archive (http://www.jstor.org).

For other lists of music periodicals, see chapter 2 under "Periodicals," pp. 34–35; for indexes of periodical articles, see under "Periodical Articles," pp. 35–38 above.

Key to Countries:
Af   Africa
Au   Australia
Aus   Austria
B   Belgium
C   Canada
D   Denmark
E   England
F   France
G   Germany
Ho   Holland
Hu   Hungary
int   international
Is   Israel
I   Italy
Sw   Switzerland
US   United States

Key to Frequency of Publication:
12   monthly
10   ten times a year
8   eight times a year
6   six times a year
5   five times a year
4   quarterly
3   three times a year
2   semiannual
1   annual
0   occasional, irregular

MUSICOLOGY

Bibliography

Fontes Artis Musicae: Review of the International Association of Music Libraries, Archives and Documentation Centres. 1954–. (int/4 from 1976) Internet address: http://www.iaml.info/fontes.php
Music Reference Services Quarterly. 1992–. (US/4)
Notes: Quarterly Journal of the Music Library Association. Nos. 1–15: 1934–42; series 2: 1943–. (US/4 [ser. 2]) Internet address: http://www.musiclibraryassoc.org/pub/pu_notes.htm

Historical Musicology

Acta Musicologica. International Musicological Society/Société Internationale de Musicologie. 1928–. (int/2)
Archiv für Musikwissenschaft. 1918–26; 1952–. (G/4) Internet address: http://www.Steiner-verlag.de/AfM/
Current Musicology. Music Department, Columbia University. 1965–. (US/2) Internet address: http://www.music.columbia.edu/~curmus/
Early Music History: Studies in Medieval and Early Modern Music. 1981–. (E/1)
International Journal of Musicology. 1992–. (int/1)

The Journal of Musicological Research. (Originally *Music and Man,* 1973–79.) 1979–. (E/4)

The Journal of Musicology: A Quarterly Review of Music History, Criticism, Analysis, and Performance Practice. 1982–. (US/4) Internet address: http://www.journalofmusicology .org/

Journal of the American Musicological Society. 1948–. (US/3) Internet address: http://www.ucpress.edu/journals/jams/

Journal of the Royal Musical Association. (Replaced *Proceedings of the Royal Musical Association,* 1874–1986 [E/1].) 1987–. (E/2) Internet address: http://www3.oup.co.uk/ roymus/

The Maud Powell Signature: Women in Music. 1995–. (US/4)

Music & Letters. 1920–. (E/4) Internet address: http://www3 .oup.co.uk/musicj/

Music Research Forum. College-Conservatory of Music, University of Cincinnati. 1986–. (US/1)

Musica e storia. 1993–. (I/1)

The Musical Quarterly. 1915–. (US/4) Internet address: http:// www3.oup.co.uk/musqtl/

Musical Times. 1844–. (E/12) Internet address: http://www .musicaltimes.co.uk/

Musicology Australia: Journal of the Musicological Society of Australia (originally *Musicology,* 1964–82). 1985–. (Au/ 1) Internet address: http://www.msa.org.au/ma.htm

Die Musikforschung. Gesellschaft für Musikforschung. 1948–. (G/4) Internet address: http://www.musikforschung .de/mf.htm

Nuova rivista musicale italiana. 1967–. (I/4)

Orbis Musicae. Department of Musicology, Tel-Aviv University. 1971–. (Is/o) Internet address: http://www.tau.ac.il/arts /publications/orbis.html

repercussions: critical and alternative viewpoints on music and scholarship. Department of Music, University of California, Berkeley. 1992–. (US/2)

Revue belge de musicologie/Belgisch Tijdschrift voor Muziekwetenschap. Société belge de musicologie. 1946–. (B/1)

Revue de musicologie. Société Française de Musicologie. 1917–. (F/2) Internet address: http://www.sfm.culture.fr/sfm/ revue.htm

Rivista italiana di musicologia. Societá Italiana di Musicologia. 1966–. (I/2) Internet address: http://www.sidm.it/

Il saggiatore musicale: rivista semestrale di musicologia. 1994–. (I/2) Internet address: http://www.muspe.unibo.it/ period/saggmus/

Schweizerische Musikzeitung/Revue musicale suisse. 1862–.
    (Sw/6) Internet address: http://wwwmusikzeitung.ch/
Studia Musicologica Academiae Scientiarum Hungaricae. 1961–.
    (Hu/2)
*Tijdschrift van de Koninklijke Vereniging voor Nederlandse
    Musiekgeschiedenis* (originally *Tijdschrift van de Vereni-
    ging voor Nederlandse Musiekgeschiedenis*). 1882–. (Ho/2)
    Internet address: http://www.kunm.nl/
*Women of Note Quarterly: The Magazine of Historical and
    Contemporary Women Composers.* 1993–. (US/4)

Limited to a Country and/or Period

American Music: A Quarterly Journal. Published for the Society
    for American Music. 1983–. (US/4) Internet address:
    http://www.american-music.org/publications/Publica-
    tioninformation.htm
*Early Music History: Studies in Medieval and Early Modern
    History.* 1981–. (E/1)
Journal of Seventeenth-Century Music. An online journal pub-
    lished by the Society for Seventeenth-Century Music.
    1995–. (US/1) Internet address: http://www.sscm-
    jscm.press.uiuc.edu/jscm/
Musica Disciplina. American Institute of Musicology, Middle-
    ton, Wisc. 1946–. (int/1) Internet address: http://www
    .corpusmusicae.com/md.htm
19th-Century Music. 1977–. (US/3) Internet address: http://www
    .ucpress.edu/journals/ncm/
Nineteenth-Century Music Review. (Replaced *The Music Review,*
    1940–2004.) 2004–. (E/4)
Plainsong and Medieval Music. Published in association
    with the Plainsong and Mediaeval Music Society. 1992–.
    (E/2)
"Recherches" sur la musique française classique. La vie musicale
    en France sous les rois Bourbons. 1960–. (F/1 or o)
Revue international de musique française. Société Internationale
    de Musique Française. 1980–. (int/3)
Tempo. Cambridge University Press. 1946–. (E/4)

Limited to a Single Composer

Acta Mozartiana. Dutsche Mozart-Gesellschaft. 1954–. (G/2)
    Internet address: http://www.deutsche-mozart-
    sesellschaft.de/mozart/acta/actamozartiana.htm
*Bach: The Journal of the Riemenschneider Bach Institute in Affil-
    iation with the American Chapter of the New Bach Society.*

Baldwin-Wallace College. 1970–. (US/3) Internet address:
  http://www.bw.edu/academics/libraries/bach/journal
Bach-Jahrbuch. Neue Bach-Gesellschaft. 1904–. (G/1)
Bonner Beethoven-Studien. (Replaced the *Beethoven-Jahrbuch,*
  1953–1999.) Veröffentlichungen des Beethovenhauses in
  Bonn. 1999–. (G/1)
Händel-Jahrbuch. Georg-Friedrich-Händel-Gesellschaft. 1955–.
  (G/1)
Haydn-Studien. Joseph Haydn Institut. 1965–. (G/1) Internet
  address: http://www.haydn-institut.de/Haydn-Studien
  /haydn-studien.html
Journal of the American Liszt Society. 1977–. (US/2) Internet
  address: http://www.Americanlisztsociety.org/jals.htm
Mozart-Jahrbuch. Internationalen Stiftung Mozarteum. 1941–43,
  1950–. (Aus/1) Internet address: http://www.nam.at/
  german/ZI_MJ.html
Schütz-Jahrbuch. Internationalen Heinrich-Schütz-Gesellschaft.
  1979–. (G/1)

Iconography

*Imago Musicae: International Yearbook of Musical Iconography/
  Internationales Jahrbuch für Musikikonographie/Annu-
  aire international d'iconographie musicale.* Répertoire
  International de l'Iconographie Musicale/ International
  Repertory of Musical Iconography/Internationales
  Repertorium der Musikikonographie. (int/1) 1984–.
  Internet address: http://www.lim.it/collane/imago.htm

Performance Practice

*Basler Jahrbuch für historische Musikpraxis: Eine Veröffentli-
  chung der Schola Cantorum Basiliensis Lehr-und For-
  schungsinstitut für alte Musik an der Musik-Akademie
  der Stadt Basel.* 1977–. (Sw/1) Internet address: http://
  www.unibas.ch/mab/scb/jb_de.htm
Concerto: Das Magazin für Alte Musik. 1996–. (G/10) Internet
  address: http://www.concerto-verlag.de
The Consort: European Journal of Early Music. Journal of the
  Dolmetsch Foundation. 1925–. (E/2)
Early Music. 1973–. (E/4) Internet address: http://www3.oup.co
  .uk/earlyj/
Early Music America: The Magazine of Historical Performance.
  (Originally *Historical Performance: The Journal of Early
  Music America,* 1988–95.) 1995–. (US/4) Internet address:
  http://earlymusic.org/Content/Publications/EMAg.htm

*The Journal of Musicology: A Quarterly Review of Music
    History, Criticism, Analysis, and Performance Practice.*
    1982–. (US/4) Internet address: http://www.ucpress
    .edu/journals/jm/
Tijdschrift oude muziek. 1996–. (Ho/4) Internet address: http://
    www.oudemuziek.nl

ETHNOMUSICOLOGY/REGIONAL STUDIES

*African Music: Journal of the International Library of African
    Music/Journal de la Discothèque Internationale de Mu-
    sique Africaine.* 1954–. (Af/o)
Asian Music: Journal of the Society for Asian Music. 1968–.
    (US/2) Internet address: http://www.skidmore.edu/
    academics/asiamusic/
Ethnomusicology: Journal of the Society for Ethnomusicology.
    1953–. (US/3) Internet address: http://www.indiana.edu/
    ~ethmusic/publications/publication.html
Ethnomusicology Forum. (Formerly *British Journal of Ethno-
    musicology.*) British Forum for Ethnomusicology. 1995–.
    (E/2)
*Latin American Music Review/Revista de música latinoameri-
    cana.* Institute of Latin American Studies, University of
    Texas. 1980–. (US/2) Internet address:
    http://www.utexas.edu/utpress/journals/jlamr.html
Popular Music and Society. Department of Sociology, Bowling
    Green State University. 1971–. (US/4) Internet address:
    http://www3.niu.edu/popms/
Selected Reports in Ethnomusicology. University of California.
    1966–. (US/o) Internet address: http://www.ethnomusic
    .ucla.edu/publications/selreprt.htm
*The World of Music: Journal of the Department of Ethnomusi-
    cology, Otto-Friedrich University of Bamberg.* 1957–.
    (int/3)

MUSIC THEORY AND NEW MUSIC

Analyse musicale. Société Française d'Analyse Musicale. 1985–.
    (F/4) Internet address: http://www.sfam.org/analmus.htm
Contemporary Music Review. 1984–. (E/4)
Dansk Musik Tidsskrift. 1925–. (D/8) Internet address: http://
    www.danskmusiktidsskrift.dk
Gamut. Georgia Association of Music Theorists. 1984–. (US/1)
In Theory Only. Michigan Music Theory Society, University of
    Michigan. 1975–. (US/o) Internet address:

http://www.bgsu.edu/colleges/music/departments/
    MUCT/theonly.html
Indiana Theory Review. Graduate Theory Association, School of
    Music, Indiana University. 1977–. (US/2) Internet address:
    http://theory.music.indiana.edu/gta/ITR/itr.htm
Journal of Music Theory. Yale School of Music. 1957–. (US/2)
    Internet address: http://www.yale.edu/jmt/
Journal of Music Theory Pedagogy. Gail Boyd Stwolinski Center
    for Music Theory Pedagogy, School of Music, University
    of Oklahoma. 1987–. (US/2) Internet address: http://music
    .ou.edu/jmtp/
Journal of New Music Research. 1972–. (B/4)
Music Analysis. 1982–. (E/3)
Music Theory Online. Society for Music Theory. 1993–. (US/6)
    An electronic journal. Subscribers receive only the table
    of contents, then may request and receive individual
    articles via e-mail. Internet address: http://www
    .societymusictheory.org/mto/
*Music Theory Spectrum: The Journal of the Society for Music
    Theory.* 1979–. (US/2) Internet address: http://www
    .societymusictheory.org/index.php?pid=44
Musiktheorie. 1986–. (G/3)
Perspectives of New Music. Fromm Music Foundation. 1962–.
    (US/2) Internet address:
    http://www.perspectivesofnewmusic.org/
Theoria: Historical Aspects of Music Theory. School of Music,
    North Texas State University. 1985–. (US/1) Internet
    address: http://www.music.unt.edu/the/Theoria.htm
Theory and Practice. Journal of The Music Theory Society of
    New York. 1974–. (US/2) Internet address: http://www
    .ithaca.edu/music/mtsnys/t&p.html
21st Century Music. 1997–. (US/12)

PERFORMING INSTRUMENT, MEDIUM, OR GENRE

*American Choral Review: The Official Journal of Chorus
    America.* 1958–. (US/4) Internet address: http://www
    .chorusamerica.org/acr_index.shtml
American Lutherie. Guild of American Luthiers. 1996–. (US/4)
    Internet address: http://www.luth.org
The American Organist. American Guild of Organists, Royal
    Canadian College of Organists, and Associated Pipe
    Organ Builders of America. 1981–. (US/12) Internet
    address: http://www.agohq.org/tao/
Annual Review of Jazz Studies. (Originally *Journal of Jazz*

Studies, 1973–81.) Rutgers Institute of Jazz Studies. 1982–. (US/1)

Ars Organi. Gesellschaft der Orgelfreunde. 1996–. (G/4) Internet address: http://www.gdo.de/veroeff/arsorgani.html

Black Music Research Journal. Center for Black Music Research, Columbia College, Chicago. 1981–. (US/2) Internet address: http://cbmr.org/pubs/bmrj.htm

Cambridge Opera Journal. 1989–. (E/3)

Chelys. Viola da Gamba Society. 1970–. (E/1) Internet address: http://www.vdgs.demon.co.uk/pubs/chelys.html

The Clarinet. The International Clarinet Association. 1974–. (int/4) Internet address: http://www.clarinet.org/ TheClarinet/index.htm

The Double Reed. The International Double Reed Society. 1978–. (int/4)

Early Keyboard Journal. Journal of the Southeastern Historical Keyboard Society and the Midwestern Historical Keyboard Society. 1982/83–. (US/1) Internet address: http://www.ekjournal.org

Flute Talk. 1981–. (US/10)

The Flutist Quarterly. The National Flute Association. 1975–. (US/4)

Galpin Society Journal. 1948–. (E/1) Internet address: http:// www.music.ed.ac.uk/euchmi/galpin/

Historic Brass Society Journal. 1989–. (US/1) Internet address: http://www.historicbrass.org

The Horn Call. Journal of the International Horn Society. 1989–. (int/3) Internet address: http://www.hornsociety.org/ HORN_CALL/

Journal of Band Research. American Bandmasters Association. 1964–. (US/2) Internet address: http://www .americanbandmasters.org/jbr.htm

Journal of Singing. National Association of Teachers of Singing. 1944–. (US/5) Internet address: http://www.nats.org/ journal.html

Journal of the American Musical Instrument Society. 1974–. (US/1) Internet address: http://www.amis.org/pubs/ journal/jindex.htm

Journal of the American Viola Society. 1985–. (US/3) Internet address: http://www.americanviolasociety.org/javs.html

Journal of the Lute Society of America. 1968–. (C/1) Internet address: http://www.cs.dartmouth.edu/~lsa/ publications/JLSA-Index.html

Journal of the Viola da Gamba Society of America. 1964–. (US/1) Internet address: http://www.vdgsa.org/pgs/pubs.html

Journal of the Violin Society of America. 1975–. (US/2) Internet
     address: http://www.vsa.to/journal.htm
Journal of Voice. The Voice Foundation and the International
     Association of Phonosurgeons. 1986–. (US/4) Internet
     address: http://www.voicefoundation.org/journal/html
The Opera Quarterly. 1983–. (US/4)
L'organo: rivista di cultura organaria e organistica. 1960–. (I/2)
Saxophone Journal. 1980–. (US/6) Internet address: http://
     www.dornpub.com/saxophonejournal.html
Tibia: Magazin für Holzbläser. (Originally *Tibia: Magazin für
     Freunde alte und neuer Bläsermusik* 1976–96.) 1996–.
     (G/4)

MUSIC EDUCATION

Australian Journal of Music Education. Australian Society for
     Music Education. 1969–. (Au/2) Internet address: http://
     asme.customer.netspace.net.au/nat/pubs/pub.htm
British Journal of Music Education. 1984–. (E/3)
Bulletin of the Council for Research in Music Education.
     1963–. (US/4)
Canadian Music Educator/Musicien éducateur au Canada.
     Canadian Music Educators Association/Association
     Canadienne des Educateurs de Musique. 1959–. (C/4)
     Internet address: http://www.musiceducationonline
     .org/cmea/CMEApublications.html
Contributions to Music Education. Ohio Music Education
     Association. 1972–. (US/1) Internet address: http://cme
     .webhop.org
General Music Today. An online journal of the Music Educators
     National Conference. 2001–. (US/2)
International Journal of Music Education. International Society
     of Music Education. 1983–. (int/3) Internet address:
     http://www.isme.org/article/archive/4/
Journal of Historical Research in Music Education. (Originally
     The Bulletin of Historical Research in Music Education
     1980–93.) 1993–. (US/2) Internet address: http://www
     .utc.edu/Faculty/William-Lee/Journal.html
Journal of Music Teacher Education. An online journal of the
     Music Educators National Conference. 2001–. (US/2)
Journal of Research in Music Education. Society for Research in
     Music Education, of the Music Educators National Confer-
     ence. 1953–. (US/4) Internet address: http://www.menc
     .org/publication/articles/journals.html

Missouri Journal of Research in Music Education. Missouri
 Music Educators Association. 1962–. (US/1)
Music Education Research. 1998–. (int/3)
Music Educators Journal. Music Educators National Conference.
 1914–. (US/5)
Philosophy of Music Education Review. 1993–. (US/2)
Southeastern Journal of Music Education. University of Georgia
 Center for Continuing Education. 1989–. (US/1)
Teaching Music. Music Educators National Conference. 1992–.
 (US/5)
Update: Applications of Research in Music Education. Music
 Educators National Conference. 1982–. (US/2) Internet
 address: http://www.menc.org/publication/articles/
 journals.html

OTHER JOURNALS

*Ars Lyrica: Journal of the Lyrica Society of Word-Music Rela-
 tions.* 1981–. (US/o) Internet address: http://www
 .h-net.msu.edu/~mustxt/lyrica/lyricj.html
Choreography and Dance: An International Journal. 1992–.
 (int/o)
College Music Symposium. The College Music Society. 1961–.
 (int/1) Internet address: http://www.music.org/Pubs/
 Sym/symp.html
Computer Music Journal. 1977–. (US/4) Internet address:
 http://www.leeds.ac.uk/cmj/
Criticus Musicus: A Journal of Music Criticism. 1993–. (int/3)
Dance Research. Society for Dance Research. 1983–. (E/2)
*La danza italiana: International Journal of the History of
 Dance.* 1984–. (int/2)
ECHO. (An online journal of the University of California at Los
 Angeles.) 1999–. (US/2) Internet address: http://www.echo
 .ucla.edu
International Review of the Aesthetics and Sociology of Music.
 Croatian Musicological Society. 1970–. (int/2)
The Journal of Aesthetic Education. University of Illinois and
 the Illinois Department of Public Instruction. 1966–.
 (US/4) Internet address: http://www.press.uillinois.edu/
 journals/jae.html
The Journal of Aesthetics and Art Criticism. American Society
 for Aesthetics. 1941–. (US/4) Internet address: http://
 www.temple.edu/jaac/
The Journal of Music Therapy. American Music Therapy Association. 1964–. (US/4)

Journal of New Music Research. (Originally *Interface,* 1972–93.)
  1994–. (Ho/4) Internet address: http://www.swets.nl/
  jnmr.html
Medical Problems of Performing Artists. 1986–. (US/4)
Music Perception: An Interdisciplinary Journal. 1983–. (US/4)
  Internet address: http://www.ucpress.edu/journals/mp/
Music Therapy Perspectives. American Music Therapy Associa-
  tion. 1982–. (US/2)
*Open Ear Journal: Dedicated to Sound and Music in Health and
  Education.* 1993–. (US/4)
*Organised Sound: An International Journal of Music and
  Technology.* 1996–. (int/3)
Popular Music and Society. 1977–. (int/4)
Psychology of Music. Society for Education, Music and Psychol-
  ogy Research. 1973–. (E/2) Internet address: http://www
  .sempre.org.uk/journal.html
Psychomusicology: A Journal of Research in Music Cognition.
  1981–. (US/2) Internet address: http://otto.cmr.fsu.edu/
  ~psychmus/index.html
*Rivista internazionale di musica sacra/The International
  Church Music Review.* 1980–. (int/4) Internet address:
  http://www.lim.it/rism.htm

CHAPTER SEVEN

Editions of Music

This chapter opens with a list of sources of information about music notation and editing. Of the three lists of musical editions that follow, "Historical Sets and Monuments of Music" and "Composers' Complete Works and Catalogs" are of a more scholarly nature, while the "Anthologies of Music" list is of a more practical intent. These lists vary in degree of selectivity and format, including representative publications rather than all or even most items in a particular category. For guides to the contents of these editions of music, see chapter 2 under "Editions of Music," pp. 59–61 above.

SOURCES IN ENGLISH ON MUSIC NOTATION AND EDITING

The three lists that follow are of basic sources in English that treat the notation and editing of music, and are applicable to the reproduction of music, whether the method used is handwriting, music typing, engraving, or computer software programs. The first list is of general sources on the history and practice of notation and music printing. It includes two of the most widely respected manuals of notation and music reproduction, Read and Ross, each of which begins with a historical summary of its subject; the three standard histories of notation, Apel, Parrish, and especially Rastall; Bent's relevant article in *The New Grove Dictionary*; Krummel and Sadie's handbook, *Music Printing and Publishing*, an update of the extensive *New Grove* (1st ed.) article on that topic; and Powell's guide to music engraving using the industry-standard software packages "Finale" and "Sibelius." Feder's work concerns the fundamentals of music philology and the application of philological methods to the critical editing of music, while Grier's monograph is a basic introduction to the history and methodology of music editing.

The second list comprises important sources dealing with the specialized area of editing early music and includes general or comprehensive discussions, those by Broude, Brown, Caldwell, Carapetyan, Dart, Emery, and Stevens, as well as treatments of individual aspects—authenticating sources, *musica ficta*, watermarks and paper analysis, handwriting, etc. The Festschrift edited by Borroff is a series of transcriptions of music arranged in chronological order, each accompanied by a discussion of editorial method, resulting in a kind of history of notation in examples. Cudworth's article is a unique and helpful source of information about certain matters—commonly misattributed, nicknamed, and misnamed compositions; pseudonyms and divergent spellings of composers' names—that are important to know when identifying and editing works to which they pertain.

The third list brings together works from about the last twenty-five years treating the notation of new music.

General Sources

Apel, Willi. *The Notation of Polyphonic Music 900–1600.* 5th ed., rev. and with commentary. Cambridge, Mass.: Mediaeval Academy of America, 1961. First published in 1942.

Bent, Ian D., et al. "Notation." In *The New Grove Dictionary of Music and Musicians.* 2nd ed. Vol. 18, pp. 73–189.

Feder, Georg. *Music Philology.* Trans. Bruce McIntyre. Hillsdale, N.Y.: Pendragon Press, 2004. First published in 1987.

Grier, James. *The Critical Editing of Music: History, Method, and Practice.* Cambridge: Cambridge University Press, 1996.

———. "Editing." In *The New Grove Dictionary of Music and Musicians.* 2nd ed. Vol. 7, pp. 885–95.

Krummel, D. W. *The Literature of Music Bibliography: An Account of the Writings on Music Printing and Publishing.* Fallen Leaf Reference Books in Music, no. 21. Berkeley, Calif.: Fallen Leaf Press, 1992.

Krummel, D. W., and Stanley Sadie, eds. *Music Printing and Publishing.* 1st American ed. The Norton/Grove Handbooks in Music. New York: W. W. Norton, 1990. First published in 1989.

Parrish, Carl. *The Notation of Medieval Music.* Reprint of corrected 1959 ed., with a new introduction by J. W. McKinnon. New York: Pendragon Press, 1978. First published in 1957.

Powell, Steven. *Music Engraving Today: The Art and Practice of Digital Notesetting.* New York: Brichtmark Music, 2002.

Rastall, Richard. *The Notation of Western Music: An Introduction.* 1st U.S. ed. New York: St. Martin's Press, 1982.

Read, Gardner. *Music Notation: A Manual of Modern Practice.* 2nd ed. Boston: Crescendo Publishers, 1969. First published in 1964.

Ross, Ted. *The Art of Music Engraving and Processing: A Complete Manual, Reference and Text Book on Preparing Music for Reproduction and Print.* Miami: Hansen Books, 1970.

Winternitz, Emanuel. *Musical Autographs from Monteverdi to Hindemith.* Enl. and corrected ed. 2 vols. New York: Dover Publications, 1965. First published in 1955.

Editing Early Music

Berger, Anna Maria Busse. *Mensuration and Proportion Signs: Origins and Evolution.* Oxford: Clarendon Press, 1993.

Berger, Karol. *Musica Ficta: Theories of Accidental Inflections in Vocal Polyphony from Marchetto da Padova to Gioseffo Zarlino.* Cambridge: Cambridge University Press, 1987.

Boorman, Stanley. "Watermarks." In *The New Grove Dictionary of Music and Musicians.* 2nd ed. Vol. 27, pp. 114–18.

Borroff, Edith. *Notations and Editions: A Book in Honor of Louise Cuyler.* Dubuque, Iowa: Wm. C. Brown Company Publishers, 1974; reprint, New York: Da Capo Press, 1977.

Broude, Ronald. "Editing Early Music: Some Notes on Procedure and Presentation." *The Choral Journal* 21 (January 1981): 5, 8–12.

Caldwell, John. *Editing Early Music.* 2nd ed. Early Music Series, vol. 5. Oxford: Clarendon Press, 1995. First published in 1985.

Carapetyan, Armen. "Problems of Editing and Publishing Old Music." *Musica Disciplina* 15 (1961): 5–14.

Cudworth, Charles L. "Ye Olde Spuriosity Shoppe, or, Put It in the Anhang." *Notes* 12 (December 1954): 25–40; (September 1955): 533–53.

Dart, Thurston. *The Interpretation of Music.* 4th rev. reimpression. London: Hutchinson's University Library, 1960. Chapter 2: "The Editor's Task," pp. 18–28. First published in 1954.

Emery, Walter. *Editions and Musicians: A Survey of the Duties of Practical Musicians and Editors towards the Classics.* Reprinted with additions. London: Novello, 1958. First published in 1957.

Grier, James. "Musical Sources and Stemmatic Filiation: A Tool for Editing Music." *The Journal of Musicology* 13 (Winter 1995): 73–102.

Krummel, Donald W. "Guide for Dating Early Music: A Synopsis." *Fontes Artis Musicae* 18 (January–August 1971): 40–59.

LaRue, Jan. "Watermarks and Musicology." *Acta Musicologica* 33 (April–December 1961): 120–46.

Routley, Nicholas. "A Practical Guide to *Musica Ficta*." *Early Music* 13 (February 1985): 59–71.

Spector, Stephen, ed. *Essays in Paper Analysis.* London: Associated University Presses, 1987.

Stevens, Denis. *Musicology: A Practical Guide.* 1st American ed. Yehudi Menuhin Music Guides. New York: Schirmer Books, 1981.

Wolf, Jean K., and Eugene K. Wolf. "Rastrology and Its Use in Eighteenth-Century Manuscript Studies." In Eugene K. Wolf and Edward H. Roesner, eds., *Studies in Musical Sources and Style: Essays in Honor of Jan LaRue.* Madison, Wisc.: A-R Editions, 1990. Pp. 237–91.

New Notation

Cole, Hugo. *Sounds and Signs: Aspects of Musical Notation.* London: Oxford University Press, 1974.

Cope, David. *New Music Notation.* Dubuque: Kendall-Hunt Publishing, 1976.

Karkoschka, Erhard. *Notation in New Music: A Critical Guide to Interpretation and Realisation.* Trans. Ruth Koenig. New York: Praeger, 1972. First published in 1966.

Pooler, Frank, and Brent Pierce. *New Choral Notation: A Handbook.* 2nd ed., rev. and exp. New York: Walton Music, 1973. First published in 1971.

Read, Gardner. *Modern Rhythmic Notation.* Bloomington: Indiana University Press, 1978.

———. *Source Book of Proposed Music Notation Reforms.* Music Reference Collection, no. 11. New York: Greenwood Press, 1987.

———. *20th-Century Microtonal Notation.* Contributions to the Study of Music and Dance, no. 18. New York: Greenwood Press, 1990.

Risatti, Howard A. *New Music Vocabulary: A Guide to Notational Signs for Contemporary Music.* Urbana: University of Illinois Press, 1975.

Stone, Kurt. *Music Notation in the Twentieth Century: A Practical Guidebook.* New York: W. W. Norton, 1980.

Warfield, Gerald. *Writings on Contemporary Music Notation:*

An Annotated Bibliography. MLA Index and Bibliography
Series, no. 16. Ann Arbor, Mich.: Music Library Association, 1976.

HISTORICAL SETS AND MONUMENTS OF MUSIC

The following selection from the many historical sets and monuments of music shows something of their diversity, as indicated
by the various categories into which they fall. They also vary greatly
in degree and type of scholarliness (i.e., amount of scholarly appa-
ratus, length of preface, presence or absence of critical commentary,
type of editorial method, and "user friendliness") as well as in size,
ranging from a handful of volumes up to hundreds per set (e.g., *Corpus Mensurabilis Musicae, Diletto musicale*). The volumes in some sets
are large, each containing many works or a single lengthy work (e.g.,
Denkmäler der Tonkunst in Österreich, Musica Britannica); at the other
end of the continuum are the scholarly performing editions, such
as *Nagels Musik-Archiv* and *Cantio Sacra*, most of which contain a
single short work or small set of works per volume.

Some of the growing output of facsimile reprint series have been
included in the list (e.g., *The Italian Cantata in the Seventeenth Century, The London Pianoforte School*), even though they are not strictly
speaking *editions* of music.

In the interest of simplicity and space-saving, editorial and publication information has been abbreviated; in many of the larger sets
it may change from time to time, and to attempt to give all of it
would serve little purpose. For most of the items in the list complete bibliographic information may be found in Hill and Stephens;
see p. 60 above.

Limited to an Era

*Concentus Musicus: Veröffentlichungen der Musikgeschich-
    tlichen Abteilung des Deutschen Historischen Instituts
    in Rom.* Cologne: Arno Volk Verlag, etc., 1973–.
Corpus Mensurabilis Musicae [CMM]. Middleton, Wisc.: Amer-
    ican Institute of Musicology, 1947–.
Fallen Leaf Publications in Contemporary Music. Berkeley,
    Calif.: Fallen Leaf Press, 1985–.
Institute of Mediaeval Music: Collected Works/Gesamtausgabe.
    Brooklyn, N.Y.: Institute of Mediaeval Music, 1957–.
Masters and Monuments of the Renaissance. Leeman L. Perkins,
    gen. ed. New York: Broude Trust, 1980–.
Monumenta Monodica Medii Aevi. Ed. Bruno Stäblein. Kassel:
    Bärenreiter, 1956–.

Monuments of Music and Music Literature in Facsimile. First
Series—Music. New York: Broude Brothers, 1965–.
Monuments of Renaissance Music. Edward Lowinsky, gen. ed.
Chicago: University of Chicago Press, 1964–.
The 19th Century/Das 19. Jahrhundert/Le 19e siècle. Kassel:
Bärenreiter, 1969–.
Paléographie musicale. Solesmes: Imprimerie Saint-Pierre, etc.,
1889–1958, 1969–.
Polyphonic Music of the Fourteenth Century. Kurt von Fischer,
gen. ed. 24 vols. Monaco: Editions de l'Oiseau-Lyre,
1956–92.
*Publikationen älterer praktischer und theoretischer Musikw-
erke, vorzugsweise des XV. und XVI. Jahrhunderts.* 29 vols.
Leipzig: Breitkopf & Härtel, etc., 1873–1905; reprint, New
York: Broude Brothers, 1967.
Recent Researches in the Music of the Baroque Era. Christoph
Wolff, gen. ed. Middleton, Wisc.: A-R Editions, 1964–.
Recent Researches in the Music of the Classical Era. Neal
Zaslaw, gen. ed. Middleton, Wisc.: A-R Editions, 1975–.
*Recent Researches in the Music of the Middle Ages and Early
Renaissance.* Charles M. Atkinson, gen. ed. Middleton,
Wisc.: A-R Editions, 1975–.
*Recent Researches in the Music of the Nineteenth and Early
Twentieth Centuries.* Rufus Hallmark, gen. ed. Middleton,
Wisc.: A-R Editions, 1979–.
Recent Researches in the Music of the Renaissance. James Haar,
gen. ed. Middleton, Wisc.: A-R Editions, 1964–.
Renaissance Music in Facsimile. Ed. Howard Mayer Brown et al.
50 vols. New York: Garland Publishing, 1986–88.
*Thesauri Musici: Musik des 15., 16. und beginnenden 17.
Jahrhunderts/Music of the 15th, 16th and the Beginning
of the 17th Centuries.* Ed. Walter Pass. 35 vols. Vienna:
L. Doblinger, 1971–74.
Three Centuries of Music in Score. Ed. Kenneth Cooper. 13 vols.
New York: Garland Publishing, 1988–90.
Unbekannte Werke der Klassik und Romantik. Munich: Walter
Wollenweber, [1969–].

Limited to a Region

L'arte musicale in Italia. Ed. Luigi Torchi. 7 vols. Milan: G.
Ricordi, 1897–1908; reprint, Milan: Ricordi, 1968.
*Biblioteca de Catalunya: Publicacions del Departament de
Música.* Barcelona: Institut d'Estudis Catalans, etc., 1921–.
*Canadian Musical Heritage: A Multi-volume Anthology of Early
Canadian Printed Music/Le patrimoine musical cana-*

dien. . . . Ottawa: Canadian Musical Heritage Society, 1983–.

I classici musicali italiani. 15 vols. Milan: I Classici Musicali Italiani, 1941–43, 1956.

Denkmäler der Musik in Salzburg. Munich: Katzbichler, 1977–.

Denkmäler der Musik in Salzburg. Facsimile editions. Bad Reichenhall, Austria: Comes, 1990–.

Denkmäler der Tonkunst in Bayern [DTB]. Denkmäler deutscher Tonkunst, ser. 2. 38 vols. Wiesbaden: Breitkopf & Härtel, etc., 1900–38. Rev. ed., 1962–. New series, 1967–.

Denkmäler der Tonkunst in Österreich [DTÖ]. Vienna: Artaria, etc., 1894–.

Denkmäler deutscher Tonkunst [DDT]. 1st series. 65 vols. Leipzig: Breitkopf & Härtel, 1892–1931. Reprint: 65 vols. + 2 suppl. vols., Wiesbaden: Breitkopf & Härtel, 1957–61.

Denkmäler norddeutscher Musik. Kassel: Bärenreiter, 1965–.

Denkmäler rheinischer Musik. Düsseldorf, etc.: Musikverlag Schwann, 1951–.

Documenta Musicae Fennica. Helsinki: Fazer, 1964–.

Earlier American Music. 30 vols. Ed. H. Wiley Hitchcock. New York: Da Capo Press, 1972–87.

Das Erbe deutscher Musik. Wiesbaden: Breitkopf & Härtel, etc.: 1935–.

Exempla Musica Neerlandica. Amsterdam: Nederlandse Muziekgeschidenis, 1964–.

Institute of Mediaeval Music: Collected Works/Gesamtausgabe. Brooklyn, N.Y.: Institute of Mediaeval Music, 1957–.

Monumenta Artis Musicae Sloveniae. Ljubljana: Slovenska Akademija Znanosti in Umetnosti, 1983–.

Monumenta Musica Neerlandica. 16 vols. Amsterdam: Nederlandse Muziekgeschidenis, 1959–85.

Monumenta Musicae Belgicae. 11 vols. Berchem: "De Ring," etc., 1932–51, 1960–74; reprint, New York: Broude Brothers, 1967.

Monumenta Musicae in Polonia. Warsaw: Polskie Wydawnictwo Muzyczne. Series A: 1966–. Series B: 1964–89. Series D: 1975–90.

Monumentos de la música española. Barcelona: Consejo Superior de Investigaciones Científicas, etc., 1941–.

Music at the Courts of Italy. Massimo Ossi, gen. ed. New York: Broude Brothers, 1994–.

Music for London Entertainment, 1600–1800. Tunbridge Wells, England: Macnutt, 1983–.

Music of the United States of America. Published for the American Musicological Society. Richard Crawford, editor-in-chief. Middleton, Wisc.: A-R Editions, 1993–.

Musica Antiqua Bohemica. Prague: Melantrich, 1934–.

Musica Britannica: A National Collection of Music. London: Stainer and Bell, 1951–. (Some volumes issued in revised editions.)

Música hispana. Series A: Música lírica. Series B: Música instrumental. Madrid: Instituto Compultense, 1992–.

Musiche renascimentali siciliane. Ed. P. E. Carapezza. Rome: De Santis, 1970–.

Musik der Mannheimer Hofkapelle. Ed. Ludwig Finscher. Stuttgart: Carus Verlag, 1995–.

Portugaliae Musica. Lisbon: Fundação Calouste Gulbenkian, 1959–.

Recent Researches in American Music. John Graziano, gen. ed. Middleton, Wisc.: A-R Editions, 1977–.

Schweizerische Musikdenkmäler/Monuments de la musique suisse. Kassel: Bärenreiter, etc., 1955–.

Society for the Publication of American Music. 81 vols. Boston: Ditson, 1920–68.

Thesaurus Musicae Bohemiae. Series A: Musik der Gotik und Renaissance. Series B: Musik des Barocks und der Klassik. Prague: Supraphon, 1989–.

Three Centuries of American Music. Ed. Martha Furman Schleifer and Sam Dennison. 12 vols. Boston: Hall, 1989–92.

Wydawnictwo dawneij muzyki polskiej [Monuments of Ancient Polish Music]. Cracow: Polskie Wydawnictwo Muzyczne, 1930–.

Zródla do historii musyki polskiej [Historical Development of Polish Music]. Cracow: Polskie Wydawnictwo Muzyczne, 1960–.

Limited to an Era and a Region

Antiquitates Musicae in Polonia. Ed. Hieronim Feicht. 15 vols. Warsaw: Warsaw University Press, 1963–76.

Magnus Liber Organi de Notre-Dame de Paris. Ed. Edward H. Roesner. Monaco: Editions de l'Oiseau-Lyre, 1993–.

Maîtres anciens de la musique française. 6 vols. Paris: Heugel, etc., 1966–73.

Les maîtres musiciens de la renaissance française. Ed. Henry Expert. 22 vols. Paris: Alphonse Leduc, 1894–1908; reprint, New York: Broude Brothers, 1952.

Monuments de la musique française au temps de la renaissance. Ed. Henry Expert. 11 vols. Vols. 1–10, Paris: Maurice Senart, 1924–29. Vol. 11, Paris: Editions Salabert, 1958.

The Old English Edition. Ed. G. E. P. Arkwright. 25 vols. Lon-

don: Joseph Williams, 1899–1902; reprint, New York:
Broude Brothers, 1970.

*Polyphonies du XIIIe siècle: Le manuscrit H 196 de la Faculté
de Médecine de Montpellier.* Ed. Yvonne Rokseth. 4 vols.
Paris: Editions de l'Oiseau-Lyre, 1935–39.

*Van Ockeghem tot Sweelinck: Nederlandse Muziekgeschiedenis
in Voorbeelden.* Ed. Albert Smijers. 7 vols. Amsterdam:
G. Alsbach, 1949–56.

Limited to a Medium or Genre

Instrumental Ensemble

Alte Musik. Munich: F. E. C. Leuckart, 1924–.

Ars Instrumentalis: Konzertante Werke alter Meister. Hamburg:
Musikverlag Hans Sikorski, 1953–.

Consortium: Eine Spiel-und Kammermusik-Reihe. Ed. Helmut
Mönkemeyer. Wilhelmshaven: Heinrichshofen's Verlag,
1963–.

Diletto musicale: Doblingers Reihe alter Musik. Vienna:
L. Doblinger, 1955–.

Hortus Musicus. Kassel: Bärenreiter, 1936–. (Primarily instrumental.)

Ludus Instrumentalis: Kammermusik alter Meister. Hamburg:
Musikverlag Hans Sikorski, 1950–.

Musica Instrumentalis. Zurich: Musikverlag vom Pelikan,
1954–.

Nagels Musik-Archiv. 256 vols. Kassel: Nagels Verlag, 1927–83.
(Primarily instrumental.)

The Symphony 1720–1840. Barry S. Brook, gen. ed. 61 vols. + *Reference Volume: Contents of the Set and Collected Thematic Indexes.* New York: Garland Publishing, 1979–86.

Keyboard

*Archives des maîtres de l'orgue des XVIe, XVIIe, et XVIIIe
siècles.* Ed. Alexandre Guilmant. 10 vols. Paris: A. Durand
& Fils, Editeurs, 1898–1910.

The Art of the Keyboard. New York: Broude Trust, 1991–.

*Cantantibus Organis: Sammlung von Orgelstücken alter Meis-
ter.* Ed. Eberhard Kraus. Regensburg: Friedrich Pustet,
etc., 1958–.

Corpus of Early Keyboard Music. Willi Apel, gen. ed. Middleton,
Wisc.: American Institute of Musicology, 1963–.

Le grand clavier. Ed. D. Moroney. Monaco: Editions de l'Oiseau-
Lyre, 1990–.

The International Library of Piano Music. 13 vols. New York:
    University Society, 1967.
Liber Organi. Mainz: B. Schott's Söhne, 1931–38, 1954–.
Die Orgel: Ausgewählte Werke zum praktischen Gebrauch.
    Lippstadt, etc., Germany: Kistner & Siegel, 1957–.
Le trésor des pianistes. Foreword by Bea Friedland. 23 vols. New
    York: Da Capo Press, 1977. First published in 1861–72.

Lute, Guitar

*Die Tabulatur: Ausgewählte Werke in ihrer Originalnotation
    mit Übertragungen für Laute (oder ein Tasteninstrument)
    und Gitarre.* 34 vols. Ed. Helmut Mönkemeyer. Hofheim
    am Taunus, Germany: Friedrich Hofmeister, 1965–82.

Vocal

Cantio Sacra: Geistliche Solokantaten. Ed. Rudolf Ewerhart.
    Cologne: Edmund Bieler, 1955–.
Chor-Archiv. Kassel: Bärenreiter, 1932–.
Das Chorwerk. Ed. Friedrich Blume. 142 vols. Wolfenbüttel:
    Möseler, 1929–39, 1956–90.
Early Romantic Opera. Ed. Philip Gossett and Charles Rosen. 44
    vols. New York: Garland Publishing, 1978–83.
*Die Oper: Kritische Ausgabe von Hauptwerken der
    Operngeschichte.* Ed. Heinz Becker. Munich: Henle, 1975–.

Limited to a Medium or Genre and to a Region and/or Era

La cantate française au XVIIIe Siècle. Geneva: Minkoff, 1984–.
Chefs d'oeuvre classiques de l'opéra français. 40 vols. Leipzig:
    Breitkopf & Härtel, 1880; reprint, Williamstown, Mass.:
    Broude Brothers, 1971.
Choeur des muses: Corpus des luthistes françaises. 35 vols. Paris:
    Editions du Centre National de la Recherche Scientifique,
    1958–91.
Clavecinistes européens du XVIIIᵉ siècle. Geneva: Minkoff,
    1986–.
Clavecinistes françaises du XVIIIᵉ siècle, 1702–1720. Geneva:
    Minkoff, 1982–.
Drammaturgia musicale veneta. Milan: Ricordi, 1983–.
Early English Church Music. London: Stainer and Bell, 1963–.
Early Keyboard Music. Thurston Dart, gen. ed. London: Stainer
    and Bell, 1956–.
The Eighteenth-Century Continuo Sonata. Jane Adas, gen. ed.
    10 vols. New York: Garland Publishing, 1991.

The Eighteenth-Century French Cantata. Ed. David Tunley.
17 vols. New York: Garland Publishing, 1990–91.
English Instrumental Music of the Late Renaissance. Ed.
Bernard Thomas. London: London Pro Musica, 1972–.
The English Lute-Songs. Ed. Edmund H. Fellowes. Ser. 2, rev.
ed. Rev. Thurston Dart. London: Stainer and Bell, 1959–69.
First published as *The English School of Lutenist Song
Writers,* 2nd series, 1920–32.
The English Madrigalists. Ed. Edmund H. Fellowes. Rev. ed. Ed.
Thurston Dart. 39 vols. London: Stainer and Bell, 1956–88.
First published as *The English Madrigalist School,*
1913–24.
*English Song 1600–1675: Facsimiles of Twenty-six Manuscripts
and an Edition of the Texts.* Ed. Elise Bickford Jorgens. 12
vols. New York: Garland Publishing, 1986–87.
German Instrumental Music of the Late Renaissance. London:
London Pro Musica, 1973–.
German Opera 1770–1800. Ed. Thomas Bauman. 22 vols. New
York: Garland Publishing, 1985–86.
The Italian Cantata in the Seventeenth Century. Carolyn Gi-
anturco, gen. ed. 16 vols. New York: Garland Publishing,
1985–86.
Italian Instrumental Music of the Renaissance. London: London
Pro Musica, 1972–.
*Italian Instrumental Music of the Sixteenth and Early Seven-
teenth Centuries.* Ed. James Ladewig. 30 vols. New York:
Garland Publishing, 1987–95.
Italian Opera 1640–1770. Ed. Howard Mayer Brown. 97 vols.
New York: Garland Publishing, 1977–84.
Italian Opera 1810–1840. Ed. Philip Gossett. 25 vols. New York:
Garland Publishing, 1985–89.
*The Italian Oratorio 1650–1800: Works in a Central Baroque
and Classic Tradition.* Ed. Joyce L. Johnson and Howard E.
Smither. 31 vols. New York: Garland Publishing, 1986–87.
*Italian Secular Song 1606–1636: A Seven-Volume Reprint Col-
lection.* Ed. Gary Tomlinson. 7 vols. New York: Garland
Publishing, 1986.
*The London Pianoforte School 1766–1860: Clementi, Dussek,
Cogan, Cramer, Field, Pinto, Sterndale Bennett, and Other
Masters of the Pianoforte.* Nicholas Temperley, gen. ed.
20 vols. New York: Garland Publishing, 1984–87.
Piano Music of the Parisian Virtuosos, 1810–1860. Ed. Jeffrey
Kallberg. 10 vols. New York: Garland Publishing, 1993.
Romantic French Song, 1830–1870. Ed. David Tunley. 6 vols. New
York: Garland Publishing, 1995.

Seventeenth-Century Keyboard Music. Alexander Silbiger, gen.
ed. 28 vols. New York: Garland Publishing, 1987–89.
Sixteenth-Century Chanson. Ed. Jane A. Bernstein. 30 vols. New
York: Garland Publishing, 1987–95.
Sixteenth-Century Madrigal. Ed. Jessie Ann Owens. 30 vols.
New York: Garland Publishing, 1987–96.
Sixteenth-Century Motet. Ed. Richard Sherr. 30 vols. New York:
Garland Publishing, 1987–96.
*Solo Motets from the Seventeenth Century: Facsimiles of Prints
from the Italian Baroque.* Ed. Anne Schnoebelen. 10 vols.
New York: Garland Publishing, 1987–89.
*Tallis to Wesley: English Organ Music . . . from the Sixteenth
to the Nineteenth Centuries.* London: Hinrichsen, 1956–.
*Treize livres de motets parus chez Pierre Attaingnant en 1534
et 1535.* Ed. Albert Smijers. 14 vols. Paris: Editions de
l'Oiseau-Lyre, 1934–36, 1960–64.
Tudor Church Music. 10 vols. + appendix. London: Oxford
University Press, 1922–29, 1948; reprint, New York:
Kalmus, 1976.

Without Specific Limitations

Accademia Musicale. Charles Sherman, gen. ed. 31 vols. Mainz,
etc.: Universal Edition, 1969–79.
Antiqua: Eine Sammlung alter Musik. Mainz: B. Schott's Söhne,
1966–.
Arts du spectacle. Paris. Editions du Centre National de la
Recherche Scientifique, 1988–.
The Attaingnant Dance Prints. Ed. Bernard Thomas. 7 vols.
London: London Pro Musica, 1972–91.
Collegium Musicum. [New Haven]: Department of Music,
Graduate School, Yale University, 1955–65. 2nd series:
Collegium Musicum: Yale University. Middleton, Wisc.:
A-R Editions, 1969–.
Early Music Institute Publications. Bloomington: Indiana Uni-
versity Press, 1990–.
Early Music Library. Brighton, England: London Pro Musica,
1987–.
Facsimile Series for Scholars and Musicians. Peer, Belgium:
Alamire, 1989–.
Harvard Publications in Music. Cambridge, Mass.: Harvard
University Press, 1967–.
Hausmusik. 186 vols. Vienna: Österreichischer Bundesverlag,
1947–57.
Mitteldeutsches Musikarchiv: Veröffentlichungen des Musikwis-

senschaftlichen Seminars der Friedrich-Schiller-Universität Jena. 7 vols. Leipzig: Breitkopf & Härtel, 1953–57.

Music in Facsimile. New York: Garland Publishing, 1983–.

Musik alter Meister: Beiträge zur Musik-und Kulturgeschichte Innerösterreichs. Ed. Hellmut Federhofer. Graz: Akademische Druck-und Verlagsanstalt, 1954–.

Musikalische Denkmäler. Mainz: B. Schott's Söhne, 1955–.

Organum. Lippstadt, Germany: Kistner & Siegel, 1924–.

The Penn State Music Series. 27 vols. University Park: Pennsylvania State University Press, 1963–71.

Publications de la Société Française de Musicologie. Ser. 1. 23 vols. Paris: Droz, 1925–79.

Publikationen älterer Musik. Ed. Theodor Kroyer. 11 vols. Leipzig: Breitkopf & Härtel, 1926–40.

Le pupitre: Collection de musique ancienne. François Lesure et al. Paris: Heugel, 1967–.

Recent Researches in the Oral Traditions of Music. Philip V. Bohlman, gen. ed. Middleton, Wisc.: A-R Editions, 1993–.

Series of Early Music. Karl Geiringer et al. Bryn Mawr, Pa.: Theodore Presser, 1968–.

Smith College Music Archives. 16 vols. Northampton, Mass.: Smith College, 1935–72.

Thesaurus Musicus. 70 vols. London: Pro Musica Edition, 1979–86.

The Wellesley Edition. Jan LaRue, gen. ed. 11 vols. Wellesley, Mass.: Wellesley College, 1950–73.

COMPOSERS' COMPLETE WORKS AND CATALOGS

This list, selective like the preceding one, is limited to some of the most famous composers, listed in alphabetical order. The two related types of sources included, complete scholarly editions and catalogs (all but a few are thematic), have been combined in a single list by composer to show the current state of affairs as it applies to these composers. As in the sets and monuments bibliography, editorial and publication information is abbreviated; full citations may be found in Hill and Stephens and in Brook and Viano (see pp. 60 and 61 above).

The order of items is chronological rather than alphabetical where there is more than one of either type of source, with editions listed first, then catalogs. The standard older complete editions are still useful, and for many composers' works for which there is such an older edition from the nineteenth or early twentieth century, a new one is in progress; this is also often the case with catalogs.

Editorial methods vary, as with historical sets and monuments, but in general the modern editions are more reliable and certainly more up-to-date than their older counterparts. (It should be noted that the complete works of many composers are contained in certain sets and monuments, e.g., Machaut, Dufay, and Giovanni Gabrieli in *Corpus Mensurabilis Musicae;* Goudimel and Cabezón in *The Institute of Medieval Music: Collected Works;* and Orlando di Lasso's complete motets in the *Recent Researches in the Music of the Renaissance* series.)

Carl Philipp Emanuel Bach Edition. E. Eugene Helm, coordinating ed.; Rachel Wade, gen. ed. London: Oxford University Press, 1989–.

Wotquenne, Alfred. *Thematisches Verzeichnis der Werke von Carl Philipp Emanuel Bach (1714–1788).* Leipzig: Breitkopf & Härtel, 1905; reprint, Wiesbaden: Breitkopf & Härtel, 1980.

Helm, E. Eugene. *Thematic Catalogue of the Works of Carl Philipp Emanuel Bach.* New Haven, Conn.: Yale University Press, 1989.

The Collected Works of Johann Christian Bach. 47 vols. Ed. Ernest Warburton. New York: Garland, 1984–93.

Warburton, Ernest, ed. *[Johann Christian Bach] Thematic Catalogue.* 3 vols. New York: Routledge, 1999.

Johann Sebastian Bach's Werke, herausgegeben von der Bach-Gesellschaft. 47 vols. Leipzig: Breitkopf & Härtel, 1851–99, 1926.

Johann Sebastian Bach: Neue Ausgabe sämtlicher Werke, herausgegeben vom Johann-Sebastian-Bach-Institut Göttingen und vom Bach-Archiv Leipzig [Neue Bach-Ausgabe]. Kassel: Bärenreiter, 1954–.

Schmieder, Wolfgang. *Thematisch-systematisches Verzeichnis der musikalischen Werke von Johann Sebastian Bach: Bach-Werke-Verzeichnis (BWV).* 2nd ed., rev. and enl. Wiesbaden: Breitkopf & Härtel, 1990. First published in 1950.

Schulze, Hans-Joachim, and Christoph Wolff. *Bach Compendium: Analytisch bibliographisches Repertorium der Werke Johann Sebastian Bachs (BC).* Frankfurt: C. F. Peters, 1985–.

Reeder, Ray, and Wolfgang Schmieder. *The Bach English-Title Index.* Fallen Leaf Reference Books in Music, no. 20. Berkeley, Calif.: Fallen Leaf Press, 1993.

Béla Bartók: A Complete Catalogue of His Published Works/Ein vollständiges Verzeichnis seiner veröffentlichten

Werke/Un catalogue complet de ses oeuvres publiées.
    London: Boosey & Hawkes, 1970.
Dille, Denijs. *Thematisches Verzeichnis der Jugenwerke Béla
    Bartóks: 1890–1904.* Kassel: Bärenreiter, 1974.
Somfai, László. *Béla Bartók: Composition, Concepts, and
    Autograph Sources.* Berkeley: University of California
    Press, 1996.

*Ludwig van Beethoven's Werke: Vollständige kritisch durchge-
    sehene überall berechtigte Ausgabe.* Leipzig: Breitkopf &
    Härtel, 1864–90. 7 suppls.: 1959–71. Reprint, New York:
    Kalmus, 1967.
*Beethoven Werke, herausgegeben vom Beethoven-Archiv
    Bonn.* Joseph Schmidt-Görg, gen. ed. Munich: G. Henle,
    1960–.
Kinsky, Georg, and Hans Halm. *Das Werk Beethovens: Thema-
    tisch-bibliographisches Verzeichnis seiner sämtlichen
    vollendeten Kompositionen.* Munich: G. Henle Verlag,
    1955; reprint, Munich: G. Henle Verlag, 1983.
Green, James F. *The New Hess Catalog of Beethoven's Works.*
    West Newbury, Vt.: Vance Brook Publishers, 2003.

Edizione critica delle opere di Vincenzo Bellini. Marco Uvietta,
    gen. ed. 14 vols. projected. Milan: Ricordi, 2003–.

Sämtliche Werke Alban Berg. Rudolf Stephan, gen. ed. The
    Alban Berg Foundation. 22 vols. in 3 series projected.
    Vienna: Universal, 1984–.

Hector Berlioz Werke. Ed. Charles Malherbe and Felix Weingart-
    ner. 20 vols. Leipzig: Breitkopf & Härtel, 1900–1907.
Hector Berlioz: New Edition of the Complete Works. Kassel:
    Bärenreiter, 1967–.
Hopkinson, Cecil. *A Bibliography of the Musical and Literary
    Works of Hector Berlioz, 1803–1869. . . .* 2nd ed. Ed.
    Richard Macnutt. Tunbridge Wells, England: Richard
    Macnutt, 1980. First published in 1951.
Holoman, D. Kern. *Catalogue of the Works of Hector Berlioz.*
    Hector Berlioz: New Edition of the Complete Works, vol.
    25. Kassel: Bärenreiter, 1987.

The Complete Works of William Billings. Ed. Hans Nathan and
    Karl Kroeger; Richard Crawford, editorial consultant. 4
    vols. Boston: American Musicological Society and Colo-
    nial Society of Massachusetts, 1977–90.

Kroeger, Karl, comp. *Catalog of the Musical Works of William Billings*. Music Reference Collection, no. 32. New York: Greenwood Press, 1991.

L'edizione critica delle opere Luigi Boccherini. Ed. Aldo Pais. Padua: Zanibon, 1977–.
Gérard, Yves. *Thematic, Bibliographical, and Critical Catalogue of the Works of Luigi Boccherini*. London: Oxford University Press, 1969.

Johannes Brahms Sämtliche Werke, Ausgabe der Gesellschaft der Musikfreunde in Wien. Ed. Hans Gál and Eusebius Mandyczewski. 16 vols. Leipzig: Breitkopf & Härtel, [1926–27].
Neue Ausgabe sämtlicher Werke Johannes Brahms. Munich: G. Henle Verlag, 1996–.
McCorkle, Margit L., with Donald M. McCorkle. *Johannes Brahms: Thematisch-bibliographisches Werkverzeichnis*. Munich: G. Henle Verlag, 1984.
Benjamin Britten: A Complete Catalogue of His Published Works. London: Boosey & Hawkes/Faber Music, 1973.
Banks, Paul. *Benjamin Britten: A Catalogue of the Published Works*. Aldeburgh, Suffolk, England: The Britten-Pears Library for The Britten Estate, 1999.

Anton Bruckner Sämtliche Werke: Kritische Gesamtausgabe. Ed. Robert Haas et al. 11 vols. Vienna: Musikwissenschaftlicher Verlag, 1930–44 (incomplete). [2nd rev. ed.], ed. Leopold Nowak, 1951–.
Grasberger, Renate. *Werkverzeichnis Anton Bruckner (WAB)*. Publikationen des Instituts für Oesterreichische Musikdokumentation, no. 7. Tutzing: Hans Schneider, 1977.

Dietrich Buxtehudes Werke. 8 vols. Hamburg: Ugrino, 1925–37, 1958 (incomplete); reprint, New York: Broude International Editions, 1977.
Dietrich Buxtehude: The Collected Works. Kerala J. Snyder, gen. ed. New York: Broude Brothers, 1987–.
Karstädt, Georg, ed. *Thematisch-systematisches Verzeichnis der musikalischen Werke von Dietrich Buxtehude: Buxtehude-Werke-Verzeichnis (BuxWV)*. 2nd rev. and enl. ed. Wiesbaden: Breitkopf & Härtel, 1985. First published in 1974.

The Byrd Edition. Ed. Philip Brett, et al. London: Stainer and Bell, 1976–2004.

Opere complete di Giacomo Carissimi. Ed. Lino Bianchi. Rome:
Istituto Italiano per la Storia della Musica,1951–.

Giacomo Carissimi: Catalogo delle opere attribuite. Milan:
Finarte, 1975.

Buff, Iva M. *A Thematic Catalog of the Sacred Works of Giacomo Carissimi.* Clifton, N.J.: European American Music
Corporation, 1979.

Friedrich Chopin's Werke. 14 vols. Leipzig: Breitkopf & Härtel,
1878–80. Critical commentary and suppl.: 1878–1902.
*Fryderyk Chopin: Complete Works, According to the Autographs
and Original Editions, with a Critical Commentary.* Ed.
Ignacy J. Paderewski et al. 21 vols. Warsaw: Fryderyk
Chopin Institute, 1949–62.
Wydanie narodowe dziel Fryderyka Chopina [National Edition].
Ed. Jan Ekier. Warsaw: Polskie Wydawnictwo Muzyczne,
1967–.
Brown, Maurice J. E. *Chopin: An Index of His Works in Chrono-
logical Order.* 2nd rev. ed. London: St. Martin's Press,
1972. First published in 1960.
Kobylanska, Krystyna. *Frédéric Chopin: Thematisch-biblio-
graphisches Werkverzeichnis.* Translated into German by
Helmut Stolze. Munich: G. Henle, 1979. First published
in 1977.
Chominski, Józef M., and Teresa Dalila Turlo. *Katalog dziel
Fryderyka Chopina/A Catalogue of the Works of Frederick
Chopin.* Cracow: Polskie Wydawnictwo Muzyczne, 1990.

Tyson, Alan Walker. *Thematic Catalogue of the Works of Muzio
Clementi.* Tutzing, Germany: Schneider, 1967.

Les oeuvres de Arcangelo Corelli. Ed. Joseph Joachim and
Friedrich Chrysander. 5 vols. London: Augener, 1888–91.
*Arcangelo Corelli: Historisch-kritische Gesamtausgabe der
musikalischen Werke.* Hans Oesch, gen. ed. Laaber,
Germany: Laaber-Verlag, etc., 1976–.
Marx, Hans Joachim. *Die Überlieferung der Werke Arcangelo
Corellis: Catalogue raisonné.* Arcangelo Corelli: His-
torisch-kritische Gesamtausgabe der musikalischen
Werke, suppl. vol. Cologne: Arno Volk Verlag, 1980.

Oeuvres complètes de François Couperin. Maurice Cauchie, gen.
ed. 12 vols. Paris: Edition de l'Oiseau-Lyre, 1932–33. Rev.
ed., 1980–.

Cauchie, Maurice. *Thematic Index of the Works of François Couperin.* Monaco: Lyrebird Press, 1949; reprint, New York: A.M.S. Press, 1976.

Lichtenwanger, William. *The Music of Henry Cowell: A Descriptive Catalog.* Brooklyn, N.Y.: Institute for Studies in American Music, Conservatory of Music, Brooklyn College of the City University of New York, 1986.

Oeuvres complètes de Claude Debussy. Paris: Durand-Costallat, 1985–.
Lesure, François. *Catalogue de l'oeuvre de Claude Debussy.* Publications du Centre de Documentation Claude Debussy, no. 3. Geneva: Editions Minkoff, 1977.
————. *Claude Debussy: Biographie critique, suivie du catalogue de l'oeuvre.* Paris: Fayard, 2003. Pp. 461–588.

Edizione critica delle opere di Gaetano Donizetti. Milan: Ricordi, 1982–.
Inzaghi, Luigi. "Catalogo generale della opera." In *Gaetano Donizetti.* Ed. Giuseppe Angeloni, Giampiero Tintori, and Luigi Inzaghi. Milan: Nuove Edizione, 1983. Pp. 133–278.

Antonín Dvořák: Souborné vydánt/Gesamtausgabe/Complete Edition/Edition complète. Prague: Artia, 1955–.
Burghauser, Jarmil. *Antonín Dvořák: Thematic Catalogue, Bibliography, Survey of Life and Work.* Prague: Artia, 1960.
Burghauser, Jarmil, and John Clapham. *Antonín Dvořák, Thematicky Katalog/Thematisches Verzeichnis/Thematic Catalogue.* 2nd ed. Prague: Bärenreiter Edition Supraphon, 1996.

Elgar Complete Edition. Ed. J. N. Moore and C. Kent. Borough Green, England: Novello, 1981–.

Hopkinson, Cecil. *A Bibliographical Thematic Catalogue of the Works of John Field, 1782–1837.* London: self-published, 1961.

Johann Jakob Froberger: Neue Ausgabe sämtlicher Werke. Ed. S. Rampe. Kassel: Bärenreiter, 1993–.

Charteris, Richard. *Giovanni Gabrieli (ca. 1555–1612): A Thematic Catalogue of His Music with a Guide to the Source Materials and Translations of His Vocal Texts.* Stuyvesant, N.Y.: Pendragon Press, 1996.

Carlo Gesualdo (Principe di Venosa): Sämtliche Werke. Ed.
    Wilhelm Weisman and Glenn E. Watkins. 10 vols. Ham-
    burg, Germany: Ugrino, 1957–67.

Christoph Willibald Gluck Sämtliche Werke. Rudolf Gerber,
    gen. ed. Kassel: Bärenreiter, 1951–.
Wotquenne, Alfred. *Catalogue thématique des oeuvres de Chr. W.
    v. Gluck.* Leipzig: Breitkopf & Härtel, 1904; reprint, Hilde-
    sheim, Germany: Georg Olms Verlag, 1983.
Hopkinson, Cecil. *A Bibliography of the Printed Works of C. W.
    von Gluck, 1714–1787.* 2nd rev. and augm. ed. New York:
    Broude Brothers, 1967. First published in 1959.

Edvard Grieg: Samlede Verker/Gesamtausgabe/Complete Works.
    Frankfurt-am-Main: Peters, 1977–95.

Georg Friedrich Händels Werke. Ed. Friedrich Chrysander. 96
    vols. + 6 suppl. vols. Leipzig: Breitkopf & Härtel, 1858–94,
    1902; reprint, New York: Kalmus, 1976.
*Hallische Händel-Ausgabe: Kritische Gesamtausgabe, heraus-
    gegeben von der Georg-Friedrich-Händel-Gesellschaft.*
    Kassel: Bärenreiter, 1955–.
Bell, A. Craig. *Handel: Chronological Thematic Catalogue.* 2nd
    ed. Darley, England: Grian-Aig Press, 1972. First published
    in 1969.
Eisen, Walter, and Margret Eisen, eds. *Händel-Handbuch: Gleich-
    zeitig Supplement zu Hallische Händel-Ausgabe (Kritis-
    che Gesamtausgabe).* 5 vols. projected. Kassel: Bärenreiter,
    1978–. (*Thematisch-systematisches Verzeichnis,* ed. Bernd
    Baselt, begins in vol. 1 and continues in vols. 2–3.)

*Joseph Haydns Werke: Erste kritische durchgesehene Gesam-
    tausgabe.* Ed. Eusebius Mandyczewski et al. 11 vols. in 10.
    Leipzig: Breitkopf & Härtel, [1907–33] (incomplete).
Joseph Haydns kritische Gesamtausgabe. Georg Feder, gen. ed.
    4 vols. Boston: The Haydn Society; Leipzig: Breitkopf &
    Härtel, 1950–51 (incomplete).
*Joseph Haydns Werke, herausgegeben vom Joseph Haydn-Institut
    Köln.* Munich: G. Henle, 1958–.
Hoboken, Anthony van. *Joseph Haydn: Thematisch-biblio-
    graphisches Werkverzeichnis.* 3 vols. Mainz: B. Schott's
    Söhne, 1957–78.
Bryant, Stephen C., and Gary W. Chapman. *Melodic Index to
    Haydn's Instrumental Music: A Thematic Locator for the
    Hoboken Thematisch-bibliographisches Werkverzeichnis,
    Volumes I and III.* New York: Pendragon Press, 1981.

Paul Hindemith Sämtliche Werke im Auftrag der Hindemith-Stiftung. Kurt von Fischer and Ludwig Finscher, gen. eds. Mainz: B. Schott's Söhne, 1975–.
Paul Hindemith Werkverzeichnis. Mainz: B. Schott's Söhne, 1985.

Host, Imogen. *A Thematic Catalogue of Gustav Holst's Music.* London: Faber, 1974.

Sinclair, James B. *A Descriptive Catalogue of the Music of Charles Ives.* New Haven, Conn.: Yale University Press, 1999.

Souborné kritické vydání del Leose Janácka/Kritische Gesamtausgabe der Werke von Leos Janácek/Complete Critical Edition of the Works of Leos Janácek. Ed. J. Vyslouzil et al. 45 vols. in 8 series projected. Prague: Supraphon, 1978–.
Simeone, Nigel, John Tyrrell, and Alena Nemcová. *Janácek's Works: A Catalogue of the Music and Writings of Leos Janácek.* Oxford: Clarendon Press, 1997.

Werken van Josquin des Prés. Ed. Albert Smijers. 55 vols. Amsterdam: G. Alsbach, etc., 1922–69.
New Josquin Edition. Utrecht: Vereniging voor Nederlandse Muziekgeschiedenis, 1988–.

Orlando di Lassus Sämtliche Werke [old series]. Ed. Franz X. Haberl and Adolf Sandberger. 21 vols. Leipzig: Breitkopf & Härtel, [1894–1927] (incomplete).
Orlando di Lasso Sämtliche Werke, neue Reihe. Kassel: Bärenreiter, 1956–.
Orlando di Lasso Sämtliche Werke. 2nd ed., rev., based on the old series. Wiesbaden: Breitkopf & Härtel, 1968–.

Franz Liszts musikalische Werke, herausgegeben von der Franz-Liszt-Stiftung. 34 vols. Leipzig: Breitkopf & Härtel, 1907–36.
Franz Liszt: Neue Ausgabe Sämtlicher Werke/Ferenc Liszt: New Edition of the Complete Works. Kassel: Bärenreiter, 1970–.
Thematisches Verzeichniss der Werke, Bearbeitungen und Transcriptionen von F. Liszt. New, augm. ed. Leipzig: Breitkopf & Härtel, 1877; reprint, London: H. Baron, 1965. First published in 1855.
Howard, Leslie, and Michael Short. *Franz Liszt (1811–1886): A Thematic Catalogue of His Works, Volume 1.* Hillsdale, N.Y.: Pendragon Press, 2004.

Oeuvres complètes de J.-B. Lully (1632–1687). Henry Prunières,
gen. ed. 10 vols. Paris: Editions de la Revue Musicale,
etc., 1930–39; reprint and suppl. vols., New York: Broude
Brothers, 1965–71.
Jean-Baptiste Lully: The Complete Musical Works. New York:
Broude Brothers, 1996–.
Schneider, Herbert. *Chronologisch-thematisches Verzeichnis
sämtlicher Werke von Jean-Baptiste Lully (LWV).*
Mainzer Studien zur Musikwissenschaft, vol. 14. Tutzing:
Hans Schneider, 1981.
Gustafson, Bruce, and Matthew Lashinskie. *A Thematic Locator
for the Works of Jean-Baptiste Lully Coordinated with
Herbert Schneider's Chronologisch-thematisches Verzei-
chnis sämtlicher Werke von Jean-Baptiste Lully (LWV).*
New York: Performer's Editions, 1989.

*Gustav Mahler Sämtliche Werke: Kritische Gesamtausgabe,
herausgegeben von der Internationalen Gustav Mahler
Gesellschaft, Wien.* Vienna: Universal Edition, etc., 1960–.

*Felix Mendelssohn Bartholdy's Werke: Kritische durchgesehene
Ausgabe.* Ed. Julius Rietz. 19 series. Leipzig: Breitkopf &
Härtel, 1874–77; reprint, New York: Kalmus, 1971.
Leipziger Ausgabe der Werke Felix Mendelssohn Bartholdys.
Internationale Felix-Mendelssohn-Gesellschaft and
Sächsische Akademie der Wissenschaften. Leipzig:
Deutscher Verlag für Musik, 1960–.
*Thematisches Verzeichniss im Druck erschienener Compositio-
nen von Felix Mendelssohn Bartholdy.* 3rd, augm. ed.
Leipzig: [Breitkopf & Härtel], 1882. First published in
1841.

Tutte le opere di Claudio Monteverdi. . . . Ed. Gian Francesco
Malipiero. 16 vols. + suppl. Vienna: Universal Edition, etc.,
1926–42, 1968; reprint, Bryn Mawr, Pa.: Theodore Presser,
1966.
Opera omnia Claudio Monteverdi. Fondazione Claudio Monteverdi. Cremona, Italy: Athenaeum Cremonense, 1970–.
Stattkus, Manfred H. *Claudio Monteverdi: Verzeichnis der
erhaltenen Werke (SV).* Bergkamen, Germany: Musikverlag Stattkus, 1985.

*Wolfgang Amadeus Mozart's Werke: Kritisch durchgesehene
Gesamtausgabe.* 24 series. Leipzig: Breitkopf & Härtel,
1876–1905; reprint, New York: Kalmus, 1968[?].
Wolfgang Amadeus Mozart: Neue Ausgabe sämtlicher

Werke, . . . herausgegeben von der Internationalen Stiftung Mozarteum, Salzburg. Kassel: Bärenreiter, 1955–. Vols. 1–20 reprinted by Kassel: Bärenreiter, 1991.

Köchel, Ludwig Ritter von. *Chronologisch-thematisches Verzeichnis sämtlicher Tonwerke Wolfgang Amadé Mozarts . . . .* 8th ed. Ed. Franz Giegling et al. Wiesbaden: Breitkopf & Härtel, 1983. First published in 1862.

Hill, George R., and Murray Gould, et al. *A Thematic Locator for Mozart's Works as Listed in Köchel's* **Chronologisch-thematisches Verzeichnis, Sixth Edition.** Music Indexes and Bibliographies, no. 1. Hackensack, N.J.: Joseph Boonin, 1970.

M. Mussorgsky Sämtliche Werke. Ed. Paul Lamm. 24 vols. Moscow: State Music Publishers, 1928–34 (incomplete); reprint, New York: Kalmus, 1969.

Modest Petrovich Mussorgskii: Polnoe akademischeske sobranie sochinenii [Complete Academic Edition of Compositions]. Moscow: Muzyka, 1996–.

New Obrecht Edition. Chris Maas, gen. ed. 18 vols. Utrecht: Vereniging voor Nederlandse Muziekgeschiedenis, 1983–99.

Jacques Offenbach: Critical Edition. Ed. Jean-Christoph Keck. 44 vols. in 8 series projected. Berlin: Boosey & Hawkes, 1999–.

Perreault, Jean M. *Thematic Catalogue of the Musical Works of Johann Pachelbel.* Lanham, Md.: Scarecrow Press, 2004.

Edizione nazionale delle opere di Niccolo Paganini. Ed. L. Ronga et al. Rome: Istituto italiano per la storia della musica, 1976–.

Pierluigi da Palestrina's Werke. Ed. Raffaele Casimiri. 33 vols. Leipzig: Breitkopf & Härtel, [1862–1907].

Le opere complete di Giovanni Pierluigi da Palestrina. Rome: Fratelli Scalera, 1939–65, 1973–2000.

Hall, Allison. *Palestrina: An Index to the Casimiri, Kalmus and Haberl Editions.* MLA Index and Bibliography Series, no. 22. Lanham, Md.: Scarecrow Press, 1980.

Giovanni Battista Pergolesi: The Complete Works. Ed. Barry S. Brook et al. New York: Pendragon Press, 1985–.

Paymer, Marvin E. *Giovanni Battista Pergolesi, 1710–1736: A Thematic Catalogue of the Opera Omnia with an Appen-*

dix Listing Omitted Compositions. New York: Pendragon Press, 1977.

Schmidt, Carl B. *The Music of Francis Poulenc (1899–1963): A Catalogue.* Oxford: Oxford University Press, 1995.

Collected Works of Sergei Prokofiev. 20 vols. Moscow: State Music Publishers, 1955–78; reprint, Melville, N.Y.: Belwin-Mills, 1979.

The Works of Henry Purcell. Published by the Purcell Society. 32 vols. London: Novello, 1878–. New series of rev. and unpub. works, 1968–.
Zimmerman, Franklin B. *Henry Purcell, 1659–1695: An Analytical Catalogue of His Music.* London: St. Martin's Press, 1963.
————. *Henry Purcell, 1659–1695: Melodic and Intervallic Indexes to His Complete Works.* Philadelphia: Smith-Edwards-Dunlap, 1975.

Threlfall, Robert, and Geoffrey Norris. *A Catalogue of the Compositions of S. Rachmaninoff.* London: Scolar Press, 1982.

Jean-Philippe Rameau (1683–1764): Oeuvres complètes. Camille Saint-Saëns, gen. ed. 18 vols. Paris: Durand et Fils, 1895–1913, 1924 (incomplete).
Jean Philippe Rameau: Opera omnia. Sylvie Boissou, ed. Paris: Billaudot, 1996–.

Catalogue de l'oeuvre de Maurice Ravel. Paris: Fondation Maurice Ravel, 1954.

Nikolay Andreievich Rimsky-Korsakov: Polnoie sobranie sochinenii [Complete Works]. Moscow: Gosudarstvennoe Muzykal'noe Izdatel'stvo, 1946–70; reprint, New York: Belwin-Mills, 1979–84.

Edizione critica delle opere di Gioachino Rossini. Philip Gossett et al., gen. eds. Pesaro: Fondazione Rossini, 1979–.

Ratner, Sabina Teller. *Camille Saint-Saëns (1835–1921): A Thematic Catalogue of His Complete Works. Volume 1: The In strumental Works.* New York: Oxford University Press, 2002.

Jenkins, Newell Owen, and Bathia Dina Churgin. *Thematic Catalogue of the Works of Giovanni Battista Sammartini:*

Orchestral and Vocal Music. Cambridge, Mass.: Harvard University Press, 1976.

Arnold Schönberg Sämtliche Werke. Joseph Rufer, gen. ed. Mainz: B. Schott's Söhne, 1966–.
Rufer, Josef. *The Works of Arnold Schoenberg: A Catalogue of His Compositions, Writings and Paintings.* Trans. Dika Newlin. London: Faber and Faber, 1962. First published in 1959.

Franz Schubert's Werke: Kritisch durchgesehene Gesamtausgabe. 21 series + critical commentary/index. Leipzig: Breitkopf & Härtel, 1884–97; reprint, New York: Dover, 1965.
Franz Schubert: Neue Ausgabe sämtlicher Werke, herausgegeben von der Internationalen Schubert-Gesellschaft. Kassel: Bärenreiter, 1964–.
Deutsch, Otto Erich. *Franz Schubert: Thematisches Verzeichnis seiner Werke in chronologischer Folge.* Franz Schubert: Neue Ausgabe sämtlicher Werke, ser. 8, vol. 4. Kassel: Bärenreiter, 1978. First published in English in 1951.

Robert Schumann's Werke. Ed. Clara Schumann. 14 series. Leipzig. Breitkopf & Härtel, 1881–93; reprint, New York: Kalmus, 1968.
Robert Schumann: Neue Ausgabe sämtlicher Werke, herausgegeben von der Robert-Schumann-Gesellschaft Düsseldorf/Robert Schumann: New Edition of the Complete Works, Published by the Robert-Schumann-Gesellschaft Düsseldorf. Ed. Akio Mayeda and Klaus Wolfgang Niemöller. Mainz: B. Schott's Söhne, 1991–.
Hofmann, Kurt, and Siegmar Keil. *Robert Schumann: Thematisches Verzeichnis sämtlicher im Druck erschienenen musikalischen Werke mit Angabe des Jahres ihres Entstehens und Erscheinens.* 5th ed., rev. and enl. Hamburg: J. Schuberth, 1982. First published in 1860.
McCorkle, Margit L., and Akio Mayeda. *[Robert Schumann:] Thematisch-bibliographisches Werkverzeichnis.* Mainz: B. Schott, 2003. Also published as *Robert Schumann: Neue Ausgabe sämtlicher Werke,* Series VIII, Supplement. Mainz: B. Schott, 2003.

Heinrich Schütz's Sämtliche Werke. Ed. Philipp Spitta et al. 18 vols. Leipzig: Breitkopf & Härtel, [1885–1927]; reprint, Wiesbaden: Breitkopf & Härtel, 1968.
Heinrich Schütz: Neue Ausgabe sämtlicher Werke, herausgegeben im Auftrag der Internationalen Heinrich-Schütz-Gesellschaft. Kassel: Bärenreiter, 1955–.

Stuttgarter Schütz-Ausgabe: Heinrich Schütz Sämtliche Werke nach den Quellen. Ed. Günter Graulich and Paul Horn. Stuttgart: Hänssler-Verlag, 1971–.

Bittinger, Werner. *Schütz-Werke-Verzeichnis (SWV): Kleine Ausgabe, im Auftrag der Neuen Schütz-Gesellschaft.* Kassel: Bärenreiter, 1960.

Miller, D. Douglas, and Anne L. Highsmith, comps. *Heinrich Schütz: A Bibliography of the Collected Works and Performing Editions.* Music Reference Collection, no. 9. New York: Greenwood Press, 1986.

D. Shostakovich: Collected Works. Dvukh Tomakh, gen. ed. 42 vols. Moscow: Izdatel'stvo "Muzyka," 1979–87.

New Collected Works of Dmitri Shostakovich. Ed. Manashir Iakubov. Moscow: Izdatel'stvo"DSCH," 2002–.

MacDonald, Malcolm. *Dmitri Shostakovich: A Complete Catalogue.* 2nd ed. London: Boosey & Hawkes, 1985. First published in 1977.

Hulme, Derek C. *Dmitri Shostakovich: Catalogue, Bibliography & Discography.* 3rd ed. Lanham, Md.: Scarecrow Press, 2002. First published in 1982.

Jan Sibelius Works. Glenda Gould, gen. ed. Wiesbaden: Breitkopf & Härtel, 1998–.

Dahlström, Fabian. *Jean Sibelius: Thematisch-bibliographisches Verzeichnis seiner Werke.* Wiesbaden: Breitkopf & Härtel, 2003.

Souborná díla Bedricha Smetany [Smetana's Collected Works]. Ed. Zdenek Nejedly. 4 vols. Prague: Státní Nakladatelství, 1924–36.

Johann Strauss Gesamtausgabe. Ed. Fritz Racek. Vienna: Doblinger, 1967–.

Winmann, Alexander. *Verzeichnis sämtlicher Werke von Johann Strauss, Vater und Sohn.* Vienna: Musikverlag L. Krenn, 1956.

Strauss-Elementar-Verzeichnis (SEV): Thematisch-bibliographischer Katalog der Werke von Johann Strauss (Sohn). Ed. N. Rubey. Vienna Institute for Strauss Research. Tutzing, Germany: H. Schneider, 1990–.

Mueller von Asow, E. H. *Richard Strauss: Thematisches Verzeichnis.* 6 vols. Vienna: Verlag L. Doblinger, 1955–74.

Schuh, Willi, and Ernst Roth. *Richard Strauss: Gesamtverzeichnis.* London: Boosey & Hawkes, 1964.

Trenner, Franz, and E. H. Mueller von Asow. *Richard Strauss Werkverzeichnis.* Veröffentlichungen der Richard-Strauss-Gesellschaft, vol. 12. Munich: W. Ludwig, 1993. Based on E. H. Mueller von Asow's *Richard Strauss: Thematisches Verzeichnis.*

The Complete Works of Igor Stravinsky (1882–1971): A Comprehensive Catalogue of Stravinsky's Music, Compiled in Honor of the Composer's 100th Anniversary. Valley Forge, Pa.: European American Retail Music, 1981.
Caesar, Clifford. *Igor Stravinsky: A Complete Catalogue.* San Francisco: San Francisco Press, 1982.

Arthur Sullivan, 1842–1900: The Operas. Ed. Steven Ledbetter. New York: Broude Brothers, 1994–.

Karol Szymanowski: Gesamtausgabe/Complete Edition. Ed. T. Chylinska. Cracow: PWM-Edition, 1973–.
Michalowski, Kornel. *Karol Szymanowski, 1882–1937: Katalog tematyczny dziel i bibliografia/Thematic Catalogue of Works and Bibliography/Thematisches Werkverzeichnis und Bibliographie.* Cracow: Polskie Wydawnictwo Muzyczne, 1967.

P. Tchaikovsky: Polnoe Sobranie Sochinenii [Complete Edition of Compositions]. 124 vols. Moscow: State Music Publishers, 1940–71.
Petr Il'ic Cajkovskij (1840–1893): New Edition of the Complete Works/Neue Ausgabe sämtlicher Werke. 12 series, of which ser. 11 will be literary works, diaries, and letters, and ser. 12, catalog of works. Moscow: Muzyka; Mainz: Schott, 1993–.
Systematisches Verzeichnis der Werke von Pjotr Iljitsch Tschaikowsky: Ein Handbuch für die Musikpraxis. Hamburg: Musikverlag Hans Sikorski, 1973.
Poznansky, Alexander, and Brett Langston. *The Tchaikovsky Handbook. Vol. 1: Thematic Catalogue of Works, Catalogue of Photographs, Autobiography. Vol. 2: Catalogue of Letters, Bibliography.* Bloomington: Indiana University Press, 2002.

Georg Philipp Telemann: Musikalische Werke, herausgegeben im Auftrag der Gesellschaft für Musikforschung. Kassel: Bärenreiter, 1950–.
Menke, Werner. *Thematisches Verzeichnis der Vokalwerke von Georg Philipp Telemann.* 2nd ed. 2 vols. Frankfurt: Vittorio Klostermann, 1988. First published in 1982–83.

Ruhnke, Martin. *Georg Philipp Telemann: Thematisch-systematisches Verzeichnis seiner Werke: Telemann-Werkverzeichnis (TWV)*. Georg Philipp Telemann: Musikalische Werke, suppl. Kassel: Bärenreiter, 1984–99.

Kennedy, Michael. *A Catalogue of the Works of Ralph Vaughan Williams*. 2nd ed. Oxford: Oxford University Press, 1996. First published in 1964.

The Works of/Le opere di Giuseppe Verdi. Philip Gossett, coordinating ed. Chicago: University of Chicago Press; Milan: G. Ricordi, 1983–.

Hopkinson, Cecil. *A Bibliography of the Works of Giuseppe Verdi, 1813–1901*. 2 vols. New York: Broude Brothers, 1973–78.

[*Antonio Vivaldi: Le opere strumentali*]. Ed. Gian Francesco Malipiero. 530 vols. Rome: G. Ricordi, 1947–72.

Antonio Vivaldi: Edizione critica. Ed. Paul Everett and Michael Talbot. Milan: Ricordi, 1982–.

Rinaldi, Mario. *Catalogo numerico tematico delle composizioni di Antonio Vivaldi*. . . . Rome: Editrice Cultura Moderna, [1945].

Pincherle, Marc. *Antonio Vivaldi et la musique instrumentale*. Book 2: *Inventaire thématique*. Paris: Fleury, 1948; reprint, New York: Johnson Reprint, 1968.

Coral, Lenore. *A Concordance of the Thematic Indexes to the Instrumental Works of Antonio Vivaldi*. 2nd ed. MLA Index Series, no. 4. Ann Arbor, Mich.: Music Library Association, 1972. First published in 1965.

[Fanna, Antonio.] *Opere strumentali di Antonio Vivaldi (1678–1741): Catalogo numerico-tematico secondo la catalogazione Fanna*. 2nd ed., rev. and enl. Milan: Ricordi, 1986. First published in 1968.

Ohmura, Noriko. *A Reference Concordance Table of Vivaldi's Instrumental Works*. Tokyo: Kawasaki, 1972.

Ryom, Peter. *Antonio Vivaldi: Table de concordances des oeuvres (RV)*. Copenhagen: Engstrøm & Sødring, 1973.

———. *Verzeichnis der Werke Antonio Vivaldis (RV)*. Leipzig: VEB Deutscher Verlag, 1974.

Ryom, Peter. *Répertoire des oeuvres d'Antonio Vivaldi: Les compositions instrumentales [RV]*. Copenhagen: Engstrøm & Sødring, 1986.

Richard Wagners musikalische Werke: Erste kritisch revidierte Gesamtausgabe. Ed. Michael Balling. 10 vols. Leipzig: Breitkopf & Härtel, 1912–ca. 1929 (incomplete).

Richard Wagner Sämtliche Werke. Ed. Carl Dahlhaus. Mainz:
  B. Schott's Söhne, 1970–.
Deathridge, John, et al. *Wagner Werk-Verzeichnis (WWV):
  Verzeichnis der musikalischen Werke Richard Wagners
  und ihre Quellen.* Mainz: B. Schott's Söhne, 1986.

William Walton Edition. David Lloyd-Jones, gen. ed. Oxford:
  Oxford University Press, 1998–.
Craggs, Stewart R. *William Walton: A Catalogue.* Rev. ed. Oxford:
  Oxford University Press, 1990. First published in 1977.

Carl Maria von Weber: Sämtliche Werke. Ed. G. Allroggen. 45
  vols. in 10 series projected. Mainz: Schott, 1998–.
Jähns, Friedrich Wilhelm. *Carl Maria von Weber in seinen
  Werken: Chronologisch-thematisches Verzeichniss
  sämtlichen Compositionen.* . . . Berlin: [n.p.], 1871; reprint,
  Berlin: Lienau, 1967.

The Kurt Weill Edition. 25 vols. in 4 series projected. New York:
  Kurt Weill Foundation for Music, 1996–.

Hugo Wolf: Sämtliche Werke. H. Jancik, gen. ed. 19 vols. Interna-
  tional Hugo Wolf Society. Vienna: Musikwissenschaftlicher
  Verlag, 1960–2001.
Berke-Müller, Paul. *Hugo Wolf: Verzeichnis seiner Werke.*
  Leipzig: C. F. Peters, 1908.

Other Thematic Catalogs

Edwards, Owain. *English Eighteenth-Century Concertos: An
  Inventory and Thematic Catalogue.* Thematic Catalogues
  Series, no. 28. Hillsdale, N.Y.: Pendragon Press, 2004.

Mayer-Martin, Donna, and Dorothy Keyser. *Thematic Catalogue
  of Troubadour and Trouvère Melodies.* Thematic Catalogues Series, no. 18. Hillsdale, N.Y.: Pendragon Press, 2004.

Whittemore, Joan. *Music of the Venetian Ospedali: A Thematic
  Catalogue.* Thematic Catalogues Series, no. 21. Hillsdale,
  N.Y.: Pendragon Press, 1995.

ANTHOLOGIES OF MUSIC

This category of musical editions is usually less scholarly and
more practical in intent, being geared to the student, teacher, or per-

former. Most are in one or two volumes, the chief exception being
the extensive multivolume Anthology of Music, whose complete
contents are given in a separate list at the end. As in the case of musical sets and monuments, the anthologies in the present list have
various delimitations by period, genre, and medium, and have been
divided into categories accordingly. Anthologies dating from the
early twentieth century or before are mostly excluded in favor of
more recent American and English ones. For further information,
see Hilton's *Index to Early Music in Selected Anthologies* and Murray's *Anthologies of Music*; see pp. 60–61 above.

General

Benjamin, Thomas, et al., comps. *Music for Analysis: Examples
    from the Common Practice Period and the Twentieth
    Century.* 5th ed. Boston: Houghton Mifflin, 2001. First
    published in 1978.
Bonds, Mark Evan. *Anthology of Scores to A History of Music in
    Western Culture.* 2 vols. Upper Saddle River, N.J.: Prentice
    Hall, 2003.
Brandt, William, et al. **The Comprehensive Study of Music.**
    1976–80.

> 1. *Anthology of Music from Plainchant through Gabrieli.*
>   New York: Harper & Row, 1980.
> 2. *Anthology of Music from Monteverdi through Mozart.*
>   New York: Harper's College Press, 1977.
> 3. *Anthology of Music from Beethoven through Wagner.*
>   New York: Harper's College Press, 1977.
> 4. *Anthology of Music from Debussy through Stock-
>   hausen.* New York: Harper's College Press, 1976.
> 5. *Piano Reductions for Harmonic Study.* New York:
>   Harper & Row, 1980.
> 6. *Basic Principles of Music Theory.* New York: Harper &
>   Row, 1980.

Briscoe, James R., ed. *New Historical Anthology of Music by
    Women.* Bloomington: Indiana University Press, 2004.
    First published in 1987 as *Historical Anthology of Music
    by Women.* CD recordings also available from Indiana
    University Press.
Burkhart, Charles. *Anthology for Musical Analysis.* 6th ed.
    New York: Thomson/Schirmer, 2004. First published
    in 1964.
Cohen, Albert, and John D. White. *Anthology of Music for
    Analysis.* New York: Appleton-Century-Crofts, 1965.
Davison, Archibald T., and Willi Apel. *Historical Anthology of*

Music. Rev. ed. 2 vols. Cambridge, Mass.: Harvard University Press, 1977. First published in 1946 [vol. 1].

DeVoto, Mark, comp., ed., and annot. *Mostly Short Pieces: An Anthology for Harmonic Analysis.* New York: W. W. Norton, 1992.

Distefano, Joseph P., and James A. Searl. *Music and Materials for Analysis: An Anthology.* Lanham, Md.: Scarecrow Press, 1995.

Forney, Kristine, ed. *The Norton Scores: A Study Anthology.* 9th ed., in 2 vols. New York: W. W. Norton, 2003. First published in 1968.

Fuller, Sarah. *The European Musical Heritage 800–1750.* New York: Alfred A. Knopf, 1987; reprint, New York: McGraw-Hill, 1993.

Kostka, Stefan M., and Roger Carper Graybill. *Anthology of Music for Analysis.* Upper Saddle River, N.J.: Prentice Hall, 2004.

Lerner, Edward R. *Study Scores of Musical Styles.* New York: McGraw-Hill, 1968.

Lincoln, Harry B., and Stephen Bonta. *Study Scores of Historical Styles.* 2 vols. Englewood Cliffs, N.J.: Prentice Hall, 1986–87.

Palisca, Claude V., ed. *Norton Anthology of Western Music.* 4th ed. 2 vols. New York: W. W. Norton, 2001. First published in 1980.

Parrish, Carl, comp. and ed. *A Treasury of Early Music: An Anthology of Masterworks of the Middle Ages, the Renaissance, and the Baroque Era.* New York: W. W. Norton, 1958; reprint, Mineola, N.Y.: Dover Publications, 2000.

Parrish, Carl, and John F. Ohl, comps and eds. *Masterpieces of Music before 1750: An Anthology of Musical Examples from Gregorian Chant to J. S. Bach.* New York: W. W. Norton, 1951; reprint, Mineola, N.Y.. Dover Publications, 2001.

Schering, Arnold, comp. and ed. *Geschichte der Musik in Beispielen: Dreihundertfünfzig Tonsätze aus neun Jahrhunderten.* Leipzig: Breitkopf & Härtel, 1931; reprint, New York: Broude Brothers, 1957.

Starr, William J., and George F. Devine. *Music Scores Omnibus.* 2nd ed. 2 vols. Englewood Cliffs, N.J.: Prentice Hall, 1974. First published in 1964.

Stein, Leon. *Anthology of Musical Forms.* Evanston, Ill.: Summy-Birchard, 1962.

Stolba, K Marie, ed. *The Development of Western Music: An Anthology.* 3rd ed. Boston: McGraw-Hill, 1998. First published in 1991.

Turek, Ralph, ed. *Analytical Anthology of Music.* 2nd ed. New York: McGraw-Hill, 1992. First published in 1984.

Walton, Charles W. *Music Literature for Analysis and Study.* Belmont, Calif.: Wadsworth Publishing, 1973.

Wennerstrom, Mary H. *Anthology of Musical Structure and Style.* Englewood Cliffs, N.J.: Prentice Hall, 1983.

Limited to an Era

Berry, Wallace, and Edward Chudacoff. *Eighteenth-Century Imitative Counterpoint: Music for Analysis.* New York: Appleton-Century-Crofts, 1969.

DeLio, Thomas, and Stuart Saunders Smith, eds. *Twentieth Century Music Scores.* Englewood Cliffs, N.J.: Prentice Hall, 1989.

Democratic Souvenirs: An Historical Anthology of 19th-Century American Music. New York: New York Public Library by C. F. Peters, 1988.

Downs, Philip G., ed. *Anthology of Classical Music.* New York: W. W. Norton, 1992.

Gleason, Harold, comp. and ed. *Examples of Music before 1400.* New York: Appleton-Century-Crofts, 1942.

Greenberg, Noah, and Paul Maynard, eds. *An Anthology of Early Renaissance Music.* New York: W. W. Norton, 1975.

Hoppin, Richard H., ed. *Anthology of Medieval Music.* The Norton Introduction to Music History. New York: W. W. Norton, 1978.

Johnson, Roger, comp. *Scores: An Anthology of New Music.* New York: Schirmer Books, 1981.

Kirby, F. E. *Music in the Classic Period: An Anthology with Commentary.* New York: Schirmer Books, 1979.

———. *Music in the Romantic Period: An Anthology with Commentary.* New York: Schirmer Books, 1986.

Marrocco, W. Thomas, ed. *Ars Antiqua.* Oxford: Oxford University Press, 1979.

Marrocco, W. Thomas, and Harold Gleason, comps. and eds. *Music in America: An Anthology from the Landing of the Pilgrims to the Close of the Civil War, 1620–1865.* New York: W. W. Norton, 1964.

Marrocco, W. Thomas, and Nicholas Sandon. *Medieval Music.* The Oxford Anthology of Music. London: Oxford University Press, 1977.

Minor, Andrew C. *Music in Medieval and Renaissance Life: Anthology of Vocal and Instrumental Music, 1200–1614.* Columbia: University of Missouri Press, 1964.

Morgan, Robert P., ed. *Anthology of Twentieth-Century Music.* The Norton Introduction to Music History. New York: W. W. Norton, 1992.

Music from the Days of George Washington: A Collection of Patriotic and Military Tunes, Piano and Dance Music, Songs and Operatic Airs. Ed. W. O. Strunk. Washington, D.C.: United States George Washington Bicentennial Commission, 1931; reprint, New York: Da Capo Press, 1983.

Plantinga, Leon, ed. *Anthology of Romantic Music.* The Norton Introduction to Music History. New York: W. W. Norton, 1984.

Simms, Bryan R. *Music of the Twentieth Century: An Anthology.* New York: Schirmer Books, 1986.

Soderlund, Gustave Fredric, and Samuel H. Scott, comps. *Examples of Gregorian Chant and Sacred Music of the 16th Century.* [Augm. ed.] Englewood Cliffs, N.J.: Prentice Hall, 1971; reprint, Prospect Heights, Ill.: Waveland Press, 1996. First published in 1937.

Wennerstrom, Mary H., comp. *Anthology of Twentieth-Century Music.* 2nd ed. Englewood Cliffs, N.J.: Prentice Hall, 1988. First published in 1969.

Wilson, David Fenwick. *Music of the Middle Ages: An Anthology for Performance and Study.* New York: Schirmer Books, 1990.

Limited to a Medium or Genre

Brody, Elaine. *Music in Opera: A Historical Anthology.* Englewood Cliffs, N.J.: Prentice Hall, 1970.

Christiansen, Rupert, ed. *The Grand Obsession: An Anthology of Opera.* London: William Collins Sons, 1988.

Dakers, Lionel, comp. and ed. *The New Church Anthem Book: One Hundred Anthems.* Oxford: Oxford University Press, 1992.

Dunn, Thomas, ed. *The Renaissance Singer.* With an introductory essay, "Some Notes on 16th Century Sacred Polyphony," by Joseph Dyer. Boston: E. C. Schirmer, 1976.

Gardner, John, and Simon Harris. *A Cappella: An Anthology of Unaccompanied Choral Music from Seven Centuries.* New York: Oxford University Press, 1992.

Gillingham, Bryan. *Medieval Polyphonic Sequences: An Anthology.* Ottawa, Canada: Institute of Mediaeval Music, 1985.

———. *Secular Medieval Latin Song: An Anthology.* Ottawa, Canada: Institute of Mediaeval Music, 1993.

[Greenberg, Noah, et al., eds.] *New York Pro Musica Choral*

Songbook: Sacred and Secular Music of Spain, England, Germany, and the Netherlands for Mixed Voices. New York: Associated Music Publishers, 1966.

Jackson, Francis, et al. *Anthems for Choirs.* 4 vols. London: Oxford University Press, 1973–76.

Jacques, Reginald, David Willcocks, and John Rutter, eds. and arrs. *Carols for Choirs.* 4 vols. London: Oxford University Press, 1961–80.

Lang, Paul Henry, comp. *The Concerto 1800–1900: A Norton Music Anthology.* New York: W. W. Norton, 1969.

———. *The Symphony 1800–1900: A Norton Music Anthology.* New York: W. W. Norton, 1969.

Le Huray, Peter, et al. *Anthems for Men's Voices.* 2 vols. Oxford: Oxford University Press, 1965.

MacClintock, Carol, ed. *The Solo Song 1580–1730: A Norton Music Anthology.* New York: W. W. Norton, 1973.

McGee, Timothy J. *Medieval Instrumental Dances.* Bloomington: Indiana University Press, 1989.

Maillard, Jean, ed. *Anthologie de chants de troubadours.* Nice: Delrieu, 1967.

———. *Anthologie de chants de trouvères.* Paris: Zurfluh, 1967.

Morris, Christopher, comp. *A Sixteenth-Century Anthem Book.* 6th ed, rev. London: Oxford University Press, 1988. First published in 1960.

Robinson, Ray, ed. *Choral Music: A Norton Historical Anthology.* New York: W. W. Norton, 1978.

Werf, Hendrik van der. *The Extant Troubadour Melodies: Transcriptions and Essays for Performers and Scholars.* Rochester, N.Y.: [Author], 1984.

Willcocks, David, and John Rutter, eds. and arrs. *100 Carols for Choirs.* London: Oxford University Press, 1987.

Limited to a Medium or Genre and to a Region

Arnold, Denis, ed. *Ten Venetian Motets.* London: Oxford University Press, 1980.

Bernstein, Jane A., ed. *French Chansons of the Sixteenth Century.* University Park: Pennsylvania State University Press, 1985.

Cori Spezzati. 2 vols. Cambridge: Cambridge University Press, 1988.

Dearmer, Percy, R. Vaughan Williams, and Martin Shaw. *The Oxford Book of Carols.* London: Oxford University Press, 1928.

Dobbins, Frank, ed. *The Oxford Book of French Chansons.* London: Oxford University Press, 1987.

Greenberg, Noah, ed. *An Anthology of Elizabethan Lute Songs, Madrigals, and Rounds.* The Norton Library. New York: W. W. Norton, 1955.

———. *An Anthology of English Medieval and Renaissance Vocal Music: Part Songs for One to Six Voices.* The Norton Library. New York: W. W. Norton, 1968.

Harman, Alec, ed. *The Oxford Book of Italian Madrigals.* London: Oxford University Press, 1983.

Hillier, Paul, ed. *The Catch Book: 153 Catches, Including the Complete Catches of Henry Purcell.* Oxford: Oxford University Press, 1987.

———. *English Romantic Partsongs.* Oxford: Oxford University Press, 1986.

Keyte, Hugh, and Andrew Parrott, eds.; Clifford Bartlett, assoc. ed. *The New Oxford Book of Carols.* Reprint with corrections. New York: Oxford University Press, 1994. First published in 1992.

Ledger, Philip, ed. *The Oxford Book of English Madrigals.* London: Oxford University Press, 1978.

Le Huray, Peter, ed. *Treasury of English Church Music, 1545–1650.* Reprint with corrections. Cambridge: Cambridge University Press, 1982. First published in 1965.

Martens, Mason, ed. *The Bicentennial Collection of American Choral Music (1760–1900).* Dayton, Ohio: McAfee Music, 1975.

Morris, Christopher, comp. *The Oxford Book of Tudor Anthems: 34 Anthems for Mixed Choir.* London: Oxford University Press, 1978.

Newman, Anthony, comp. and ed. *Anthology of Early English Harpsichord Music.* New York: G. Schirmer, 1984.

Patterson, Willis C., comp. *Anthology of Art Songs by Black American Composers.* New York: E. B. Marks, 1977.

———. *The Second Anthology of Art Songs by African American Composers.* [Willis C. Patterson], 2002.

Pedrell, Felipe, comp. *Anthology of Classical Spanish Organists (16th, 17th & 18th Centuries).* 2 vols. New York: Associated Music Publishers, 1968.

Roche, Jerome, ed. *The Flower of the Italian Madrigal: For Mixed Voices.* 2 vols. Renaissance Voices. New York: Galaxy Music, 1988.

Roche, Jerome, et al., eds. *The Flower of the Italian Madrigal: For Mixed Voices. Vol. 3: Light Madrigals and Villanellas.* New York: Gaudia Music and Arts, 1995.

Smith, James G., comp. and ed. *The New Liberty Bell: A Bicentennial Anthology of American Choral Music.* Champaign, Ill.: Mark Foster, 1976.

Young, Percy M., ed. *The English Glee.* New York: Oxford University Press, 1990.

Comprehensive Multivolume Set

Anthology of Music: A Collection of Complete Musical Examples Illustrating the History of Music. Ed. Karl Gustav Fellerer. 48 vols. + index. Also published as **Das Musikwerk.** Cologne: Arno Volk Verlag, 1955–76.

1. *Four Hundred Years of European Keyboard Music.* 2nd ed. By Walter Georgii. 1959. First published in 1959.
2. *Troubadours, Trouvères, Minne-, and Meistersinger.* By Friedrich Gennrich. 1960.
3. *The Sixteenth-Century Part Song in Italy, France, England and Spain.* By Hans Engel. 1961.
4. *European Folk Song: Common Forms in Characteristic Modifications.* By Walter Wiora. 1966.
5. *The Opera from Its Beginnings until the Early 19th Century.* By A. A. Abert. 1962.
6. *The Classics.* By Kurt Stephenson. 1962.
7. *The Italian Trio Sonata.* By Erich Schenk. 1955.
8. *The Character Piece.* By Willy Kahl. 1961.
9. *Medieval Polyphony.* By Heinrich Husmann. 1962.
10. *The German Part Song from the 16th Century to the Present Day.* By Helmuth Osthoff. 1955.
11. *The Variation.* By Kurt von Fischer. 1962.
12. *Improvisation in Nine Centuries of Western Music.* By Ernest T. Ferand. 1961.
13. *The Music of the Byzantine Church.* By Egon Wellesz. 1959.
14. *The German Solo Song and the Ballad.* By Hans Joachim Moser. 1958.
15. *The Solo Sonata.* By Franz Giegling. 1960.
16. *The Solo Song outside German Speaking Countries.* By Frits Noske. 1959.
17. *The Toccata.* By Erich Valentin. 1958.
18. *Gregorian Chant.* By Franz Tack. 1960.
19. *The Fugue I: From the Beginnings to J. S. Bach.* By Adam Adrio. 1961.
20. *Hebrew Music.* By Eric Werner. 1961.
21. *Romanticism in Music.* By Kurt Stephenson. 1961.
22. *The Art of the Netherlanders.* By René Bernard Lenaerts. 1964.
23. *The Concerto Grosso.* By Hans Engel. 1964.
24. *History of Instrumentation.* By Heinz Becker. 1964.

25. *The Solo Concerto.* By Hans Engel. 1964.
26. *The Suite.* By Hermann Beck. 1966.
27. *The Dance.* By Georg Reichert. 1974.
28. *Pre-Classical Polyphony.* By Karl Gustav Fellerer. 1965.
29. *The Symphony.* By Lothar Hoffmann-Erbrecht. 1967.
30. *History of the Mass.* By Joseph Schmidt-Görg. 1968.
31. *The Monody.* By Karl Gustav Fellerer. 1968.
32. *The Cantata.* By Richard Jakoby. 1968.
33. *The Fugue II: From Handel to the Twentieth Century.* By Josef Müller-Blattau. 1968.
34. *The Serenade for Orchestra.* By Günter Hausswald. 1970.
35. *The Trio Sonata outside Italy.* By Erich Schenk. 1970.
36. *Program Music.* By Wolfgang Stockmeier. 1970.
37. *The Oratorio.* By Günther Massenkeil. 1970.
38. *The Opera I: 17th Century.* By Hellmuth Christian Wolff. 1971.
39. *The Opera II: 18th Century.* By Hellmuth Christian Wolff. 1971.
40. *The Opera III: 19th Century.* By Hellmuth Christian Wolff. 1975.
41. *Original Vocal Improvisations from the 16th-18th Centuries.* By Hellmuth Christian Wolff. 1972.
42. *The Fantasia I: 16th to 18th Century.* By Peter Schluening. 1971.
43. *The Fantasia II: 18th to 20th Century.* By Peter Schluening. 1971.
44. *Non-European Folklore and Art Music.* By Marius Schneider. 1972.
45. *The Music of the Figured Bass Era.* By Günter Hausswald. 1974.
46. *Chamber Music.* By Hubert Unverricht. 1975.
47. *The Motet.* By Heinrich Hüschen. 1975.
48. *Survey and Index.* Karl Gustav Fellerer, ed. and comp. 1976.

CHAPTER EIGHT

Miscellaneous Sources

This final chapter brings together two bibliographies concerning sources that are more or less complementary or peripheral to the subject of research in music, but above all *practical* in their intent. The first is a selective listing of currently available guides to aspects of research and writing in English, varying from general discussions of research techniques to manuals of style used in the humanities and other guides to proper English usage, and concluding with some representative guides to getting work published. The second list, "The Music Industry," assembles useful information pertaining to the business of music—publishing, careers, grants, competitions, etc.—especially as it is practiced in the United States.

MANUALS OF STYLE AND OTHER AIDS TO RESEARCH, WRITING, AND PUBLICATION

Some of the following lists are geared to a general readership and some to writers on music. They emphasize sources that are recent or that have demonstrated staying power. The various subdivisions and the titles of the works are for the most part self-explanatory. Particular mention should be made of the important and burgeoning field of computer applications to music research and writing (for further information, consult also the computer journals listed in chapter 6, under "Other Journals," pp. 244–45 above).

The third list, "General Manuals of Style and Other Guides to English," is particularly selective, there being innumerable guides of this type in print, but it includes some of the most commonly used general manuals of style in the field—*The Chicago Manual of Style, MLA Handbook,* and Turabian's *Manual for Writers*—as well as several other guides to English usage.

"Guides to Writing about Music" lists the best-known special-ized style manuals in music, including the recent ones by Wingell and Boyle et al. "Guides to the Publication Process" features a few representative recent guides to the often complicated venture of getting works into print.

General Aids to Research

Barzun, Jacques, and Henry F. Graff. *The Modern Researcher.*
    6th ed. Belmont, Calif.: Thomson/Wadsworth, 2004. First
    published in 1957.
Beasley, David. *Beasley's Guide to Library Research.* Toronto:
    University of Toronto Press, 2000.
———. *How to Use a Research Library.* London: Oxford Univer-
    sity Press, 1988.
Booth, Wayne C., et al. *The Craft of Research.* 2nd ed. Chicago:
    University of Chicago Press, 2003. First published in 1995.
Borg, Walter R., and Meredith Damien Gall. *Educational Re-
    search: An Introduction.* 7th ed. Boston: Allyn and Bacon,
    2003. First published in 1963.
Directory of Music User Guides for Libraries. Music Library
    Association, 1998–. Internet address: http://www.library
    .yale.edu/%7Eegglstn/mugdir/
Druesedow, John E., Jr. *Library Research Guide to Music:
    Illustrated Search Strategy and Sources.* Library Research
    Guides Series, no. 6. Ann Arbor, Mich.: Pierian Press, 1982.
Frederick, Janet, and Drew Smith. *Library and Internet Research
    Skills: A Guide for College Students.* Dubuque, Iowa:
    Kendall/Hunt Publishing Co., 2000.
Hacker, Diana, and Barbara Fister. *Research and Documentation
    in the Electronic Age.* Boston: Bedford Books, 1998.
Helm, E. Eugene, and Albert T. Luper. *Words & Music: Form
    and Procedure in Theses, Dissertations, Research Papers,
    Book Reports, Programs, Theses in Composition.* Rev.
    ed. Totowa, N.J.: European American Music, 1982. First
    published in 1971.
Herbert, Trevor. *Music in Words: A Guide to Researching and
    Writing about Music.* London: Associated Board of the
    Royal Schools of Music, 2001.
Lunsford, Andrea, et al. *The New St. Martin's Pocket Guide
    to Research and Documentation.* Boston: Bedford/St.
    Martin's Press, 2001.
Madsen, David. *Successful Dissertations and Theses: A Guide to
    Graduate Student Research from Proposal to Completion.*
    2nd ed. San Francisco: Jossey-Bass Publishers, 1992. First
    published in 1983.

Mann, Thomas. *A Guide to Library Research Methods.* New
    York: Oxford University Press, 1987.
Poulton, Helen J., with Marguerite S. Howland. *The Historian's
    Handbook: A Descriptive Guide to Reference Works.*
    Norman: University of Oklahoma Press, 1972.
Ruben, Roberta Lynn, and Janice K. Brewer. *Finding Informa-
    tion: A Guide to Research in Academic Libraries.* Salem,
    Wisc.: Sheffield Publishers, 1991.
Watanabe, Ruth T. *Introduction to Music Research.* Prentice Hall
    History of Music Series. Englewood Cliffs, N.J.: Prentice
    Hall, 1967.
Whiteley, Sandra. *The American Library Association Guide to
    Information Access: A Complete Handbook and Directory.*
    New York: Random House, 1994.
Wingell, Richard J., and Silvia Herzog. *Introduction to Research
    in Music.* Upper Saddle River, N.J.: Prentice Hall, 2001.

Computer Aids to Music Research

Bartle, Barton K. *Computer Software in Music and Music Edu-
    cation: A Guide.* Metuchen, N.J.: Scarecrow Press, 1987.
Brinkman, Alexander R. *Pascal: Programming for Music Re-
    search.* Chicago: University of Chicago Press, 1990.
Davis, Deta S. *Computer Applications in Music: A Bibliography.*
    The Computer Music and Digital Audio Series, vol. 4.
    Madison, Wisc.: A-R Editions, 1988.
————. *Computer Applications in Music: A Bibliography,
    Supplement 1.* Computer Music and Digital Audio Series,
    vol 10. Madison, Wisc.: A-R Editions, 1992.
Hammond, Ray. *The Musician and the Micro.* Poole, Dorset,
    England: Blandford Press, 1983.
Harrison, David B. *Computer Applications to Music and Musi-
    cology: A Bibliography.* Waterloo, Ont.: University of
    Waterloo, 1977.
Hewlett, Walter B., and Eleanor Selfridge-Field, eds. *Computing
    in Musicology: An International Directory of Applications.*
    Menlo Park, Calif.: Center for Computer Assisted Research
    in the Humanities, 1989–. Originally entitled *Directory of
    Computer Assisted Research in Musicology,* 1985–88.
Lincoln, Harry B. *Development of Computerized Techniques in
    Music Research with Emphasis on the Thematic Index.*
    Washington, D.C.: U.S. Office of Education, Bureau of
    Research, 1968.
————, ed. *The Computer and Music.* Ithaca, N.Y.: Cornell
    University Press, 1970.
Lister, Craig. *The Musical Microcomputer: A Resource Guide.*

Garland Reference Library of the Humanities, vol. 854. New York: Garland Publishing, 1988.

Mathews, Max V., and John R. Pierce, eds. *Current Directions in Computer Music Research.* System Development Foundation Benchmark Series, vol. 2. Cambridge, Mass.: MIT Press, 1989.

Waters, William J., comp. *Music and the Personal Computer: An Annotated Bibliography.* Music Reference Collection, no. 22. New York: Greenwood Press, 1989.

General Manuals of Style and Other Guides to English

Barney, Stephen A., ed. *Annotation and Its Texts.* University of California Humanities Research Institute Series. New York: Oxford University Press, 1991.

Barzun, Jacques. *Simple & Direct: A Rhetoric for Writers.* Rev. ed. Chicago: University of Chicago Press, 1994. First published in 1975.

Bates, Jefferson D. *Writing with Precision: How to Write So That You Cannot Possibly Be Misunderstood.* New exp. ed. New York: Penguin Books, 2000. First published in 1990.

Bernstein, Theodore M. *The Careful Writer: A Modern Guide to English Usage.* New York: Atheneum, 1965.

Berry, Thomas Elliott. *The Craft of Writing.* New York: McGraw-Hill, 1974.

———. *The Most Common Mistakes in English Usage.* New York: Chilton Book Company, 1961.

The Chicago Manual of Style: The Essential Guide for Authors, Editors, and Publishers. 15th ed. Chicago: University of Chicago Press, 2003. First published in 1937.

Ehrlich, Eugene H. *The Bantam Concise Handbook of English.* Toronto: Bantam Books, 1986.

Fowler, H. W. *The New Fowler's Modern English Usage.* Rev. 3rd ed. Rev. R. W. Burchfield. New York: Oxford University Press, 2000. First published in 1926 as *A Dictionary of Modern English Usage.*

Gibaldi, Joseph, and Walter S. Achtert. *MLA Handbook for Writers of Research Papers.* 6th ed. New York: Modern Language Association of America, 2003. First published in 1977.

Guinagh, Kevin, comp. and trans. *Dictionary of Foreign Phrases and Abbreviations.* 3rd ed. New York: H. W. Wilson, 1983. First published in 1965.

Heacock, Paul. *Which Word When? The Indispensible Dictionary of 1500 Commonly Confused Words.* New York: Dell Publishing, 1989.

Howard, V. A., and J. H. Barton. *Thinking on Paper: Refine, Express, and Actually Generate Ideas by Understanding the Processes of the Mind.* New York: William Morrow, 1986.

Kane, Thomas S. *The Oxford Essential Guide to Writing.* New York: Berkeley Books, 2000. First published in 1988 as *The New Oxford Guide to Writing.*

Kaye, Sanford. *Writing under Pressure: The Quick Writing Process.* New York: Oxford University Press, 1989.

Leunen, Mary-Claire van. *A Handbook for Scholars.* Rev. ed. New York: Oxford University Press, 1992. First published in 1978.

Longyear, Marie, ed. *The McGraw-Hill Style Manual: A Concise Guide for Writers and Editors.* New York: McGraw-Hill Book Co., 1983.

Maggio, Rosalie. *The Nonsexist Word Finder: A Dictionary of Gender-Free Usage.* Phoenix: Oryx Press, 1988.

Martin, Phyllis. *Word Watcher's Handbook: A Deletionary of the Most Abused and Misused Words.* 3rd ed. New York: St. Martin's Press, 1990; reprint, Lincoln, Neb.: IUniverse.com, 2000. First published in 1977.

Merriam-Webster's Manual for Writers and Editors. Completely rev. ed. of *Webster's Standard American Style Manual.* Springfield, Mass.: MerriamWebster, 1998. First published in 1985.

Nicholson, Margaret. *A Dictionary of American-English Usage: Based on Fowler's Modern English Usage.* New York: Oxford University Press, 1957.

Perrin, Porter G. *Reference Handbook of Grammar and Usage.* New York: William Morrow, 1972.

———. *Writer's Guide and Index to English.* 6th ed. Rev. David R. Ebbitt and Wilma R. Ebbitt. Glenview, Ill.: Scott, Foresman, 1978. First published in 1939 as *An Index to English.*

Roget's International Thesaurus. 6th ed. Rev. Robert L. Chapman and Barbara Ann Kipfer. New York: HarperResource, 2001. First published in 1911; other revisions of Roget's original classic of 1852 also available.

Schwartz, Marilyn, et al. *Guidelines for Bias-Free Writing.* Bloomington: Indiana University Press, 1995.

Soles, Derek. *The Essentials of Academic Writing.* New York: Houghton Mifflin Co., 2004.

Strunk, William, Jr. *The Elements of Style.* 4th ed. With revisions, introduction, and a new chapter by E. B. White. New York: Longman, 2004. First published in 1918.

Turabian, Kate L. *A Manual for Writers of Term Papers, Theses, and Dissertations.* 6th ed. Rev. John Grossman and Alice

Bennett. Chicago: University of Chicago Press, 1996. First
published in 1969.

Urdang, Laurence, ed. *The New York Times Dictionary of Misunderstood, Misused, Mispronounced Words.* New York:
Black Dog & Leventhal Publishers, 2002. First published in
1972 as *The New York Times Everyday Reader's Dictionary of Misunderstood, Misused, Mispronounced Words.*

Williams, Joseph M. *Style: Toward Clarity and Grace.* Chicago:
University of Chicago Press, 1990.

Words into Type. Based on Studies by Marjorie E. Skillin, Robert
M. Gay, et al. Ed. Catherine B. Avery and Linda Pelstring.
3rd ed., completely rev. Englewood Cliffs, N.J.: Prentice
Hall, 1974. First published in 1948.

Guides to Writing about Music

Bellman, Jonathan. *A Short Guide to Writing about Music.* New
York: Longman, 2000.

Boyle, J. David, Richard K. Fiese, and Nancy Zavac. *A Handbook
for Preparing Graduate Papers in Music.* 2nd ed. Houston,
Tex.: Halcyon Press, 2004. First published in 2001.

Helm, E. Eugene, and Albert T. Luper. *Words & Music: Form
and Procedure in Theses, Dissertations, Research Papers,
Book Reports, Programs, Theses in Composition.* Rev. ed.
Totowa, N.J.: European American Music, 1982. First published in 1971.

Holoman, D. Kern. *Writing about Music: A Style Sheet from the
Editors of 19th-Century Music.* Berkeley: University of
California Press, 1988.

Poultney, David. *Studying Music History: Learning, Reasoning,
and Writing about Music History and Literature.* 2nd ed.
Englewood Cliffs, N.J.: Prentice Hall, 1996. First published
in 1983.

Radice, Mark A., ed. *Irvine's Writing about Music.* 3rd. rev. and
enl. ed. Portland, Ore.: Amadeus Press, 1999. First published in 1956 as *Writing about Music: A Style Book for
Reports and Theses.*

Wingell, Richard J. *Writing about Music: An Introductory Guide.*
3rd ed. Upper Saddle River, N.J.: Prentice Hall, 2002. First
published in 1990.

Guides to the Publication Process

The Association of American University Presses Directory. New
York: Association of University Presses, issued annually.

Balkin, Richard. *How to Understand and Negotiate a Book*

Contract or Magazine Agreement. Cincinnati: Writer's
    Digest Books, 1985.
————. *A Writer's Guide to Contract Negotiations.* 2nd ed. New
    York: Hawthorn/Dutton, 1981. First published in 1977.
Banks, Michael A., and Ansen Dibell. *Word Processing Secrets
    for Writers.* Cincinnati: Writer's Digest Books, 1989.
Basart, Ann P. *Writing about Music: A Guide to Publishing
    Opportunities for Authors and Reviewers.* Fallen Leaf
    Reference Books in Music, no. 11. Berkeley, Calif.: Fallen
    Leaf Press, 1989.
*Chicago Guide to Preparing Electronic Manuscripts for Authors
    and Publishers.* Chicago Guides to Writing, Editing, and
    Publishing. Chicago: University of Chicago Press, 1987.
*Directory of Publishing Opportunities in Journals and Periodi-
    cals.* 5th ed. Chicago: Marquis Academic Media, 1981.
    First published in 1971.
International Directory of Scholarly Publishers. Paris: UNESCO,
    1977–.
Luey, Beth. *Handbook for Academic Authors.* 4th ed. Cambridge:
    Cambridge University Press, 2002. First published in
    1987.
Parsons, Paul. *Getting Published: The Acquisition Process at
    University Presses.* Knoxville: University of Tennessee
    Press, 1989.
Powell, Walter W. *Getting into Print: The Decision-Making
    Process in Scholarly Publishing.* Chicago: University of
    Chicago Press, 1985.

Miscellaneous

Biguenet, John, and Rainer Schulte, eds. *The Craft of Transla-
    tion.* Chicago Guides to Writing, Editing, and Publishing.
    Chicago: University of Chicago Press, 1989.

THE MUSIC INDUSTRY

The following varied lists of sources all pertain to the *business*
of music, and thus may be of practical use to those desiring to en-
ter it as much as to those who are engaged in doing research on it.
It begins with general guides to the music industry and to finding
careers in the field. It then addresses specific aspects: "Performing
Arts, Competitions, and Festivals," "Musical Instrument Makers,"
"Music Publishing and Copyright," "Music Recording, Production,
and Digital Technology," "Grant Support for the Arts," and "Arts
Management," and concludes with a list of relevant periodicals, all

American except for the British *International Arts Manager* and the
Canadian *International Journal of Arts Management*. For further in-
formation about competitions and festivals, see chapter 2 under
"International Music Guides," pp. 55–56 above.

General Sources

Baskerville, David. *Music Business Handbook and Career Guide.*
    7th ed. Thousand Oaks, Calif.: Sage Publications, 2001.
    First published in 1979.
Brabec, Jeffrey, and Todd Brabec. *Music, Money, and Success:
    The Insider's Guide to Making Money in the Music Indus-
    try.* 4th ed. New York: Schirmer Trade Books, 2004. First
    published in 1994.
———. *Music, Money, Success and the Movies: The Basics of
    "Music in Film" Deals.* New York: ASCAP, 2002.
Fink, Michael. *Inside the Music Industry: Creativity, Process,
    and Business.* 2nd ed. Belmont, Calif.: Thomson/Schirmer,
    1996. First published in 1989 as *Inside the Music Business:
    Music in Contemporary Life.*
Hale, Cecil I. *The Music Industry: A Guidebook.* 1st ed. Dubuque,
    Iowa: Kendall/Hunt Publishing, 1990.
Halloran, Mark, ed. and comp. *The Musician's Business and Le-
    gal Guide.* 3rd ed. Upper Saddle River, N.J.: Prentice Hall,
    2001. First published in 1979 as *The Musician's Manual.*
Livingston, Robert Allen. *Livingston's Complete Music Business
    Reference.* 2 vols. Cardiff by the Sea, Calif.: La Costa Music
    Business Consultants, 1988.
———. *Livingston's Complete Music Industry Business and
    Law Reference Book.* Cardiff by the Sea, Calif.: La Costa
    Music Business Consultants, 1981.
Music Industry Directory. 7th ed. Chicago: Marquis Professional
    Publications, 1983. Formerly *The Musician's Guide: The
    Directory of the World of Music,* 1954–80.
Passman, Donald S. *All You Need to Know about the Music
    Business.* 5th ed. New York: Free Press, 2003. First pub-
    lished in 1991.
Pavlakis, Christopher. *The American Music Handbook.* New
    York: Free Press, 1974.
Rachlin, Harvey. *The Encyclopedia of the Music Business.* New
    York: Harper and Row, 1981.
Rapaport, Diane Sward. *A Music Business Primer.* Upper Saddle
    River, N.J.: Prentice Hall, 2003.
Schulenberg, Richard. *Legal Aspects of the Music Industry: An
    Insider's View.* New York: Billboard Books, 1999.
Shemel, Sidney, and M. William Krasilovsky. *More about This*

Business of Music: A Practical Guide to Four Additional Areas of the Music Industry Complex. Rev. and enl. 5th ed. New York: Billboard Books, 1994. First published in 1967.

————. *This Business of Music: A Practical Guide to the Music Industry for Publishers, Writers, Record Companies, Producers, Artists, Agents.* 9th ed. New York: Billboard Books, 2003. First published in 1964.

Sly, Lesly. *Power and the Passion: A Guide to the Australia Music Industry.* North Sydney, New South Wales, Australia: Warner/Chappell, 1993.

Weiss, Mitch, and Perri Gaffney. *Managing Artists in Pop Music: What Every Artist and Manager Must Know to Succeed.* New York: Allworth Press, 2003.

Weissman, Dick, et al. *Navigating the Music Industry: Current Issues and Business Models.* Milwaukee, Wisc.: Hal Leonard, 2003.

Worrel, John William. *The Directory of the Music Industry.* Evanston, Ill.: The Instrumentalist, 1970.

Zalkind, Ronald. *Getting Ahead in the Music Business.* Zadoc Music Business Series. New York: Schirmer Books, 1979.

Careers in Music

Baskerville, David. *Music Business Handbook and Career Guide.* 7th ed. Thousand Oaks, Calif.: Sage Publications, 2001. First published in 1979.

Beeching, Angela Myles. *Beyond Talent: Creating a Successful Career in Music.* New York: Oxford University Press, 2004.

Bernstein, Seymour. *Monsters and Angels: Surviving a Career in Music.* [U.S.A.]: 1stBooks Library, 2002.

Bessom, Malcolm E., and John T. Aquino, eds. *Careers and Music.* Reston, Va.: Music Educators National Conference, 1977.

Bjorneberg, Paul. *Exploring Careers in Music.* 2nd ed. Reston, Va.: Music Educators National Conference, 2000. First published in 1982.

Black, Sharon, and Brigid Rafferty. *The Gigs Handbook: A Beginner's Guide to Playing Music Jobs.* Rev. 2nd printing. Skokie, Ill.: Benny Publishing, 2002. First published in 2000 as *The Gigs Handbook: A Beginner's Guide to Playing Professionally.*

Boytim, Joan Frey. *The Private Voice Studio Handbook: A Practical Guide to All Aspects of Teaching.* Milwaukee, Wisc.: Hal Leonard, 2003.

Busnar, Gene. *Careers in Music.* New York: Julian Messner, 1982.

Butler, Mimi. *The Complete Guide to Running a Private Music Studio*. 3rd ed. Haddonfield, N.J.: self-published, 2003. First published in 2001.

Cahill, Greg. *Making Your Living as a String Player: Career Guidance from the Experts at Strings Magazine*. Milwaukee, Wisc.: String Letter Publications, 2004.

Caprez, Emma. *Getting into Performing Arts*. 2nd ed. Richmond, England: Trotman, 2002. First published in 1998 as *Getting into Drama, Music, and Dance*.

Careers in Focus: Music. New York: J. G. Ferguson Publishing, 2005.

Cornell, Richard. *Exploring Music Careers: A Student Guidebook*. Washington: U.S. Government Printing Office, 1976.

Des Pres, Josquin, and Mark Landsman. *Creative Careers in Music*. 2nd ed. New York: Allworth Press, 2004. First published in 2000.

Field, Shelly. *Career Opportunities in the Music Industry*. 5th ed. New York: J. G. Ferguson Publishing, 2004. First published in 1986.

Gerardi, Robert. *Opportunities in Music Careers*. 4th ed. VGM Opportunities Series. Lincolnwood, Ill.: VGM Career Books, 2002.

Goldberg, Jan. *Opportunities in Entertainment Careers*. Lincolnwood, Ill.: VGM Career Horizons, 1999.

Goldberg, Jan, Stephen E. Lambert, and Julie DeGalan. *Great Jobs for Music Majors*. 2nd ed. Chicago: VGM Career Books, 2004. First published in 1998.

Hammond, Ray. *Working in the Music Business*. Poole, Dorset, England: Blandford Press, 1983.

Hannan, Michael. *The Australian Guide to Careers in Music*. Sydney: University of New South Wales, 2003.

Highstein, Ellen. *Making Music in Looking Glass Land: A Guide to Survival and Business Skills for the Classical Musician*. 4th ed. New York: Concert Artists Guild, 2003. First published in 1991.

Hoover, Deborah A. *Supporting Yourself as an Artist: A Practical Guide*. 2nd ed. New York: Oxford University Press, 1989. First published in 1985.

Jevnikar, Jana, comp. *Careers in the Arts: A Resource Guide*. New York: Center for Arts Information: Opportunity Resources for the Arts, 1981.

Kerner, Kenny. *Going Pro: Developing a Professional Career in the Music Industry*. Milwaukee, Wisc.: Hal Leonard, 1999.

Knab, Christopher, and Bartley F. Day. *Music Is Your Business: Helping Musicians Help Themselves with the Business of*

Music. 2nd ed., newly rev. and exp. Seattle, Wash.: Four-Front Media and Music, 2003. First published in 1975.

Kusek, David, et al. *Building Your Music Career.* DVD (36 min.). Boston: Berklee Press, 2003.

The Orchestral Musician's Complete Career Guide. Toronto: Orchestras Canada, 1999.

Papolos, Janice. *The Performing Artist's Handbook.* Cincinnati: Writer's Digest Books, 1984.

Popyk, Bob. *The Business of Getting More Gigs as a Professional Musician.* Milwaukee, Wisc.: Hal Leonard, 2003.

Rourke, Kelley. *Career Guide for Singers.* 6th ed. Washington, D.C.: Opera America, 2003. First published in 1992.

Sharp, Erica. *How to Get an Orchestra Job—and Keep It: A Practical Guide Book.* Encinitas, Calif.: Encinitas Press, 1985.

Spellman, Peter. *The Musician's Internet: On-line Strategies for Success in the Music Industry.* Boston: Berklee Press, 2002. Distributed by Hal Leonard Publications.

———. *The Self-Promoting Musician: Strategies for Independent Music Success.* Boston: Berklee Press, 2000. Distributed by Hal Leonard Publications.

Stearns, Betty, and Clara Degen, eds. *Careers in Music.* Rev. ed. Wilmette, Ill.: American Music Conference, 1980. First published in 1966.

Stiernberg, John. *Succeeding in Music: A Business Handbook for Performers, Songwriters, Agents, Managers, and Promoters.* San Francisco: Backbeat Books, 2001.

Summers-Dossena, Ann. *Getting It All Together: A Handbook for Performing Artists in Classical Music and Ballet.* Metuchen, N.J.: Scarecrow Press, 1985.

Weissman, Dick. *Music Business: Career Opportunities and Self-Defense.* 3rd rev. ed. New York: Three Rivers Press, 2003. First published in 1979.

Zager, Michael. *Writing Music for Television and Radio Commercials: A Manual for Composers and Students.* Lanham, Md.: Scarecrow Press, 2003.

Performing Arts, Competitions, and Festivals

Alink, Gustav A. *Piano Competitions Worldwide.* 4th ed. The Hague, Netherlands: G. A. Alink, 2003. First published in 1988.

Canning, Hugh, ed. *International Music and Opera Guide.* London: Tantivy Press, 1986–. Replaces *International Music Guide,* 1977–85.

Carlino, Angelo. *The Evils of Music Management, an Exposé:*

The Facts of Life Every Singer, Pianist and Musician Should Know about Opera and Concert Management. New York: LaCar Publishing, 1975.

Chamber Music Festivals, Schools, and Workshops. New York: Chamber Music America, 2000–. (Annual.)

Classical Music America: The Music-Lover's Guide to the Cities of North America. Peterborough, N.H.: BC Music Magazine, 1998.

Concert Artists Guild's Guide to Competitions. New York: The Guild, 1987–. (Annual.)

Directory of Music Competitions. Desloge, Mo.: MDA Music Placement Services, 1978.

Finell, Judith Greenberg, comp. *The Contemporary Music Performance Directory: A Listing of American Performing Ensembles, Sponsoring Organizations, Performing Facilities, Concert Series, and Festivals of 20th Century Music.* New York: American Music Center, 1975.

Gottesman, Roberta, ed. *The Music Lover's Guide to Europe: A Compendium of Festivals, Concerts, and Opera.* New York: John Wiley & Sons, 1992.

Gusikoff, Lynne. *Guide to Musical America.* New York: Facts on File Publications, 1984.

Handel, Beatrice, et al., eds. *Handel's National Directory for the Performing Arts.* 4th ed. 2 vols. Dallas: NDPA, 1988–. First published in 1973.

Musical America's Festivals. New York: Musical America, 1991–. (Annual.)

Rabin, Carol Price. *Music Festivals in America.* 4th ed. Great Barrington, Mass.: Berkshire Traveller Press, 1990. First published in 1979.

———. *Music Festivals in Europe and Britain, Including Israel, Russia, Turkey and Japan.* Rev. and enl. Stockbridge, Mass.: Berkshire Traveller Press, 1984. First published in 1980.

Smith, Douglas, and Nancy Barton. *International Guide to Music Festivals.* New York: Quick Fox, 1980.

Musical Instrument Makers

Farrell, Susan Caust. *Directory of Contemporary American Musical Instrument Makers.* Columbia: University of Missouri Press, 1981.

Laskin, Grit. *The World of Musical Instrument Makers: A Guided Tour.* Oakville, Ont.: Mosaic Press, 1987.

Music Publishing and Copyright

Althouse, Jay. *Copyright: The Complete Guide for Music Educa-
    tors.* 2nd ed., rev. and updated. Van Nuys, Calif.: Music in
    Action, 1997. First published in 1984.
Axford, Elizabeth C. *Song Sheets to Software: A Guide to Print
    Music, Software, and Web Sites for Musicians.* Lanham,
    Md.: Scarecrow Press, 2001.
Beck, Joseph M., et al. *Understanding Basic Copyright Law,
    2003.* New York: Practising Law Institute, 2003.
Bruwelheide, Janis H. *The Copyright Primer for Librarians and
    Educators.* 2nd ed., updated. Chicago: American Library
    Association; Washington, D.C.: National Education Asso-
    ciation, 1998. First published in 1987.
Chickering, Robert B., and Susan Hartman. *How to Register a
    Copyright and Protect Your Creative Work: A Basic Guide
    to the Copyright Law and How It Affects Anyone Who
    Wants to Protect Creative Work.* Updated ed. New York:
    Charles Scribner's Sons, 1987. First published in 1980.
*Copying under Copyright, A Practical Guide: Dos and Don'ts
    about the U.S. Copyright Law.* New York: Music Publish-
    ers Association, 1999.
*Copyright Law Symposium: Nathan Burkan Memorial Compe-
    tition.* Sponsored by the American Society of Composers,
    Authors and Publishers. New York: Columbia University
    Press, 1939–.
Copyright Registration for Musical Compositions. Washington,
    D.C.: Library of Congress and the Government Printing
    Office, 2004. Internet address: http://purl.access.gpo.gov/
    gpo/lps44029
Dannay, Richard. *Advanced Seminar on Copyright Law, 2004.*
    New York: Practising Law Institute, 2004.
Dranov, Paula. *Inside the Music Publishing Industry.* White
    Plains, N.Y.: Knowledge Industry Publications, 1980.
Erickson, J. Gunnar, et al. *Musician's Guide to Copyright.* Rev.
    ed. New York: Charles Scribner's Sons, 1983. First pub-
    lished in 1979.
*Final Report of the National Commission on New Technologi-
    cal Uses of Copyrighted Works, July 31, 1978.* Washington,
    D.C.: Library of Congress, 1979.
Fisher, William W. *Promises to Keep: Technology, Law, and the
    Future of Entertainment.* Stanford, Calif.: Stanford Univer-
    sity Press, 2004.
Gertz, Ronald H., et al. *Music Licensing in the Digital Age.* Little
    Falls, N.J.: Glasser LegalWorks, 2000.
Gordon, Sherri Mabry. *Downloading Copyrighted Stuff from the*

Internet: Stealing or Fair Use? Aldershot, Hants, England: Enslow Publishers, 2004.

Green, Richard G. *Copyright Q & A for Orchestra Managers, Librarians, and Artistic Administrators.* Washington, D.C.: American Symphony Orchestra League, 1996.

Heald, Paul J. *Reviving the Rhetoric of the Public Interest: Choir Directors, Copy Machines, and New Arrangements of Public Domain Music.* Durham, N.C.: Duke University School of Law, 1996.

Hurst, Walter E., and Don Rico. *How to Be a Music Publisher.* 2nd ed. Hollywood: Seven Arts Press, 1979. First published in 1976.

Moser, David J. *Music Copyright for the New Millennium.* Vallejo, Calif.: ProMusic Press, 2002.

Music Copyright for Educators. (A directory of Internet resources providing information on music copyright issues.) Internet address: http://staff.lib.muohio.edu/%7eshocker/copyright/music/

Strong, William S. *The Copyright Book: A Practical Guide.* 5th ed. Cambridge, Mass.: MIT Press, 1999. First published in 1981.

The United States Copyright Law: A Guide for Music Educators. Updated ed. Music Educators National Conference. New York: National Music Publisher's Association, 1998. First published in 1978.

United States Copyright Office website: http://www.copyright.gov

Using Copyrighted Music. Atlanta: American Society of Composers, Authors and Publishers, 2000.

Wager, Willis. *A Musician's Guide to Copyright and Publishing: New Copyright Law.* New York: Carousel Publishing, 1990. First published in 1975.

Wilson, Lee. *Making It in the Music Business: The Business and Legal Guide for Songwriters and Performers.* 3rd ed. New York: Allworth Press, 2004. First published in 1995.

Wolff, Robert. *How to Make It in the New Music Business: Lessons, Tips, and Inspiration from Music's Biggest and Best.* New York: Watson-Guptill, 2004.

Music Recording, Production, and Digital Technology

Aldrich, Nika. *Digital Audio Explained.* San Francisco: Backbeat, 2004.

Alten, Stanley R. *Audio in Media.* 6th ed. Belmont, Calif.: Wadsworth/Thomson Learning, 2002. First published in 1981.

Ballora, Mark. *Essentials of Music Technology.* Upper Saddle River, N.J.: Prentice Hall, 2003.

Borwick, John, ed. *Sound Recording Practice for the Association of Professional Recording Studios.* 3rd ed. New York: Oxford University Press, 1987.

Bosi, Marina, and Richard E. Goldberg. *Introduction to Digital Audio Coding and Standards.* Boston: Kluwer Academic Publishers, 2003.

Brice, Richard. *Music Engineering.* 2nd ed. Oxford: Newnes, 2001. First published in 1998.

Cary, Tristram. *Dictionary of Musical Technology.* New York: Greenwood Press, 1992.

Chappell, Jon. *Digital Home Recording: Tips, Techniques, and Tools for Home Studio Production.* San Francisco: Backbeat Books, 2003.

Collins, Mike. *A Professional Guide to Audio Plug-Ins and Virtual Instruments.* Oxford: Focal Press, 2003.

Delson, Donn, and Walter E. Hurst. *Delson's Dictionary of Radio and Record Industry Terms.* Thousand Oaks, Calif.: Bradson Press, 1986.

Derry, Roger. *PC Audio Editing: For Broadcast, Desktop, and CD Audio Production.* 2nd ed. Oxford: Focal Press, 2003. First published in 2000.

Eargle, John. *Handbook of Recording Engineering.* 4th ed. Boston: Kluwer Academic Publishers, 2003. First published in 1986.

Franz, David, and Susan Gedutis. *Recording and Producing in the Home Studio: A Complete Guide.* Boston: Berklee Press, 2004. Distributed by Hal Leonard.

Greenebaum, Ken, and Ronen Barzel. *Audio Anecdotes: Tools, Tips, and Techniques for Digital Audio.* Natick, Mass.: A. K. Peters, 2004.

Gronow, Pekka, and Ilpo Saunio. *An International History of the Recording Industry.* London: Cassell, 1998.

Hallifax, Andrew. *The Classical Musician's Recording Handbook.* London: SMT, 2004.

Hill, Brad. *Going Digital: A Musician's Guide to Technology.* Belmont, Calif.: Thomson/Schirmer, 1998.

Huber, David Miles, and Robert E. Runstein. *Modern Recording Techniques.* 5th ed. Boston: Focal Press, 2001. First published in 1974.

Hull, Geoffrey. *The Recording Industry.* 2nd ed. New York: Routledge, 2004. First published in 1998.

Hurst, Walter E. *The Record Industry Book.* 7th ed. Entertainment Industry Series, no. 1. Hollywood: Seven Arts Press, 1978. First published ca. 1960.

Katz, Robert A. *Mastering Audio: The Art and the Science.* Boston: Focal Press, 2003.

Kompanek, Sonny. *From Score to Screen: Sequencers, Scores, and Second Thoughts: The New Film Scoring Process.* New York: Schirmer Trade Books, 2004.

Laycock, Roger. *Audio Techniques for Television Production.* Oxford: Focal Press, 2002.

Leonard, John A. *Theatre Sound.* New York: Routledge, 2001.

Mandell, Jim. *The Studio Business Book.* Rev. and exp. 2nd ed. Vallejo, Calif.: Mixbooks, 2000. First published in 1989.

Marshall, Gary. *Guide to Making a Record.* Iver Heath, England: Artemis, 2003.

McCartney, Tom. *Recording Studio Technology, Maintenance, and Repairs.* New York: McGraw-Hill, 2004.

McGee, Marty. *Encyclopedia of Motion Picture Sound.* Jefferson, N.C.: McFarland, 2001.

Menasché, Emile. *The Desktop Studio: A Guide to Computer-Based Audio Production.* Milwaukee, Wisc.: Hal Leonard, 2002.

Middleton, Chris. *The Complete Guide to Digital Audio.* Lewes, England: Ilex, 2004.

Middleton, Chris, and Allen Zuk. *The Complete Guide to Digital Audio: A Comprehensive Introduction to Digital Sound and Music-Making.* Boston: Muska and Lipman Publications, 2003.

Morton, David: *Sound Recording.* Westport, Conn.: Greenwood Press, 2004.

Moylan, William. *The Art of Recording: The Creative Resources of Music Production and Audio.* New York: Van Nostrand Reinhold, 1992.

———. *The Art of Recording: Understanding and Crafting the Mix.* Boston: Focal Press, 2002.

Nisbett, Alec. *The Sound Studio: Audio Techniques for Radio, Television, Film, and Recording.* 7th ed. Boston: Focal Press, 2003. First published in 1993.

Pellman, Samuel. *Introduction to the Creation of Electroacoustic Music.* Belmont, Calif.: Thomson/Schirmer, 1994.

The Professional Audio Sourcebook. 2 vols. New York: B & H Photo-Video-Pro Audio, Inc., 2003.

Rapaport, Diane Sward. *How to Make and Sell Your Own Record: The Complete Guide to Independent Recording.* Rev. 3rd ed. Jerome, Ariz.: Jerome Headlands Press, 1988. First published in 1978.

Roberts-Breslin, Jan. *Making Media: Foundations of Sound and Image Production.* Boston: Focal Press, 2003.

Rudolph, Thomas E., and Vincent A. Leonard. *Recording in the Digital World: Complete Guide to Studio Gear and*

Software. Boston: Berklee Press, 2001. Distributed by Hal Leonard.

Rumsey, Francis. *Desktop Audio Technology: Digital Audio and MIDI Principles.* Boston: Focal Press, 2004.

Rumsey, Francis, and Tim McCormick. *Sound and Recording: An Introduction.* 4th ed. Oxford: Focal Press, 2002. First published in 1992.

Russ, Martin. *Sound Synthesis and Sampling.* 2nd ed. Boston: Focal Press, 2004. First published in 1996.

Ryan, John. *The Production of Culture in the Music Industry: The ASCAP-BMI Controversy.* Lanham, Md.: University Press of America, 1985.

Sams, Howard W., Colin MacQueen, and Steve Albanese. *Digital Audio Dictionary.* Indianapolis, Ind.: Prompt Publications, 1999.

Slone, G. Randy. *The Audiophile's Project Sourcebook.* New York: McGraw-Hill, 2002.

Souvignier, Todd. *Loops and Grooves: The Musician's Guide to Groove Machines and Loop Sequencers.* Milwaukee, Wisc.: Hal Leonard, 2003.

Sterne, Jonathan. *The Audible Past: Cultural Origins of Sound Production.* Durham, N.C.: Duke University Press, 2003.

Talbot-Smith, Michael. *Audio Engineer's Reference Book.* Oxford: Focal Press, 1999.

———. *Sound Engineering Explained.* 2nd ed. Oxford: Focal Press, 2001. First published in 1997.

Utz, Peter. *Introduction to Audio.* Middleton, Wisc.: A-R Editions, 2003.

Volanski, John J. *Sound Recording Advice: An Instruction and Reference Manual That Demystifies the Home Recording Studio Experience.* San Diego, Calif.: Pacific Beach Publications, 2003.

Wadhams, Wayne. *Dictionary of Music Production and Engineering Terminology.* New York: Schirmer Books, 1988.

———. *The Musician's Guide to the Recording Studio.* New York: Schirmer Books, 1989.

———. *Sound Advice: The Musician's Guide to the Record Industry.* New York: Schirmer Books, 1990.

Watkinson, John. *Introduction to Digital Audio.* 2nd ed. Oxford: Focal Press, 2001. First published in 1994.

Whitaker, Jerry C. *Audio/Video Professional's Field Manual.* New York: McGraw-Hill, 2002.

———. *Master Handbook of Audio Production: A Guide to Standards, Equipment, and System Design.* New York: McGraw-Hill, 2003.

Whitaker, Jerry C., and K. Blair Benson. *Standard Handbook of Audio and Radio Engineering.* 2nd ed. New York: McGraw-Hill, 2002. First published in 1988.

White, Paul. *Basic Digital Recording.* London: Sanctuary, 2000.

———. *The Sound on Sound Book of Recording and Production Techniques for the Recording Musician.* 2nd ed. London: Sanctuary, 2002. First published in 1997.

Williams, David, and Peter R. Webster. *Experiencing Music Technology: Software, Data, and Hardware.* 2nd ed. Belmont, Calif.: Thomson/Schirmer, 1999. First published in 1996.

Grant Support for the Arts

Annual Register of Grant Support: A Directory of Funding Sources. Wilmette, Ill.: National Register Publishing, 1969–.

Barbato, Joseph, and Danielle S. Furlich. *Writing for a Good Cause: The Complete Guide to Crafting Proposals and Other Persuasive Pieces for Nonprofits.* New York: Simon and Schuster, 2000.

Coley, Soraya M., and Cynthia A. Scheinberg. *Proposal Writing.* 2nd ed. Thousand Oaks, Calif.: Sage Publications, 2000. First published in 1990.

Conrad, Daniel Lynn, et al. *The Grants Planner: A Systems Approach to Grantsmanship.* [Rev. ed.] San Francisco: The Institute, 1979. First published in 1976.

Edelson, Phyllis, and Rebecca Alvin. *Foundation Grants to Individuals.* 11th ed. New York: The Foundation Center, 1999. First published in 1977.

Falkenstein, Jeffrey A., and David G. Jacobs. *The Foundation Directory: 2001 Edition.* 22nd ed. New York: The Foundation Center, 2001. First published in 1960.

Foundation Grants Index on CD-ROM. New York: The Foundation Center, 2003.

Gray, Susan Heinrichs. *How to Find and Win Federal Grants: The Complete Guide for Nonprofit Organizations.* North Little Rock, Ark.: Federal Grant Guide, 2003.

Jacobs, David G. *Guide to U.S. Foundations, Their Trustees, Officers, and Donors.* New York: The Foundation Center, 2003.

Johnson, Pattie J., and Margaret Morth. *Foundation Fundamentals: A Guide for Grantseekers.* 6th ed. New York: The Foundation Center, 1999. First published in 1980.

Lefferts, Robert. *Getting a Grant in the 1980s: How to Write Successful Grant Proposals.* 2nd ed. Englewood Cliffs, N.J.: Prentice Hall, 1982.

Millsaps, Daniel, et al., eds. *The National Directory of Arts and*

Education Support by Business Corporations. 2nd ed. Arts Patronage Series, no. 10. Washington, D.C.: Washington International Arts Letter, 1982. Rev. ed. of *National Directory of Arts Support by Business Corporations,* first published in 1979.

————. *The National Directory of Arts Support by Private Foundations: Volume Five.* Arts Patronage Series, no. 12. Washington, D.C.: Washington International Arts Letter, 1983. First published in 1977.

————. *The National Directory of Grants and Aid to Individuals in the Arts, International.* 8th ed. Des Moines, Iowa: Allied Business Consultants, 1993. First published in 1970.

Olson, Stan, et al., eds. *Foundation Grants to Individuals.* 6th ed. New York: Foundation Center, 1988. First published in 1977.

Pfeiffer, William S., and Charles H. Keller. *Proposal Writing: The Art of Friendly and Winning Persuasion.* Upper Saddle River, N.J.: Prentice Hall, 2000.

Porter, Robert A., ed. *Guide to Corporate Giving in the Arts, 4.* New York: American Council for the Arts, 1987.

————. *The Subsidized Muse: Public Support for the Arts in the United States.* Cambridge: Cambridge University Press, 1978.

Sarbacher, Jennifer J. *Guide to Funding for Emerging Artists and Scholars.* Washington, D.C.: President's Committee on the Arts and Humanities, 1991.

Taniguchi, Jason. *Canadian Directory to Foundations and Grants.* 15th ed. Toronto: Canadian Centre for Philanthropy, 2001. First published in 1975.

Tehan, Rita. *Grants and Foundation Support: Selected Print, Electronic, and Internet Sources of Information on Government and Private Funding.* Washington, D.C.: Congressional Research Service, Library of Congress, 1999.

White, Virginia P. *Grants for the Arts.* New York: Plenum Press, 1980.

Yuen, Francis K. O., and Kenneth L. Terao. *Practical Grant Writing and Program Evaluation.* Pacific Grove, Calif.: Brooks/Cole Thomson Learning, 2003.

Arts Management

ArtsNet: Arts Management Information Service. A comprehensive online resource for Internet sites in all areas of the arts. Pittsburgh: Master of Arts Management Program, Carnegie Mellon University, 1997–. Internet address: http://artsnet.heinz.cmu.edu

Benedict, Stephen, ed. *Public Money and the Muse: Essays on Government Funding for the Arts.* New York: W. W. Norton, 1991.

Byrnes, William J. *Management and the Arts.* 3rd ed. Boston: Focal Press, 2003. First published in 1993.

Chong, Derrick. *Arts Management: Critical Perspectives on a New Sub-Discipline.* New York: Routledge, 2001.

Colbert, François. *Marketing Culture and the Arts.* 2nd ed. Montreal: Presses H. E. C., 2001. First published in 1994.

Dickman, Sharron. *Arts Marketing: The Pocket Guide.* Kew, Victoria, Australia: Centre for Professional Development, 1997.

———. *What's My Plan? A Guide to Developing Arts Marketing Plans.* Surrey Hills, New South Wales: Australia Council for the Arts, 2000.

Diggle, Keith. *Arts Marketing.* London: Rheingold, 1994.

Dimaggio, Paul. *Managers of the Arts: Careers and Opinions of Administrators of U.S. Resident Theaters, Art Museums, Symphony Orchestras, and Community Arts Agencies.* Bethesda, Md.: Seven Locks Press, 1987.

Dunbar, Roger, ed. *Managing Organizations: For Music, Professional Art, and Visual Art Professionals.* Boston: Pearson Custom Publishing, 2002.

Fishman, James J., and Stephen Schwarz. *Nonprofit Organization: Statutes, Regulations, and Forms.* Westbury, N.Y.: Foundation Press, 1995.

Freakley, Vivien, and Rachel Sutton. *Essential Guide to Business in the Performing Arts.* London: Hodder and Stoughton, 1996.

Hagoort, Giep. *Art Management: Entrepreneurial Style.* 3rd ed. Delft, The Netherlands: Eburon, 2003. First published in 2000.

Hill, Elizabeth, Catherine O'Sullivan, and Terry O'Sullivan. *Creative Arts Marketing.* 2nd ed. Boston: Butterworth Heinemann, 2003. First published in 1995.

Kaiser, Michael M., and Paul S. Engler. *Strategic Planning in the Arts: A Practical Guide.* New York: Kaiser/Engler Group, 1995.

Langly, Stephen, and James Abruzzo. *Jobs in Arts and Media Management: What They Are and How to Get One!* New York: ACA Books, 1990.

Levy, Alan Howard. *Government and the Arts: Debates over Federal Support of the Arts in America from George Washington to Jesse Helms.* Lanham, Md.: University Press of America, 1997.

McCombie, Mel. *Art and Policy: The National Endowment for*

the Arts and Art in Public Places. New York: Peter Lang, 1999.

McDaniel, Nello, George Thorn, and Catherine Cartwright. *Arts Planning: A Dynamic Balance.* New York: ARTS Action Issues, 1997.

Mokwa, Michael P., et al. *Marketing the Arts.* New York: Praeger, 1980.

Mulcahy, Kevin V., and Margaret Jane Wyszomirski. *America's Commitment to Culture: Government and the Arts.* Boulder, Colo.: Westview Press, 1995.

Nakamoto, Kent, and Kathi Levin, comps. *A Selected and Annotated Bibliography on Marketing the Arts.* Updated in 1983 by H. Perry Mixter. [Madison, Wisc.]: Association of College, University and Community Arts Administrators, 1983. Updated ed. of *Marketing the Arts: A Selected and Annotated Bibliography,* first published in 1978.

The National Endowment for the Arts. Internet address: http://www.arts.gov

The National Endowment for the Arts 1965–2000: A Brief Chronology of Federal Support for the Arts. Washington, D.C.: National Endowment for the Arts, 2000.

Nelson, Charles A., and Frederick J. Turk. *Financial Management for the Arts: A Guidebook for Arts Organizations.* New York: Associated Councils of the Arts, 1975.

Newman, Danny. *Subscribe Now! Building Arts Audiences through Dynamic Subscription Promotion.* New York: American Council for the Arts, 1977.

Orobko, William. *The Musician's Handbook: A Practical Guide to the Law and Business of Music.* 1st ed. Self Counsel Series. Vancouver: International Self-Counsel Press, 1985.

Pick, John, and Malcolm Hey Anderton. *Arts Administration.* 2nd ed. London: Spon, 1996. First published in 1980.

Porter, Robert, ed. *Community Arts Agencies: A Handbook and Guide.* New York: American Council for the Arts, 1978.

Radbourne, Jennifer, and Margaret Fraser. *Arts Management: A Practical Guide.* St. Leonards, New South Wales, Australia: Allen and Unwin, 1997.

Rentschler, Ruth. *The Entrepreneurial Arts Leader.* St. Lucia, Queensland, Australia: University of Queensland Press, 2002.

Suber, Charles, and J. Dennis Rich. *Dictionary for Artists and Performers and Managers.* Needham Heights, Mass.: Simon and Schuster Custom Publishing, 1998.

Taubman, Joseph. *In Tune with the Music Business.* New York: Law-Arts Publishers, 1980.

————. *Performing Arts Management and Law.* 2 vols. New York: Law-Arts Publishers, 1972. Suppls., 1974 and 1981.

————. *Performing Arts Management and Law: Forms.* 4 vols. New York: Law-Arts Publishers, 1973–76.

Tipton, Harmon H. "Study of the Role of Federal Subsidy and the American Political Economy in American Classical Music." M.A. thesis, San Diego State University, 1996.

Tschirhart, Mary. *Artful Leadership: Managing Stakeholder Problems in Nonprofit Arts Organizations.* Bloomington: Indiana University Press, 1996.

Turk, Frederick J., and Robert P. Gallo. *Financial Management Strategies for Arts Organizations.* New York: ACA Books, 1984.

Wolf, Thomas. *The Nonprofit Organization: An Operating Manual.* Englewood Cliffs, N.J.: Prentice Hall, 1984.

Periodicals and Periodical Database

ABI/Inform. Ann Arbor, Mich.: University Microfilms International, 1989–. An index of business-related periodicals. (Exists only on CD-ROM.)

International Arts Manager. 1988–. (Bimonthly.)

International Journal of Arts Management. 1998–. (Triannual.)

International Musician. American Federation of Musicians. 1901–. (Monthly.)

Musical America: International Directory of the Performing Arts. Continues *Musical America: Directory of the Performing Arts.* 1974–. (Annual.)

Index of Authors, Editors, Compilers, and Translators

Index of Titles

PHILLIP D. CRABTREE and DONALD H. FOSTER are
both retired from the faculty at the University of Cincinnati
College–Conservatory of Music. ALLEN SCOTT is Associate
Professor of Music History at Oklahoma State University.